Second Edition

FORENSIC PODIATRY

Principles and Methods

Second Edition

FORENSIC PODIATRY

Principles and Methods

John A. DiMaggio
Wesley Vernon

CRC Press
Taylor & Francis Group
Boca Raton London New York

CRC Press is an imprint of the
Taylor & Francis Group, an **informa** business

Preface

The first edition of *Forensic Podiatry: Principles and Methods* was published by Humana Press. The authors would like to thank them for that opportunity and permissions granted to reuse various figures from the original edition as well as the areas of text that remain still current and applicable to the second edition.

The first edition was written for the general audience, that is, podiatrists, forensic podiatrists, and nonpodiatrists with an interest in the field. Given that the specialty of forensic podiatry has rapidly developed from relative obscurity to a discipline that many have now heard about, and it is being practiced in a changed operating context, this second edition is primarily aimed at the needs of training and practicing forensic podiatrists. It covers most areas of importance to practice safely and effectively within the current requirements of all forensic disciplines. We note instances where the subject matter is more fully covered in a text dedicated to that subject. The book should still be of interest to the more general readership, however, with up-to-date details of current practice being covered within this reference text for those who wish to understand the work of forensic podiatrists.

Production of this second edition, which reflects the many changes that have recently taken place in forensic podiatry, would not have been possible without the help and support from family, friends, colleagues, and various organizations and officials who have always given support to the discipline and its development. Although these are too numerous to mention in a single acknowledgments section, particular thanks must go to the following: Dr. Sarah Reel, Selina Reidy, Jeremy Walker, Professor Ivan Birch, Dr. Claire Gwinnett, Dr. Norman Gunn, Dr. Owen Facey, Lesley Hammer, Matt Johnson, Mark Hatcher, Dwane Hilderbrand, Robert Tavernaro, Larry Brennan, and Iain Wilson.

Special thanks to Michael J. Nirenberg, DPM, for contributing Chapter 10 on the Frye test and Daubert standard.

Special thanks to my parents Denis and Irene Vernon and our wives, Val Vernon and Andriana DiMaggio.

John A. DiMaggio
Bandon, Oregon

Wesley Vernon
University of Huddersfield, Huddersfield, UK

Authors

John A. DiMaggio, DPM, BS, started his private practice in Tempe, Arizona, in 1974, and his forensic practice in 1989.

In 1984, he was sponsored by the city of Mesa, Arizona to be a reserve police officer. He served as a certified peace officer in the state of Arizona and worked in the patrol division for 15 years. He often assisted the Crime Scene Unit and processed crime scenes. He has testified as an expert witness in cases for both the prosecution and the defense. He is a member of the American Academy of Forensic Sciences and the International Association for Identification. He has written many articles and lectured widely in the United States and also internationally. He founded the American Society of Forensic Podiatry in 2003.

Wesley Vernon, OBE, was employed as the head of Podiatry Services, a research lead, and the lead of Deputy Allied Health Professions for Sheffield Primary and Community Services (Sheffield Teaching Hospitals NHSFT), prior to his retirement in 2015. He was a seconded (now visiting) professor at the University of Huddersfield and a visiting professor at Staffordshire University. He served as the first Chair of the Forensic Podiatry Science and Practice Sub-Committee of the International Association for Identification from 2007 to 2015. From 2013 to 2016, he served as the Hon. Chair of Quality Standards of the Chartered Society of Forensic Sciences. Vernon has also served as Chair of the Podiatric Research Forum (later the Society of Chiropodists and Podiatrists Research and Development Committee), and Chair of the Research Forum for Allied Health Professions. He was also elected as the President of the Society of Shoefitters (UK) in 2015.

Professional recognitions include being a Fellow (retired) of the Chartered Society of Forensic Sciences; Founding Fellow of the Faculty of Podiatric Medicine, the Royal College of Physicians and Surgeons of Glasgow; Fellow in Podiatric Medicine; and Fellow of the Faculty of Management of the College of Podiatrists. In 2015, he received the Dedication to Service Award of the International Association for Identification. He is a meritorious award holder of the Society of Chiropodists and Podiatrists, Distinguished Member of the International Association for Identification, and, in 2016, was awarded Honorary Membership of the American Society of Forensic Podiatrists.

He has extensive experience in forensic podiatry casework from 1995 within the United Kingdom and also, internationally has been involved in forensic podiatry research from 1989 (being awarded a PhD for research into the potential of shoe wear patterns in forensic identification in 2000). He has undertaken extensive work to develop, adopt, and implement governance arrangements for the practice of forensic podiatry. Vernon has regularly presented worldwide and has authored or coauthored more than 60 journal articles. He has contributed to forensic textbooks, including coauthoring the first textbook on forensic podiatry, published in 2011.

In 2009, he was made an Officer of the Order of the British Empire (OBE) for his invaluable service to medicine and health care.

Organic electrolytes, such as $TEABF_4$/ACN and $TEABF_4$/PC, currently dominate the commercial ES market. There are several ways to increase the energy density of ESs including:

a. Development of electrolytes with a higher electrochemical stability. The commercial ESs with $TEABF_4$/ACN or $TEABF_4$/PC organic electrolytes have a cell voltage of 2.7–2.8 V. Since the energy density of the ES is proportional to the square of operating voltage, increasing the cell voltage remarkably enhances the energy density. In most cases, the operative cell voltage is limited by the electrochemical stability of the electrolyte. Therefore, the enhancement of the electrochemical stability of the electrolytes will significantly increase the energy density of ESs. The electrochemical stability of organic electrolytes depends on the cation and anion of the conducting salt, the organic solvents (single solvent or solvent mixture), and their interactions. Therefore, it is possible to increase the electrochemical stability of organic electrolytes by optimizing or modifying conventional organic electrolytes, and by developing new conducting salts and organic solvents through proper formulation. For example, the electrochemical stability of sulfone-based or adiponitrile (ADN) solvents is higher than that of commercial ACN and PC solvent-based electrolytes. As mentioned previously, increasing the electrochemical stability of electrolytes may sacrifice other properties such as viscosity and ionic conductivity. Therefore, one should also consider all the other important properties of electrolytes. For example, the use of an organic solvent or solvent mixtures with a high electrochemical stability combined with a conducting salt with an acceptable ionic conductivity maybe a promising solution. In addition, an IL electrolyte-based ESs can have high-energy density due to the high electrochemical stability of an IL. To date, huge numbers of ILs have been synthesized and many of them have not yet been tested and investigated for use in ESs. It is rather promising to design and prepare ILs with both high electrochemical stability and sufficient ionic conductivity by carefully selecting or designing the cation and anion of ILs.

b. Enhancement of the charge storage ability by using pseudocapacitance. The pseudocapacitance enhancement can result from not only pseudocapacitive electrode materials but also from redox-active electrolytes. On the basis of these electrode materials and/or electrolytes, a dramatically higher energy density can be obtained, even for aqueous electrolyte-based ESs (especially hybrid or asymmetric ESs). Owing to the low cost and simplified fabrication processes without the need of strictly controlled environments, hybrid ESs with aqueous electrolytes or ESs with redox-active aqueous electrolytes remain promising candidates for ESs with high-energy density.

2. Development of further fundamental understanding, by both advanced experimental investigations and theoretical modeling. This understanding will lead to the design and optimization of new electrolytes with improved

electrochemical stability, ionic conductivity, and thermal stability. It is particularly recommended to pay more attention to recently developed electrolytes such as electrolytes mixed with IL and organic solvents or mixtures of different ILs, solid-state electrolytes, redox-active electrolytes, and multivalent ions containing electrolytes. In addition, considering the rapid development of newly developed electrode materials, it is essential to fundamentally understand the dynamics and behavior of electrolyte ions in materials such as complex hierarchical-structured carbon-based materials, pseudocapacitive electrode materials, and hybrid/composite materials. An understanding of these fundamental aspects can be facilitated by utilizing *in situ* experimental characterization approaches such as spectroelectrochemistry, nuclear magnetic resonance, and Fourier transform infrared spectroscopy, combined with theoretical work based on the molecular/electron level. To ensure the development of long-term ES stability, an in-depth understanding of the degradation mechanisms of electrolytes requires further research through *in situ* or online analysis methods such as Raman microscopy and differential electrochemical mass spectroscopy.

3. Development of appropriate, standardized methods to evaluate electrolyte performances. With the rapidly increasing research in the field of ESs and development of new electrolytes such as solid-state or quasi-solid-state electrolytes, it is highly desirable to establish appropriate, standardized methods to characterize and compare the performance metrics of various electrolytes and the assembled ESs with the investigated electrolyte. When evaluating the performance of ESs, the mass and volume of the tested electrolyte must also be considered. To obtain the true performance of electrolytes, it is necessary to standardize a series of factors, such as the loading amount, the thickness of electrode materials, binders (if any), current collectors, and testing conditions. Furthermore, it is also required to develop reliable and standard methods for evaluating the performance of solid electrolyte-based ESs under applied stresses.

5.4 SUMMARY

To facilitate wide applications of ESs, it is essential to develop ESs with remarkably higher energy densities while retaining other advantages such as high-power performances. To achieve this target, a wide variety of novel electrolytes and promising electrode materials have been explored for ESs. Increasing the operative cell voltages of ESs is an extremely practical way to improve the energy density. Since the operative voltage windows of ESs are strongly limited by the electrochemical stability of electrolytes, various types of electrolytes have been investigated for ESs. The electrolytes developed so far are summarized and classified into aqueous electrolytes, organic electrolytes, ILs, solid-state or quasi-solid-state electrolytes, and redox-active electrolytes. In spite of considerable achievements in this field, several major challenges still exist. These challenges include (a) improving the energy density of ESs while maintaining high-power capability and good cycling stability; (b) a lack of standard methods to evaluate the performance of electrolytes for ESs; (c) the high cost of some electrolytes especially ILs; and (d) an insufficient fundamental understanding of charge storage mechanisms for some newly developed electrolytes in more realistic and complex electrode materials. To address the above challenges, some possible research directions were also proposed in this chapter.

REFERENCES

1. Jiang, D. E., Z. H. Jin, D. Henderson, and J. Z. Wu. 2012. Solvent effect on the pore-size dependence of an organic electrolyte supercapacitor. *Journal of Physical Chemistry Letters* 3:1727–1731.
2. Chmiola, J., G. Yushin, Y. Gogotsi, C. Portet, P. Simon, and P. L. Taberna. 2006. Anomalous increase in carbon capacitance at pore sizes less than 1 nanometer. *Science* 313:1760–1763.
3. Largeot, C., C. Portet, J. Chmiola, P. L. Taberna, Y. Gogotsi, and P. Simon. 2008. Relation between the ion size and pore size for an electric double-layer capacitor. *Journal of the American Chemical Society* 130:2730–2731.
4. Centeno, T. A., O. Sereda, and F. Stoeckli. 2011. Capacitance in carbon pores of 0.7 to 15 nm: A regular pattern. *Physical Chemistry Chemical Physics* 13:12403–12406.
5. Jiang, D. E., Z. Jin, and J. Wu. 2011. Oscillation of capacitance inside nanopores. *Nano Letters* 11:5373–5377.
6. Feng, G., J. Huang, B. G. Sumpter, V. Meunier, and R. Qiao. 2011. A "counter-charge layer in generalized solvents" framework for electrical double layers in neat and hybrid ionic liquid electrolytes. *Physical Chemistry Chemical Physics* 13:14723–14734.
7. Shim, Y., Y. Jung, and H. J. Kim. 2011. Graphene-based supercapacitors: A computer simulation study. *Journal of Physical Chemistry C* 115:23574–23583.
8. Fedorov, M. V., and A. A. Kornyshev. 2014. Ionic liquids at electrified interfaces. *Chemical Reviews* 114:2978–3036.
9. Ozolinš, V., F. Zhou, and M. Asta. 2013. Ruthenia-based electrochemical supercapacitors: Insights from first-principles calculations. *Accounts of Chemical Research* 46:1084–1093.
10. Liu, Y. D., F. Zhou, and V. Ozolins. 2012. *Ab initio* study of the charge-storage mechanisms in RuO_2-based electrochemical ultracapacitors. *Journal of Physical Chemistry C* 116:1450–1457.
11. Tompsett, D. A., S. C. Parker, P. G. Bruce, and M. Saiful Islam. 2013. Nanostructuring of β-MnO_2: The important role of surface to bulk ion migration. *Chemistry of Materials* 25:536–541.
12. Cormier, Z. R., H. A. Andreas, and P. Zhang. 2011. Temperature-dependent structure and electrochemical behavior of RuO_2/carbon nanocomposites. *Journal of Physical Chemistry C* 115:19117–19128.
13. Kang, J., S. H. Wei, K. Zhu, and Y. H. Kim. 2011. First-principles theory of electrochemical capacitance of nanostructured materials: Dipole-assisted subsurface intercalation of lithium in pseudocapacitive TiO_2 anatase nanosheets. *Journal of Physical Chemistry C* 115:4909–4915.
14. Zhong, C., Y. Deng, W. Hu, J. Qiao, L. Zhang, and J. Zhang. 2015. A review of electrolyte materials and compositions for electrochemical supercapacitors. *Chemical Society Reviews* 44:7484–7539.
15. Miller, J. R., and A. F. Burke. 2008. Electrochemical capacitors: Challenges and opportunities for real-world applications. *Electrochemical Society Interface* 17:53–57.

For Product Safety Concerns and Information please contact our EU representative GPSR@taylorandfrancis.com Taylor & Francis Verlag GmbH, Kaufingerstraße 24, 80331 München, Germany

Batch number: 10726532

Printed by Printforce, the Netherlands

CRC Press
Taylor & Francis Group
6000 Broken Sound Parkway NW, Suite 300
Boca Raton, FL 33487-2742

First issued in paperback 2021

ISBN 13: 978-0-367-77839-2 (pbk)
ISBN 13: 978-1-4822-3513-5 (hbk)

Library of Congress Cataloging-in-Publication Data

Names: DiMaggio, John A., author. | Vernon, Wesley, author.
Title: Forensic podiatry : principles and methods / by John A. DiMaggio and Wesley Vernon.
Description: Second edition. | New York : CRC Press, [2017] | Includes bibliographical references and index.
Identifiers: LCCN 2016033392| ISBN 9781482235135 (hardback : alk. paper) | ISBN 9781315395029 (ebook)
Subjects: LCSH: Forensic podiatry. | Forensic sciences. | Footprints.
Classification: LCC HV8077.5.F6 D55 2017 | DDC 614/.1--dc23LC record available at https://lccn.loc.gov/2016033392

Visit the Taylor & Francis Web site at
http://www.taylorandfrancis.com

and the CRC Press Web site at
http://www.crcpress.com

This book is dedicated to the memory of Norman H. Gunn, DPM

A pioneer in the field of forensic podiatry

Contents

Introduction

During the time between these first and second publications, it is apparent that much has changed. The new publication has more than doubled in size. Forensic podiatry practice has developed to the point that although it is still a relatively small forensic specialty, it is becoming known by many as a valuable forensic discipline. The true test of awareness is how well known a specialty or discipline is outside the professional sphere within which it operates. In recent times, forensic podiatry cases have been reported positively in the media (ABC News 2012; Brisbane Times 2012; Malagon 2015); forensic podiatrists have been invited to take part in television documentaries (Daily Mail Reporter 2013; KCPTO 2016); and perhaps even more notably, forensic podiatrists and their work have begun to be used in works of fiction, including crime novels (Cowley 2015; Spinella 2013) and television crime dramas (Hughes 2010; IMDb 2011).

Despite this notable increase in awareness, there are still relatively few regularly practicing forensic podiatrists worldwide. Although various private consultants and academics provide forensic podiatry services, at the time of writing there is only one dedicated forensic podiatry unit known that employs several forensic podiatrists to provide the full range of forensic podiatry services to commissioning agencies (Walker et al. 2016).

The current situation in which awareness of forensic podiatry is increasing dramatically, with relatively few practitioners being able to provide forensic podiatry services, could become problematic. However, one master's degree course in forensic podiatry is available and this course, in conjunction with other courses that anecdotally are being considered in various universities, will be essential in training additional forensic podiatrists who could then respond to the increased demand. If this demand continues, the discipline will need and can expect more advanced study courses in forensic podiatry to help prepare additional practitioners to meet such increasing demands.

The American Society of Forensic Podiatry (ASFP), established in 2003, is an entry-level professional organization that has members currently from the United States, but also the United Kingdom (UK), Canada, Australia, India, and Spain. Through its efforts, an undergraduate course on forensic podiatry has been established at the New York College of Podiatric Medicine. There are currently four student forensic podiatry clubs established at educational institutions.

Inclusion of podiatrists in other professional organizations, such as the International Association for Identification, which has its own section, the Chartered Society of Forensic Sciences, and the American Academy of Forensic Sciences has been accomplished.

Additional research to develop and support the work of forensic podiatrists has taken place since the first edition was published, although the forensic podiatry discipline has the potential to develop itself much further. Practice is undertaken within the boundaries of the forensic podiatry evidence base and experience, with forensic podiatry practitioners needing to make it clear as to whether their submitted work has been based on research-based understandings, experience, or both. As further research is undertaken to investigate the parameters of practice and to develop knowledge underpinning such practice, it is likely that forensic podiatrists will be in a position to offer much more to the criminal justice system than is currently possible. Improved understandings through research and development have the potential to widen forensic podiatry practice (i.e., forensic podiatrists will be able to offer more services with greater value than currently possible) and deepen understanding of specific aspects of practice (e.g., evidential conclusions presented by forensic podiatrists can be strengthened further, thereby becoming more valuable forms of evidence than is the current situation). As such, further forensic podiatry research has been and is expected to continue to drive these developments.

The above anticipated developments relate specifically to the discipline of forensic podiatry. Other changes have been taking place that can be anticipated to continue across the criminal justice system that will require and drive change for forensic podiatry as well as all other forensic disciplines. The majority of these changes relate to the universal demand for improved standards, governance, and ethics in forensic science and practice (Home Office 2016; NRC 2009). In line with such demands, forensic podiatrists have needed and will continue to need to improve their own practices to ensure that their work meets such requirements. Having made these improvements, they will also be required to demonstrate their compliance through monitoring systems, including audits and peer reviews.

Forensic podiatry has developed considerably since it was first used in the early 1970s and more recently since it began to be formally accepted by mainstream professional bodies in the field of forensic science. Many further developments can be expected over the next few years to build on this previous foundation work and keep practice in line with external expectations.

References

ABC News. (2012). Questions over Corryn Rayney's boot scuffs. *ABC News*. September 28. Available from: http://www.abc.net.au/news/2012-09-28/rayney-trial/4286496 (Accessed September 29, 2016).

Brisbane Times. (2012). Murder scene footprints could be Sica's. *Brisbane Times*. April 30. Available from: http://www.brisbanetimes.com.au/queensland/murder-scene-footprints-could-be-sicas-court-20120430-1xu0e.html (Accessed March 15, 2016).

Cowley, Emma. (2015). *Forensic podiatry and crime fiction. Careers in podiatry.* Available from: http://careersinpodiatry.com/2015/11/04/forensic-podiatry-crime-fiction/ (Accessed March 15, 2016).

Daily Mail Reporter. (2013). Amanda Knox documentary reconstructs Italian apartment murder scene in CSI-style probe to try to answer five key questions. Mail Online. September 25. Available from: http://www.dailymail.co.uk/news/article-2432112/Amanda-Knox-documentary-reconstructs-Italian-apartment-murder-scene-CSI-style-probe-try-answer-key-questions.html#ixzz42yHjFnUa (Accessed March 15, 2016).

Home Office. (2016). *Forensic Science Strategy: A national approach to forensic science delivery in the criminal justice system*. London: The Williams Lea Group on behalf of the Controller of the HMSO.

Hughes, Gwyneth. (2010). Five days: Season 2. BBC TV. March.

IMDb. (2011). Bones: The feet on the beach: Plot summary. Available from: http://www.imdb.com/title/tt1628113/plotsummary?ref_=tt_ov_pl (Accessed March 15, 2016).

KCPTO. (2016). *How Sherlock changed the world*. KCPTO. Available from: http://kcpt.org/highlights/how-sherlock-changed-the-world/ (Accessed March 15, 2016).

Malagon, Elvia. (2015). Local doctor helps net Wisconsin murder conviction. nwi.com. January 9. Available from: http://www.nwitimes.com/news/local/lake/local-doctor-helps-net-wisconsin-murder-conviction/article_36dffda2-92c1-5b2b-9f99-4c07175f7c1e.html (Accessed March 15, 2016).

NRC (National Research Council). (2009). *Strengthening Forensic Science in the United States—A Path Forward. National Academy of Sciences.* Washington, DC: The National Academies Press.

Spinella, Art "Drago #6: And the City Burned" 2013. Available from: http://www.DragoMysterySeries.com (Accessed July 20, 2013).

Walker, Jeremy, Selinha Reidy, Sarah Reel, and Ivan Birch. (2016). The work of the Sheffield Teaching Hospital's Forensic Podiatry Unit. *Podiatry Now* 19(4): 20–22.

General Forensic Concerns

I

The Crime Scene and Crime Laboratory 1

Evidence collection is one of the most important components of a criminal investigation and subsequent prosecution. Physical evidence can positively link a suspect to a crime, or it can prove one's innocence. Continued advancements in technology and instrumentation then assist law enforcement and crime scene professionals in piecing together the forensic information from the materials collected at the crime scene. Some of these materials may not end up having evidentiary value, but they still need to be discovered, identified, collected, and analyzed, and technological advances assist the crime scene investigation team with such tasks. The reliability of and dedication to crime scene processing and evidence collection have also become more important to the general public, possibly because of the increased awareness of forensic techniques viewed widely on TV. This public expectation places an additional obligation on a crime scene investigation team to solve local crimes in a similar manner to those of the publicized cases on TV.

1.1 General Concerns Regarding Pedal Evidence

It would not be usual for forensic podiatrists to recover evidence from the scene of a crime; this duty belongs to the scene of crime officer (SOCO), crime scene investigator (CSI), or crime scene officer (CSO), depending on the country of origin (Vernon et al. 2009). It can however be helpful for the forensic podiatrist to understand the general processes involved and what has taken place before the evidence is placed in his or her possession. It is also possible that advice from the forensic podiatrist may be requested from crime scene specialists where pedal evidence is apparent at the scene, providing a further need for the processes involved to be understood by the podiatrist.

If a single footprint is present at a crime scene, then it is possible that additional footprints are also present; however, often only one footprint is found. In many cases, only a partial footprint is found and in some circumstances, none are found. The theory postulated by French forensic scientist Edward Locard (Locard's exchange principle) stated that "every contact between people and/or objects will result in the exchange of evidence of the contact between the two" (Siegel 2007, 12). Knowing that such transference and exchange is to be expected suggests that diligent searching for additional prints could be productive. Until recently, pedal evidence was not considered to be of great value, especially if there were no suspects; however, with the advent of the certified footwear examiner/footmarks examiner and the forensic podiatrist, such thinking has changed. After entry into the crime scene and visual overall observation, the investigator has crime scene personnel look for pedal evidence in the most obvious locations. In many cases the crime scene is chaotic, and there may be multiple crime scene shoeprints, some of which are from emergency medical teams (EMTs) or police officers. It is therefore advisable to collect all shoeprints and exclude those of officers and EMTs later, as opposed to not collecting these prints at all. There is always the chance that one of these shoeprints belongs to the suspect. In addition, every bare footprint has the potential for providing information about the person who made it. A bare footprint can offer a high level of individuality, including differences between the right and left foot of the same person.

In addition to searching the obvious areas, systematic searches need to be performed that include the exterior and peripheral areas of the crime scene.

1.2 Crime Scene

The main objectives of personnel at the crime scene are to protect, identify, record, collect, and preserve evidence and to maintain a chain of custody. The investigator should maintain a general knowledge of the protocols required at the crime scene, even though it will not usually be necessary for the forensic podiatrist to attend the crime scene. Some considerations relative to footprint evidence include climatic conditions. For example, a recent rain at an outdoor scene may be conducive to the formation of three-dimensional footprints or shoeprints. Conversely, heavy precipitation may destroy these prints or make them less usable. Often, the point of entry can be the most productive area of the crime scene for finding evidence such as tool marks, foot or shoe impressions, and fingerprints related to that entry. A very thorough search around the perimeter of the crime scene can be valuable and needs to be diligently performed by crime scene personnel.

Securing the crime scene is most important to prevent unnecessary contamination and to allow for the preservation and subsequently the best representation of the physical evidence. Protocols usually involve an officer securing the scene and logging in only those individuals who are required to be at that scene. In a high-profile case it can be difficult to keep a crime scene under control. One of the main problems, albeit unintentional, is with the arrival of the EMTs and other emergency personnel. Their primary task is to save lives and as they enter a crime scene they may inadvertently leave their own prints at the scene, possibly obliterating pedal evidence as they do so. Where there has been the potential for this contamination, prints should be taken from all who were present at the crime scene. Although this approach will not bring back obliterated prints, it will allow the prints of all personnel present to be identified and then eliminated from the inquiry as appropriate.

1.3 Discovery of Physical Evidence

By the time that a podiatrist becomes involved in identification of bare footprints, crime officers have often already found and collected the bare footprint for comparison purposes. It is however useful to briefly consider the process used, both for contextual understanding and to provide a basic knowledge of the procedures involved, should the podiatrist be asked to assist in the location and collection of bare footprints. Inevitably, the perpetrator of a crime will have entered and left the crime scene and in doing so will have left shoeprints, or occasionally bare footprints at that scene (Hilderbrand 1999). These shoe or footprints may not initially be apparent and need to be discovered to be of use. The investigator will thus need to view the crime scene in its entirety and consider within that scenario where shoe or footprints are likely to be found. If, for example, entry was through a broken window, there would be a reasonable possibility of prints being present on either side of this window. In a case involving acts of direct physical violence, usually involving blood loss by the victim, bare footprints may be anticipated in the vicinity of the body. After considering the scene in this way, there may be a requirement to use specialized lighting techniques or chemicals to indicate the presence of bare footprints in these areas, as these prints may not be immediately obvious to the naked eye. The investigator then notes any bare footprints present and records their positions for later image capture and collection. The investigator may also continue to look for bare footprints, either when footprints are not present or to increase the number of prints available for later comparison. Bare footprints can be discovered in either two- or three-dimensional form. Three-dimensional prints are those made in a substrate that lead to an impression consisting of length, width, and breadth measurements. These prints may occur in dirt or sand. Two-dimensional prints are those made on a harder surface, thus they provide only length and width measurements (DiMaggio 2005). Three-dimensional footprints of adequate quality are usually, by definition, obvious, whereas two-dimensional prints may be more hidden from view. When searching for two-dimensional prints, both the surface form and possible substrates that may present on the print need to be considered because some surface–substrate combinations are more conducive to the formation of prints than others (Bodziak 2000; DiMaggio 2005).

1.4 Enhancing Bare Footprint Evidence

After the areas in which bare footprints may be present at a crime scene have been defined, the task then is to collect and, if necessary, enhance the prints for examination purposes. Collection can take place before or after enhancement. Enhancement before collection would usually take place when the method of collection at the scene is photography. Experience has shown that footprints captured at crime scenes by photography are the most usual form of evidence presented to podiatrists for later examination, as opposed to the use of the actual removed footprints, or the collection of three-dimensional footprints through casting techniques.

To either optimize the detail in prints, which are already apparent, or search for prints, which are not immediately obvious, the investigator may undertake the enhancement of footprints before collection. This task is often facilitated by the introduction of lighting variables that can be used in combination with chemical enhancement of the prints, if indicated. The simplest lighting variable is the introduction of oblique light to the scene. An oblique light source is angled to the print to make the print, the detail within the print, or both more apparent (Figure 1.1). Oblique lighting can be used with equal

(a) (b)

Figure 1.1 Comparison of foot impressions under (a) normal and (b) oblique lighting.

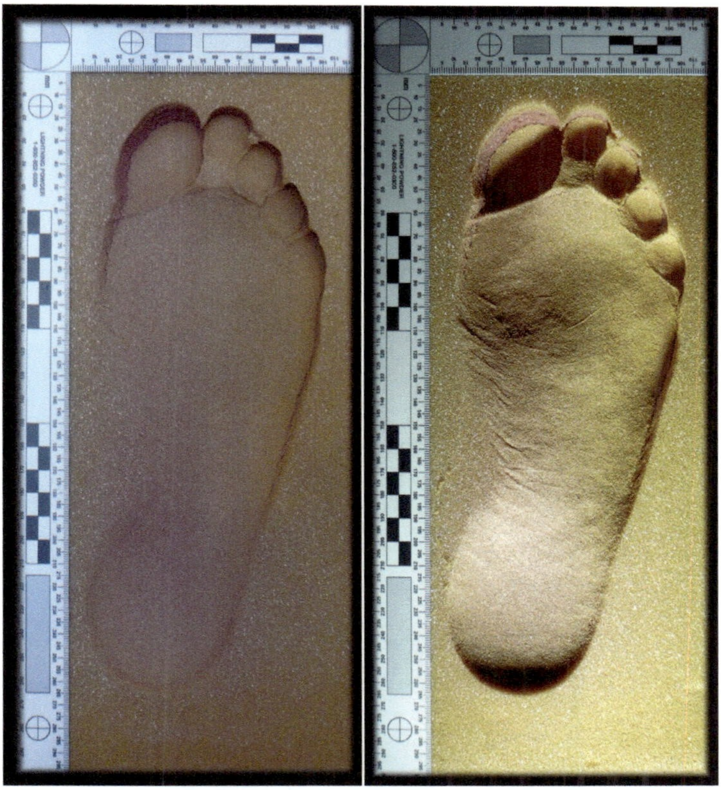

(a) (b)

Figure 1.2 Effect of (a) overhead and (b) oblique lighting on a three-dimensional foot impression.

success in two- and three-dimensional prints. With three-dimensional prints, the print can become optimized by oblique lighting techniques through the introduction of shadow effects and greater contrast between various areas of the print (Figure 1.2).

Specialized forms of lighting can also be used by the SOCO, CSI, or CSO, and they are most commonly described as forensic light sources or alternate light sources. Together, they span the visible spectrum plus infrared and ultraviolet wavelengths. By adjusting the wavelength within the visible spectrum, already visible prints can be enhanced and show details that may not be immediately apparent under basic white light illumination. The use of wavelengths outside the visible spectrum can be used to show the presence of prints not immediately apparent to the observer (Figure 1.3). Of particular note in relation to the enhancement of footprints is the use of luminol to chemically enhance prints that may have been left in blood and that are not visible to

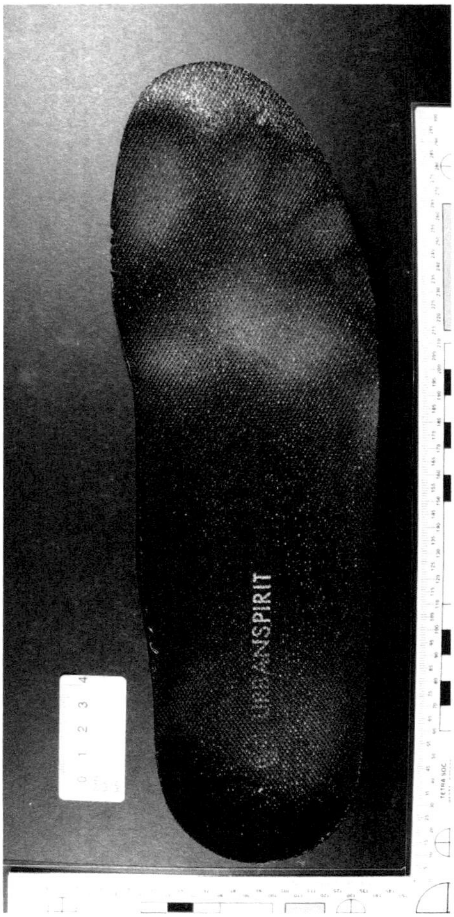

Figure 1.3 Enhancement of foot impressions through the use of specialized lighting sources.

the naked eye. Luminol has been described as "a chemicoluminescent compound that is used as a presumptive, catalytic test for the presence of blood," where it is said to be so sensitive that it fluoresces with blood present in just 1 part in 5 million (Redsicker 2001). When used, luminol is sprayed onto the area under consideration and then viewed in the dark, the luminol would fluoresce and glow in areas where it has contacted traces of blood [although it also is known to react in contact with paint, porcelain, metal, and hypochlorite (bleach)] (Eckert 1997). In dealing with prints, where the foot has trodden in blood at the crime scene, those areas of the foot that have contacted the blood would show up clearly with the luminol test. If the entire plantar surface has contacted blood, there is the potential for the whole footprint to become apparent through the application of luminol. Once the print has been

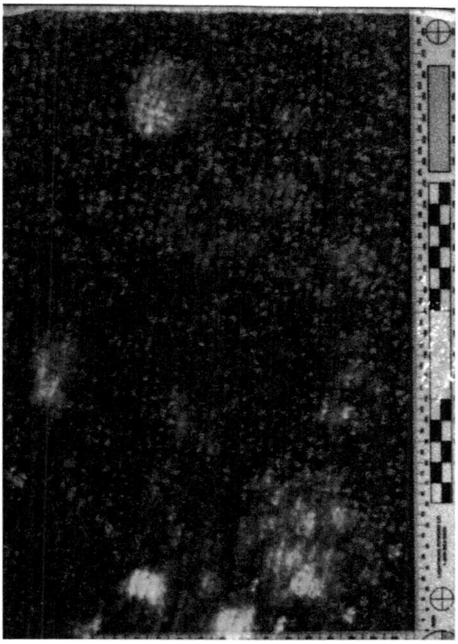

Figure 1.4 Enhancement of bloody bare footprint on carpet by using luminol.

treated with luminol, it is possible to photograph this luminol-enhanced print for later assessment and comparison (Figure 1.4).

Bluestar® Forensic is a new reagent that creates chemiluminescence with blood and has certain the following advantages over luminol:

- Nontoxic and easy to prepare
- Long-lasting and bright images
- Good-quality photos obtained with an ordinary camera
- No alteration of DNA
- Same solution can be used repeatedly to fluoresce the same bloodstain
- No need to use in total darkness

Both luminol and Bluestar Forensic can reveal evidence of blood years after the incident occurred and can be of benefit in cold cases where remnants of blood still remain.

1.5 Collecting Questioned Bare Footprint Evidence

There are several textbooks that comprehensively consider the process of discovering, enhancing, and collecting shoeprints for identification purposes. The techniques of capture and enhancement of footwear as described in these books translate directly to the capture and enhancement of bare footprints present at the scene of the crime. See Bodziak (1999) and Hildebrand (2013) to gain a comprehensive understanding of these tasks and processes.

Although, as mentioned, it is unlikely that the forensic podiatrist will be required to collect footprint evidence directly, his or her understanding of this process can be useful for contextual reasons. A variety of techniques are used to collect footprints for examination purposes, and these techniques are considered in brief below.

Physical removal of bare footprint evidence: It may be possible to physically remove a bare footprint from a crime scene for later examination and comparison purposes. Examples of situations in which a footprint would be removed include those in which the footprint has been made on a door, enabling the door to be physically removed from its hinges; or where the footprint has been made on a loose item at the scene, e.g., a sheet of paper that can then be easily taken away for examination. If necessary, material containing a clear bare footprint can be physically cut away from the scene before removal. This removal could apply to bare footprints present on a section of carpet, or to prints on a wooden floorboard or tile floor.

Lifting: Lifting techniques are used when a two-dimensional bare footprint is available for examination purposes. It is defined as "a way of transferring a two-dimensional impression from its original surface to a surface that will provide better contrast" (Bodziak 1999). Through lifting, the footprint can be removed for later examination. There are many techniques of lifting two-dimensional impressions, each with its own distinct advantages and disadvantages. Such techniques include adhesive and gelatin lifts, both of which allow dusty prints to be collected (Hilderbrand 2013); electrostatic lifts that rely on the use of static electricity to collect dusty prints (Bodziak 1999); and various silicone-based products that adhere to the prints and that when set allow the print to be removed. The choice of lift used depends on the type of bare footprint available for removal, the surface upon which the bare footprint is present, and the contrast available through the background color of the lifting surface. Whichever lifting method is selected, the print should always be photographed before lifting in case anything goes wrong during the lifting process, thereby spoiling the print.

Casting: Although lifting is the method of choice for the removal of two-dimensional impressions, casting is the preferred method for the capture and removal of three-dimensional bare footprints/foot impressions. The purpose of casting is to collect the bare footprint while retaining as much fine detail as possible. This process has been defined in the context of footwear as "the filling of a three-dimensional footwear impression with a material that will acquire and retain the characteristics that were left in that impression by the footwear" (Bodziak 1999). Various materials are available for casting and include differing grades of dental stone, silicon-based materials, alginates, paraffin wax, and sulfur. Because properties of these materials are diverse, the casting method needs be selected carefully, according to the circumstances. Some of these methods, e.g., sulfur and paraffin wax, allow casts to be taken from prints in snow. As in the lifting techniques, it is usual for the three-dimensional prints to be photographed before casting in case damage to the print occurs during casting.

Photography: It can be considered in capturing the bare footprint and should invariably be used in conjunction with any of the other methods of footprint capture. The photography process is considered in detail in Chapter 3. As stated, although podiatrists are unlikely to find themselves at crime scenes, it is important that any evidence-quality photographic images that are passed to them later for examination have been taken to the standards required. It is essential that the examining podiatrist ensures such standards before starting the examination and comparison of the images.

1.6 Collection of Evidence

Each item of evidence must be placed in a separate and appropriate secure container. All items must be appropriately marked and packaging must be sealed using standard protocols. When selecting the type of container, several factors should be considered: whether the material represents a biohazard, thereby requiring special precautions and labeling; whether the material is fragile, thereby needing additional protection; and whether the evidence is or is not suitable for placing into packaging that is occlusive, thereby heightening the risk of undesirable effects such as mold growth. In general, plaster/stone foot mold casts and footwear should be packaged in a paper receptacle. Each item should be packaged separately and sealed in an appropriate manner with evidence tape. Each item should be labeled with the examiners initials, date, case number, and other relevant information.

1.7 Chain of Custody

The purpose of maintaining a chain of custody is to be able to clearly identify the evidence and show that it has remained secure and free from external influence at all times from seizure to conclusion. To this end, a continuous audit trail is required in which it can be shown, in order, exactly who had secure possession of and access to the evidentiary item. Included in this process there needs to be a log with certain information:

- Case number
- Date
- Time
- Item(s)
- Means of delivery
- From
- To
- Received by
- Comments

If the exhibit has been properly identified by this method, the chain of custody is complete.

The evidence must at all times be kept in a secure (locked) location until it is needed elsewhere, and at which time all chain of custody protocols are adhered to again.

1.8 Crime Laboratory

Crime laboratories have been present in the United States since 1924, when the first laboratory attached to a police department was instigated by the Los Angeles Police Department (Eckert 1997). Later, laboratories were introduced by the federal government across the country, and now include the Federal Bureau of Investigation, Drug Enforcement Agency, and Alcohol Tobacco and Firearms Bureau laboratories (Eckert 1997). Today, crime laboratories are often operated on a local, independent basis by the various agencies involved in law enforcement.

Currently in the UK, forensic work is undertaken either in-house within police forces or by private laboratories.

In Canada, forensic science services are provided through three government-funded institutes: the Institute of Legal Medicine of Police Science, the Centre of Forensic Sciences, and the Royal Canadian Mounted Police regional laboratories. More than 100 countries worldwide have at least one laboratory facility offering forensic science services (Saferstein 2009). A full-service forensic laboratory offers many services, and laboratory personnel can also supply expert testimony in court. Laboratory personnel also provide answers to many technical questions that may be asked of the laboratory. The various services offered include latent fingerprints, toxicology, photographic unit, firearms unit, document examination, and footwear and barefoot examination. In the United States, pedal evidence concerns are usually addressed by the photographic unit of the laboratory with the task to use photography to capture such evidence for later evaluation. The photographic personnel can also use various techniques to enhance photographs for better visualization.

The maintenance of a close working relationship between a forensic podiatrist and laboratory personnel is very important, and close communication with the podiatrist will help the laboratory staff to understand what they can do to assist. After the capture of the questioned bare footprint or footwear, its transport to a laboratory, and possible subsequent examination by a forensic scientist, a forensic podiatrist may then be asked to become involved in a case of identification involving bare footprints or footwear. In the case of bare footprints, the task is to compare a bare footprint or prints that were present at the crime scene with bare footprints made by a known person (usually the suspect) to determine whether he or she is the owner of the questioned, or unknown, print. In the case of footwear, the task of the forensic podiatrist is usually to examine the potential for a link between the footwear and the person who is suspected of wearing that footwear.

References

Bodziak WJ. (2000). *Footwear Impression Evidence: Detection, Recovery and Examination*, 2nd edn. CRC Press, London.

DiMaggio J.A. (2005). The role of feet and footwear in medico legal investigations. In *Forensic Medicine of the Lower Extremity*, edited by J. Rich, D.E. Dean, and R.H. Powers. pp. 375–400. Totawa, NJ: Humana Press.

Eckert WG. (1997). *Introduction to Forensic Sciences*, 2nd edn. CRC Press, Boca Raton, FL.

Hilderbrand D.S. (1999). *Footwear, the Missed Evidence*. Temecula, CA: Staggs Publishing.

Hilderbrand D.S. (2013). *Footwear, the Missed Evidence*, 3rd edn. Staggs, Wildomar, CA.

Redsicker, David R. (2007). *Forensic Photography*. 2nd ed. Boca Raton: CRC Press.

Saferstein R. (2009). *Forensic Science: From the Crime Scene to the Crime Lab*. Prentice Hall, Englewood Cliffs, NJ.

Siegel JA. (2007). *Forensic Science: The Basics*. CRC Press, Boca Raton, FL.

Vernon W, Brodie B, DiMaggio J, Gunn N, Kelly H, Nirenberg M, Reel S, and Walker J. (2009). *Forensic Podiatry: Role and Scope of Practice (In the Context of Forensic Human Identification)*. International Association for Identification. http://www.theiai.org/disciplines/podiatry/podiatry_role_and_scope.pdf (Accessed November 3, 2011).

Human Identification and General Principles and Definitions Relevant to Forensic Podiatry Practice

2

This chapter discusses human identification, the science and practice of forensic podiatry, and its role and purpose of forensic podiatry in assisting the criminal justice system to identify people and answer other legal questions through the application of podiatric knowledge. A thorough explanation of what is needed for evidential purposes, a discussion of class and individual characteristics, and a short explanation of the likelihood ratio approach to forming conclusions in the consideration of pedal evidence are provided. A discussion of evidence handling and the methodology that would be used that parallels that of other disciplines is given [including the analysis, comparison, and evaluation of the evidence with independent peer verification (ACE-V) approach].

2.1 Human Identification

2.1.1 Purpose of Human Identification

> In modern Society, ordinary citizens accept certain personal responsibilities. In return, society guarantees fundamental personal and civil rights. These facts constitute the major reason why every citizen must retain personal identity throughout life and beyond death.
>
> *Keiser-Neilson 1980, 1*

The fact that personal identification is required within society is widely understood. The reasons why personal identity is required are however rarely considered in depth by the public. In the quote above, Keiser-Neilson succinctly defined the reasons why the maintenance of identity is so important throughout both life and death. In death, every single body, once discovered, does at that point belong to someone missing, so in an orderly society, every human body must be identified as quickly as possible (Keiser-Neilsen 1980) to enable societal order to continue. Problems that can occur in the case of a missing person can involve the settlement of estates, the need to pay out insurance awards, ascertainment that no foul play is involved, and the need to avoid the possibility of bigamy (Reisner and Wooldridge 1977).

If the missing person supports a family and it is not known whether that person is alive or dead, financial burdens may be placed on the family until the person is officially pronounced as dead. In such cases, "assumed death" can replace the death certificates, but a period up to several years can be stipulated before an application for this verdict can be made. In England and Wales, a Presumption of Death Act requires that a person must have been thought to be dead or "have not been known to be alive" for at least seven years before their death can be formally assumed and their property passed to others and their marriage or civil partnership ended (Fairbairn 2015). The United States typically has a seven-year period of declared death in absentia, but that period can vary from state to state. Thus, serious legal complications are created when a person becomes missing. By law, minimum nonphysical data are recorded for everyone on birth certificates representing social identity, and death certificates are used to officially record death. Both are important legal documents and until a death certificate is issued, missing persons must be considered alive and entitled to the full protection of their personal, human, and civil rights as well as being held accountable for their legal and other societal responsibilities.

Where a crime has taken place and the perpetrator has left human evidence, that person must be identified as quickly as possible. While that person is alive, he or she remains fully responsible for keeping and having kept actions within the acceptable constraints defined by the society within which he or she lives, with there being legal implications when the rules of society have been broken. In a crime scene, the requirement is to identify the perpetrator of the crime (as well as the victim) as soon as possible to prevent further occurrence and to allow justice to be administered for the misdemeanor.

2.1.2 Personal Identity

Personal identity is formed from infinite combinations of physical and mental features, few of which in isolation can be seen as individual. In the deceased person, loss of identity may occur through the body becoming severely traumatized, through the person being unknown, and through decomposition. In the living person, loss of identity most commonly occurs in relation to crime, where a perpetrator can deliberately attempt to hide his or her identity at varying levels and in several ways. Such attempts can range from simply leaving the scene of crime and hoping to never be associated with the event to being forensically aware and going to great lengths to prevent leaving any evidence of their presence at the scene, or possibly destroying such evidence after the event.

To establish the identity of an unknown person, the process of person identification is used in which data of an unknown person, either the dead, the amnesiac, or the criminal, are compared with data available from a known person, in an effort to establish a match (identification) or mismatch (exclusion) with the unknown person. When authorities are satisfied of a match, and identity is re-established, subsequent actions can include the issuing of death certificates, undergoing rehabilitation, or charging and criminal conviction of the person concerned.

Personal identity is therefore important in society and its loss through denial, death, or memory loss, particularly in relation to crime situations, may require help from forensic examiners to re-establish personal identity.

2.2 General Principles and Definitions Relevant to Forensic Podiatry Practice

2.2.1 Scientific Practice

Thomas Samuel Kuhn was a science philosopher of great significance. It was Kuhn's belief that normal science "meant research firmly based upon one or more past scientific achievements, which within that community provides the foundation for further practice" (Kuhn 1996, 10). Kuhn referred to these scientific achievements as paradigms that he described as essentially a set of agreements shared by scientists as to how problems are to be understood. He believed that paradigms are essential to scientific inquiry, because "no natural history can be interpreted in the absence of an implicit body of theoretical and methodological belief that allows selection, evaluation, and criticism" (Kuhn 1996, 16–17). A paradigm therefore guides the research efforts of scientific communities, and as such its presence most clearly identifies a field of knowledge as a science.

After the establishment of paradigms, the formation of professional groups and their attendant activities (e.g., journals, conferences and educational programs) usually takes place, all of which are centered on those with assumed knowledge of the paradigm in question. Kuhn believed that a scientific community could not practice its trade without such a set of received beliefs that rigorously prepare and authorize the student for professional practice within that science.

The knowledge used by podiatrists as part of their forensic practice should ideally be that component of their knowledge base that can be described as scientific: the research-based foundation knowledge of professional practice.

2.2.2 Forensic Scientific Practice

Forensic science is science used for the purposes of the law, particularly in the detection of crime and the administration of justice (House of Commons Science and Technology Committee 2005). In its broadest sense, the full spectrum of forensic science includes all related activities within that field from basic research to applied technology. The term "forensic science" therefore refers not only to the typical services offered by the main forensic science providers, such as analyses involving toxicology, DNA, hair, fiber, footwear, tool marks, firearms, drugs and documents, but also to the research that underpins the development, testing, and introduction of new forensic technology. Forensic pathology, the examination of human bodies to determine the cause and manner of death in criminal or suspicious circumstances, is also included within this definition, as is the use of fingerprints for identification purposes. Previously, in the UK, approximately 85% of forensic services were delivered by the Forensic Science Service (FSS) (House of Commons Science and Technology Committee 2005); however, in March 2012 the FSS was closed down by the UK government (UKFSR 2011). Since this closure, forensic services have been contracted out to the private and independent sectors or provided in-house within the police services (House of Commons Science and Technology Committee 2013). According to information listed on the University of Kent website in 2012, it is believed that around 5000 people work in forensic science in the UK, with 200 graduates being recruited each year. Given that there are much lower numbers of forensic podiatrists practicing regularly in the UK, forensic podiatry is a highly specialized, non-mainstream area of forensic practice that nevertheless has responsibilities to operate within the same framework as the more mainstream disciplines.

In the United States, forensic services are provided through many organizational levels of crime laboratories: municipal laboratory departments, state laboratory facilities, and the national Federal Bureau of Investigation that offers services to all police departments in the United States. As in the UK, forensic podiatry is currently practiced outside this context, but again it should still ideally be scientific, by definition used for forensic purposes, and operated within the same framework of practice and responsibility as that of the established crime laboratories.

Irrespective of the country in which it is performed, the practice of forensic science concerns the application of science in relation to forensic problems. A forensic scientist is expected to be able to think and reason in a scientific way, bringing together theory and practice to address the issue at hand. Each forensic case requires the scientific testing of a working theory and the approach usually adopted is that of analysis, comparison, and evaluation of the evidence with independent peer verification (ACE-V). It has been suggested that the following qualities, abilities, and requirements make a competent forensic scientist:

1. Knowledge
2. Ability to work a case correctly
3. Ability to obtain a correct answer
4. Ability to present evidence to a reasonable standard

5. Use of appropriate methods
6. Acceptable ways of recording observational results
7. Accepted scientific criteria for interpretation (Allen 2002, 66)

2.2.3 Scientific Interpretation of Evidence

The term "science" has been defined as follows:

1. The systematic study of the nature and behavior of the material and physical universe, based on observation, experiment and measurement, and the formulation of laws to describe these facts in general terms
2. The knowledge so obtained and the process of obtaining it
3. Any particular branch of this knowledge
4. Any body of knowledge organized in a systematic manner
5. Skill or technique
6. Knowledge (Makins 1994, 1386)

Although these definitions of science are individually clear, they are wide ranging and suggest that the term can literally imply knowledge and its organization, the process of its acquisition, and the application of that knowledge. The philosophers however find these definitions over-simplistic and instead ask what common features these areas share that would "make them a science"—a much more complex question (Okasha 2002, 1). It has been suggested that there may not in fact be an essential nature to science; instead, science may be represented by loosely clustered features as opposed to fixed features (Okasha 2002).

Irrespective of the difficulties in defining science precisely, it certainly concerns knowledge and how that knowledge is appropriately acquired. Philosophers have previously stated that the only knowledge we can be certain about is that relating to arithmetic and geometry (North-Whitehead 1925), although this has been heavily debated over many years (Robinson and Groves 1999), and it has also been suggested that "we cannot know anything with 'perfect' certainty" (Mitroff and Turoff 1975). As such, processes of reasoning are needed to gain a best understanding of the world. These processes are known as deductive and inductive reasoning and inference to best explanation (Okasha 2002), and are best described by giving examples of how they may work in practice. As such, an example of deductive reasoning could be as follows:

- All podiatrists must be registered with the UK Health and Care Professions Council (HCPC) to be legally allowed to practice as a podiatrist in the UK as stated by the HCPC on its website on February 5, 2016.
- Sarah is legally allowed to practice as a podiatrist in the UK.
- It can therefore be reasoned that Sarah is registered with the Health and Care Professions Council.

As illustrated by this example, although it is not directly known that Sarah is registered with the HCPC, the applied logic leaves no room for doubt that if the two given statements are absolutely correct and all-encompassing, as Sarah is legally allowed to practice as a podiatrist, she must therefore be registered with the HCPC. It has been suggested that the term “proof” should strictly only be used when dealing with deductive inferences (Okasha 2012).

An example of inductive reasoning could be as follows:

- Six members of a podiatric surgery team use the same locker room for changing before a long operating theater (room) session. They all change in the locker room, each leaving wallets containing a large amount of money on open view on a table in the room. The room itself can be easily accessed from the public waiting area, and the room has not been secured.
- Five of the team members go to the locker room immediately after the operating theater session, but the sixth member of the team stays in the theater area to do an equipment audit.
- The five team members who have gone to the locker room find that during the long theater session, someone has entered the room and stolen all of their money from their wallets, all six of which had been on open view in the room.
- It can be reasoned that money left in the wallet of the sixth person (who has not yet been in the room to check) will also have been stolen.

Although the logic involved in inductive reasoning is clear to follow, the reasoning involved is not as tight as that involved in deductive reasoning and may not be correct. Although it may seem reasonable to assume that the thief has emptied all wallets of money, this may not necessarily have been the case. It could be that the thief concerned ran out of time before he or she was able to search and empty all wallets, or that the thief found the final wallet more difficult to open than the others, or that the thief knew the owner of the sixth wallet and as such did to want to steal from this person, or even that the sixth team member had been the one who stole money from the others. Inductive reasoning is therefore much more prone to reaching false conclusions in ways that deductive reasoning is not.

In relation to the above-mentioned hypothetical scenario, an example of the third form of reasoning, inference to best explanation, could be as follows:

- On investigation by the police, it was found that the sixth member of the surgery team had left the long operating session for 15 minutes halfway through that session.
- The following evening, the sixth member of the team had purchased an expensive meal for themselves and a partner for

£200 (US$267)—slightly less than the total amount of money that had been stolen from the wallets of the other team members.
- The police had previously interviewed the sixth member of the team when a wallet had been stolen from the team member's previous workplace in the same town.

Inference to the best explanation is another form of non-deductive reasoning, albeit considerably weaker than that of inductive reasoning. Although suggesting links between that staff member and the missing money, there could be alternative explanations for each of the given facts that could imply that the sixth member of the surgery team had stolen the money from the wallets of his or her colleagues. Leaving the long theater session could have related to little more than the need to visit the restroom, to make a personal phone call, or simply to seek fresh air or a drink of water in the middle of what had been a long session. The purchase of an expensive meal could have simply related to an anniversary celebration of the type that most people experience throughout the year or simply relate to that staff member being a gourmet food aficionado who regularly eats in expensive restaurants. Being interviewed by the police previously could simply relate to there being long-term occurrences of crimes of this type in the area concerned. While suggesting possible links between this person and the theft of money, there are several alternative explanations. However, from the information available, it could be that the explanation provided from this available information is the best or most plausible and therefore can be seen as the most reasonable in the absence of a better explanation.

Ideally, scientists should follow deductive reasoning only; however, this approach is often not possible in real-world situations where inductive reasoning is also used regularly as well as inference to the best explanation. As such, much of scientific interpretation is based on assumption to varying degrees, and as demonstrated above, such an interpretation is not necessarily reliable. We cannot therefore solely rely on scientific "fact" where science often provides the best explanation at a particular point in time—an explanation that can change with additional information.

The expert opinion provided by forensic scientists is, in effect, the final result of decision making under conditions of different degrees of uncertainty. Irrefutable knowledge is not guaranteed—there is usually some element of doubt, even if that doubt is infinitesimally small. Because there cannot be 100% certainty in relation to some of the knowledge used in forensic practice and scientific interpretation is an essential aspect of reaching a conclusion where (as is often the case to some extent) doubts can exist, all casework requires a degree of interpretation using the forms of reasoning described above. As shown, such interpretation can potentially be prone to error and bias, and the forensic practitioner should be aware of this potential and use safeguards to compensate for the potential for such error (e.g., the use of verification—the "V" aspect of ACE-V).

As noted above, any competent forensic scientist must be able to use accepted scientific criteria for interpretation (Allen 2002, 66). Interpretation itself should be distinguished from observation: observation represents what one sees, i.e., in a scientific context, data that are presented without explanation, with interpretation being the attempt to use reasoning to explain what it is that has been observed (what has happened).

The term "phenomenology" is a method of philosophical inquiry that is concerned with description (Jasper 1994; Koch 1995), whereas the term "hermeneutics," developed as a methodology for text interpretation, concerns the principles of interpretation and explanation (Palmer 1969). The use of these methodologies has widened since their development, and methods analogous to the classic meaning of both approaches have been used successfully in past research of direct relevance to forensic science and practice (Vernon 2000).

Hermeneutic methodologies can be considered a form of inductive analysis (Vernon 2000), and they provide a reasonable basis for understanding and approaching scientific interpretation in forensic practice. In achieving hermeneutic understanding, separate items of information are considered together (unified) in the context within which they exist. This unification process is described as drawing a Hermeneutic circle (Kvale 1987) with what is described as "a leap of understanding" taking place when the circle containing all the elements required for that understanding is complete (Vernon 2000, 30). There are two key elements to this process. First, all elements should be known before making that interpretation, and second any interpretation should always be made within context. If the context is not fully understood, the interpretation may be erroneous.

It is therefore inevitable that the forensic scientist will need to use interpretation routinely in his or her practice to bridge the gap between information available and understanding. Knowledge of the limitations of the different forms of reasoning should lead to appropriate cautions being taken in this task that in turn, will limit the potential for error at this essential stage of casework.

2.2.4 Physical Evidence

Pedal evidence is one of many forms of physical evidence. Physical evidence is diverse and can include, e.g., body fluids, fibers, fingerprints, footprints, and explosive materials. This type of evidence has the following functions:

- Prove that a crime has been committed
- Provide investigative leads

- Link a crime to a suspect
- Corroborate or refute a suspect's position
- Identify a suspect
- Induce a confession from a suspect
- Exonerate the innocent
- Provide expert testimony in court (Eckert and James 1997, 33–34)

2.2.5 Criteria for Usable Physical Evidence

The physical evidence considered by podiatrists needs to meet certain criteria to be of value. These criteria are considered in brief below.

Physical evidence needs to be available: Without the availability of physical evidence, very little can be done to identify a person. Forensically aware criminals try to exploit this fact when they attempt to destroy all evidence that could link their presence to a scene of crime.

Physical evidence needs to be of reasonable quality and quantity: Even if physical evidence is present and available, this evidence will be of minimal to no value if it is not of reasonable quality. Examples of physical evidence of inadequate quality in forensic podiatry terms include footprints that have been heavily smeared through slippage, the insoles of shoes in which the barefoot impression is unclear, and closed-circuit TV images in which the gait of the person of interest is blurred and indistinct. For these reasons, one of the first tasks that should be undertaken by a forensic podiatrist is that of a quality check to determine whether the evidence presented is usable.

The quantity of evidence, e.g., a partial bare footprint versus a complete bare footprint, can affect the course of an evaluation even if good quality evidence is present.

Physical evidence needs to be able to express individuality: Even if physical evidence is available and of high quality and quantity, this evidence may still be of limited value if it does not express some degree of individuality. An example of this issue in podiatric terms would be the obvious presence of five toes in a barefoot impression. Although the fact that the barefoot impression contains five toes may be incontrovertible, where comparison with the general population is required, this fact on its own will be of limited use because the majority of the general population exhibits this same feature.

Physical evidence ideally needs to be stable as a feature: Physical evidence can be present, of high quality and quantity, and present a high degree of individuality, yet still could be of limited value if that evidence is not stable. "Stable" in this context means that the evidence is unlikely to be altered in any way, e.g., through the effects of function, external influence during the passage of time, which may include the impact of the aging process. Assuming that a feature demonstrates a high degree of individuality, the more stable that feature is, the stronger its evidential value will be. An example of a stable feature would be a bony deformity of the foot (e.g., a true hammer toe), which is only likely to be amended through surgery or trauma. An example of instability could be the presence of a corn, which is associated with the wearing of a poorly fitting shoe. In this example the corn may later resolve when that person has addressed the poorly fitting footwear situation. Where instability is a factor, the evidence can still be of value albeit for a shorter time.

The need for stability brings in complications in relation to some podiatric aspects of forensic identification. For example, it has been demonstrated that shoe outsole wear patterns are not as stable a feature as was first thought; they are subject to the influence of multiple variable effects (Vernon 2000). Such features should therefore be handled cautiously in the identification process. Similarly, when using podiatry records where superficial skin lesions are being considered (e.g., corns, callus, pressure points) in the identification process, it may not be possible to state that these lesions are stable. Antemortem records showing the presence or absence of such lesions do not necessarily mean that they are going to be present or absent at a later date. This does not mean that such features cannot be used, but instead that the podiatric examiner must be aware of their limitations if stability is not guaranteed. In the forensic work of the footwear, or marks examiners, accidental characteristics of shoe outsoles are known to be virtually unique[1] and as such, accidental characteristics are one of the most valuable sources of evidence in identification. Despite this, the causative shoe may need to be found quickly after the shoe impression has been left because it is possible for the accidental features that were then present to be obliterated and replaced in time by new areas of trauma and damage.

2.2.6 Class and Individual Characteristics

Physical evidence can express different levels of individuality ranging from features, which a large proportion of the population can demonstrate, through to features, which can be considered unique. An understanding of this fact is fundamental to the use of evidence in casework. In this sense, two different levels of physical evidence have been described and are in use in the

[1] Stone's presentation in 1984 (as quoted in Bodziak 2000).

general forensic disciplines—class-level and individual-level characteristics. It has however previously been suggested that in relation to pedal evidence specifically, the term "class characteristic" could be further usefully subdivided into class and intermediate levels (DiMaggio 2005; Kennedy 1995), and this suggestion is also considered in this section.

Class-level characteristics have been given a number of different definitions (Bodziak 2000; Cassidy 1987; Cooke 1984; Osterberg 1967). Common to these definitions however is an implicit understanding that these features are not unique, but do instead demonstrate incontrovertible compatibility between similar items within a particular group. In footwear terms, the marked size would be an example of a class-level feature. The marked size of a shoe is certainly not a unique feature, but where a shoe impression is being compared with the same make and type of shoe which has a different marked size, it can be stated with certainty that the shoe impression has not been formed by that shoe. Other examples of class characteristics in relation to footwear would include the shoe style, make as described in the attached logos, the outsole shape, and the tread pattern. In relation to pedal evidence, class characteristics would be nonunique features of, affecting or relating to, human feet. Examples of class characteristics in this group would include size, shape (of heel or rear-foot, arch, mid-foot, forefoot, ball of foot, toe stems, and toes), and common conditions of, and affecting, the feet.

Class characteristics show consistency and compatibility. They do not show uniqueness. Importantly, however, in combination, class characteristics can create a picture of much stronger individuality than they would on their own as long as those characteristics are independently variable from one another. The use of class characteristics in this way involves considerations of known data, for example, prevalence and survey data for the class features under consideration.

It has also been suggested that as far as pedal evidence is concerned, it could be useful to consider an additional descriptive category, namely that of intermediate characteristics (DiMaggio 2005; Kennedy 1995) which could describe features of, and affecting, the foot that are not unique but nevertheless are unusual and represent high levels of individuality. Although forensic podiatry evidence exists predominantly at the class level, the evidential weight of each item of evidence can differ considerably. The presence of a condition which is known to be present in 20% of the population, for example, would be weaker in evidential value than that present in just 0.1% of the population, which in turn would be weaker than something present in just 0.001% of the population. Examples of highly unusual features occasionally encountered could include conditions such as Ectrodactyly which can occasionally affect the feet and which is believed to affect between 1:10,000 and 1:90,000 people worldwide (Durowaye and Adegboye 2011). Crease marks, infrequently encountered bony deformities of the feet, and specific details of conditions such as "bunions" and toe deformities could also be examples of such features. It could therefore be appropriate for conditions, which are highly unusual albeit not unique to be described as "intermediate characteristics" in relation to pedal evidence.

Individual-level characteristics are features, which are unique.[2] They have also been described as identifying unique, random (Bodziak 2000), and accidental (Cassidy 1987) characteristics, depending on the context of use. When dealing with this level of evidence, the probability of a chance match is so remote as to be considered impossible.[3] In footwear terms, examples of individual characteristics include the random cut and nick marks under the outsole, which have formed through damage as the shoe has been worn. These can then transfer to a surface through a shoe print and can be used for comparison purposes when a suspected shoe is available for examination.

It is fundamentally important to note that the evidence considered and utilized by forensic podiatrists is usually at class level only. Individual characteristics of the bare foot or print are extremely rare, although their existence cannot be ruled out. The presence of a scar on the plantar surface of the foot created by trauma or injury or through surgery or a hard keratin "tract" visible as a discrete corn or callus caused by a puncture from a nail or piece of glass may be distinct for that person and could assist greatly in the comparison of bare footprints, or in mass disaster identification situations. However, the presence and value of such individual characteristics compared with what one might find on the outsole of a shoe are extremely limited at best. In the future, this situation may change as knowledge and understanding improve.

2.2.7 Investigative and Evaluative Uses of Evidence

The uses of evidence can be categorized as either investigative or evaluative; each use is required at different stages of a forensic investigation and requires different approaches (Jackson and Jones 2009). Investigative uses involve the production of explanations for case-related observations, whereas evaluative uses relate to evidential weight (Association of Forensic Science Providers 2009). An investigative approach tends to occur at an earlier stage of the investigation than an evaluative approach and aims to explain observations at the scene of crime (Jackson and Jones 2009). In doing so, the evidence can be used to help guide the investigators to future work that may be required on the case. These approaches could typically be used in a "suspect-less" situation (Jackson 2009). Evaluative use of the evidence usually comes at a later stage of the investigation when a suspect is available and both prosecution and defense propositions can be made (Jackson 2009). Comparison of

[2] Paulisick's presentation in 1994 (as quoted in Bodziak 2000).
[3] Stone's presentation in 1984 (as quoted in Bodziak 2000).

questioned (unknown) and reference (known) evidence items would typically take place in the evaluative use of the evidence.

2.2.8 Likelihood Ratio (Bayesian) Approaches

In the United Kingdom and continental Europe, Bayesian approaches to dealing with evidence have been developed. These approaches involve the use of likelihood ratios to express the strength of an item of evidence. The statistical theories underlying this approach were developed by a team of forensic statisticians lead by Dr. Ian Evett (Cook et al. 1998; Evett et al. 1998, 2000), and they have been adopted and further developed across Europe by the European Network of Forensic Science Institutions (Ytti 2006). A Bayesian approach involves creating a framework of propositions that are formed from likelihood ratio calculations. In these calculations, the proposition that a particular person has undertaken an action that has led to the transfer of evidence is compared with an alternative proposition that someone other than that person could have undertaken that particular action resulting in the transfer of that evidence. Although widely used in many areas of forensic practice, these approaches can be somewhat complicated to understand and incorrect working of the likelihood ratios can lead to erroneous results. Alternately, basic probability estimates can be used to determine the evidential value of compared items in which the probability of independently recognized variable features occurring in the same item of evidence is considered.

Lately, the Bayesian approach and accompanying use of likelihood ratios in forensic practice has been criticized (UKFSR 2013). These criticisms followed the R. v. T [2010] All ER (D) 240 (Oct) appeal case in the United Kingdom (UKFSR 2013). In this case, a person (T) had been convicted of murder. A footwear marks expert had recovered training shoe marks from the crime scene. These marks were then compared with training shoes that had been seized from the defendant. After the comparison, the expert concluded that there was "a moderate degree of scientific evidence" to support the view that the trainers recovered from the defendant had made the marks found at the crime scene in question. This conclusion presented by the expert had been derived through the use of certain limited population data and the use of mathematical formulae, although the approach to the data synthesis had not been shown in the expert report.

The appeal court considered the reliability of evaluative expert evidence in relation to footwear marks and how such evidence is presented to a jury. Criticism of the approach taken was made on several areas as follows:

- *The inappropriate use of data:* The appeal court commented that it is essential that population data used "should be applicable to the population potentially present at the scene." The application of data that applied to the general as opposed to the specific population under consideration could therefore be misleading. The appeal court also noted that any database used should be of sufficient size and in this case, said that the database had been too small to allow its meaningful use in the approach used.

- *The inappropriate use of mathematical formulae:* In noting that an approach based on mathematical calculations "is only as good as the reliability of the data used," the appeal court criticized the use of calculations based on the limited availability of data noted above. It was further noted that the figures used in the calculation lacked precision, only enabling a rough approximation of the probative[4] value of the evidence and that the area concerned (the purchase and use of footwear) was subject to so many variables that mathematical formulae could not enable their statistical measurement as attempted by the expert in this case. It was further noted that the Bayesian approach should not be seen as a standard with universal acceptance that had been fully explored in the court.
- *The inappropriate presentation of the work as "scientific":* The appeal court stated that although the work was presented as scientific, within the context of this case there was "no sufficient reliable scientific basis for providing reliable matches between recovered marks and footwear recovered months later" (R. v. T 2010).

The appeal court found the conviction to be unsafe and the appeal was upheld. At face value the judgment potentially caused consternation amongst those using the likelihood ratio approach in forensic practice (including forensic podiatrists), but the criticisms made by the appeal court need to be seen in context. As such, the following observations can be made in connection with this ruling and can be used to guide future practice.

Note that the judgment was a relatively narrow interpretation on work presented by a footwear examiner and in relation to the working of this case only (UKFSR 2013).

Although cautions had been expressed in the way that likelihood ratios had been used in this particular case, the judgment did not seem to preclude the use of such approaches in relation to forensic practice. Instead, by noting how the use of likelihood ratios had been inappropriately used in this case, the ruling could be seen conversely as providing guidance as to when approaches involving the use of likelihood ratios could be appropriate and safe (i.e., where the database information to be used is reliable and of sufficient size as to be considered meaningful, appropriate to the population concerned, and able to withstand or be interpreted in the presence of variable factors). It also seems apparent that the use of likelihood ratios should

[4] Probative = whether the evidence helps prove a fact or issue.

be seen as an expression of the expert's underpinning logic that has informed his or her opinion as opposed to a formal calculation in itself that may imply, or be perceived as representing a greater degree of precision than may be possible in a real-world context.

The working presented in the R. v. T case had not been transparent. As such, where (appropriate) data has been used to inform an expert opinion in a case, the expert should make it explicitly clear in his or her report the source of this information and how it has been used to inform the concluding opinion expressed in the report.

Finally, a major criticism had been that the work was presented as being scientific where the appeal court ruled that it was not. This aspect of the ruling did not actually state that work presented must always be scientific, and indeed a later appeal court judgment in another case ruled that opinions based on experience are allowable [R. v. Otway (2011) All ER (D) 75 (Jan)]. Therefore, when presenting casework it should be made explicitly clear whether the approach to the work presented in a case has been scientific and when it has not, and whether the expert judgment has been based on science or subjective (expert) opinion; where a combination of both approaches are noted, which aspects of the expert report are scientific and which are not should be clear.

Where collections of materials have been taken to improve knowledge in a discipline, it is important that the expert clearly understands the difference between simple collections of samples used for reference purposes and formal databases.

Survey data, small ad hoc collections of casework information, population studies, and physical reference sample collections can be useful when interpreting evidence in a case, but many of these simple collections can be outdated and geographically limited and the measurements or observations may not be applicable to the case in which they are being used. Inevitably, interpretations using data from simple collections are general and should be used carefully, especially when attempting to apply the Bayesian approach. Comprehensive data collections, organized in an easily searchable manner have the potential to provide greater confidence in an expert's conclusions and can provide greater meaning to evidence in court. These robust databases allow quick integration of large amounts of data that have been generated to try and represent the population from which they have come. These databases are time-consuming to produce and maintain, but they ultimately provide a much-improved foundation upon which likelihood calculations can be formed (Gwinnett 2009). A study by Champod et al. (2004) looked at several different types of forensic samples, including glass, footwear, DNA, fingerprints, and handwriting, to develop a set of guidelines for the production of appropriate databases so as to identify whether samples came from the same source or from different sources.

From this research it is possible to see that a series of databases may be required to gather appropriate prevalence information.

A database created to assist the work of forensic scientists should be able to function not only as a tool to assist identification, but also as a robust statistical tool, the interrogation of which can allow characteristic or dimensional frequency of the contained data to be determined (Heuser et al. 2012). Such a database would contain appropriate data fields that must "allow easy and reliable interrogation" of the database where "integrity of the data is paramount" (Heuser et al. 2012), and design features are present to reject any erroneous or incorrectly formatted data (Biermann and Grieve 1996).

At the time of writing, it is possible that other court rulings may provide further criticism and guidance in relation to forensic practice. As such, anyone working in forensics should maintain an up-to-date awareness of published information and where additional rulings, advice, or both are published to be prepared to adapt their practice accordingly. In relation to the R. v. T case, practitioners should be aware of the key points of the case and their possible implications, but they should not blindly change practice without considering the appeal court comments in the context of each specific case worked.

The Bayesian approach or likelihood ratios have been developed and used in the United Kingdom and continental Europe, although other designations for conclusions are still used, too. This system has not been generally used in the United States to date, not because of any deficiency with this system, but simply as a matter of using different approaches that have also proved satisfactory (see Section 8.3).

2.2.9 Physical Evidence and the Chain of Custody

Even powerful evidence can have its value completely destroyed through not maintaining what is described as a chain of custody. At its most basic level, the chain of custody is the demonstrable care and isolation of the evidence under consideration. From seizure to court, all persons holding the item of evidence, including the podiatric examiner, must be able to demonstrate that the evidence has been free from external influence and contamination at all times. Individual responsibility is limited to the period that the evidence is held in a person's possession. Maintaining the chain of custody includes the following care and isolation procedures:

- Using sealed bags to isolate the evidence under consideration
- Storing the sealed evidence bags in a safe, lockable area accessible only to known personnel who need to have legitimate access to the case files (typically the reporting investigator, verifier, and designated administrative staff)

- Recording with signature and personal details the names, date, and time of opening and possession of the evidence
- Working with the evidence in an appropriately clean area
- Ensuring appropriate care is given to the storage of such evidence (e.g., sealing a wet shoe in a polythene bag can lead to mold damage and placing weights on top of a shoe to be used as evidence in storage can interfere with podiatric considerations in relation to functional distortion of that shoe)

2.2.10 ACE-V(R) Approach

ACE-V or ACE-V(R) simply refers to the outline process (standard methodology) that should be followed by forensic practitioners, including forensic podiatrists in the investigation. The abbreviation ACE-V(R) is expanded as follows:

Analysis: In the analysis phase of work the evidence is assessed for both the known and unknown items that are to be compared. Here, it is important to observe, note, measure, and record what is seen by using justified approaches. This assessment also includes consideration of the evidence to ensure that it is of reasonable quality and quantity to determine whether it is possible to proceed.

Comparison: It is made between what has been observed in both the unknown (questioned) and known (reference) items being compared together. Any similarities and differences are noted between these items. These similarities and differences can relate to both descriptive and quantifiable aspects of the evidence under consideration. Typically, the known is compared to the unknown.

Evaluation: It is the crux of the work and is where the examiner must come to a conclusion as to the strength of evidence in terms of match or mismatch between the items examined. The value of similarities in terms of individuality would be considered and stated. Where dissimilarities are apparent, whether these dissimilarities would preclude the compared items from relating to the same person or whether instead they represent justifiable differences that can be expected within the context of the situations within which the compared materials have been produced would be considered. It is here that the strength of conclusion is stated and may be expressed as a likelihood ratio, level of certainty, or other form of support for the hypothesis presented.

Verification: It is similar to a second opinion in medical practice, is an independent quality check of the work undertaken before submission of that work. Verification is important because there can be a subjective opinion element involved in reaching conclusions in forensic work. Verification involves a peer colleague with an understanding of the processes involved working through the case materials independently after the analysis, comparison, and evaluation phases of the ACE-V approach. He or she would do this verification without prior knowledge of the draft findings of the reporting expert and would independently record observations; contextual comments, including any variable factors that may have affected the evidence being observed; and features that match or mismatch and the evidential value of this comparison, leading to the production of draft conclusions. The peer colleague would then check through the work of the reporting expert, including the draft report on which an editorial check for layout and typographical and phraseology corrections would be performed. On completion, if in agreement with the observations, conclusions derived, and evidential weight ascribed, the peer colleague would countersign the work to indicate that he or she is in agreement with the findings of the reporting expert. The working through of this process without prior knowledge of the findings and conclusions of the work undertaken by the reporting expert would be described as "blind verification."[5] As in all scientific approaches, the work should be replicable by any other competent examiner and in effect, this replicability is what the verification is confirming. If differences in observations occur, these differences would be recorded and then worked through with the reporting expert to determine whether they can be resolved. If resolution of such differences cannot be achieved, then this conclusion would be recorded and consideration would be given to involving a third party expert as a second verifier whose independent assessment could help to resolve these differences.

Reporting: The reporting component of the ACE-V(R) approach refers to the need produce a report that is the anticipated output on conclusion of the process. This report is tested in court, should this later be required, and the examiner should be certain that all aspects of the report will stand up to scrutiny and challenge. The report will be read by nonexperts and must be clear, easily understood, and accurate throughout (see report writing as discussed in Chapter 8).

[5] Blind verification has been described by another forensic discipline as independent examination of case materials by another competent examiner (the blind verifier) "who has no, or limited, contextual information" and "no expectation or knowledge of the determinations or conclusions of the original examiner" with the aim of this process being "to test the reproducibility of the determinations or conclusions made at any step during Analysis, Comparison, Evaluation, and Verification (ACE-V)" (SWGFAST 2012).

2.2.11 Forensic Podiatry Practice

Although the scientific aspects of the podiatry knowledge base are used in clinical practice, in forensic podiatry work, the context of practice and the way that science is used are fundamentally different. For example, in making a clinical diagnosis, the formal propositional knowledge of the profession is used, with scientific adjustments and excursions being made. The adjustments are often informed by nonpropositional experience-based understandings where that approach is not immediately successful. Conversely, in forensic practice, the approach must use the principles of applied science from the start, and although experience-based understandings can be transparently incorporated, there is no potential for "diagnostic" adjustments to be repeatedly made as the work progresses or after the report has been submitted (although the expert must be prepared to adjust his or her opinion considering additional information). Forensic podiatry work therefore needs to be approached cautiously because scientific forensic work requires a different overall approach than that of clinical practice.

Forensic podiatry is concerned with considering whether or not known persons can be associated with a scene of crime by using the podiatry knowledge base, expertise, and experience. Less frequently, forensic podiatry can be concerned with the identification of the deceased. There are many approaches within forensic science that are available to identify people by using features as wide ranging as fingerprints, DNA, teeth, bone structure, and shoeprints. Many of the techniques used in the identification can be considered mainstream and are used as standard approaches because they are often evidence based, proven in practice, tested, and frequently available. Occasionally, however, material available for identification requires the involvement of a forensic podiatrist as opposed to any other specialist. The forensic podiatrist may typically be required in the following circumstances:

1. Where there is no material available to enable any of the standard approaches to identification to be used
2. Where the standard approaches have elicited conclusions of limited value or are inconclusive and the investigators wish to strengthen their overall conclusions
3. Where more complex questions that fall within the expertise of the forensic podiatrist need to be addressed and for which the standard, mainstream forensic approaches cannot assist
4. In criminal cases, where the defense position requires additional work to be undertaken to investigate the validity of the link between compared items already suggested to be associated

The usual task in forensic podiatry is to identify features of podiatric relevance in the questioned (unknown) and reference (known) items being compared for identification purposes. The individuality represented by these features is determined by considering population prevalence and the likelihood of all such independent variables being present within the same evidential item. Concurrently, features that would suggest that the evidential items do not match are addressed using likelihood ratios appropriately (see Section 2.2.8 covering the lessons learned from the R. v. T appeal case) or by using basic probability consideration through the application of appropriate information (e.g., survey data published or unpublished) or even professional experience. Whichever approach is used, it is essential to be comfortable with the methods involved. Once adopted, and where the likelihood ratio approach is being considered, the forensic podiatrist is directed to relevant literature, including literature demonstrating how likelihood ratios can be used in forensic practice (Cook et al. 1998; Evett et al. 1998, 2000; Lucy 2005) and articles that have critically considered these approaches to help avoid pitfalls (UKFSR 2014).

2.3 Concluding Comments

This chapter has addressed the most basic principles of, or relating to, forensic podiatry practice. Any podiatrist working in the forensic context should be familiar with these principles and adhere to these principles at all times to avoid problems during casework.

References

Allen M.J. 2002. A professional body for forensic scientists (editorial). In *Fifty Years of Forensic Science: A Commentary*, edited by N. NicDaeid, pp. 65–67. Chichester: Wiley-Blackwell.

Association of Forensic Science Providers. 2009. Standards for the formulation of evaluative forensic science expert opinion. *Science and Justice* 49: 161–164.

Biermann T.W. and Grieve M.C. 1996. A computerised database of mail order garments: A contribution towards estimating the frequency of fibre types found in clothing. Part 1: The system and its operation. *Forensic Science International* 77: 65–73.

Bodziak W.J. 2000. *Footwear Impression Evidence: Detection, Recovery and Examination.* 2nd ed. London: CRC Press.

Cassidy M.J. 1987. *Footwear Identification.* Ottawa: RCMP.

Champod C., Evett I.W. and Jackson G. 2004. Establishing the most appropriate databases for addressing source level propositions. *Science and Justice* 44: 153–164.

Cook R., Evett I.E., Jackson G., Jones P.J. and Lambert J.A. 1998. A hierarchy of propositions deciding which level to address in casework. *Science and Justice* 38: 231–239.

Cooke C.W. 1984. *A Practical Guide to the Basics of Physical Evidence.* Springfield, IL: Charles C. Thomas.

DiMaggio, J.A. 2005. The role of feet and footwear in medico legal investigations. In *Forensic Medicine of the Lower Extremity*, edited by J. Rich, D.E. Dean, and R.H. Powers. pp. 375–400. Totawa, NJ: Humana Press.

Durowaye M., and Adegboye A. 2011. Familial ectrodactyly syndrome in a Nigerian child: A case report. *Oman Medical Journal* 26(4): 275–278.

Eckert W.G. and James S.H. 1997. The role of the forensic laboratory. In *Introduction to Forensic Sciences*, 2nd ed., edited by W.G. Eckert, pp. 33–55. Boca Raton, FL: CRC Press.

Evett I.E., Jackson G. and Lambert L. 2000. More on the hierarchy of propositions: Exploring the distinction between explanations and propositions. *Science and Justice* 38: 3–10.

Evett I.E., Lambert J.A. and Buckleton J.S. 1998. A Bayesian approach to interpreting footwear marks in forensic casework. *Science and Justice* 38: 241–247.

Fairbairn C. 2015. *Briefing Paper 04890: Missing Persons and the Presumption of Death.* London: House of Commons Library.

Gwinnett C. 2009. The use of inexperienced personnel in the analysis of synthetic textile fibres using polarized light microscopy for the generation of data suitable for the production of a synthetic fibres database. PhD dissertation, Staffordshire University.

Heuser L., Gwinnett C., Reel S., Vernon W. and Walton L. 2012. *Project Proposal: Development of a Bare Footprint Database.* Stoke-on-Trent: Staffordshire University.

House of Commons Science and Technology Committee. 2005. *Forensic Science on Trial, Seventh Report of Session 2004–2005.* London: The Stationary Office Ltd.

House of Commons Science and Technology Committee. 2013. *Forensic Science, Second Report of Session 2013–2014,* Vol. 1. London: The Stationary Office Ltd.

Jackson G. 2009. Understanding forensic science opinions. In *Handbook of Forensic Science*, edited by J. Fraser and R. Williams, pp. 419–445. Cullompton: Willan Publishing.

Jackson G. and Jones, P.J. 2009. Case assessment and interpretation. In *Wiley Encyclopedia of Forensic Sciences*, edited by A. Jamieson and A. Moenssens, pp. 1–15. Chichester: Wiley.

Jasper M.A. 1994. Issues in phenomenology for researchers of nursing. *Journal of Advanced Nursing* 19: 309–314.

Keiser-Neilsen S. 1980. *Person Identification Be Means of the Teeth.* Bristol: John Wright and Sons.

Kennedy R. 1995. Barefoot impressions. Paper presented at the Canadian Identification Association Annual Conference, Halifax, July.

Koch T. 1995. Interpretive approaches in nursing research: The influence of Husserl and Heidegger. *Journal of Advanced Nursing* 21: 827–836.

Kuhn T.S. 1996. *The Structure of Scientific Revolutions*, 3rd ed. Chicago, IL: University of Chicago Press.

Kvale S. 1987. Validity in the qualitative research interview. *Methods: A Journal for Human Science* 1: 37–72.

Lucy D. 2005. *Introduction to Statistics for Forensic Scientists.* Chichester: Wiley.

Makins M. 1994. *Collins English Dictionary.* Glasgow: HarperCollins.

Mitroff I.I. and Turoff M. 1975. Philosophical and methodological foundations of Delphi. In *The Delphi Technique: Methods and Applications*, edited by H.R. Linstone and M. Turoff, pp. 17–34. Boston, MA: Addison-Wesley.

North-Whitehead A. 1925. *Science and the Modern World.* New York: The Free Press.
Okasha S. 2002. *Philosophy of Science: A Very Short Introduction.* Oxford: Oxford University Press.
Osterberg J.W. 1967. *The Crime Laboratory.* Bloomington, IL: Indiana University Press.
Palmer R.E. 1969. *Hermeneutics.* Evanston, IL: North Western University Press.
Reisner N.R. and Wooldridge E.D. 1977. Forensic odontology—An overview. *Annals of Dentistry* 36: 74–76.
Robinson D. and Groves J. 1999. *Introducing Philosophy.* Cambridge: Icon Books Ltd.
SWGFAST (Scientific Working Group on Friction Ridge Analysis, Study and Technology). 2010. *Document #14 Standard for the Application of Blind Verification of Friction Ridge Examinations (Latent/Tenprint).* http://www.swgfast.org/documents/blind-verification/121124_Blind-Verification_2.0.pdf (Accessed November 14, 2012).
UKFSR (UK Forensic Science Regulator). 2011. *Newsletter No. 17.* Birmingham: The Forensic Science Regulator.
UKFSR (UK Forensic Science Regulator). 2013. *Information: Legal Obligations. FSR-I-400. Issue* 2. Birmingham: The Forensic Science Regulator.
UKFSR (UK Forensic Science Regulator). 2014. *Forensic Science Regulator Codes of Practice & Conduct for Forensic Science Providers in the Criminal Justice System: Version 2.* Birmingham: The Forensic Science Regulator.
Vernon W. 2000. The functional analysis of shoe wear patterns. PhD Diss., Sheffield Hallam University.
Ytti A. (ed.). 2006. *Information Bulletin for Shoeprint/Toolmark Examiners* 12(1).

Podiatric Forensic Concerns

II

Digital Photographic Techniques

3

Digital photography is essential to many aspects of the work of the forensic podiatrist and is used to capture images of footprints, footwear, insoles (sock liners), shoe wear, the feet of those under consideration, and closer detail from any of this evidence (objects). Those undertaking this work need to become familiar with the necessary equipment and practiced in the techniques required. In this chapter, consideration is given initially to the selection of equipment for forensic podiatry use and then to instructions and recommendations in relation to procedures. All of these techniques can be practiced without cost, and for the "trainee" forensic podiatrist such practice is recommended to develop the skills and experience required in actual casework.

It is essential for the forensic podiatrist to have a general knowledge of the digital photographic techniques, equipment, and terminology involved to ensure the best representation of the evidence that is available for examination. If for any reason the podiatrist is not able to do the photography, the crime scene unit or other knowledgeable personnel, depending on the needs of the case, can perform this task.

3.1 Digital Camera Revolution

Photography for the forensic podiatrist has become simpler and more accessible since the digital photography revolution. The early first-generation digital cameras were acceptable for leisure photography purposes, but they had poor resolution and were inadequate for forensic image capture. Subsequent improvements in resolution led to their widespread adoption in forensics. Through the use of digital photography, the costs involved in image capture have lowered considerably compared to those via traditional photography. Digital photography allows the forensic podiatrist to practice the techniques involved without the costs of film or processing where electronically stored images alone are used. There are a few drawbacks with digital photography (e.g., images can potentially be falsified through manipulation, technological failures), but as long they are understood and a rigorous protocol is adopted, they should not be problematic.

3.2 Equipment Requirements

3.2.1 Camera

The range of digital cameras available is extensive, somewhat confusing, and subject to frequent change as further technological advances are made. In this specialized area of photography, a digital single-lens reflex (DSLR) camera has many advantages and is the camera of choice, allowing lenses to be changed as required during use. A conventional single-lens reflex (SLR) camera uses film, but a DSLR camera uses an electronic image sensor to capture images. The main advantages of such a system over film-based photography are as follows:

- The image is created instantly within the camera.
- Instant checking of the image can be undertaken on capture of that image.
- The process does not require time-consuming and relatively expensive darkroom-based development.
- The less experienced photographer can now simply delete mistakes before committing the image to expensive photographic paper.
- Where the images are kept in electronic form only, images can be kept in small digital storage systems as opposed to the large volume of space required to keep hard copies.

Although pitfalls are few for digital photography compared to traditional film photography, digital photography does carry the potential for accusations that the digital image can be falsified through manipulation. There is also the potential for data (image) loss through technological failure. Similar issues are also present with traditional photography, but the manipulation or technological failure is nondigital in nature.

There are three types of sensor in use in DSLR cameras: charge-coupled device, complementary metal oxide sensor, and the Foveon X3 sensor (Freeman 2011). The resolution of these sensors is expressed in pixels. The term "pixel" is a play on the two words *pic*ture and *el*ement, and each pixel is a unit of information containing data describing the color and intensity of a small area of an image (Cambridge in Colour 2015). The pixel is a measure of sizes of the image sensor of the camera: the larger the image sensor, the higher amount of image data captured by the camera (Grotta and Grotta 2004, 14). The pixel rating is referred to extensively in relation to digital camera resolution.

In one study it was noted that "digital cameras of six and 14 megapixel resolution are both acceptable substitutes for the 35 mm film camera" in most regular shoeprint cases (Blitzer et al. 2007). The Scientific Working Group on Imaging Technology of the International Association for Identification has recommended that for photographing footwear evidence, a "Professional camera, minimum 35 mm or digital SLR with a minimum eight megapixel native resolution" is required (SWGIT 2013). Although a camera's ability to use a higher number of pixels indicates higher sensor resolution, higher numbers of pixels do not in themselves show the overall resolution of the camera. Pixel ratings are only one factor to consider in relation to the quality of image that the camera is capable of producing, with such quality being dependent on the entire camera system, including "metering, white balance control, image processing and … the lens" (Freeman 2011, loc. 173).

In forensic work, the more image data captured the better; however, the data required for forensic podiatry purposes is less than that required for example in fingerprint analysis. This difference is because the forensic podiatrist will mainly be dealing with larger objects, such as whole footprints, or shoe insoles (sock liners).

More recent recommendations suggest that a camera of at least 8 megapixels be used in forensic podiatry work to match the more stringent recommendations made for forensic footwear examiners. This pixel rating should allow the image to be enlarged to a life-size image as required in forensics without pixilation, i.e., the point where the individual square pixels become visible to the eye, thereby affecting the quality of the displayed image, occurring. All currently available DSLR cameras should have a pixel rating acceptable for forensic podiatry use.

In addition, pixels also vary in size according to the sensor within the camera. The sensors capable of producing larger and deeper pixels allow more light to be collected before the information is sent on to the camera processor, thereby providing a higher quality image with sharper detail (Grotta and Grotta 2004, 15). Generally, larger sensors produce larger pixels; therefore, a larger sensor within the camera is also an important factor in equipment selection.

It is equally important to consider the quality and type of lens of the camera. For lens quality, it is advisable to research the camera market carefully and seek the advice of a specialist retailer at the time of purchase.

The focal length of the camera lens is critical in forensic podiatry work. In digital cameras the focal length is the distance between the surface of the lens and the camera image sensor. This distance is measured in millimeters. As the focal length changes, the angle of view also changes. A 50-mm lens "when used with the 35 mm format" (Freeman 2011, loc. 249) is generally considered to represent the same field of view as that of the human eye, with lenses of a longer focal length "producing telephoto effects and lenses with shorter focal lengths producing wide-angle distortion" (Staggs 2005, 14). This setting is required for photography in forensic podiatry. The use of markedly different focal length settings can create changes in perspective that then affect scale and compromise the quality of the photographic evidence. Because digital cameras often have an adjustable focal length, the camera selected should be capable of adjustment over a range that covers the 50-mm focal length equivalent. There is however an important point to note in relation to digital cameras. Because digital cameras function differently from traditional 35-mm film cameras, the given focal length of the digital camera may differ from that of the film camera; i.e., a digital camera set at a focal length of 50 mm will not necessarily have the same focal length as the film camera. Whether the digital camera focal length is the same as that of a 35-mm film camera depends on the sensor size of the digital camera. If the sensor within the digital camera is an equivalent size to the 35-mm film format (24 × 36 mm), the lens on the digital camera functions as a lens of the same marked focal length on the 35-mm film camera (Freeman 2011). If the sensor of the digital camera is smaller than the 35-mm film format size, the lens of the digital camera has a greater focal length than a lens of the same marked focal length on a 35-mm film camera.

For this reason, the manufacturers of digital cameras with the smaller sensors give a focal length multiplier value for these cameras. This value is a number by which the focal length of the digital camera lens needs to be multiplied to show how it would be functioning in terms of focal length if it was a 35-mm film camera. For example, if a digital camera has a focal length multiplier of 1.6 and is set at a focal length of 50 mm, this camera functions as a film camera with a focal length of 80 mm. Given that the camera is required to be set around an equivalent focal length of 50 mm, it is important to consider this when taking the image. The full-frame DSLR cameras do not require such a calculation to be carried out, although note that these cameras tend to be the more expensive high-end DSLR cameras.

It is essential to know the focal length multiplication for a particular camera being purchased so that the proper lens can be used on the correct setting, thereby allowing the camera to be operated correctly in the context of evidence-quality image capture. It is clearly advantageous to have a camera that does not require such multiplication to be carried out, although such a camera may incur considerable additional costs.

When film cameras were used for forensic photography, it was generally recommended that the camera have a detachable lens (Bodziak 2000). For digital photography, and considering the less comprehensive photographic requirements of the forensic podiatrist, a DSLR camera with the right specifications fitted with a standard lens of 50-mm equivalence should be an adequate or even preferred arrangement.

In addition to having a viewfinder, most DSLR cameras also have a liquid-crystal display (LCD) screen situated centrally on the back of the camera that allows the user to see the image within the frame of the picture without having to look through the viewfinder. This capability is essential for forensic podiatry purposes because it allows the user to set up the camera to capture the image without the difficulty of bending over the camera in what may be an awkward situation to do so. Some cameras have LCD screens that hinge from the camera and are capable of swivelling to a multitude of positions, thereby allowing relatively easy viewing of the framed image and removing the need for the operator to move into awkward positions or to use step-up equipment during framing.

Most digital cameras have an integral flash unit. This type of flash unit is not adequate for capturing evidence-quality images in forensic podiatry work; a more flexible flash unit is essential. The camera must have a hot shoe to allow the attachment of an external flash unit. The camera also must have a wide range of user control options as opposed to offering automatic and programmable photography only. Particularly important in this respect is the ability to manually adjust the lens to the exact focal length required.

The camera should also be equipped with a mechanism to enable the camera shutter to be released by the operator remote from the camera, particularly while the camera is fitted onto a tripod or copy stand. Such mechanisms minimize the potential for movement, especially where slow shutter speeds are in operation. Two such release mechanisms are commonly found on digital cameras. The first mechanism is a delayed shutter release (or self-timer) that allows the operator to compose the image and then trigger the delay feature, which counts down before shutter release and allows the operator to be free of direct contact with the camera at the point of exposure. The second mechanism is involves a remote-controlled handset that allows the operator to directly control the shutter release away from the camera. This remote-controlled operation can be through wired or wireless connection with the camera. Ideally, both features should be available on the chosen camera. In practice, the delayed shutter release option takes up a considerable amount of additional time during the working day. A delay function of 12 seconds would take approximately 20 seconds to set up and operate. If, e.g., 180 images were to be captured during the working day, the use of the delay feature would add an additional 36 minutes of time to the overall operation. Conversely, a remote function can be used almost instantaneously. Both methods produce equally good results. The use of camera delay does not require the additional expense of a remote; however, the use of a remote would be preferable because of the improved efficiency associated with this device.

It is recommended that the camera itself be equipped with either a spot meter or an exposure compensation feature. The spot meter is a camera function in which the metering for each shot is taken from a defined "spot" in the center of the frame irrespective of the metering value of the surrounding detail. This function allows the exposure to optimally bring out important details for later analysis under certain circumstances, particularly where extremes of light and dark are present within the image being photographed. In the absence of a spot meter, the exposure can be compensated for through the camera's compensation adjustment, a feature that is present on most DSLR cameras. Alternately, the exposure can be adjusted later using digital imaging software. However, if this adjustment can be accounted for at source through the use of a spot meter or compensation adjustment, the stages involved in producing evidence-quality images will be reduced and time saved accordingly.

Some thought should also be given to the quality of camera construction. In professional use, a camera is subjected to a hard life, and it is important that the camera is robust and strong enough to cope with a relatively high degree of trauma. It is also recommended that the camera be of a professional appearance. Even if the camera has a technical specification that matches recommendations, the use of bargain equipment that seems to lend itself to a holiday (snapshot) scenario does not enhance professional standing. Importantly, should a case reach court presentation stage, the use of such a camera could provide a legal representative with ammunition to attack personal credibility. It is also recommended that a second or even a third camera be available as backup should there be technical problems with the primary equipment, and such equipment should also meet the recommended specifications. All cameras used should have spare power sources that could include a second battery pack and a line power (mains) or alternating current (A/C) adaptor where available.

Digital cameras store data on memory cards, with various formats available. When taking forensic-quality images, the camera is used on its highest quality image setting that, in turn, occupies more of the card memory than the default settings. In addition, a large number of images may be required when working a case. The card used in the camera should therefore be of the largest capacity possible. At the time of writing, cards of up to 128-gigabyte capacity are available in many formats, although not all digital cameras are capable of taking these larger capacity cards. If in doubt, compatibility should be checked with the retailer or manufacturer. Spare cards should be carried for additional capacity and in case technical failure of a card occurs. It is recommended that the photographer have the capacity to take at least 200 examination-quality photographs when attending a typical case, although capturing more than 100 images would not be frequently required, with 60–100 images being more typical. For practical purposes, it is recommended that the backup camera equipment share a common digital memory card format to the primary camera.

Previous recommendations from film-based photography advised that manual focusing should be possible on the camera selected for evidence photography (Bodziak 2000). A wide range of flexibility is required of the camera used in forensic podiatry photography for the camera to cope with different conditions of lighting, varying degrees of evidence clarity, and varying wear impression topography. The camera should therefore have functions in addition to automatic or program-based use to enable the operator to deal with these variables through manual adjustment. Such functions should include manual override, the ability to switch off the flash function, and aperture priority selection.

3.2.2 Camera Support

In forensic podiatry evidence photography, the use of an appropriate support for the camera is as important as the camera itself. Two forms of support are available: a copy stand and a tripod. The type of support used is influenced by the working situation.

3.2.3 Copy Stand

A copy stand is used widely by amateur and professional photographers alike. A copy stand is a heavy-based unit with a calibrated vertical sliding mount upon which a camera is mounted (Figure 3.1). The camera is attached to the mount and used to take photographs of an object placed on the stand base unit. The base unit is typically a neutral color to reduce the potential for interference with the exposure of the image of interest. The stand is also used in conjunction with adjustable side lighting units, and many stands are sold with such lighting units already integrated into the product.

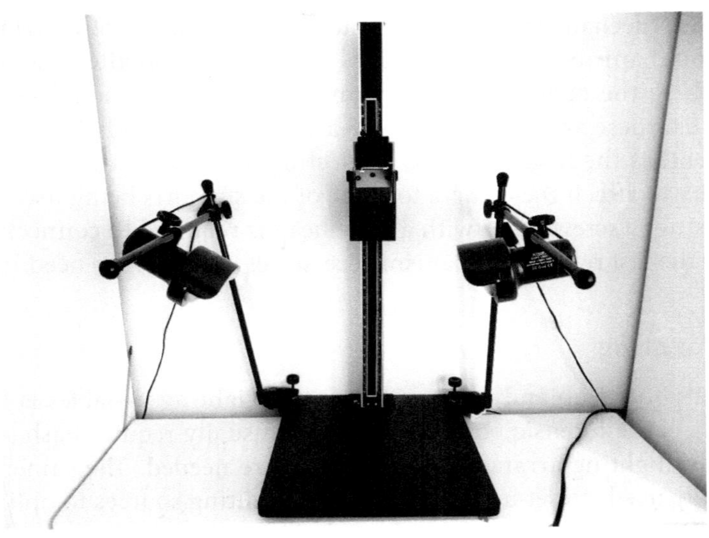

Figure 3.1 Copy stand.

The copy stand is the preferred support for the capture and handling of evidence photography in the typical laboratory or workbench situation. A copy stand provides the advantages of serving as a robust, vibration-free platform and offers adjustability and minimal potential for error when setting up the item(s) to be photographed. It also allows the use of integral and well-placed lighting. A drawback of a copy stand is that it is not easily transported to a site for evidence examination, such as may often be required in casework scenarios; however, if the evidence can be brought to the photographer's own workplace for bench examination, a copy stand is ideal.

3.2.4 Tripod

A major advantage of a tripod over a copy stand is that it is designed to be portable; thus, for forensic podiatry, a tripod can be transported and used in any situation. Although more adjustment variables are introduced with a tripod, which may be less robust than the copy stand, the tripod's greater flexibility means that, in practice, it will invariably have more overall case use. Although there are a multitude of tripods on the market, many are unsuitable for the capture of forensic podiatry evidence. The tripod selected should be robust. It is also highly advantageous for the tripod to have a feature for suspending the camera between its legs to allow vertical image capture from directly above the evidence under consideration without the legs of the tripod coming into the frame (Figure 3.2). It is also useful for the tripod to be used in conjunction with a fast camera release mechanism, because the camera may be required to take different images of specific evidence items in different situations during the casework. Some tripods are available with such fast release mechanisms integrated into their design. For other tripods, fast release mechanisms can be purchased separately as an after-market accessory. Where the operator uses such mechanisms, care should be taken to ensure that these are of the same type across all of the individual operator's equipment, as the formats differ. Neglecting to consider this could prevent the ability to attach the camera to some of the supports being used. A small coin or stubby screwdriver with a wide head is required to connect and disconnect the fast release mechanism accessories according to need.

3.2.5 Lighting

The ability to set up and use a wide range of lighting variables is essential. In practice, the forensic podiatrist does not usually require flash, although alternative lighting arrangements certainly are needed. The camera operator usually needs to set up various external lighting sources to optimize the detail in the evidence being considered. Although two-dimensional image capture (e.g., inked footprints) are relatively simple to photograph, taking

Figure 3.2 Tripod set up for forensic podiatry use.

evidence-quality photographs of three-dimensional images, such as shoe insoles (sock liners), is more complicated. The objective in this case is to capture detailed images of the impressions caused by the foot, and these impressions may be very shallow or faint in appearance; contrast therefore needs to be optimized. Here, the ability to adjust lighting to define borders or the manipulation of lighting and shadows to bring out the minor color changes associated with staining are fundamental. The lighting equipment selected should be capable of a wide range of adjustments in the type, color, and angle of light to the image being captured.

3.2.6 Flash

Flash may not be required in forensic podiatry photography, but where its use is indicated, the integral flash units of a digital camera are inadequate, as stated in Section 3.2.1, because such units cannot be adjusted to alter the angle of light to the object being captured. Thus, where flash is required, a separate flash unit of good quality is needed with a bounce facility to allow the flash head to be angled and light from the unit to be reflected from another surface. It can also be advantageous for the flash unit to function off the camera, through for example the use of a dedicated bracket and off-shoe camera cord. The flash unit should also be compatible with the digital camera being used. This compatibility may be more critical for digital cameras than nondigital cameras, as some manufacturers warn of the potential for damage to the camera when an inappropriate unit is used. If in doubt, the manufacturer's recommendation should be followed. It may also be helpful to obtain a slave flash unit with connection lead for use with a second flash situated off the camera. The slave unit is a flash-sensitive attachment that sets off a second flash at the same time as the primary flash. Such a feature can allow experimentation with lighting angles, when attempting to optimize the image detail.

3.2.7 External Lighting

In practice, the podiatrist relies on external lighting far more than flash photography to capture the images required in forensic work. In its most basic form, such external lighting can be the simple use of oblique natural light in which the object to be photographed is positioned in such a way as to be illuminated by natural light entering from the side (Figure 3.3). More sophisticated lighting conditions, however, are usually required. In the workbench situation, where copy stands are in use, these stands often have integral lighting sources situated at either side of the object to be photographed, allowing angles of lighting to be adjusted to bring out the detail required. The ideal position is determined through adjustment, while observing the image through the camera's viewfinder or screen.

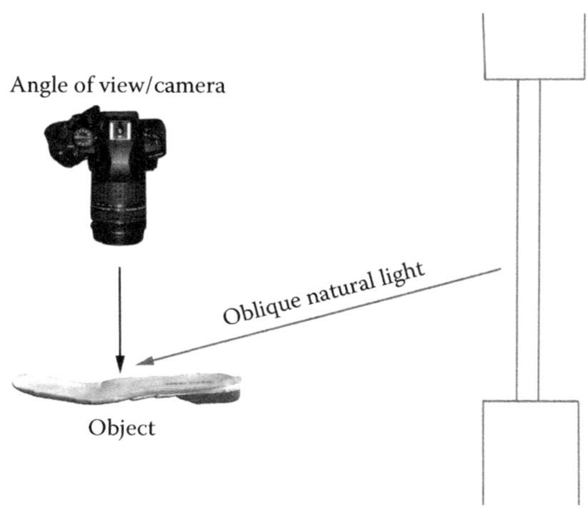

Figure 3.3 Oblique natural lighting conditions.

Such adjustment may involve either one or both side lights using an infinite range of angle variations.

When working away from the workbench with a tripod-based approach, there are often practical difficulties in transporting copy stand–based lighting equipment to a field site. In this case, a cost-effective and portable alternative can be used in the form of two adjustable table lamps, with one lamp placed on either side of the image. Such lamps allow side lighting to be introduced in the same way as on the copy stand, again allowing a wide range of adjustments to optimize the image to be captured. Such lights are not as powerful as the dedicated copy stand alternatives, and they may not be as robust in construction; however, they can produce acceptable results and are usually preferable to, and less limited than, the flash alternative.

3.2.8 Forensic Light Sources

Forensic light sources are used widely in identification work to bring out images that may not be readily apparent to the naked eye. The use of such equipment has proven value in highlighting very faint footprint images that may be present on shoe insoles or sock liners (Kennedy 1996). These light sources consist of powerful adjustable lamps that cover a wide range of wavelengths within the ultraviolet, visible, and infrared spectrums.

These light sources can be so powerful that safety features may be required to protect the operator from eye damage. Most of these light sources are also very expensive and as such may be too costly for independently operating forensic podiatrists. More cost-effective alternatives are now available in the form of diode (LED) light sources. These alternatives are gradually gaining in popularity, and although they do not have the adjustability features of the traditional forensic light sources, they are available in a range of wavelengths, covering a wide portion of the light spectrum. The task of such light sources is to optimize contrast to show the detail required in later analysis, and experimentation is required in almost every case to find the most appropriate combination of lighting and lighting position. Filters are also essential when using a specialized light source to optimize the image to be captured. Such filters would also be worn as eye goggles to prevent damage to the eyes and to allow the operator to view the image in precisely the same way as it would be captured by the filtered camera.

3.2.9 Accessory Equipment

Accessory equipment is required in evidence-quality image capture for processes involved in preparation. Such equipment provides essential detail within the image and general support to these processes.

3.3 Preparing for Image Capture

In preparing the setting for evidence-quality image capture of an object, it is not sufficient to simply place the camera on a support over the object to be photographed with adequate lighting. The camera needs to be aligned in the same plane as the object to be photographed, and as such, a small, accurate spirit (bubble) level is required. Dedicated photographic spirit levels are available that fit into the hot shoe of a camera, and these spirit levels are ideal for this purpose. The use of two such levels is recommended so that one level can be mounted on the camera, and the other level would be used simultaneously to verify the level of the surface on which the object to be photographed has been placed, enabling both lens and object to exactly be within the same plane. It is advisable to check that both levels are functioning to the same degree of accuracy before their use.

In setting up the image, an often overlooked, but vital, accessory is that of the line power extension lead and A/C adapter. An electricity supply may be required for lighting or to directly power the camera by using a line power connection and invariably, the work area may be too distant from an electrical source. A cable reel extension lead is then essential. This lead should be at least 5 m long and should have the ability to connect two or more electrical items simultaneously. For work abroad, a selection of line power adapters for international use should also be held as standard equipment.

It is also important to keep spare batteries or alternative power sources for all electrically powered items. Here, a spare camera battery and alternative line connection should be obtained along with batteries for the flash unit and a flashlight. Rechargeable batteries can be useful and are more cost-effective in the long term; however the rechargeable batteries tend to lose their charge before long-life nonrechargeable batteries. Thus, a selection of both rechargeable and long-life nonrechargeable batteries should be kept.

To capture essential detail in an image, each object to be photographed should be carefully labeled with an identifying code, description, and date of image capture. A labeling method is therefore required and although dedicated pro forma labels can be purchased, it is acceptable for the operator to create his or her own labels by using cardstock and marker pens. It is also desirable to have a range of label options, including different-sized cardstock and adhesive and nonadhesive labels to suit a wide range of working situations. A range of colors is recommended for the marker pens to assist in differentiating separate sequences or categories of image.

Evidence-quality images should always include a size scale. Although any known object (e.g., a coin, paper clip, business card) placed into the image could serve as a scale (Hilderbrand 1999, 44–45), this is not the best practice and a dedicated measurement scale should preferably be used within the image. Whatever scale is used, that same scale should be retained for later reexamination of the work. Although simple rulers of varying types have been used as scales in such photographs, variations can occur between these rulers, so a high-quality dedicated scale is recommended instead. The ideal scale for use in evidence-quality photography is the Bureau Reference Scale (Figure 3.4) developed in the United States by Federal Bureau of Investigation (FBI)–based footwear examiners for this specific purpose. The Bureau Reference Scale is L-shaped with a 30-cm long side and 15-cm short side. One side of the scale is dark and the other side is light, allowing flexibility according to lighting conditions. Both sides are nonreflective and the construction contains alternate black-and-white bars that can assist in reading the scale, where over- or underexposure has been necessary to produce a correct exposure of the object of interest. Crosshair circles are also present on the scale and can be used to verify perspective and assist in correction where errors affecting perspective have occurred. As a reference scale, manufacturing is to FBI specifications to provide a more standardized product. When purchased, a shorter separate 15-cm straight scale is often provided with the

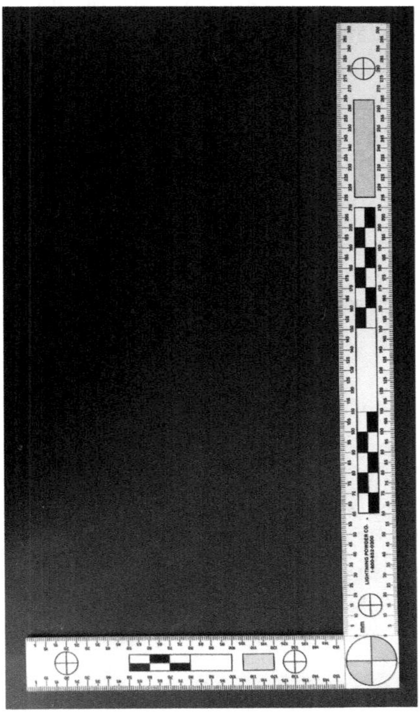

Figure 3.4 Bureau reference scale.

large L-shaped scale, and this scale can be used elsewhere in the image to facilitate easier scale checking. The Bureau Reference Scale is the gold standard scale for use in evidence-quality photography, and it is recommended for every image taken for forensic podiatry purposes.

When photographing images with a scale incorporated into the frame, it is essential for the scale to be placed on the same plane as the detail of the object being photographed. Failure to take this precaution can create misleading impressions of the dimensions of the object being examined. In this sense, it may sometimes be necessary to elevate the scale. This elevation can be achieved very simply through the use of wedges or piles of coins that are placed underneath the scale until the correct height is achieved (Figure 3.5).

It also may be necessary to indicate the angle of lighting within the image for reference purposes, should there be a need to replicate the conditions for later comparison. This determination can be achieved through the use of a simple golf tee placed upside down (point upward) within the frame. Any accompanying shadow indicates the angle of light for future reference (Hilderbrand 1999, 45).

Another recommended item of equipment is a good flashlight that can be useful in setting up the equipment in dark areas. The beam from the flashlight can also be shone at various angles onto the object to be photographed, thereby giving an indication of the optimal position for placing any light source to be used when capturing the image.

A selection of backgrounds for the object being captured is required. A plain dark green cloth is suitable for some images and can be easily transported from site to site. Dark and light cardstocks in both A3 (tabloid) and A2 (poster) sizes are also be useful, and although not as portable as cloth, these cardstocks provide a cheap and stable background that can easily be set up. With these backgrounds, it is also recommended to include masking and electrical tape and a pressure adhesive (e.g., Blu-Tack), so that the operator

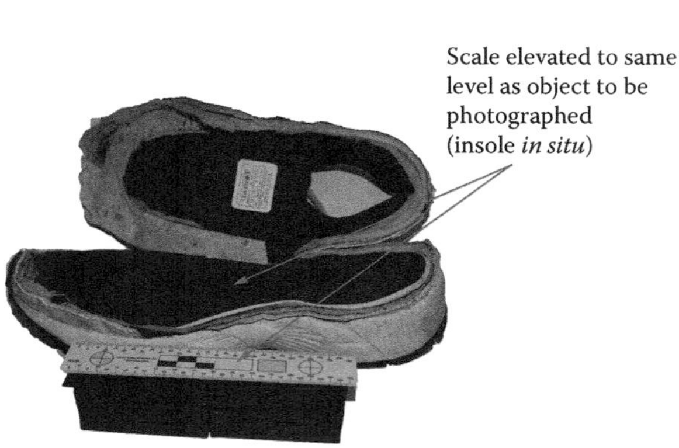

Figure 3.5 Same level placement of scale as the object to be photographed.

can secure objects for photography as required. A white board at least 50 cm square is also useful to reflect light onto the object to be captured, to vary and optimize the lighting conditions.

3.4 General Support of the Process

3.4.1 Hardware

Digital photography requires a computer system for the captured images to be saved, managed, and printed out for assessment and comparison purposes. Most modern personal computers are capable of managing the images required in forensic podiatry work. As such work involves graphic images with higher memory demands than those of text processing it is recommended that careful research be undertaken before purchasing a system for this purpose. Greater RAM memory and faster processors enable the operator to complete the work with less frustration as the images are managed, saved, and printed, whereas a large internal memory allows the significant number of high-resolution images that will inevitably need to be stored to be held on that computer. Although desktop personal computers tend to have great power and work capability, the more portable laptops and notebooks have that advantage of being portable to the preferred site of use. A computer should therefore be selected that is capable of superior power and performance in terms of image management.

Whatever system is used, care should be taken to ensure that the system is secure from accidental loss/damage, tampering, or theft; simultaneously, the practitioner should be able to show that the integrity of the files has been maintained (SWGIT 2012).

Although it is possible for any computer to be stolen, laptops/notebooks are particularly vulnerable to theft. Appropriate physical security measures should therefore be in place to prevent such loss. The computers used should always be physically secured when not in the possession of the operator (e.g., locked away, secured with a security cable). All data files should be copied at the earliest opportunity onto at least one external storage device, such as a large memory capacity external hard drive, and stored away from the primary files. Some devices of this type have two separate integral hard drives that can be configured for either maximum capacity or maximum security. For maximum security, the device can be configured as RAID (Redundant Array of Inexpensive Disks) 1, thereby providing mirrored storage of two identical copies of the backed up data on each of the separate drives. Although reducing the storage capacity of the external drive by half, it is recommended that if such a feature is available, it should be used.

Although the images can also be archived to CD (compact disc) or digital versatile disc (DVD) (again with adequate security measures being taken), these forms of storage are becoming less commonly used, and some computers are being produced without a built-in feature to play such media, thereby limiting their usefulness in such a backup role.

The computer and any associated data storage facilities should be password protected, and in the case of the computer have up-to-date virus and firewall protection. It is also recommended that the computer used for this purpose is only connected to the Internet for virus protection and other essential software updates. The backup facility should be subjected to the same security measures as the primary computer involved.

Details of such security measures along with management of the equipment within that framework should be documented in a standard operating procedure (SOP) file. More detailed information on maintaining the integrity of digital images and digital video recordings is available online via SWGIT (2012).

3.4.2 Printer

The printer required for forensic purposes should be capable of printing out full-size foot, insole, and shoeprint images for examination and comparison purposes. The widely available A4 (letter) printers are not adequate for this purpose; some shoeprints (typically those above U.K. size 9/U.S. size 10) are too large to fit completely on A4-sized paper when printed out. An A3 (tabloid) printer is therefore required and should be of graphics quality. Although an inkjet printer is capable of printing high-quality images, if the printer is not used regularly, there is a potential problem of expensive ink cartridges drying out, causing inconvenience, delay, and potentially high running costs. A laser printer will not dry out in between use and is therefore likely to incur much lower running costs. In addition, it is capable of much faster graphics printing than the inkjet alternative; however, a laser printer will inevitably have a lower resolution than an inkjet printer.

3.4.3 Software

Digital photography also relies on appropriate software to manage and produce the captured image. Most digital cameras are purchased with their own dedicated software that is adequate for taking basic digital images; downloading these images to a computer; and processing, enhancing, and printing these images. These dedicated software packages however do not necessarily have the varied functions required to manage and print out images for forensic podiatry evidence management purposes. Adobe produces reasonably priced software packages that are ideal for these purposes; one example is Adobe Photoshop.

This program allows the image to be downloaded, saved, and printed as a life-size image by the operator, thereby enabling meaningful comparisons of questioned and reference images. Adobe offers a range of digital image processing software, but some of these programs are expensive. The more basic programs are considerably cheaper and contain all the functions required for forensic podiatry purposes, although some of the tasks required during analysis and comparison of the images (e.g., measurement of detail) may take longer to perform with the basic Adobe Elements software than with the more expensive Adobe Photoshop products and software. Adobe Photoshop is highly capable and widely regarded as the industry standard for this type of software.

An alternative to the Adobe programs is the GIMP (GNU Image Manipulation Program) software. This program is currently in Version 2.8 form and can be downloaded free from the GIMP developers' website (www.gimp.org). Created for use with digital images, GIMP has a wide range of image management features and works on a wide range of computer operating systems. GIMP is an example of open source software, with the developers website making information about its source code freely available (Reel 2012). GIMP was used by Reel (2012) in her PhD work, and several advantages, many of which related to the open source nature of GIMP in the context of forensic practice were noted. Not only was GIMP noted to be cost-effective, stable, and user friendly, but also its open source nature was seen as being able to facilitate constant peer review of the product. Reel (2012) and others (Carrier 2003) have also noted that open source tools can be seen as preferable to closed source tools in the context of Daubert criteria through such peer review, which can demonstrate the general acceptance criterion of Daubert.

One disadvantage noted by Reel (2012) in relation to GIMP was the absence of an audit tool. Such a tool would allow the user's actions to be recorded as he or she worked through a file image, making changes to those images. With the current version of GIMP (Version 2.8), basic information such as size and resolution is shown about an image and although the number of steps taken in management of the image is shown, detail of what was undertaken in these steps is not. As Reel (2012) pointed out, this lack of detail could be problematic in the context of forensic casework where guidelines have suggested that steps taken in digital image analysis should be documented in detail to allow another expert to obtain the same results when repeating the process (FBI 2001).

3.5 Digital Image Capture Techniques

The techniques of digital image capture that need to be used by the forensic podiatrist differ from those of the conventional leisure photographer. There are, however, some common considerations such as the need to immobilize the camera, framing, image quality, focus, and lighting, although in a different context. Here, a step-by-step guide is presented to lead the examiner through the process of basic evidence-quality digital image capture for forensic podiatry purposes.

3.5.1 Equipment Selection

First, the immediate task should be considered, particularly regarding what is required to be photographed and where. As per the equipment requirements stated in Section 3.2, equipment should be selected according to the circumstances of the case. The type of stand and lighting are considered, with issues of portability in mind. Although the camera and various other items (including scale) are mandatory, other accessory equipment may be needed according to the required task. It is advisable to prepare a checklist of such requirements before working each individual case.

3.5.2 Equipment Inspection

Once the required equipment has been selected, the user should carefully examine each item to verify that it is in working order and that, if applicable, any statutory electrical testing is up to date. Test shots should be taken with the camera by using all memory cards (main and backup) and immediately deleted. The camera, flash unit backup cameras, and all other rechargeable electrical items should be fully charged. Nonrechargeable batteries should be unused and within their shelf life, and the line power lead extension cord should be tested by use. The lighting source should be inspected carefully to verify that all bulbs are in working order and within their shelf life, and if transportation is required, this equipment should then be packed carefully to prevent breakage. Marker pens to be used for frame labeling should be tested to ensure that they have not dried out since their previous use. In relation to the camera support, if an optional quick-release mechanism has been obtained, this mechanism and any adapters for the camera base should be in place to ensure compatibility of the attachments.

3.5.3 Setting Up the Equipment

At the site where the evidence is to be considered, a clean, private, and secure area should be sought, with access to a line power supply and preferably a sturdy table. The line power supply should be within range of the line power extension lead and there should be space to store equipment where it will not be in the way. The camera support is then considered. If the work is to be carried out in an office, a copy stand is likely to be used. If the work is to be undertaken away from the workbench, a tripod is selected, opened, adjusted to the approximate height required, and placed into position. The lighting to be used should also be placed in the approximate position required.

Having selected the working area and support, the object to be photographed is selected and the appropriate background is considered for the image. The forensic podiatrist should attempt to provide some contrast between the object and background to allow the outline of the image to be clearly defined; however, extreme contrast should be avoided between the object and background (e.g., a very dark object being placed over a very light background and vice versa). Such a mismatch may lead to lost detail through the effect of these extreme contrasts on exposure. If a copy stand is being used, the copy stand base itself may present an appropriately plain and moderately contrasting background and may not require covering with an alternative background material.

The camera is then mounted securely onto the support. If the viewing screen of the camera is capable of adjustment, it is at this stage that the screen would be tilted into its optimal position for ease of operation. Checks are then made on the camera mounting, commencing with the security of the camera on this mount. The camera should be set at the 50-mm lens position (or its equivalent if a focal length multiplication or crop factor is applicable), and the camera should be set at the approximate height required to fill the frame with the object to be photographed. A check should be made to ensure that there are no cords, straps, or the lens cap dangling from the camera because they could interfere with the image. The level of the camera would then be matched with the level of the base upon which the object of interest will be placed. The important factor here is that the images are on the same plane as the camera because problems with scale will occur if either the camera or bases are set at different planes to each other.

The object to be captured is then placed onto the chosen background in a central position, where it is checked to ensure that it is securely placed. If the image to be photographed is a two-dimensional footprint, this print may be secured carefully with tape, while ensuring that the tape is not placed over the object to be captured and that it will not damage the evidence under consideration. If the object is three-dimensional (e.g., an insole or footwear item), then the object should have enough inherent stability to remain in place on its own accord.

The Bureau Reference Scale and additional second scale, if required, are then placed neatly by the side of the object, close enough to be seen in a cropped version of the image, yet not so close as to obscure any detail (Figure 3.6). If the detail to be captured is elevated above the background base, then the scale needs to be elevated using stacks of coins or wedges so that the scale sits in the same plane as the detail of interest. A label is created and placed in an appropriate position by the side of the object. It is essential that neither scale nor labels used be placed over any aspect of the object because this obstruction will inevitably lead to later problems when the

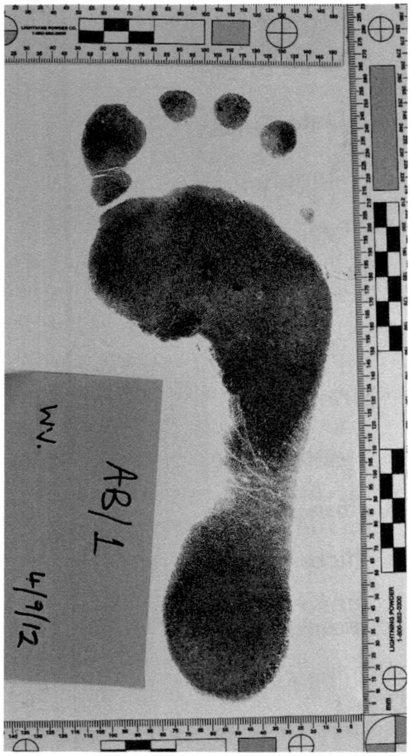

Figure 3.6 Bureau Reference Scale positioning.

image is being evaluated. The camera should next be switched on and the image checked in the viewfinder. The object, scale, and label should fill the screen, although care should be taken to ensure that no detail has been lost through the object being situated too close to the borders of the frame. If necessary, the camera should be raised or lowered slightly on its support until a satisfactory framed image is shown.

At this stage, the lighting should be considered. If the object is two dimensional, lighting should be straightforward, but if the object is three dimensional some experimentation may be required. Shining a flashlight around the object, while observing the effects through the viewfinder, gives an indication of the best lighting angle to capture the image detail required. Experimentation should also consider the effects of reflected light by using a white reflecting board to direct the light source to the optimal angle for the detail required to be shown. This approach may be especially useful in situations where flash photography is preferred. The lighting set at the angle required is then switched on in preparation for the image capture. If a forensic light source is being used, the required protective goggles should be selected and worn and any associated filters placed on the camera before use. Where filters are placed on the camera, the level should be carefully rechecked to ensure that filter placement has not been disturbed, with any remedial adjustments to level being made as necessary.

Having determined the required lighting angles, unless the lighting preparation work has suggested that flash photography would be a preferable option (which may be an infrequent preference), the automatic flash mode of the camera should be switched off to ensure that the built-in flash does not operate. If a photographer is less experienced or lacks confidence, it is recommended that the camera be set to automatic to ensure that when the appropriate lighting adjustments have been made, the exposure will be correct for the image to be captured. If color images are to be used, care should be taken to match the white balance settings of the camera with the light source in use. In professional photography, there is a concept of color temperature, and different light sources exhibit a different range of temperatures that, in turn, can affect the color of the image captured. Digital cameras of the quality required will have a feature to allow the white balance to be changed to compensate for the color temperature conditions experienced. For example, domestic light bulbs are usually tungsten, and without compensation the color will take on a more golden yellow overall appearance than that observed. With advancements in cameras technology, many cameras can now automatically make adjustments. If such adjustments are not possible on the camera being used (either automatically or manually), this can be compensated for later, with the photo management software package; however, it is better to deal with this issue at source. The camera should also be placed on its highest resolution setting, and the image should be captured either in TIFF, or RAW format, not JPEG. Unlike JPEG, TIFF and RAW are described as lossless formats, i.e., that every time a JPEG file is opened, some detail will be lost through the way in which this format operates, whereas this is not the case with TIFF and RAW. Of the two formats, TIFF and RAW, TIFF is often preferable, because with RAW, there can be compatibility issues between different manufacturing systems, which may be problematic at a later stage should there be a need to play back or look further at the image on a computer that does not hold the required proprietary software for the RAW images involved.

If the camera has the facility to adjust the focusing area, this should now be placed on its widest setting. If the spot meter is to be used, this function should be selected on the camera, the focus should be checked, and the remote function or timer delay should be set in final preparation for the image capture which can then proceed. The first image taken should be checked carefully to ensure it is of the required quality. This check can be done on some cameras by using the zoom function to gain a close-up view of known detail within the captured image (e.g., a section of the Bureau Reference Scale), to check for pin-sharp focusing. If this feature is not available, the image should be immediately downloaded onto a laptop, where quality can be checked using digital image software. Once satisfied that the image is going to be of the required quality, it is recommended that several images be taken with varying lighting conditions and that each image is protected on the camera immediately by using the camera image protection function to prevent accidental deletion.

3.5.4 Image Management

When the images to be used in a case have been captured digitally, they must then be stored safely and securely, on a suitable computer, again using TIFF or RAW formats and prepared for printing out to scale. Although the images should have been protected on the camera at the first available opportunity, this protection is now temporarily removed, and all images are downloaded onto a computer via USB connection or alternately by removal of the camera's memory card and insertion of the card into a computer. Wi-Fi and Bluetooth connections have become available on some cameras, allowing wire-free transfer of the images from camera to computer. Because of the sensitive nature of case evidence, the computer should be password protected with security measures applied at all times to prevent unauthorized access and guard against theft. Because multiple images may be involved, it is important to manage these images very carefully from the start, with suitably named and categorized files related to the case being prepared and with the images being logically and clearly named and copied into these files accordingly. Each image should be examined and any of poor quality should not be deleted but instead transferred to a nonworking file where it can still be accessed, should that be required in the future. The software cropping function can be used to "trim" the edges of each image to improve its appearance; however, care should be taken to not accidentally remove any aspect of the object being examined, or leave any aspect of the object too close to the borders of the photograph. Likewise, care should be taken to avoid accidental removal of detail shown in the scale used within the image, because this scale is essential to demonstrate the true size of the object and enable the object to be printed out as a life-size image. It is recommended that before cropping, all original photographs be kept without amendment and the cropped image "saved as" a copy. The copy would then be worked on, but all original images are still present and can be returned to later in case of error.

When the images of the quality required have been selected, the next task is to consider whether color or black-and-white images are preferred. The image management software should allow the color to be changed to black and white as required, and where color images are preferred, it should allow color and contrast to be enhanced by slight adjustments. It is important to note that at all stages of image management, contemporaneous notes must be kept.

Digital images are potentially prone to challenges that the images may have been manipulated and in doing so that the information present in these images may have been corrupted. If notes are kept of each stage of the image management, then these notes are available, if required, to show exactly what has taken place, to allow others to replicate and verify that work and to refute accusations of inappropriate or erroneous manipulation. Adobe Photoshop is capable of collecting audit data to show exactly how and when any changes to the image were made; and in addition to note taking, this information can be printed out and kept with the case file as evidence of the image management procedures performed. This function however is not available through the more basic Elements program or with the GIMP program. The color hue, saturation, brightness, and contrast functions of the software can all be adjusted slightly to optimize the detail required within the image presented on screen. The reason for restricting any adjustments to slight changes only is that if the image is subject to major alterations in color or contrast, such alterations can change positioning of the periphery of features seen within the image, therefore affecting any measurements taken. If the image is clear enough without such adjustment, the recommendation would be to work without adjustment.

One of the most important needs is to be able to print out the image showing the object as life sized. At this stage, the scale used within the image becomes essential. The following instructions given for this task are based on the Elements 9 program. Adobe Elements and Photoshop are updated regularly, and the exact manner in which this task would be undertaken can and does vary according to the program version.

Life sizing the image by using Adobe Elements 9

- Open the required image file.
- Ensure that the image visible on the screen clearly shows the horizontal and vertical aspects of the contained Bureau Reference Scale or other scale.
- Use the layer function to flatten the image, in effect placing all layers that may be present together. If the layer function is grayed out when displayed, this action is not required.
- Place a grid on the screen by selecting the View/Grid function. Simultaneously, ensure that the "Snap to Grid" function has not been selected (located under View/Snap to/Grid).
- Use the Image/Rotate/Free Rotate layer function to rotate the image. Using the mouse, left click on one of the small "handles" visible within the box bordering the image and while continuing to hold down the left mouse button, move the handle so that the vertical aspect of the scale seen within the image aligns perfectly with the corresponding vertical lines of the grid.

- When the alignment described above has been achieved, left mouse click on the green check mark visible within the image to commit to the action just taken.
- Remove the grid by deselecting the View/Grid function.
- Using the Zoom tool present within the Adobe Elements toolbox to magnify the image using the associated + (Zoom in) option (found on the top left of the screen) so that a given length of the scale within the image (e.g., 10 cm) extends from top to bottom of the computer screen. If the toolbox is not visible, go to the Windows menu at the top of the screen and select "Tools" from the dropdown list.
- Ensure that the Window/Info Tab is selected.
- From the Tools menu, select the Rectangular Marquee tool. Place the cursor on a defined position on the scale (e.g., at scale point zero) and holding down the left mouse button, drag the cursor down the scale carefully to reach another defined position on the scale (e.g., the 10-cm position). As such, you will have created a box along the scale present within the image to a defined length (in this case, a convenient 10 cm).
- The height reading (H:) present within the Info Tab now shows the length of the line that has been placed along the scale in millimeters. This information is the length that line would be if the image were printed out at this particular moment.
- Calculate the percentage difference between the image size shown at this stage and that of the life-size image required. To perform this calculation, divide the height reading selected on the scale by using the Marquee tool (e.g., 10 cm) by the length shown for that line, should the image be printed out at that stage and multiply by 100.
- From the top menu, select Image/Resize/Image Size.
- The display shows the document width and length in centimeters, should the document be printed out at this stage.
- Click on the arrow to the right of the width display, and select document width and length as percentage values to display the document height and width as 100%, based on its current size.
- Ensure that the Constrain Proportions box within the Image Size menu is checked.
- Enter the percentage value of the difference between the current image size shown and the life-size image required (as calculated above) into the document size (length) box.
- Click OK.
- Using the Rectangular Marquee tool, repeat the measurement as described above. The measurement shown in the Info Tab should now match that indicated by the defined length of the line placed along the scale.

- If a minor variation is shown, repeat the procedure with an emphasis on accuracy.
- When the vertical width has been matched to life size in this way, check the horizontal dimension of the scale in the same way. This should match (or very closely match within 0.05%). If any significant discrepancy is shown, there may have been a problem with alignment of the image and camera lens at the image capture stage. If this occurs and it is not possible to retake the image, seek professional assistance via a digital photo laboratory unless the photographer has personal extensive knowledge of the software required to adjust such images. Notes should be taken of the work required to adjust the image in this way, should such adjustments be questioned later (Figure 3.7a–g).

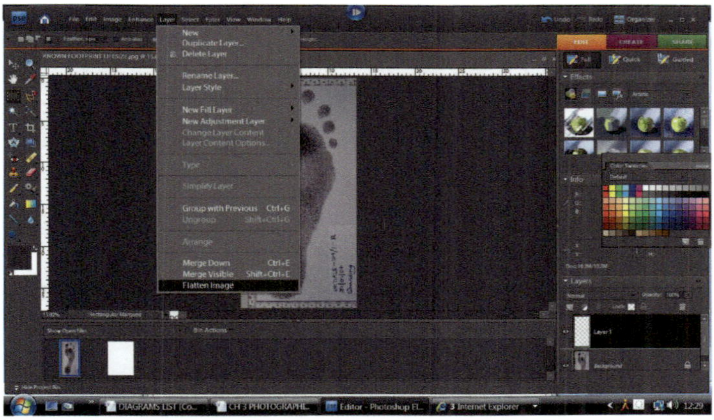

(a)

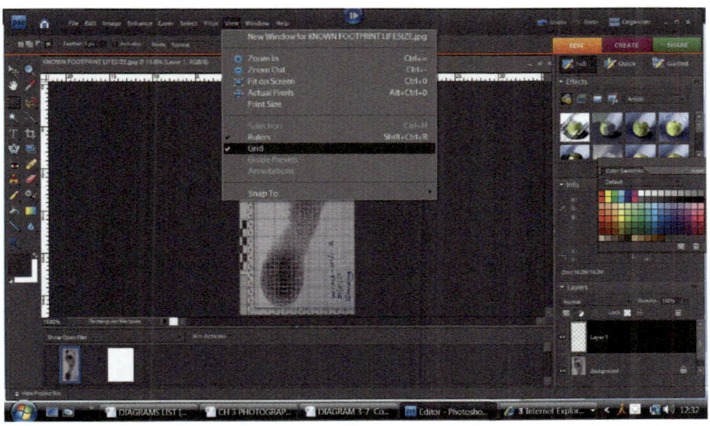

(b)

Figure 3.7 (a–g) Conversion of captured image to life size by using Adobe Elements. *(Continued)*

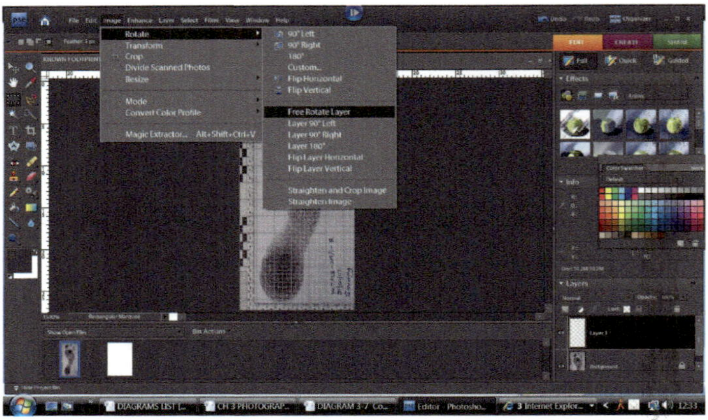

(c)

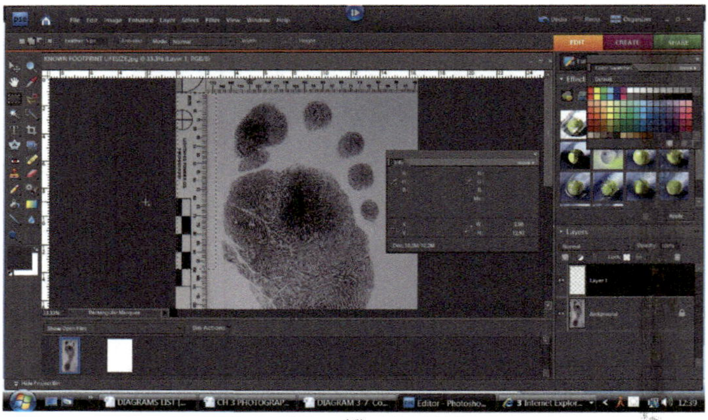

(d)

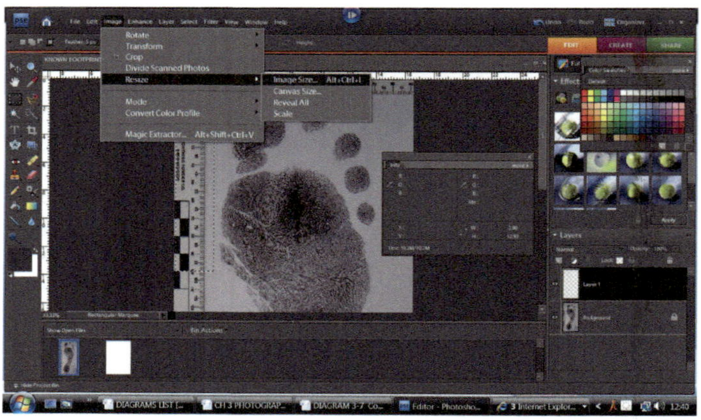

(e)

Figure 3.7 (Continued) (a–g) Conversion of captured image to life size by using Adobe Elements. *(Continued)*

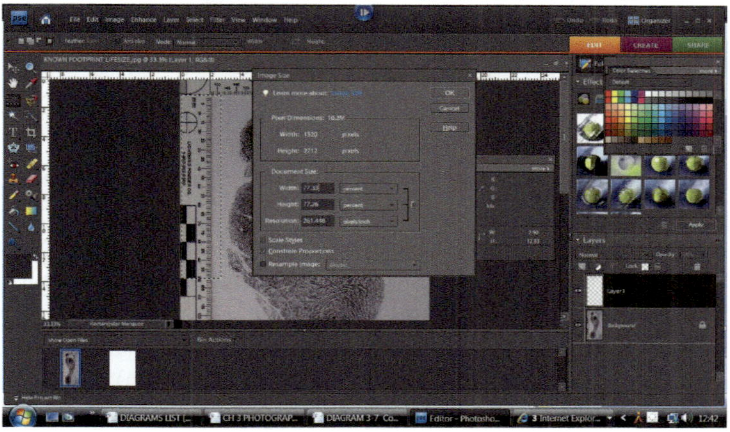

(f)

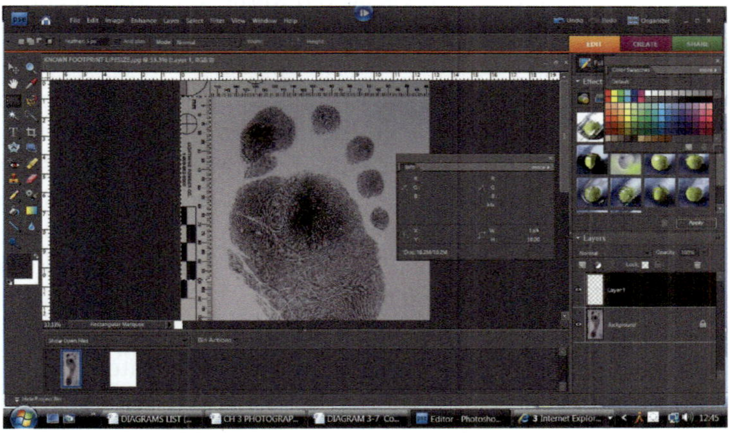

(g)

Figure 3.7 (Continued) (a–g) Conversion of captured image to life size by using Adobe Elements.

Life sizing the image by using Adobe Photoshop CS5.1

Although Adobe Elements will perform the task of life sizing images very well, this software is, in effect, a budget version of Adobe Photoshop. There are many differences between Adobe Elements and Adobe Photoshop, but also similarities. With regard to the task of life sizing an image, Adobe Photoshop is much faster and can be easier to operate than Adobe Elements. This task is helped by the presence of a Ruler (measuring) tool within the program that can be used to simply measure between two lines without needing to orientate the image to line up a scale and grid within the image. To use this tool to convert an image to life size, the following steps are taken:

- Open the required image file.
- Ensure that the image visible on the screen clearly shows the horizontal and vertical aspects of the contained Bureau Reference Scale or other scale.
- Use the layer function to flatten the image, in effect placing all layers that may be present together. If the layer function is grayed out when displayed, this action is not required.
- Use the Zoom tool present within the Adobe Photoshop toolbox to magnify the image by using the associated + (Zoom in) option (found on the top left of the screen) so that a given length of the scale within the image (e.g., 10 cm) extends from top to bottom of the computer screen. If the toolbox is not visible, go to the Windows menu at the top of the screen and select "Tools" from the dropdown list.
- Ensure that the Window/Info Tab is selected.
- From the Tools menu, select the Rectangular Ruler tool. If the tool is not immediately obvious within the visible menu, right click on the Eyedropper, Color Sampler, or Note tool (whichever is displayed), and the Ruler tool can then be seen and selected from a subset of tools within that tool subsection.
- Place the cursor on a defined position on the scale (e.g., at scale point zero) and holding down the left mouse button drag the cursor down the scale carefully to reach another defined position on the scale (e.g., the 10-cm position). As such, you will have created a Ruler tool line along the scale present within the image to a defined length (in this case, a convenient 10 cm).
- The height reading (H:) present within the Info Tab now shows the length of the line that has been placed along the scale in millimeters. This information is the length that line would be if the image were printed out at this particular moment.
- Calculate the percentage difference between the image size shown at this stage and that of the life-size image required. To perform this calculation, divide the height reading selected on the scale using the Ruler tool (e.g., 10 cm) by the length shown for that line, should the image be printed out at that stage and multiply by 100.
- From the top menu, select Image/Image Size.
- The display shows the document width and length in centimeters, should the document be printed out at this stage.
- Click on the arrow to the right of the width display and select document width and length as percentage values to display the document height and width as 100%, based on its current size.

- Ensure that the Constrain Proportions box within the Image Size menu is checked.
- Enter the percentage value of the difference between the current image size shown and the life-size image required (as calculated above) into the document size (length) box.
- Click OK.
- Using the Ruler tool, repeat the measurement as described above. The measurement shown in the Info Tab should now match that indicated by the defined length of the line placed along the scale.
- If a minor variation is shown, repeat the procedure with an emphasis on accuracy.
- From this point on, the same checks as would be undertaken per Adobe Elements are performed, and comprehensive notes are taken throughout (Figure 3.8a–i).

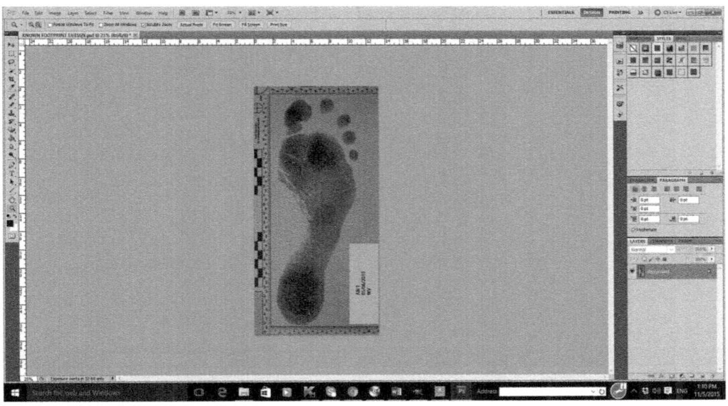

(a)

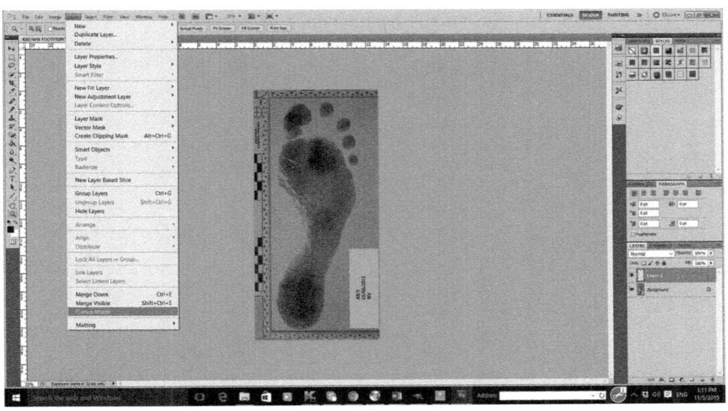

(b)

Figure 3.8 (a–i) Conversion of captured image to life size by using Adobe Photoshop. *(Continued)*

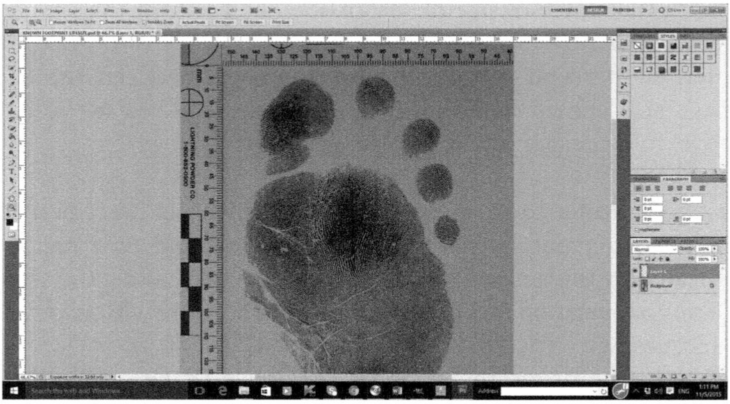

(c)

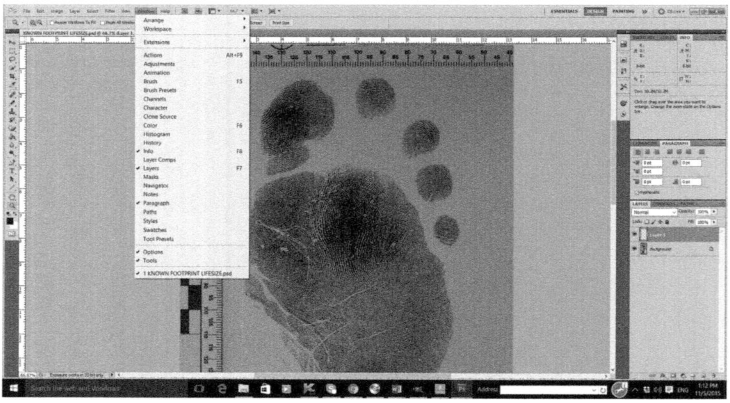

(d)

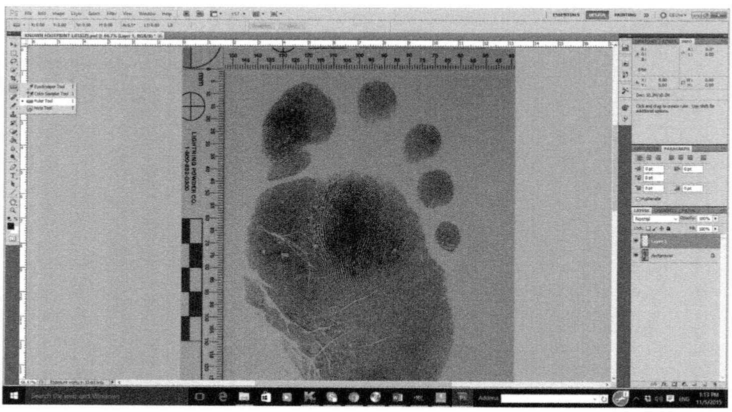

(e)

Figure 3.8 (Continued) (a–i) Conversion of captured image to life size by using Adobe Photoshop. *(Continued)*

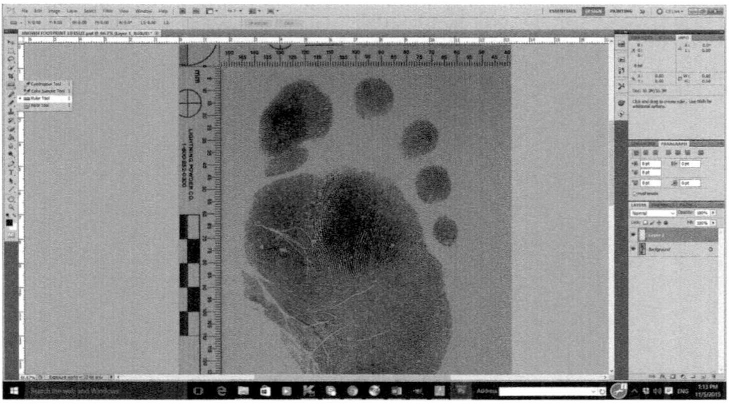

(f)

(g)

(h)

Figure 3.8 (Continued) (a–i) Conversion of captured image to life size by using Adobe Photoshop. *(Continued)*

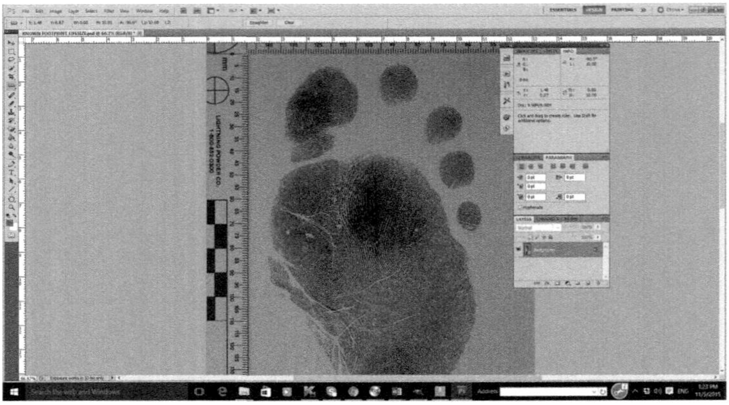

(i)

Figure 3.8 (Continued) (a–i) Conversion of captured image to life size by using Adobe Photoshop.

Life sizing the image by using GIMP Version 2.8

As an alternative, open source software GIMP can also be used for forensic applications, and the captured images can be converted to life-size images with this program. The GIMP approach differs from that of the Adobe programs with details as follows:

- Open the required image file.
- Ensure that the image visible on the screen clearly shows the horizontal and vertical aspects of the contained Bureau Reference Scale or other scale.
- Use the Zoom tool present within the GIMP dropdown menu (View/Zoom) to magnify the image by using the associated + (zoom in) so that a given length of the scale within the image (e.g., 10 cm) extends from top to bottom of the computer screen.
- Select the Zoom tool from the top dropdown menu (View/Zoom) and zoom in on a 10-cm section of the Bureau Reference Scale present within the image by using the Zoom in option).
- Select the Measure tool from the top dropdown menu (Tools/Measure). At the bottom of the screen, you will have the option to select the measure unit to be used (e.g., pixels, centimeters, millimeters, inches). Select millimeters as the option.
- Place the cursor on a defined position on the Bureau Reference Scale present within the image and holding down the left mouse button drag the cursor along the scale carefully to reach another defined position on the scale (e.g., from the 0-cm to the 10-cm position). As such, you will have created a Measure tool line along the scale

present within the image to a defined length (in this case, a convenient 10 cm).

- The reading (H:) present within an information box at the bottom of the screen along with the angle of the line drawn (which is not required) now shows the length of the line that has been placed along the scale in millimeters. This is the length that line would be if the image were to be printed out at this particular moment.
- Calculate the percentage difference between the image size shown at this stage and that of the life-size image required. To perform this calculation, divide the height reading selected on the scale using the Measure tool (e.g., 10 cm) by the length shown for that line should the image be printed out at that stage and multiply by 100.
- From the top menu select Image/Scale Image. The display box shows information relating to the image size and quality. Using the option box present, ensure that the image size is displayed as 100%, based on its current size. This shows the document width and length in centimeters, should the document be printed out at this stage.
- Click on the arrow to the right of the width display and select document width and length as percentage values. This displays the document height and width as 100%, based on its current size.
- Ensure that the small chain logo visible to the right of the image size height and width boxes shows a connected as opposed to a broken chain. Enter the percentage value as calculated above into the document size (length) box.
- Click on the scale box. The program now rescales the image.
- Using the Measure tool again, repeat the measurement as described above. The measurement shown in the information box at the bottom of the screen should now match that indicated by the defined length of the line placed along the scale.
- If a minor variation is shown, repeat the procedure with an emphasis on accuracy.
- From this point on, the same checks as would be undertaken per Adobe Elements and Adobe Photoshop are preformed, and comprehensive notes are taken throughout (Figure 3.9a–i).

When the image size has been set to life size, the image can be cropped as necessary to improve the clarity of the presented image by removing extraneous peripheral detail. It is important however to retain not only the full outline of the object to be considered presented but also the scale and label used in the digital photograph. After cropping, the image should be printed out using an A3 (Tabloid) color graphics printer onto the photographic paper recommended for use with that printer. Care is required at this stage to adjust the printed settings to those required for photographic paper of the

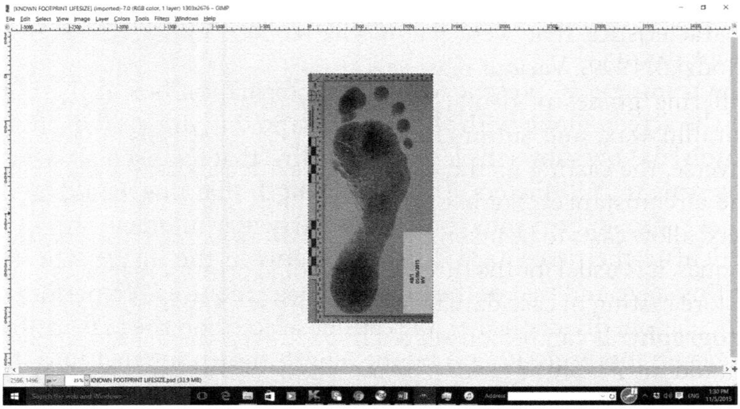

(a)

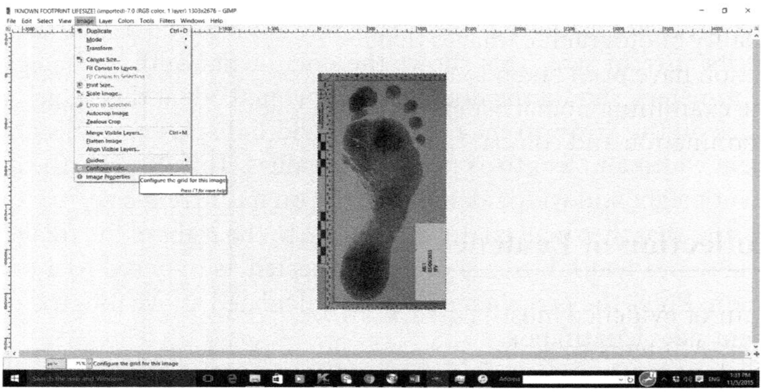

(b)

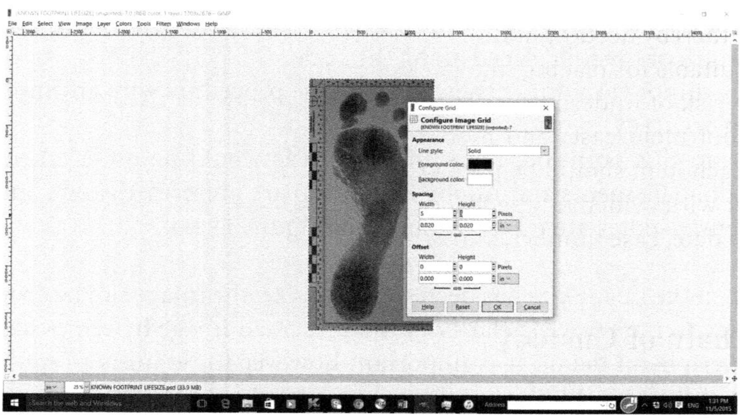

(c)

Figure 3.9 (a–i) Conversion of captured image to life size by using GIMP. *(Continued)*

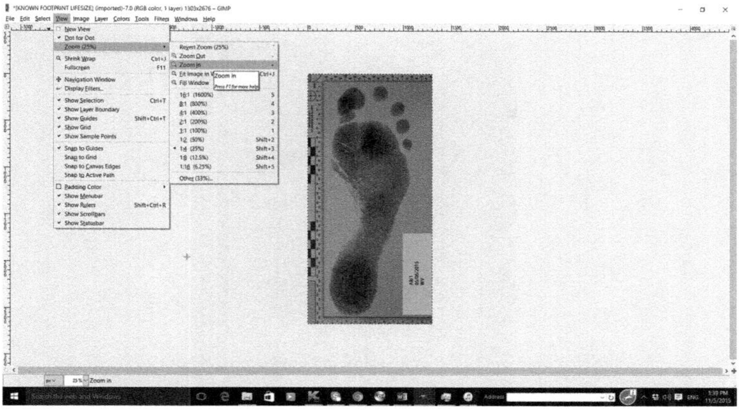

(d)

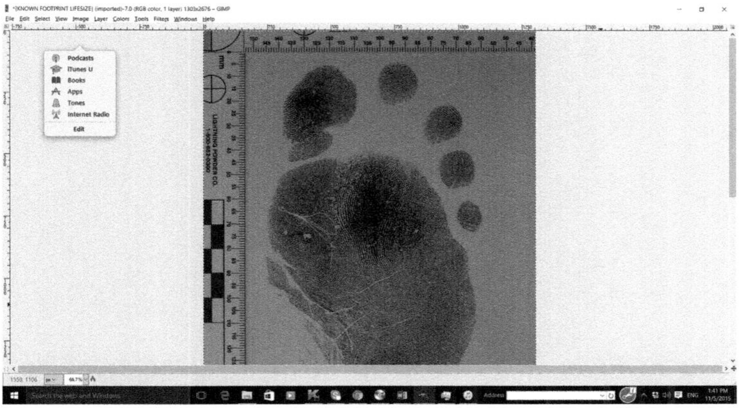

(e)

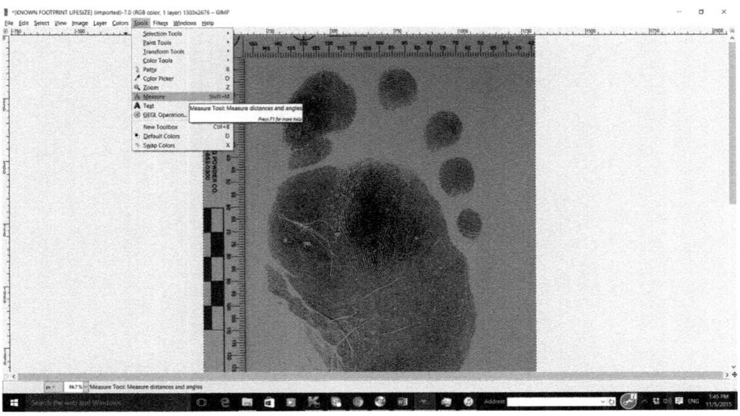

(f)

Figure 3.9 (Continued) (a–i) Conversion of captured image to life size by using GIMP. *(Continued)*

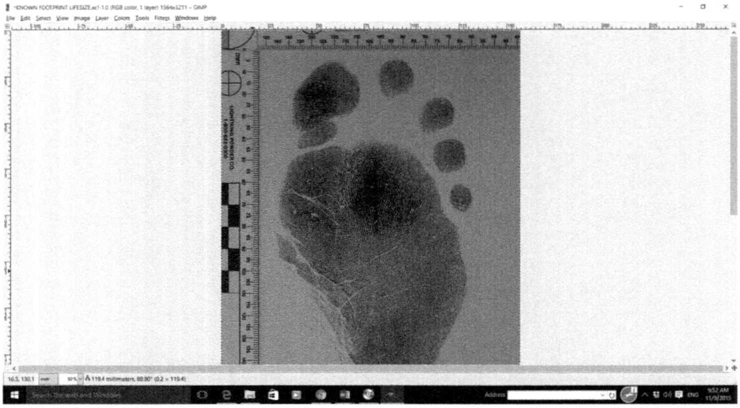

(g)

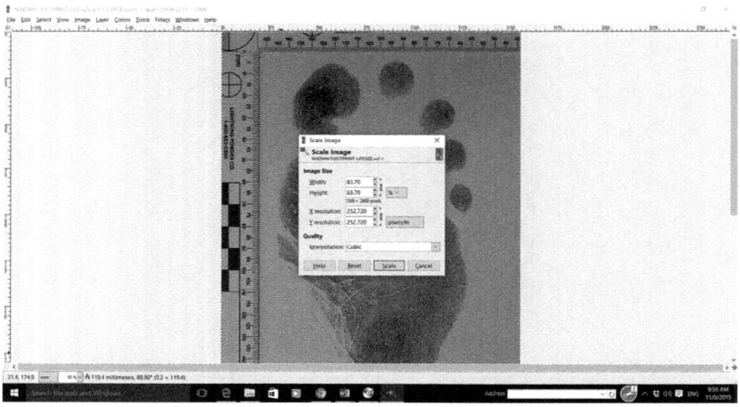

(h)

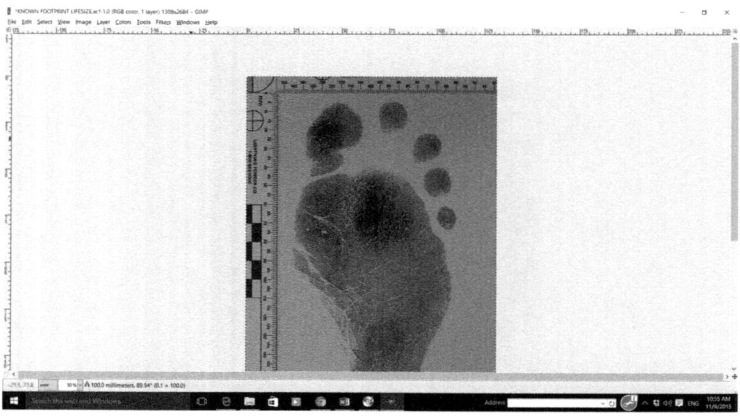

(i)

Figure 3.9 (Continued) (a–i) Conversion of captured image to life size by using GIMP.

type used. Failure to follow this final step could lead to image problems at the printing stage. It is also advisable to use the print preview function as a final check that the image will fit successfully on the selected paper size and by previewing the image to be printed; this approach provides final confirmation that no major errors of scale have occurred when adjusting the image to life size. When the image has successfully printed out, a final manual check should be made of the scale within the image by using the very same scale present within that image. If all stages mentioned above have been followed, this image should be perfectly matched, and the image is ready for comparison and evaluation.

References

Blitzer H., Hammer R. and Jacobia J. 2007. Effect of Photographic Technology on Quality of Examination of Footwear Impressions. *Journal of Forensic Identification*, 57(5): 641–657.

Bodziak W.J. 2000. *Footwear Impression Evidence: Detection, Recovery and Examination*. 2nd ed. Boca Raton, FL: CRC Press.

Cambridge in Colour. 2015. Basics of Digital Camera Pixels. http://www.cambridgeincolour.com/tutorials/digital-camera-pixel.htm (Accessed October 6, 2015).

Carrier B. 2003. *Open Source Digital Forensic Tools: The Legal Argument*. Technical Report. Stake Research Report. http://www.digital-evidence.org/papers/opensrc_legal.pdf (Accessed October 2, 2016).

FBI. 2001. Definitions and Guidelines for the Use of Imaging Technologies in the Criminal Justice System. *Forensic Science Communications*, 3(3): 1.

Freeman J. 2011. *Digital SLR Handbook*. London: HarperCollins.

Grotta D. and Grotta S.W. 2004. *Guide to Digital Photography*. Indianapolis, IN: Wiley.

Hilderbrand D.S. 1999. *Footwear, the Missed Evidence*. Temecula, CA: Staggs Publishing.

Kennedy R. 1996. Barefoot Impressions. Paper presented at the Annual Conference of the Canadian Identification Society, Halifax, Canada, 25 July.

Reel S. 2012. Development and Evaluation of a Valid and Reliable Footprint Measurement Approach in Forensic Identification. PhD Thesis, The University of Leeds, York St. John University.

Staggs S. 2005. *Crime Scene and Evidence Photographer's Guide*. 2nd ed. Temecula, CA: Staggs Publishing.

SWGIT (Scientific Working Group, Imaging Technology). 2012. Section 13: Best Practices for Maintaining the Integrity of Digital Images and Digital Video. https://www.swgit.org/pdf/Section%209%20General%20Guidelines%20for%20Photographing%20Footwear%20and%20Tire%20Impressions?docID=124 (Accessed October 15, 2016).

SWGIT (Scientific Working Group, Imaging Technology). 2013. Section 9: General Guidelines for Photographing Footwear and Tire Impressions.

Bare Footprint Identification

4

This chapter commences with a brief history of the use of bare footprints in identification, in particular, in areas in which several disciplines may be involved. A competent technician can perform some of these tasks as well as an initial assessment to determine whether the evidence is of adequate quality and quantity to proceed. There are times however when it is desirable for this entire process to be lead specifically by the forensic podiatrist. Methods of collecting exemplar (reference or standard) prints are presented along with variations of these methods and a comparison of these approaches. The assessments of various features of bare footprints that may be of interest to the forensic podiatrist also are presented, along with situations that could compromise the quality of bare footprints. The chapter then discusses techniques for the "measurement," comparison, and assessment of bare footprints and the podiatric assessment that involves interpretation of the features apparent within such prints. Research on the reliability and validity of bare footprints measurement approaches is presented, along with work that examines the cause of "ghosting" features found at the anterior and posterior aspects of dynamic bare footprints. The chapter closes with an evaluation of bare footprints after assessment and comparison, and the significance of similarities and differences between the known and unknown (questioned) bare footprint items that may be important in reaching the final conclusion.

4.1 Brief History

Bare footprint identification is an identification technique that uses a bare footprint; this bare footprint has usually been left at a scene of crime by the perpetrator of that crime. In the Western world where the shod foot predominates, bare footprint identification is a relatively unusual technique used in the identification process. Bare footprint identification is however more frequently used as a method in identification in countries where barefoot walking is commonplace (Qamra et al. 1980). There are however circumstances where bare footprints can be associated with crime scenes in the West. These circumstances can include crimes of a sexual nature (Barker and Scheuer 1998), where the perpetrator has removed his clothing before or during the crime and where the offender with forensic awareness has removed his or her footwear before the criminal act in the mistaken belief that if caught, conviction is less likely when leaving only a bare footprint at the scene. There have also been examples of bare footprints being used as evidence in crimes of violence, where the criminal has removed and destroyed bloodstained clothing and footwear, inadvertently leaving bare footprints in blood at the scene (Newsquest 2006).

Human footprints have been the subject of various publications that have considered their use in human identification (Bodziak 2000; Gunn 1991; Reel et al. 2010, 2012; Robbins 1985; Vernon 2006a). Human footprints have also been the subject of various research studies (Barker and Scheuer 1998; Kennedy 1996, 2005; Kennedy et al. 2003, 2005; Laskowski and Kyle 1988; Reel 2012; Reel et al. 2010, 2012). One of these studies was a significant long-term project involving a sample of 24,000 bare footprints collected from 12,000 volunteers (Kennedy 2005). Various approaches have been suggested and tested that could be used to express the individuality of the human footprint and to allow one footprint to be compared against another to determine whether the footprints could have been formed by the same person, or whether the dimensions and features would preclude that possibility. Reel (2012) tested the reliability and validity of the various approaches available for the measurement and comparison of bare footprints. Of the preexisting methods available for bare footprint measurement, Reel (2012) found that some are more repeatable in practice than others, and the Gunn method was particularly consistent in use across different examiners. Through this research, a new approach to the measurement of the features of bare footprints was recommended, and it represented an amalgamation of the most repeatable aspects of preexisting approaches to measurement.

Several specialists have been involved in the consideration of bare footprint evidence, including forensic identification specialists (Kennedy 1996), anthropologists (Robbins 1978; Topinard 1877), and podiatrists (Reel 2012; Reel et al. 2010, 2012; Vernon 2006a, 2006b). The added value podiatrists bring to the process is their understanding of the functioning foot and the effects that this function may have on the form of the human footprint. Anthropologists can assist with interpreting the dimensions of the print, and forensic identification specialists have general knowledge of the identification process across many areas that can bring additional understanding to considering footprints as evidence.

4.2 Obtaining Exemplar Prints

Although it possible to make some assumptions from a footprint in isolation, the true value of a bare footprint in identification relates to the ability to compare the questioned print with a print collected from a known person under controlled conditions, with the latter print being known as the exemplar (reference or standard) print. The circumstances of collecting exemplar prints vary and may include collection from prisoners in custody or on remand, from willing volunteers where the examiner has been instructed by a defense team, or from a person assisting the police in the investigation. It may also be necessary to compare the questioned prints with those of persons known to have been at the scene and not involved in the crime (e.g., relatives; attending personnel such as paramedics, or victims). The process should however follow the same approach irrespective of circumstances and requires the following equipment:

- Inkless paper system
- Long roll of brown or white paper
- Black (printers) ink and roller
- Marker tape
- Masking tape
- Permanent writing equipment
- Video-recording equipment (×2)

One of the first things to consider before collecting exemplar bare footprints for comparison with the questioned prints is whether the questioned prints are of dynamic or static form. Dynamic prints are prints left by a subject during ambulation (walking), whereas static prints are prints left when the subject is standing, not during ambulation.

Previous publications have noted that foot structure alters between its static and dynamic states, affecting the form of the plantar surface of the foot/bare footprint (Barker and Scheuer 1998; Kippen 1993; Mathieson et al. 1999; Tsung et al. 2003). One consequence of this alteration is the presence of a ghosting-type effect that can regularly be seen at the posterior heel, and anterior toe areas of dynamic prints (Figure 4.1). The term "ghosting" has been described as "the lighter shading of the footprint which extends beyond the areas that would or should be normally captured during collection of the barefoot print" (Burrow 2015). The term ghosting is believed to have first been used in 1996 to explain this phenomenon to the court.[1] Although ghosting can, on occasion, occur in static prints (Burrow 2015), the phenomenon is particularly and usually associated with dynamic footprints and is one feature that can be used to help distinguish between static and dynamic prints present at a crime scene. In addition, the situation of the footprint at a crime scene would provide contextual information to help determine whether a print is static or dynamic. If present within a sequence of footprints, the examiner

[1] Description use by Vernon while presenting evidence to the Court in R. v. Clarke 2006.

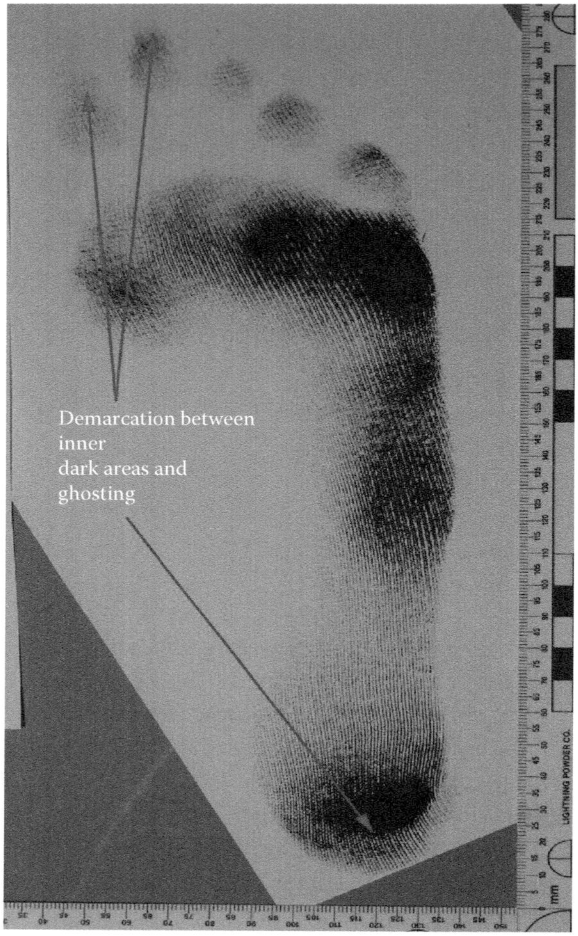

Figure 4.1 Ghosting phenomena occurring in dynamic bare footprints.

could confidently state that a print must be dynamic, whereas a print close to and facing a wall, e.g., is most likely to be static.

Once a print has been determined to be static or dynamic, collection of exemplar prints is undertaken. Using the principle of comparing like-with-like items, questioned static prints would be compared with exemplar static prints and questioned dynamic prints with exemplar dynamic prints. The nature of the questioned prints then determines what form of exemplar print collection is required.

In the collection of dynamic exemplar prints, an uninterrupted straight walkway is required, ideally of the minimum length required for podiatric gait analysis, typically approximately 20 feet. It is recommended that two podiatrists be present to observe the subject walking during the dynamic footprint collection process and that a four-step protocol be used. In previous research, this protocol produced pressure and force values more akin to midgait protocols than one-step approaches (Meyers-Rice et al. 1994) where the subject may not have achieved his or her habitual gait form at the point that the bare footprint is left. The four-step approach also has benefits over midgait protocols in which targeting difficulties can be experienced (Meyers-Rice et al. 1994). In this context of collecting dynamic footprints for forensic analysis, placement of the foot onto the inkless paper during midstance would represent such a targeting difficulty.

The recommended procedures for collecting dynamic bare footprints are as follows:

- The subject is asked to walk barefoot while the walkway is being prepared, to help achieve their habitual gait form before footprint collection.
- A line is selected or made on the floor with marker tape and the subject asked to stand behind this line and look straight ahead, with the toes of both feet touching the line.
- A mark is then selected or taped onto the wall surface at the subject's eye level, and the subject is asked to look toward this line.
- The subject is asked to walk at a normal pace toward the wall marker, stepping off with the foot opposite that from which the exemplar print is to be taken.
- At the end of the first stride (the second step) and the second stride (the fourth step), the landing positions of the foot in question should be noted.
- The impregnated mat of the inkless print kit should be placed approximately in line with, but not at that stage directly over the second step position, and an inkless paper sheet should be placed loosely in line with, but not at that stage directly over the fourth step position.
- This process is then repeated several times until reasonably consistent landing places are identified for the second and fourth step positions of the foot.
- The impregnated mat is then moved directly over the indicated second step position, and the inkless paper sheet is quickly and securely taped at the indicated fourth step position.
- Recording equipment, placed to the side and rear of the selected landing position, is then switched on and the subject is asked to walk again, this time with the intention being that the foot in question should land completely within the confines of the impregnated mat and then the secured inkless paper sheet, upon which a complete footprint would then be left.

- The participant walks forward at a normal pace, stepping off with the right foot as described above.
- The process is then repeated until a collection of six or more good-quality footprints have been obtained, and then the whole procedure is repeated for the opposite foot.
- Clinical wipes are made available for the subject to clean his or her feet on completion of the exercise.

It is inevitable that from time to time, several prints will be spoiled or partial, and these prints should be carefully filed away separate from the exemplar prints. On each occasion that the foot in question lands on the inkless paper, the observing podiatrists should note whether the step onto the paper seemed to reflect the typical/anticipated walking pattern of the subject, particularly noting whether there had been any attempt by the subject to amend the gait pattern to alter the form of the footprint. Typical examples of such amendments include pulling back the toes to avoid leaving a toe imprint, contracting the foot during the stance phase of walking to leave only a partial impression, attempting to smudge the footprint by introducing shearing or torsion movements during the stance phase, and leaving only a partial footprint by not placing the foot within the confines of the inkless paper during collection of the bare footprint. The observing podiatrists should compare their observational notes after each footprint has been left to verify areas of doubt and confirm whether the stance phase observed was acceptable in terms of apparent normality for that subject's gait.

An alternative approach to collecting exemplar dynamic bare footprints involves the use of a 20-foot-long sheet of white butcher paper, black printers ink, and a roller. Here, instead of using an inkless paper system, the walkway is covered with the white butcher paper taped to the floor and as before, a marker is placed on the wall. The subject's feet would be comprehensively inked with the roller and black printers ink. The subject would then be asked to walk across the paper toward the marker, leaving inked footprints as he or she progress. One option to prevent the subject from intentionally altering his or her gait when that is a problem is to ask a question, such as "What is your age?" When the subject begins the sequence, a sequence of 10 footprints is usually collected by this method, with at least a minimum of eight steps required. Three separate sequences should be taken to allow the examiner to choose the most accurate and consistent footprints, which are usually steps 4–8.

Each of these approaches has its own advantages and disadvantages. Although the inkless paper method is clean and has the potential to collect extremely clear footprints, it can nevertheless be difficult to set up, time-consuming (especially where the subject is being uncooperative), and incapable of collecting a sequence of prints. However where extreme targeting difficulties are experienced, consideration could be given to taping several inkless sheets together, thereby increasing the size of target area and reducing the potential for this area to be partially missed by the participant's foot.

The ink and roller method can be messy, but it is much quicker to set up and use than the inkless paper approach. This method also collects a sequence of multiple prints from which those of the best quality can easily be selected for later examination. The method selected should be that which is the most applicable to each particular circumstance.

A cream has been developed (Bond 2013) that could be wiped onto the subject's foot as a substitute for the impregnated mat used in the inkless paper kit. If used in conjunction with rolls of fax paper, this method would provide a clean, nonmessy solution that would simultaneously eliminate the need for participants to target the impregnated mat. As such, this method could provide the advantages of each method described above, without any of the disadvantages. This cream method is however relatively new, and real-world testing is required before its widespread adoption in practice.

The above-mentioned methods would be used where the collection of exemplar dynamic prints is required in casework. Where static prints have been found at the crime scene, these prints need to be compared with exemplar static prints, and the collection process for this form of bare footprint differs from dynamic print collection.

Reel (2012) noted that static print collection protocols have been poorly described in the literature. Thus, Reel (2012) described a detailed protocol that was used in her PhD study of bare footprints to ensure consistency. The recommended approach for the collection of exemplar static bare footprints is as follows:

- The subject stands with his or her hands on hips and places the feet on either side of an inkless pad.
- The subject is asked to raise the right foot, and place it onto the pad.
- While the subject's foot is situated on the pad, the examiner securely tapes a sheet of inkless paper in the position just vacated by that foot.
- The subject returns the foot to its original position, where a print is formed on the inkless paper that has been placed in situ.
- The foot is again raised in an upward direction, allowing the examiner to remove and store the inkless paper.

In addition to the recommendations of Reel (2012), it is also advantageous to place a firm support in the vicinity of the subject that he or she can hold onto for security purposes when standing on one leg while the inkless paper is being removed after collection.

Although Reel (2012) recommended that three prints be collected, this number was for research purposes. In casework, a minimum of six prints for each foot should be collected. Although there is the slight risk of subject fatigue, the collection of larger numbers of prints is helpful when dealing with a subject who may be uncooperative and thus have potential for greater variation in footprint form.

The American Society of Forensic Podiatry (ASFP) presents another method that has been in use for some time in the United States, following protocols established. This technique uses an inkless paper method similar to that described above – in this case, the Identicator® Inkless Shoeprint System LE-25. This system is composed of a yellow chemically treated pad and a supply of white paper sheets. A chemical reaction is created on the white sheet after contact of the bottom of the foot with the yellow chemical pad, leading to the production of a black footprint. This technique also uses a tracing of the foot (foot outline).

The reasoning behind this technique is the black footprint produced is an indication of the internal osseous foot structure against the immediate soft tissue contact area to the receiving surface (weight-bearing surface), but not a true morphological picture of the foot.

This black footprint is often used as a basic "picture" to define a foot as flat, neutral, or high arch, depending on the contact area or is measured and termed "foot length." This approach, however, overlooks the soft tissue component not related to the osseous structure as such. Hence, the recommendation is to include a footprint outline (tracing) when possible to give a truer morphological profile, e.g., narrow, broad, medial bulge indicating a hypermobile flat foot.

Looking at the bare footprint does not always coincide to what is seen in the fleshed foot. The soft tissue not evident in the "osseous" footprint can be estimated to give the length of the foot that actually fits in a shoe. These distinctions are important, and many subscribe to the foot outline when at all possible.

"Two-Step" Method for Barefoot Impressions with Foot Outline:

1. Have the subject march in place for 3 seconds and then stop with feet side by side.
2. Place the chemical pad (yellow pad) in front of the right foot and take one step forward at a normal step length (one might consider a test step length first without the pad to gauge the proper distance as it will vary between subjects) with right on to the treated pad and stop. Do not apply any pressure to the foot; step placement should be satisfactory.
3. Step forward with the left foot to be side by side with the right foot.
4. Place the treated paper in front of the right foot at the appropriate step length distance; repeat steps 2 and 3.
5. Using a thin lead or ink pen, outline (trace) the foot. Importantly, the device must be held perpendicular to the ground surface.

The thickening of the marking instrument may add 5–6 mm to total length.
6. Have the subject step off. Inspect and redo if necessary.
7. Repeat with the left foot.
8. At least three samples from each foot should be taken.

Note: If questioned footprints were socked, then all exemplars should be made in socked feet.

4.3 Variations in Exemplar Footprint Collection Phase

Although the inkless paper method is a common method used to collect exemplar bare footprints, it is sometimes advisable to collect bare footprints that reflect the conditions at the scene of crime. For example, the examiner may want to replicate the type of surface on which the questioned bare footprints have been found. The examiner would plan the approach according to the surface to be replicated e.g., carpet, wooden boarding, or concrete slabs. If carpet is involved, the plantar surfaces of the subject's feet could be liberally covered with ink before he or she walks across a roll of appropriate carpet. From the sequence of prints left, the examiner would select the highest quality prints for examination, bearing in mind observations made with regard to attempts to alter the footprint form. Where slabs or wooden surfaces are being considered, the examiner would place a sample of the surface type at the point at which the footprint is to be collected and would collect and examine inked prints as described above.

Having collected exemplar bare footprints for comparison with the questioned bare footprints, the examination and comparison process would continue using the analysis, comparison, and evaluation of the evidence with independent peer verification (reporting) [ACE-V(R)] approach described in Chapter 2.

4.4 Assessment of the Bare Footprint

The initial task is to assess each footprint selected for comparison, and the usual approach is to examine the questioned prints before the exemplar prints are examined. In this assessment, each footprint is evaluated in isolation using an appropriate combination of objective measurement and descriptive tools, where possible. For the assessment, objective dimensions of the print are stated, outline morphology is traced, and any features apparent within the footprint are factually described. Such features could relate to the positioning of toes, or missing aspects of the footprint (e.g., an absence of toe impressions, the presence of only partial heel or ball impressions). Footprints may also show friction ridge detail or blemishes may be apparent within the print, the presence of which of which should be recorded along with the area within the print that such detail was observed. The podiatrist would normally forward such information to an appropriate expert, because expertise in the examination of such features falls outside the specialized knowledge of podiatrists.

The forensic podiatrist's examination would not follow the same approach as marks examiners who would focus on outline physical shape matches/mismatches as opposed to podiatric understanding of the human foot. Regardless, it is necessary to recognize the need to consider bare footprint morphology before using podiatric understanding in the footprint analysis and comparison process. Although the podiatrist's weighted conclusions are not founded on issues of outline shape, such features would be used as a gateway to proceeding with a podiatric analysis of the footprints. Thus, although the podiatrist focuses on podiatric features, it would be a mistake to blindly proceed with podiatric comparison in the presence of obvious preclusive, repeatable shape differences between compared footprints.

A complete bare footprint consists of five toe prints (sometimes with stem prints), a ball of foot impression, web ridge line (anterior portion of the ball of foot area) heel impression, lateral midfoot impression, and an arch profile (Figure 4.2). It is the size, orientation, and shape of these features that provide information that can help in the identification process. The information

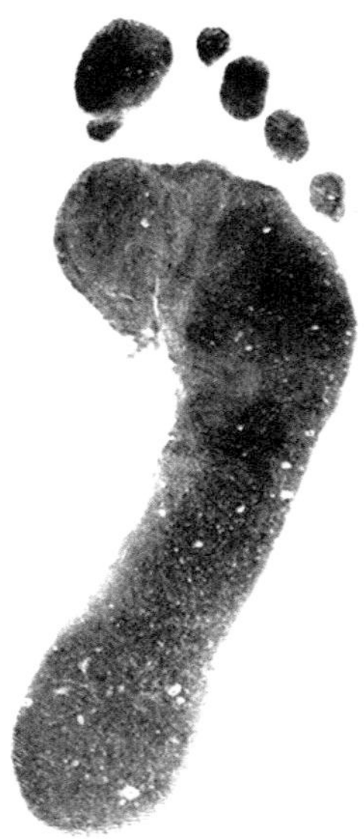

Figure 4.2 Bare footprint.

expressed by these features in an unknown footprint can be compared with that of exemplar footprints collected from someone suspected of leaving an unknown bare footprint at a crime scene. Without the possibility of exemplar footprints being available for this comparison, the questioned footprint is little use in identification. The questioned bare footprint may however have some value in providing an indication of the approximate shoe size of the person responsible for the print.[2] In addition, Reel (2012) and Reel et al. (2012) suggested a means of estimating height from static and dynamic bare footprints. In static prints, Reel's work determined that the heel- to fourth-toe measurements represented the highest stature correlations in static prints and that the heel- to fifth-toe measurements represented the highest stature correlations in dynamic prints. This approach differed from previous work that usually investigated relationships between overall foot length and stature (Anderson et al. 1956; Barker and Scheuer 1998; Giles and Vallandigham, 1991; Kanchan et al. 2012; Krishan and Sharma 2007; Nataraja Moorthy 2011; Oberoi et al. 2006; Robbins 1985). Although based on a relatively small sample, Reel's work estimated that when using her defined measurements, the standard error estimate for height estimation from bare footprints was 4.16 cm. This is the closest correlation to date between footprint dimensions and height, and Reel's work suggested that the anatomical structure of the lateral border of the foot contributes to the more stable height indication than simple comparison of height with the longest foot measurement.

Although it is possible to collect clear and accurate bare footprints from the suspected person for comparison purposes, the presence of a near-perfect questioned footprint is unusual. Footprints can be compromised in a variety of ways, some of which are considered below, that compromise their usefulness in the identification process.

First, the bare footprint can be partial (incomplete). This problem can take many forms, including absent or partial heel prints, missing toe prints, and a general incompleteness across the medial dimension, where the person may have placed his or her foot into ground contact while exhibiting an excessive amount of inversion (Figure 4.3).

Second, the footprint may be complete, but smeared through the act of slippage or through a turning movement that occurred at the time of leaving the footprint. Thus, areas of the footprint can be rendered unclear through smearing or smudging of the features; through an apparent lengthening of the footprint, where the slippage has been linear; or both. Slippage involving both a linear and a turning motion concurrently can lead to the footprint suggesting the presence of a different toe formula than would have been

[2] This would however not be possible with any degree of accuracy, and at the time of writing, this should be approached cautiously, with careful reference to the various differing findings in the literature around foot length versus height estimations.

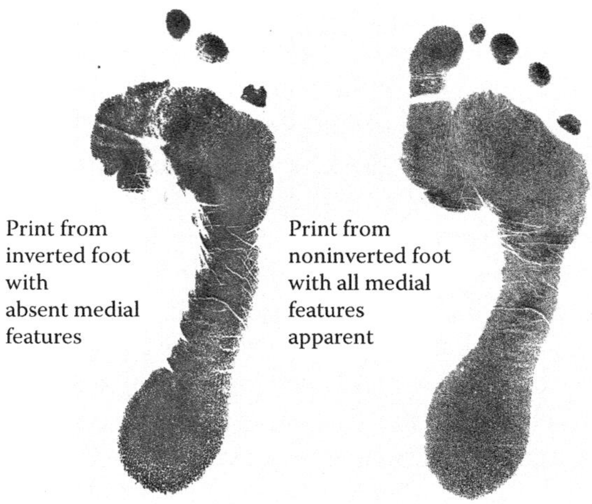

Figure 4.3 Effect of inversion on the barefoot print.

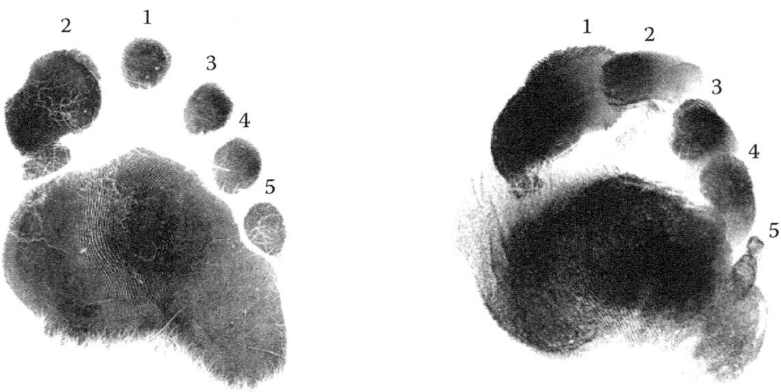

Figure 4.4 Potential effect of slippage on toe formulae. Both bare footprints are from the same person, but because of slippage the footprint on the right appears to have a 1st toe of slightly greater length than the 2nd toe.

created by the foot under more ideal conditions (Figure 4.4). Slippage can be typically seen in footprints made in blood, where the nature of the substrate predisposes the foot to such movement.

Bare footprints can also be compromised where they have been partially obliterated by additional footprints over the footprint being examined, thereby obscuring or even obliterating the features of interest. Such additional footprints can come from the one person, either where there has been a high level of personal activity at the scene, or where the foot has been lifted and placed twice in the same area as part of a single attempted movement.

They can also be left by third parties such as the victim, where there may have been frantic activity during acts of violence; someone who assisted with the crime; or an unconnected third party (e.g., someone who discovered the crime scene after the event). Footprints may also be compromised by the shoeprints of those officially visiting the scene of crime after the event, such as ambulance drivers, scenes of crime officers, or police personnel who may have been unaware of the possible presence of such evidence and its evidential value.

Where a high-quality bare footprint has been left at a crime scene, footprint evidence can be extremely valuable. The value, however, will decrease where the footprint has been compromised as in the circumstances described above. Investigators should be aware of this fact and be prepared to deal with uncertainties associated with such data loss through adjusting levels of certainty expressed in their report-based conclusions about the strength of such evidence.

Various approaches have been devised to allow footprints to be objectively "measured" and compared for identification purposes. The most commonly used approaches are the Gunn method, the optical center method, the Reel method, and the overlay method/DiMaggio modified overlay method.

4.4.1 Gunn Method

Dr. Norman Gunn began forensic podiatry work in Canada in the early 1970s. In his casework, Gunn was asked to compare unknown footprints found at a scene of crime with footprints of suspected perpetrators of that crime, and he needed to develop an objective process to assist with that comparison. He produced a system in which various linear measurements were taken from each of the footprints involved and used these measurements to describe and compare these prints (Vernon 2006a). This approach helped to form a conclusion as to whether there was a match or mismatch between the footprints being compared. The technique commences with the drawing of six lines. Five of these lines are drawn from the rearmost aspect of the heel of the footprint to the tips of each of the five toes. A sixth line is then drawn across the widest part of the ball of foot area. These six lines represent the most basic form of the Gunn method (Figure 4.5). The lines are then carefully measured, and the measurements are used to compare the footprints being examined. Additional lines can be introduced into this approach if necessary, e.g., to deal with a partial footprint (Figure 4.6) or to strengthen the evidence provided. When adding additional lines, any of the points used to draw the basic six lines of this approach can be used as reference points for adding further lines (Figure 4.7). This technique is simple to use in practice and is likely to be one of the primary methods selected by the examining podiatrist in the footprint comparison process.

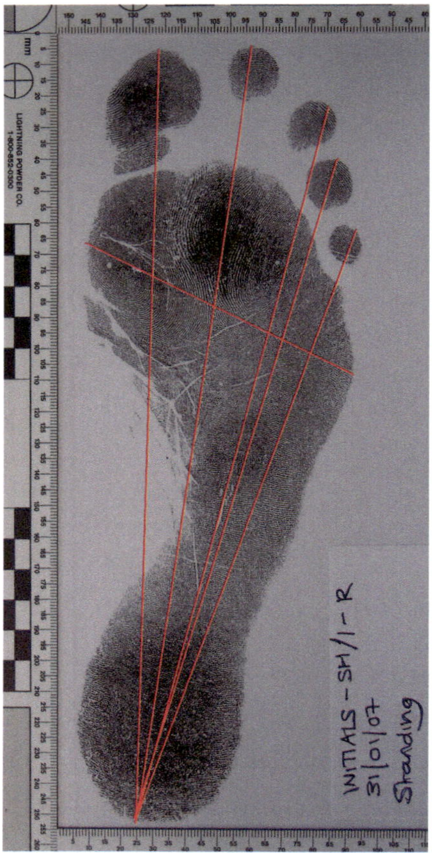

Figure 4.5 Gunn method.

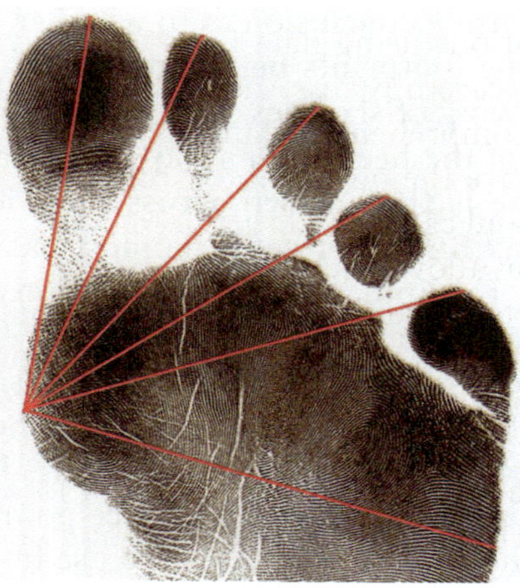

Figure 4.6 Gunn method utilized for partial print analysis.

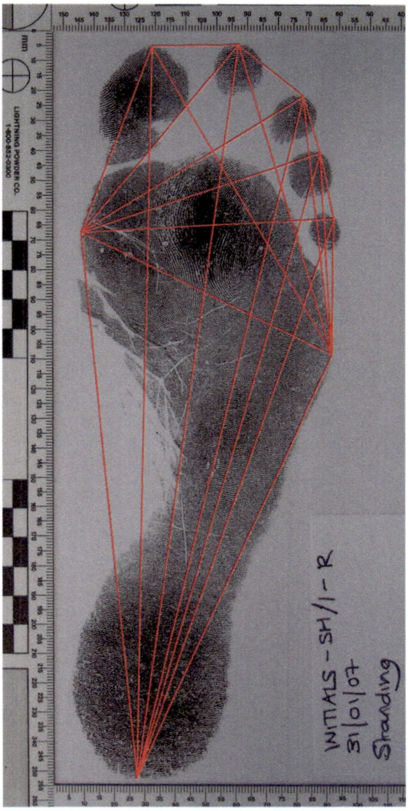

Figure 4.7 Extended Gunn method.

4.4.2 Optical Center Method

The optical center method was used in the 1990s by the Royal Canadian Mounted Police as part of a long-term study intended to strengthen the value of the human footprint in identification (Kennedy 1996, 2005; Kennedy et al. 2003, 2005, Kennedy and Yamashita 2007). It is a development of the Gunn method and shares similarities with Gunn's approach in that it is based on the measurement and comparison of lines drawn between various morphological landmarks of the footprint. It differs from the Gunn method in the source and destination points from which many of these lines are drawn. Instead of using peripheral reference points on which to base the connecting lines, optical centers are used. An optical center is the dead center of a morphological feature as represented by the center of a circle when placed into a position of "best fit" within that particular feature (Figure 4.8). This optical center can be calculated by software used for design purposes (e.g., AutoCAD®2010 software), or by a manual approach in which the investigator places a series of

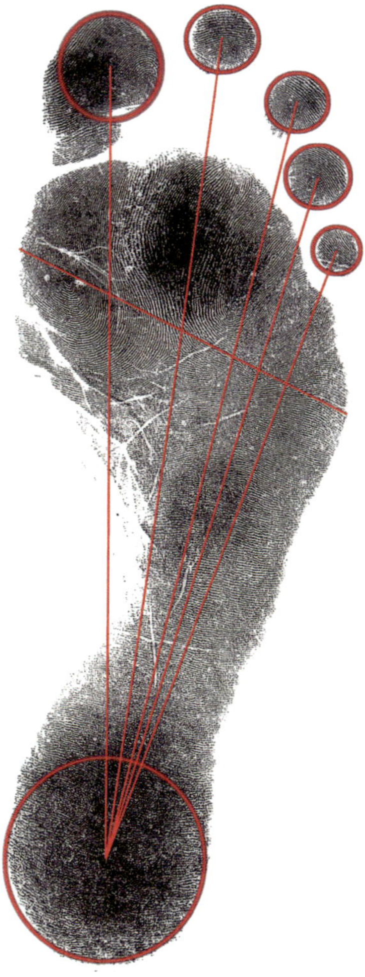

Figure 4.8 Optical center method.

concentric circles over the feature being examined into the best-fit position and marks the center of the concentric circles. The mark thus created would be used as one of the reference points for a measurement taken using this approach (Figure 4.8). As in the Gunn method, six basic measurements are taken. Five separate lines are drawn from the optical center of the heel to the optical center of each toe, and a line is also drawn directly across the widest part of the ball of foot area. Because the optical center cannot be used to determine medial and lateral positions of the ball of the foot, no attempt is made to calculate optical centers for this measurement. Although simple to use in practice, this approach may be more useful when the examiner has access to the relevant software because personal experience has suggested that human error when this approach is used manually can create a higher level of ambiguity than that afforded by the Gunn approach.

4.4.3 Reel Method

One of the key outcomes of the PhD work of Reel (2012), as reflected in the title of that project, was the development and validation of a new and reliable method of footprint measurement for use in forensic identification. Reel (2012) critically evaluated the literature relating to the previously available measurement approaches by using the knowledge gained from this evaluation to create a new pragmatic method for collecting and measuring two-dimensional bare foot impressions for use in forensic analysis and comparison.

Both the Gunn and Reel methods are based around an initial series of measurements taken from the very rearmost aspect of the heel. It is important that when used for comparison purposes, this measurement is taken from the same position every time because even very small variations in the selected measurement point can lead to apparent differences in measurement (Kennedy et al. 2003). It is therefore important that an objective means of locating the rearmost aspect of the heel is adopted. In the Reel method, this objectivity is inherent within the approach described and is based on the measurement technique advocated in the Rossi system of podometrics (Rossi 1992). Rossi developed a series of measurements for the clinical description and categorization of the human footprint. Although this system was not developed by Rossi for forensic identification purposes, two of the initial measurements he advocated connect the outermost lateral aspect of the heel print with the lateral aspect of the ball of foot area, and the innermost medial aspect of the heel with the medial aspect of the ball of foot area (Figure 4.9). In considering most footprints, these lines would be expected to intersect at a point posterior to the heel. This intersection then forms a reference point from which the rearmost aspect of the heel could be objectively selected for measurements taken for identification purposes.

A second alternative approach to defining the rearmost aspect of the heel would be to place a grid line over the footprint image. The grid would be aligned over the image in such a way that the most lateral aspects of the forefoot and the heel are perfectly aligned with one of the vertical grid lines. At this point, the rearmost aspect of the heel can be determined from its proximity to the first horizontal grid line distal to the heel (Figure 4.10). This second approach was not advocated by Reel, although is known to have been used in practice for many years. Further evaluation is therefore indicated to determine the reliability and validity of such an approach in identifying the rearmost aspect of the heel.

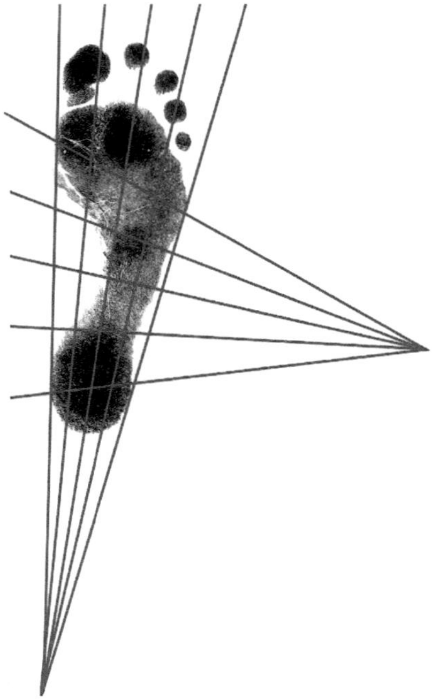

Figure 4.9 Rossi's system of podometrics.

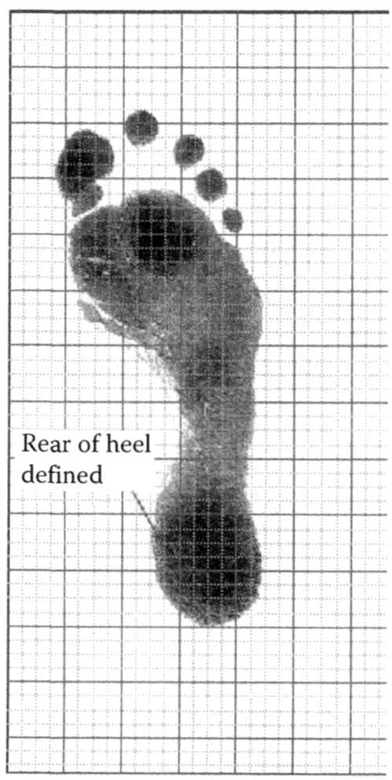

Figure 4.10 Defining the rearmost aspect of the heel.

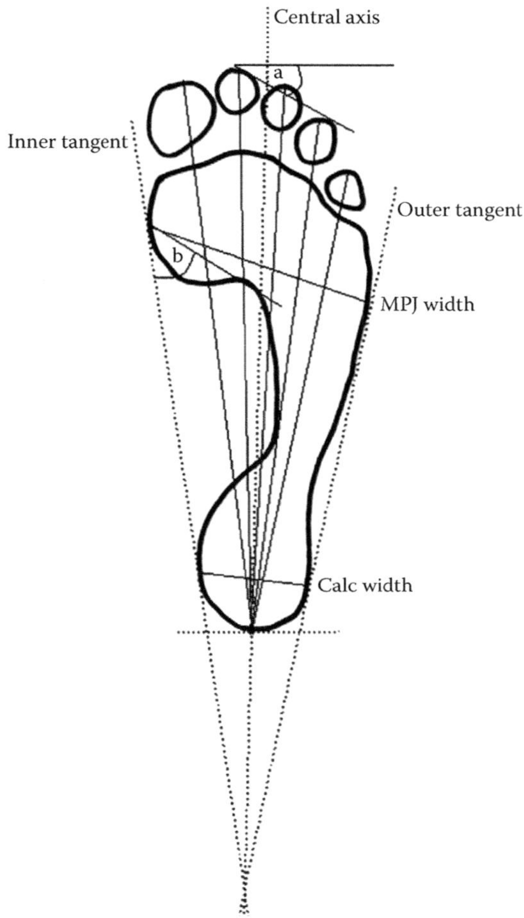

Figure 4.11 Reel method.

The approach involved in the Reel method is described in detail by Reel (2010) and is as follows (Figure 4.11):

- The inner and outer tangents of the footprint are identified and bisected to create a "central axis."
- A grid is placed over the image, which is then rotated until the central axis is in parallel alignment with the grid.[3]
- A horizontal line (heel line) is drawn to traverse the most proximal pixel of the heel as shown by this new alignment.

[3] Reel (2012) advocated using the GIMP software program for this task. It is also possible to use alternative digital image management software (e.g., Adobe Photoshop) or a manual approach using a hard copy transparent grid.

- Where the central axis and the heel line intersect, five lines are drawn to the apices of each toe.
- The widest parts of the heel and the ball of the footprint, as shown by the inner and outer tangents are drawn.
- The toe angle of declination is measured.
- If desired, the footprint angle is measured.

Similar to the Gunn method with the additional steps taken to define the rearmost aspect of the heel and, if required, toe and footprint angles, the Reel method is simple to use and pragmatic in its approach to bare footprint analysis.

4.4.4 Overlay/DiMaggio Modified Overlay Method

The overlay method was originally developed as a tool for comparisons of plantar impressions of footprints. In the United Kingdom, Dr. Owen Facey was a primary proponent of this method, and it was also being used in the United States by the Federal Bureau of Investigation and other agencies, and in Canada by the Royal Canadian Mounted Police (O. Facey, pers. comm., 2005). This method was modified by DiMaggio (2005), when descriptive terms were added to the various morphological features apparent on the bare footprint (Figure 4.12). Linear measurements are not used in this approach; the

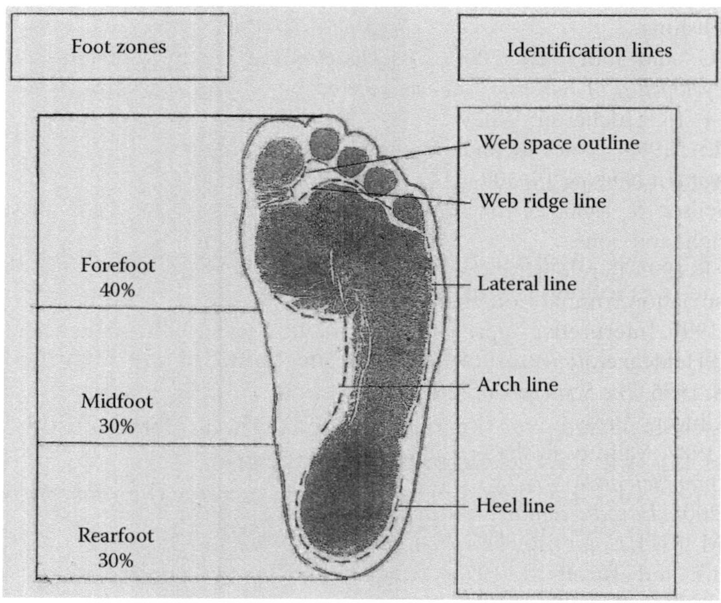

Figure 4.12 DiMaggio morphological identification lines and foot zones.

technique instead relies on tracing (by various methods) of the outline of a known footprint onto a clear background and placing this tracing on top of an unknown footprint being examined, thereby allowing comparison of various features these two footprints to determine compatibility (Figure 4.13). Such features include the position, shape, and outline detail of toes; the anterior ball of foot (web ridge line); arch area; lateral foot contour; and the heel area. The web space outline is used for images usually present when evaluating the sock liner of the shoe. The foot zones allow for proportional analyses, especially when partial bare footprints are examined. Soft tissue deformities, scarring, and creasing of the plantar print can also be compared using this method. In practice, the overlay method is simple to perform and the accuracy of the technique has improved with the development of digital cameras that allow for tighter depictions of the footprint outline to be collected than that afforded by traditional manual tracings. Some digital imaging software allows the superimposition of two or more images, and these images can be used for an overlay comparison in addition to the manual approach.

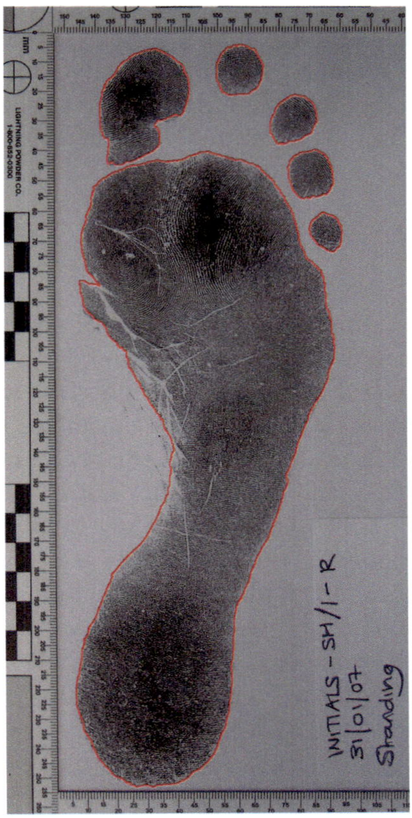

Figure 4.13 Overlay method.

4.4.5 Method Selection in Practice

As part of her PhD work, Reel (2012) assessed the concurrent validity and reliability of the three linear measurement approaches (Gunn, optical center, and Reel methods). Thirty randomly selected bare footprints were used in Reel's assessment: 14 were static, 14 were dynamic, and 2 were randomly selected. Correlations between one measurement (heel to first toe) from each technique were assessed for similarity. In this assessment, for each method and using each of the 30 footprints, the same assessor constructed and recorded all measurements twice on separate occasions in a repeated-measures analysis.

Using this approach, the highest reliability estimates occurred with the Reel method, closely followed by the Gunn method. The lowest estimate occurred with the optical center method. This work suggests that either the Reel or Gunn method should be the approach of choice when selecting a linear measurement approach for casework application. Whichever approach is used, it is essential that it is used consistently throughout the case to ensure standardization.

In practice, the forensic podiatrist would be advised to use at least two of the measurement systems mentioned above: one involving linear measurements in conjunction with the overlay method. This approach would allow the collection of both quantitative and descriptive comparison data and the collection of additional points for comparison to strengthen the value of the evidence. It would also provide some form of triangulation to support any conclusions reached.

4.4.6 Ghosting

In Section 4.2, the commonly seen presence of ghosting accompanied by inner dark areas observed in dynamic as opposed to static prints was noted. Vernon (2015) has studied what causes the ghosting and inner dark effects on the grounds that for these features to be considered in forensic analysis, it is important to understand what they are, what causes them, how erroneous results can be controlled, and the limitations of any technical methods (of analysis) (UKFSR 2016). By understanding how these features are formed, it is possible to consider the limitations of their use in identification and to be confident of their replicability under defined conditions (such as during normal gait). Improved understanding of the causes of these features could also lead to their further development in the forensic analysis of bare footprints.

Vernon's (2015) project itself was an observational, practice-based action research approach taking place within a gait laboratory. All participants who were male provided bare footprints through the use of an inkless paper print collection kit. For the print collection, the inkless paper was taped to a Kistler force plate with high-resolution cameras situated on either side to capture detail of foot movement as the prints were being formed. Ground reaction force (GRF) data were collected via the force plate and the print form. Video recordings and GRF data were later compared to determine what correlations, if any, were apparent.

Comparison of the bare footprints, GRF data, and digital image recordings recorded data comparisons taken as part of this project showed that in all cases examined the inner dark area of the heel corresponded with the initial heel strike, the main body of the heel, large GRF peak, and the longer contact time of this area of the heel during stance. The outer ghosting features corresponded with a backward splaying of the fat pad as heel loading was taking place with minimal ground contact time. In all cases, the backward splaying of the fat pad of the heel occurred when the anticipated small transient peak in GRF was seen during heel loading (Figure 4.14a–d).

It was noted that those project participants who contacted the ground in a more "flat-footed" manner tended to exhibit a smaller transient spike during heel loading as seen in the GRF graphs and less ghosting.

For the toe area of the bare footprints, the inner dark area corresponded with the body of the toes, which was in longer ground contact time with the ground surface, and with the second GRF peak, which occurs at heel lift. The outer ghosting feature corresponded with a rapid reduction in the GRF and with the shorter contact time of the anterior aspect of the toes as the toes

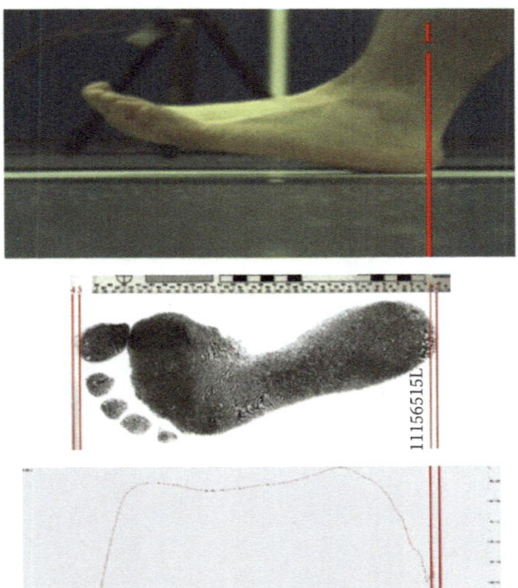

(a)

Figure 4.14 Correlation between visual recordings, ground reaction force vs. time graphs, and the toe ghosting/inner dark areas of prints. (a) Heel strike. *(Continued)*

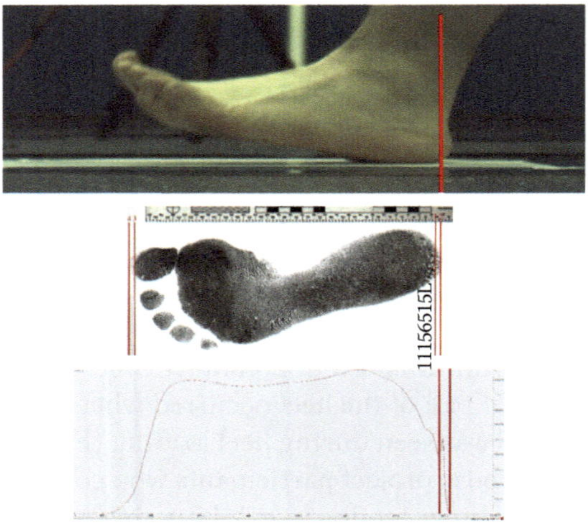

(b)

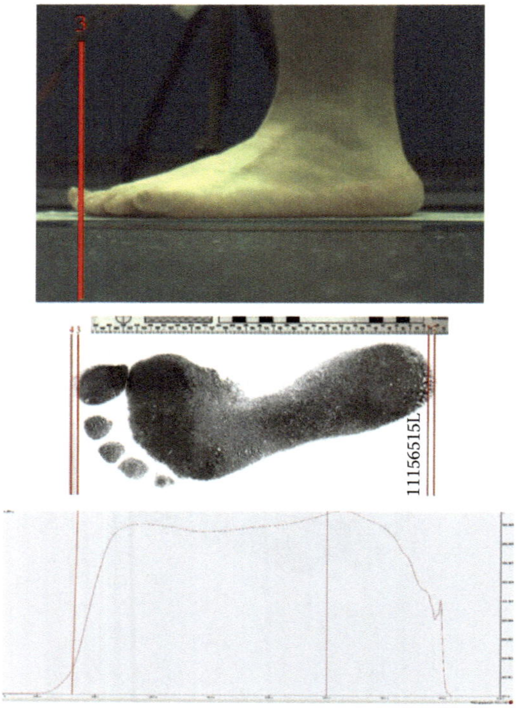

(c)

Figure 4.14 (Continued) Correlation between visual recordings, ground reaction force vs. time graphs, and the toe ghosting/inner dark areas of prints. (b) splaying of heel pad; (c) toes, prior to toe-off. *(Continued)*

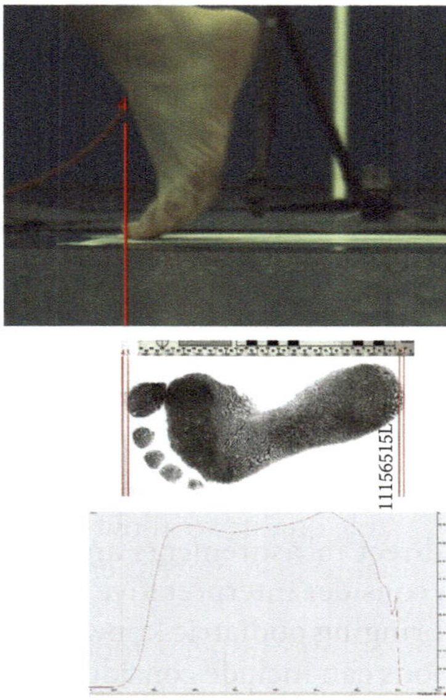

(d)

Figure 4.14 (Continued) Correlation between visual recordings, ground reaction force vs. time graphs, and the toe ghosting/inner dark areas of prints. (d) toes, prior to toe-off.

commenced leaving the ground at the start of the swing phase as the stance period reached its conclusion (Figure 4.14) (Vernon 2015).

This project provided new insight into the causes of ghosting and the inner dark features seen in the heel and toe areas of dynamic bare footprints—with the inner dark areas seeming to represent the true stance period—those aspects of the plantar surface that have been in ground contact for the longest times and the outer ghosted areas representing transient contacts at the most posterior aspect of the of the heel and most anterior aspects of the toes that have come into ground contact during stance.

Although these are new and useful appreciations, the project did have some limitations that mainly centered around the small, limited sample studied in this project that focused exclusively on the bare footprints of seven male-only participant volunteers. Future work to repeat these methods using larger sample sizes and with other population groups (e.g., females, other cultural groups) is now recommended to further improve understanding of the ghosting and inner dark features seen in dynamic bare footprints.

Because there are continuing demands for improved governance in forensic practice (NAS 2009; UKFSR 2016), evidence to show that the ghosting and inner dark features of bare footprints are not randomly created artifacts and what they represent in terms of their functional creation should help to support the use of these features in forensic identification.

These new appreciations also suggest that the outer demarcation points of the inner dark features of bare footprints could be measured and evaluated for forensic identification purposes as well as the outer ghosting features. The validity and reliability of different approaches to the measurement of ghosting has previously been studied, and similar studies of the measurement of the inner dark areas are now indicated. The additional points for comparison offered by the inner dark areas can potentially enhance footprint individuality and the value of this form of evidence in human identification.

4.4.7 Assessment of Bare Footprints: Interpretative Aspects

In addition to the use of direct measurements and descriptions, the podiatric examiner would also consider interpretative aspects of each bare footprint being examined via bringing podiatric knowledge and understanding into play. Such interpretations can include consideration of the implied foot size and the toe and metatarsal formula as represented within the bare footprint. A barefoot print on a hard surface would represent only those aspects of the foot that have contacted the ground. The extreme aspects of toes, heel, and cross-ball width that would represent the true length and width of the foot would not have contributed to formation of the bare footprint unless that barefoot print was formed in a soft substrate that had allowed the foot to sink deeper into the surface. A footprint on a firm surface would therefore seem shorter than and not as wide as the actual foot responsible for that bare footprint (Figure 4.15). An approximate rule of thumb has been used to suggest the overall foot length implied by a complete two-dimensional footprint, in which 1.5–2 cm is added to the overall footprint length to suggest an implied overall foot length. Unpublished research has also considered an objective formula from which the length of a foot can be calculated (Grant 2006). Because of the small sample size and the wide confidence intervals involved, this work is not conclusive. It must be stressed that the approximation of the true foot size by adding 1.5–2 cm to the total barefoot print length is an approximation only, and as such it should be dealt with accordingly in the resultant evidence report, if used at all. Ongoing currently unpublished data collection via the University of Northampton in the United Kingdom is showing that although the 1.5–2-cm approximation can often apply, there can also be wider variations in the relationship between bare footprint and foot length, hence the need for particular caution in this respect.[4]

[4] This work is being considered in further depth before publication, which will take place after further data collection.

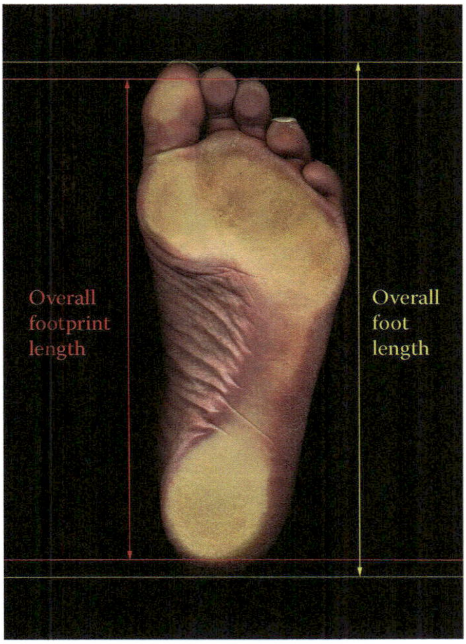

Figure 4.15 Overall foot length vs. overall barefoot print length.

Related to interpretative aspects of the footprint is the recognition of the presence of toe features such as a Greek ideal, where the second toe is situated distally in relation to the first toe position (Figure 4.16). Other features indicated by toe position could include the presence of hallux valgus, mallet toes, hammer toes, and surgically or congenitally shortened toes (Figure 4.17). Within the footprint, missing toe prints may also be apparent. The examiner thus needs to consider whether these findings relate to actual missing toes, whether they relate to contracted/retracted toes that have not contacted with the ground during stance, or whether the foot function itself could have led to an absence of ground contact at the site of the apparently missing toe. Indications of the foot type suggested by the footprint form can also be apparent, and scuffing or smearing patterns related to the print may indicate functional considerations involved in the footprint formation.

In considering the ball of foot area, the presence of pathological or unusual features may be indicated. For example, the presence of an extreme bunion deformity or tailor's bunion may be demonstrated through the ball of foot extending beyond its usual confines compared to the toe positions observed. The presence of higher pressure areas can also be apparent through darker patterns observable within the print (Figure 4.18) that relate to either functional or structural features.

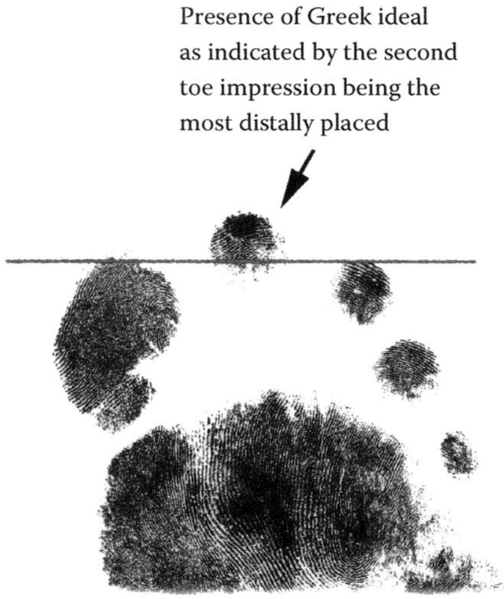

Figure 4.16 Greek ideal.

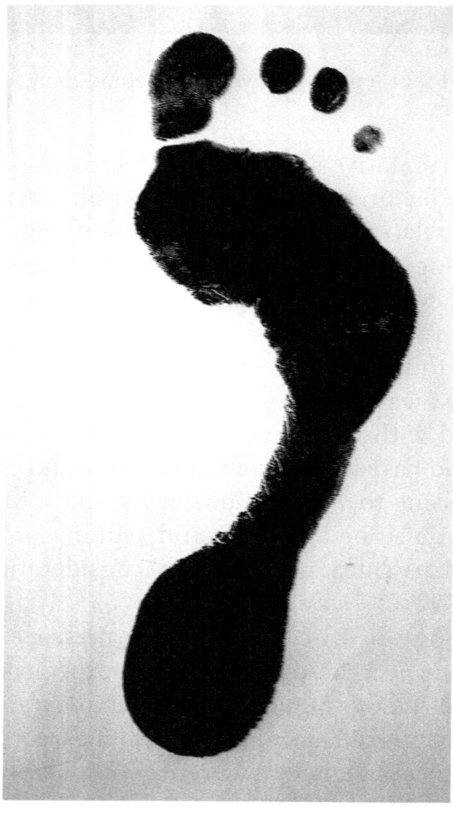

Figure 4.17 Congenitally short fifth toe (no purchase).

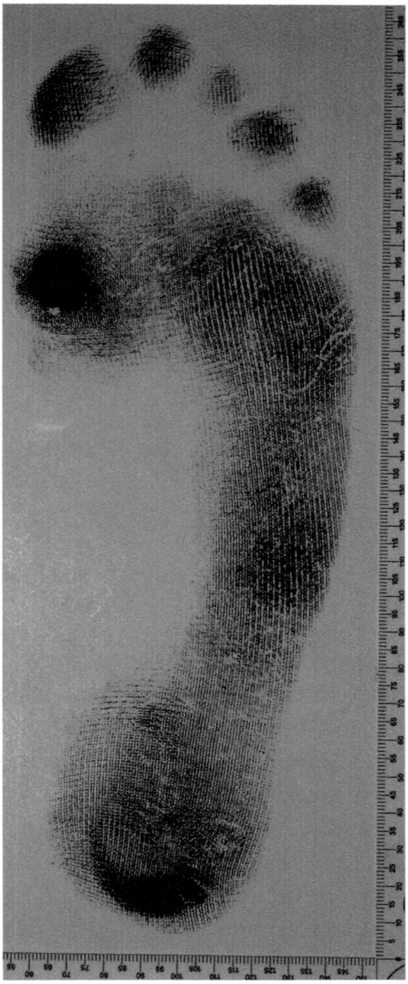

Figure 4.18 Effect of high-pressure areas on the bare footprint, with the darker areas relating to areas of relatively higher pressure in the socked print.

The morphological detail of the arch area of the bare footprint may also indicate the presence of foot pathology. Pesplanus (flat feet); pronatory tendencies; or when viewed in conjunction with toe positions, indications of pescavus (high arch) in the causative foot can become apparent through the shape of the arch area of the examined footprint (Figure 4.19).

Similarly, the foot width-versus-length ratio can be calculated, and these particular footprint dimensions may be used to describe the overall foot shape. It has also been suggested that the foot can be subdivided into three distinct zones and that the ratio of the sizes of each zone can be used in this comparison process (DiMaggio 2005). In addition to the identification

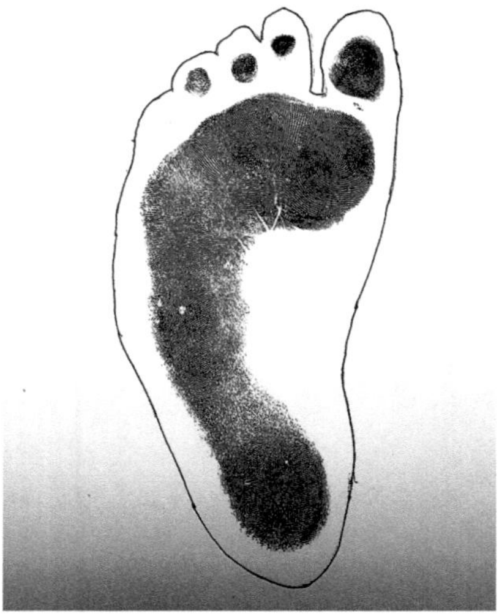

Figure 4.19 Arch shape (narrow) and lateral "C" shape of cavus foot type.

of broad feet, or long narrow feet, pathological aspects may be apparent in relation to hallux valgus or pescavus foot types, where they have affected the foot shape. It would only be advisable to undertake such an assessment if the footprint is clear and complete because attempting to calculate the foot width-versus-length ratio could be misleading in the presence of incomplete measurement data. It has also been suggested by a podiatrist with an interest in podiatric archaeology that foot dimensions can relate to the ancestral origin of the "owner" of the foot (Jackson 2007) and, in turn, could be theoretically interpreted from the footprint. Extreme caution in using such interpretations in forensic podiatry work is recommended until further research is undertaken to validate these observations.

Various blemishes may be noted in the detail apparent within the footprint, and it is possible to interpret these blemishes as sites of scar tissue and of preexisting skin lesions (Figure 4.20). In a bare footprint, the site and nature of such lesions should be carefully recorded alongside the interpretive description. Friction ridge detail may also be apparent within the examined footprint, and the presence of such detail should be noted for the later involvement of an examiner with expertise in the examination and comparison of such detail. Other features that can be apparent from the bare footprint include detailed variations in morphological outlines (Figure 4.21) and the presence of crease lines within the footprint (Massey 2004). The site and nature of such lesions should be recorded and described when present, in case a ridge detail analyst becomes involved in the case.

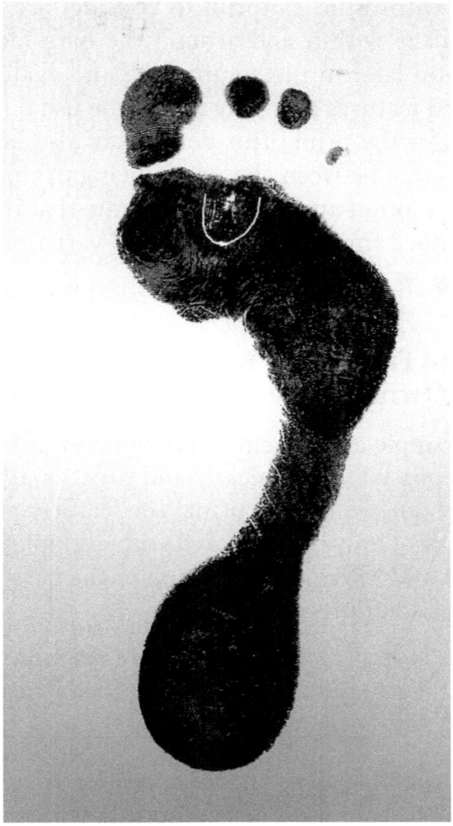

Figure 4.20 Scar tissue.

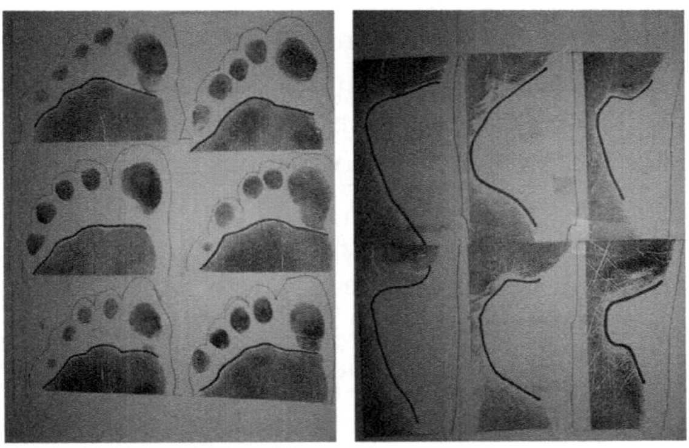

(a) (b)

Figure 4.21 Morphological variations of (a) web ridge line and (b) arch line.

Other features within the footprint to consider are signs of smudging, smearing, and slippage within and around the bare footprint. This information may be useful later in the comparison and evaluation stages, when considering repeated features that may reflect the usual foot function of the person responsible for the print. This detail may also be useful when considering any differences between the prints being examined as indications of slippage or other motion and may demonstrate that the form of the footprint has been amended through the functional variation that has led to the smudging, smearing, or slippage.

4.4.8 Clinical and Functional Examination of the Suspected Owner of the Questioned Footprint

In addition to the simple assessment of known and unknown footprints, it is also advisable, if possible, to clinically and functionally examine the suspected owner of the questioned footprint. The features present on the questioned footprint can not only be compared with exemplar footprints but also with the foot status and lower limb function of the person leaving a known footprint for comparison purposes.

4.5 Comparison

After assessing the available footprints as described above, the next task is to compare the unknown bare footprint/footprints with the known exemplar bare footprint/footprints that have been collected from a suspect as well as the foot status and lower limb function of that person.

In practical terms, it can be useful to first use a basic preliminary comparison process to eliminate the more obvious mismatched bare footprints. This comparison would take the form of initial "rough" tracing comparisons of known and unknown prints to eliminate the mismatches as well as the creation of a "shortlist" of apparently matched prints for more accurate evaluation (Figure 4.22). Once this shortlist has been created, more accurate comparisons would be undertaken on the shortlisted prints by using proprietary digital image programs such as Adobe Photoshop.

The comparison process should sequentially work through the comparison of all measurements, shapes, and features that have been recorded and determined using the following approaches and considerations.

Objective measurement comparisons: Any measurements taken using either the Gunn, optical center, or Reel methods are compared directly, with any differences between each measurement also being recorded in tabular form.

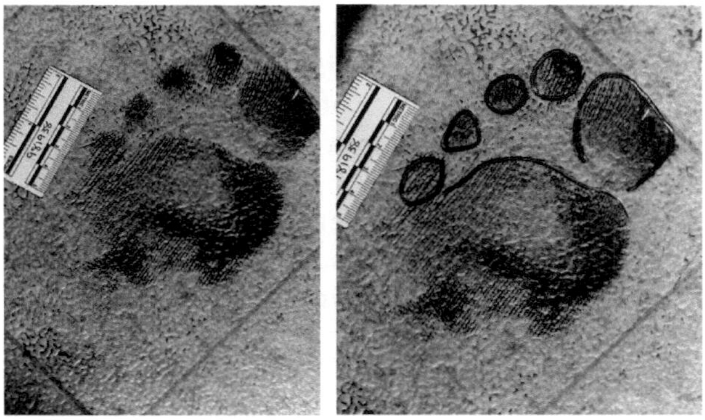

Figure 4.22 Initial tracing of questioned partial bloody footprint.

Morphological comparisons: Similarly, morphological similarities and differences as indicated by the overlay (or DiMaggio modified overlay method using the identification lines) would be compared and recorded feature by feature. This comparison would typically include compatibility position of the toes, heel line, arch line, lateral line, web ridge line, and web space outline (usually reserved for sock liner image comparisons).

Pathological feature comparisons: A podiatrist is a highly specialized health professional/physician trained in the recognition and treatment of the various pathologies of the foot and structural and functional problems that affect the foot. If such conditions are apparent from examination of the bare footprint, they should be recorded in tables relating to both known and unknown footprints with a view to assessing compatibility.

Detailed comparisons: The assessment process may have noted the presence of many additional details such as the presence of skin lesions, the position and shape of crease lines, close morphological details, unusual features, and friction ridge detail. Relevant podiatric information of this type from both known and unknown footprints should be compared item by item, with the presence or absence of such features and their position and shape being recorded for all footprints examined with a view to assessing compatibility. A comparison of friction ridge detail features is beyond the expertise of a podiatrist, and the involvement of a ridge detail analyst should be sought.

Missing feature comparisons: It is possible that some features may be missing from the footprints being examined. Any areas of such missing data from the bare footprints should be compared point by point. Such comparisons have two uses during evaluation. First, they can show that a comparison of a particular area of the footprint could not be carried out because of missing "data." Second, they could potentially indicate the presence of a repeated feature in relation to a repeated foot function or stance position.

Foot ratio comparisons: Where it has been possible to calculate foot ratios, these ratios should be compared side by side for similarity and compatibility. The foot zones, i.e., rearfoot 30%, midfoot 30%, and forefoot 40%, can be helpful in these situations, as proposed by DiMaggio (2005).

Interpretative comparisons: Where forensic podiatrists have been able to interpret various aspects of the bare footprint and make implications in relation to the causative foot from their observations, these observations should be compared between known and unknown footprints feature by feature.

Functional aspect comparisons: Functional aspect comparisons are also interpretative. Any features that have been noted within the bare footprints being examined that have functional significance should also be compared. For example, the presence of a toe or toes that have not come into ground contact could be compared, as should print anomalies indicating, e.g., inversion of the foot, smudging, smearing, and slippage, or lack of heel strike.

4.6 Evaluation

Finally, the examiner needs to evaluate the evidence through careful consideration of the detail that has been subject to examination and comparison. This step is the crux of the process: without an evaluation, a conclusion cannot be reached. The first consideration of the examiner is whether it is possible to reach a conclusion in cases where the evidence is "spoiled," inadequate, or erroneous. This effect can be due to, e.g., problems in photographic perspective, wherein errors have been made in setting the image to evidence-quality standards. Evidence can also be inadequate if the print is partial or very old and therefore not necessarily still relevant in a comparison with the foot status of the suspect, thereby making it impossible to reach a valid conclusion. If this is the case, the examiner should be prepared to state this and at the point that this has become apparent, to not proceed any further with the investigation. It could be however that recommendations can be made as to the potential for other expert involvement, or for remedial action to be taken to correct the situation (e.g., perspective correction in evidence photography, a search for further evidence, photography of the evidence with a strength scale).

Assuming that it is deemed possible to reach a conclusion, the comparison made of class characteristics; gross measurements, interpretations, and observations will need to be evaluated. Those factors that are compatible and those that are incompatible are stated, and a conclusion is made as to whether the compared prints could belong to the same person or whether differences are apparent that could only demonstrate a mismatch. If any incompatible features are found, a conclusion that a mismatch is apparent can be made at this stage, with typical excluding features being a clear discrepancy in the length and shape of the compared footprints and obvious pathological features being present on one footprint and not the other. If the compared footprints are found to be similar in these respects, more detailed consideration can then be given to the overall length of the questioned and known footprints. This evaluation would be an interpretive evaluation in which the implied lengths of the causative feet could be suggested as far as possible, to determine whether they are similar. In turn, the suggested sizes could be related to population data specifically to suggest the proportion of the population (often the male population) known to have a foot size within the implied range. An example of such available information in the United Kingdom is the population foot size table published by the Shoe and Allied Trade Research Association (Peet 1999). In the United States, similar tables regarding foot (shoe) sizes are available through the National Shoe Retailers Association and other sources.

Where common pathologies or other features have been noted between known and unknown bare footprints, published data on the prevalence of that feature in the general population can be considered to show how unusual such features are in this population. Where published information is not available, other data sources that can be considered include personal database information (i.e., a collection of footprints held by the examiner). Personal experience could also be referred to in formulating an opinion as to the significance of matched/mismatched features, with any accompanying limitations being stated. Such opinions can be supplemented, supported, triangulated, by the collection of additional bare footprint/foot survey data specifically for the purposes of demonstrating evidential weight in the subsequent report. Where subjective opinion has informed these considerations, it is essential that this is made clear in the report. Similarly, where any survey data or combinations of survey and other prevalence data have been presented, it is important to clarify that these data have been included to show the logic of the expert decision making as opposed to these data being presented as scientific calculations.

At the time of writing, work is being undertaken in two separate organizations—ASFP and Staffordshire University in the United Kingdom to prepare databases or libraries of bare footprints. The intention in both cases is for such bare footprint data to be made available as reference sources to all forensic podiatry professionals to assist with their casework needs. Known data on functional conditions that may be present in bare footprints can be used in the same way, where they are apparent from the footprints examined.

In considering the prevalence of any features apparent within the examined bare footprints, it is essential that prevalence within the specific population being considered informs the expert's opinion. For example, if the subject of the investigation is a white male, then it could be misleading to use prevalence data for the general, female, or other racial group populations where prevalence of the features being considered may differ.

The next consideration as part of the evaluation process is whether toe positions between the known and unknown samples are broadly compatible, or whether they are too dissimilar for the compared prints to have been made by the same person. The examiner needs to give careful attention to the possible confounding effects of function, bringing known functional understanding into play in this particular interpretation. Factors relating to the questioned footprint position and sequence may need to be considered. Of particular interest would be whether the position or sequence of the footprint suggests that the footprint has been produced in standing, walking, running, turning, or jumping situations, or in circumstances in which a person had made the print while manipulating a burden. If so, the examiner should consider to what extent the suggested variable could have amended the toe positioning and whether any differences observed could still be within the range that could have been produced by the same person. If a footprint has been found, e.g., on a landing at the top of a flight of stairs, positioned at 90° to the flight of the stairs, it is probable that the individual responsible for that print was in the process of turning at the time that the print was formed. A footprint at the base of a high wall, facing away from that wall and adjacent to the opposing footprint, could very well have been produced by someone landing after jumping from the wall, again with the potential for the form of the footprint to have been amended. Conversely, a complete footprint situated midway within a sequence of footprints present along a short corridor is unlikely to have been formed by anything other than a basic walking function, unless there are indications that the person had been dragging or carrying an object at the same time.

Taking all these factors into account, it should be possible for the examiner to determine whether any differences observed between known and unknown footprints examined could be justified, or whether a true incompatibility between the person responsible for each footprint is implied.

The next consideration relates to how objective linear measurements recorded by the Gunn, optical center or Reel methods compare. Kennedy and Yamashita (2007) used an error margin of ±5 mm in comparisons of bare footprints within their research database, and this error margin should be considered for each measurement compared. The more compared measurements there are that fall within these limits, the greater the likelihood that the same person has formed the prints. Where measurements have fallen outside this range, the footprints should be examined closely for signs of the prints being incomplete, having been amended by function, sources of error, or whether this seems to be a true difference. Where true differences are found, consideration should be given as to whether these differences are great enough in terms of the size and number of differences present to preclude the possibility of these prints having being made by the same person.

The next stage of the evaluation is to consider fine morphological detail comparisons. The detail recorded and compared in relation to outline shape and highly individual features (e.g., presence of scarring, crease lines, skin lesions) would be considered. The examiner would consider whether the features observed have been apparent in both compared prints and whether the absence of such features in one print or the other would preclude the possibility of a match, or whether this difference could be justified through, e.g., print incompleteness or smudging. Where dermatoglyphic detail comparison is required, it should be referred on to a friction ridge detail analyst for further examination.

Similarly, it is almost inevitable that some aspects of the questioned footprint will be missing; unclear; or show signs of slippage, torsion, or other movement. During the evaluation, the examiner should consider such areas and what they imply in relation to the footprint, particularly whether such implied movements could have amended the footprint form, or whether differences observed could only have been caused by the footprints being created by different persons. Slippage, repeated feature absence, or evidence of torsion during movement is apparent within the questioned footprint may imply that the person responsible for producing the questioned footprint has a particular repeatable foot/lower limb function. Where this function is apparent, the implications in terms of individualization should be noted in the evaluation, again referring to known research, surveys, population databases, or experience for considerations of prevalence. Any observations of this type have the potential to be triangulated through the results of a full clinical and functional analysis of the suspect.

Finally, the conclusion derived through the evaluation should be stated in terms of how strong the evidence is that is being presented. The level of support offered for the proposition that the questioned and known bare footprints have been made by the same person and also that the prints have been made by different people would be derived. Each and every feature that has been compared and evaluated would be considered with regard to current understanding. In dealing with footprints, central to this is the understanding gained from the work of Kennedy and colleagues (Kennedy 1996, 2005; Kennedy et al. 2003, 2005; Kennedy and Yamashita 2007) in that every one of the footprints in their database of 24,000 prints has been proved to be different. Kennedy's database however consists of footprints that had been collected under standardized conditions, and it is inevitable that this given state will not apply to questioned footprints found in real-world situations. Similarly, the work did not go on to consider whether any observed similarities between different bare footprints could represent interpopulation differences as opposed to individual differences. If any differences between bare footprints simply reflect characteristics of the population type (e.g., Chinese population, Indian population, Caucasian population), then these features would be much more commonly encountered than they would be if they reflected individual characteristics alone. As such, Kennedy's work to consider the individuality of bare footprints would not be applied directly in casework, but it makes an underpinning point that bare footprints may be potentially quite individual in form, if not actually unique.

After all independent variables have been considered in bare footprint comparisons for identification purposes, as per the above-mentioned methods, these prints would finally be subjected to considerations regarding the level of individuality represented by the common characteristics apparent within each print. This approach would essentially take into account the likelihood of all observed independent features being present within the population being considered using the approaches outlined in Chapter 2. In the past, a likelihood ratio calculation would have been used for this purpose to help the court understand how unusual an apparent match would be in relation to real-life evidential comparisons. Since the R. v. T case in the United Kingdom, there are moves away from the likelihood ratio approaches in favor of the presentation of evaluative opinion, particularly where there are doubts as to the appropriateness and reliability of available data (The Forensic Institute 2011).

4.7 Additional Case Considerations

In a case involving bare footprint evidence, such as a bloody bare footprint, the primary exemplar (standard) for comparison of a suspect's footprint to the questioned footprint and fabricating such in both static and dynamic modes has been comprehensively presented. There are other exemplars, however, that are collected by some examiners, depending on the case needs or as a matter of preference. The use of such exemplars may or may not be helpful and sometimes this need is not apparent until the later stages of the casework. For this reason, the following three exemplars are often taken for the purpose of more completeness, although their use is a personal choice of the examiner according to the needs of the case being worked.

To summarize, we have for our use examination-quality photographs, static bare footprints (with foot outline), and a dynamic gait pattern that one would collect routinely if there are footprints in sequence at the scene.

1. *Photographs:* Standing anteroposterior, lateral, medial, and posterior views can be photographed for reference, along with plantar aspects of the foot and head-to-toe views of suspect.
2. *Foot measurements:* The Brannock Device® is most commonly used system, but there are other systems that could be used such as the pedoGRID© system (DiMaggio/Hilderbrand) and other grids (see Chapter 5).
3. *Foam impressions:* Foam impression blocks are available through several manufacturers. A weight-bearing impression can be taken or a one-step impression for more of a dynamic mold fabrication. Molds are fabricated using basic dental stone material or similar. These impressions can be helpful in corroborating size and also can be used in courtroom presentation.

4.8 New Area to the Scope of Pedal Evidence

The four main areas of podiatric involvement to date are as follows:

1. Bare or socked footprints or foot impressions
2. Associated footwear evaluation in relation to pedal concerns
3. Forensic gait analysis/closed-circuit TV
4. Mass disaster identification

Over the past several years, we have been approached regarding cases involving requests for comparing an adult's footprint to an infant's footprint (taken at birth) with a view to considering whether or not the two as same. This task has not previously been broached by forensic podiatrists, but it seems worthy of research and evaluation. There have been several citations in the literature, but with limited decisiveness. It is mentioned here only for the sake of completeness.

References

Anderson M., Blais M. and Green W.T. 1956. Growth of the normal foot during childhood and adolescence; length of the foot and interrelations of foot, stature, and lower extremity as seen in serial records of children between 1–18 years of age. *American Journal of Physical Anthropology* 14: 287–308.

Barker S.L. and Scheuer J.L. 1998. Predictive value of human footprints in a forensic context. *Medicine, Science and the Law* 38: 341–46.
Bond J.W. 2013. Capturing finger and palm impressions using a hand cream and thermochromatic paper. *Journal of Forensic Science* 458: 1297–99.
Burrow J.G. 2015. Ghosting of images in barefoot exemplar prints collection: Issues for analyses. *Journal of Forensic Identification* 65: 884–900.
DiMaggio J.A. 2005. The role of feet and footwear in medico legal investigations. In *Forensic Medicine of the Lower Extremity*, edited by J. Rich, D.E. Dean, and R.H. Powers. pp. 375–400. Totawa, NJ: Humana Press.
Giles E. and Vallandigham P.H. 1991. Height estimation from foot and shoeprint length. *Journal of Forensic Sciences* 36: 1134–51.
Grant J.-A. 2006. Correlations between 2D Footprint Impressions and Foot Length. BSc (hons) project, The University of Northampton.
Gunn N. 1991. New methods of evaluating footprint impressions. *Royal Canadian Mounted Police Gazette* 53: 1–3.
Jackson P. 2007. Footloose in Archaeology. *Current Archeology*, June 8, 2014. http://www.archaeology.co.uk/articles/features/footloose-in-archaeology.htm (Accessed December 3, 2015).
Kanchan T., Krishan K., ShyamSundar S., Aparna K.R. and Jaiswal S. 2012. Analysis of footprint and its parts for stature estimation in Indian population. *The Foot* 22: 175–80. doi: 10.1016/j.foot.2012.02.010.
Kennedy R.B. 1996. Uniqueness of bare feet and its use as a possible means of identification. *Forensic Science International* 82: 81–7.
Kennedy R.B. 2005. Ongoing research into barefoot impression evidence. In *Forensic Medicine of the Lower Extremity*, edited by J. Rich, D.E. Dean, and R.H. Powers. pp. 401–413. Totawa, NJ: Humana Press.
Kennedy R.B., Chen S., Pressman I.S., Yamashita A.B. and Pressman A.E. 2005. A large-scale statistical analysis of barefoot impressions. *Journal of Forensic Science* 50: 1071–80.
Kennedy R.B., Pressman I.S., Sanping C., Petersen P.H. and Pressman A.E. 2003. Statistical analysis of barefoot impressions. *Journal of Forensic Science* 48: 55–63.
Kennedy R.B. and Yamashita B. 2007. Barefoot morphology comparisons: A summary. *Journal of Forensic Identification* 57: 383–413.
Kippen S.C. 1993. A preliminary assessment of recording the physical dimensions of an inked footprint. *Journal of British Podiatric Medicine* 48: 74–80.
Krishan K. and Sharma A. 2007. Estimation of stature from dimensions of hands and feet in a North Indian population. *Journal of Forensic and Legal Medicine* 14: 327–32.
Laskowski G.E. and Kyle V.L. 1988. Barefoot impressions—A preliminary study of identification characteristics and population frequency of their morphological features. *Journal of Forensic Science* 33: 378–88.
Massey S.L. 2004. Persistence of creases on the foot and their value for forensic identification purposes. *Journal of Forensic Identification* 54: 296–315.
Mathieson I., Upton D. and Birchenough A. 1999. Comparison of footprint parameters calculated from static and dynamic footprints. *The Foot* 9: 145–9.
Meyers-Rice B., Sugars L., McPoil T. and Cornwall M.W. 1994. Comparison of three methods for obtaining plantar pressures in nonpathologic subjects. *Journal of the American Podiatric Medical Association* 84: 499–504.

NAS (National Academy of Sciences). 2009. *Strengthening Forensic Science in the United States: A Path Forward*. Washington, DC: The National Academies Press.

Nataraja Moorthy E.T., Khairulmazidah M., Mohamed H.Y. and Jayaprakash P.T. 2011. Estimation of stature based on foot length of Malays in Malaysia. *Australian Journal of Forensic Sciences* 43: 13–26.

Newsquest Media Group. 2006. Chemical tests not conclusive. http://www.thisiswiltshire.co.uk (Accessed November 26, 2009).

Oberoi D., Kuruvilla A., Saralaya K.M., Rajeev A., Ashok B., Nagesh K. and Nageshkumar R. 2006. Estimation of stature and sex from foot print length using regression formulae and standard foot print length formula respectively. *Journal of Punjab Academy of Forensic Medicine and Toxicology* 6: 1–9.

Peet M.J. 1999. *Proportion of the UK Population with a Given Shoe Size*. SATRA Report. Northampton: SATRA.

Qamra S.R., Sharma B.R. and Kaila P. 1980. Naked foot marks—A preliminary study of identification factors. *Forensic Science International* 162: 145–52.

Reel S., Rouse S., Vernon W. and Doherty P. 2010. Reliability of a two-dimensional footprint measurement approach. *Science and Justice* 50: 113–18.

Reel S., Rouse S., Vernon W. and Doherty P. 2012. Estimation of stature from static and dynamic footprints. *Forensic Science International* 219: 283.e1–83.e5.

Reel S.M.-L. 2012. Development and evaluation of a valid and reliable footprint measurement approach in forensic identification. PhD diss., The University of Leeds.

Robbins L.M. 1978. The individuality of human footprints. *Journal of Forensic Science* 32: 778–85.

Robbins L.M. 1985. *Footprints: Collection, Analysis and Interpretation*. Springfield, MA: Charles C. Thomas.

Rossi W.A. 1992. Podometrics: A new methodology for foot typing. *Journal of Testing and Evaluation* 20: 301–11.

The Forensic Institute. 2011. Commentary on the case of R v T involving footwear evidence and Bayes' approach. http://www.theforensicinstitute.com/Articles/Comment ary%20on%20RvT.htm (Accessed December 11, 2014).

Topinard P. 1877. *L'Anthrologie*. 2nd ed. Paris: C. Reinwald.

Tsung B., Fan Y.B., Zhang M. and Boone D.A. 2003. Quantitative comparison of plantar foot shapes under weight-bearing conditions. *Journal of Rehabilitation Research and Development* 40: 517–26.

UKFSR (UK Forensic Science Regulator). 2016. *Forensic Science Regulator Codes of Practice & Conduct for Forensic Science Providers in the Criminal Justice System: Version 3*. Birmingham: The Forensic Science Regulator.

Vernon W. 2006a. The foot in identification. In *Forensic Human Identification: An Introduction*, edited by T. Thompson and S. Black. pp. 303–320. Boca Raton, FL: CRC Press.

Vernon W. 2006b. The development and practice of forensic podiatry. *Journal of Clinical Forensic Medicine* 13: 284–7.

Vernon W. 2015. A work based observational action research project involving males of working age to determine the cause of the inner darker areas and outer lighter areas of ghosting seen in two-dimensional dynamic bare foot-prints. MSc diss. University of Huddersfield.

Footwear Examination and Analysis

5

In the context of identification, the examination of footwear that has been associated with a crime scene is a multidisciplinary task. Podiatrists usually become involved in forensic footwear examination where a suspect has been found, and the task is to consider whether that person can be associated or disassociated with footwear already linked with the crime scene. A podiatrist's assessment of shoes in this context involves the analysis, comparison, and evaluation of wear features of the insole/sock liner, the internal and external aspects of the upper structure of the shoe, and the outsole. In addition to comparing known and unknown (questioned) footwear items together, the forensic podiatrist may also examine the suspected wearer or wearers of the shoes to look for features of the foot that may provide additional linking or disassociating factors. This chapter describes the processes involved in the forensic podiatry analysis of footwear in the identification process.

5.1 Introduction

Footwear can be associated with a scene of crime in a wide variety of ways. For example, shoeprints at the scene of crime could potentially be linked to the outsole of the shoe that made these prints. Where the shoeprint is available at the crime scene, the task is to match that print to a shoe later found or seized from a suspect. This task is assigned to forensic footwear examiners (in the United States) or to marks examiners (in the United Kingdom), and the frequency with which this work is required means that these are the main specialists involved in the forensic examination of footwear outsoles. The techniques predominantly used by these specialists to link a shoe outsole to a shoeprint found at a scene of crime are the matching of compatible features usually relating to the shoe manufacturing process (i.e., class characteristics) and areas of damage on the shoe outsole (i.e., accidental characteristics) apparent on the questioned shoeprint and known shoe outsole. Because the accidental characteristics are randomly formed, they are considered to be unique[1] and therefore extremely powerful sources of evidence.

[1] The term "unique" is used in its formal sense, meaning that the feature or features are so individual that it can reasonably be assumed that they represent the only example anywhere in the natural world.

Other scenarios that can be encountered are those in which footwear has been directly left at a crime scene. This scenario can occur with crimes involving rape, where the perpetrator has removed his or her clothing. It also can occur in crimes involving other forms of violence, such as during a struggle and the person has been separated from his or her footwear and has fled from the scene of crime, leaving the footwear behind. The task required then is not that of determining whether a shoe can be linked to the scene, but instead of whether the shoe can be linked to a suspected wearer of that shoe. Other forms of evidence that could be involved in making this connection include DNA-based evidence (e.g., the victim's blood is on the shoes), or fibers or other trace evidence is present within the shoe that may associate the shoe with the crime. Cases also occur where footwear not found at the crime scene has been seized later and linked to the scene through shoeprints or other forms of evidence as considered above (e.g., DNA, fibers) and the suspected wearer then denies ownership of these shoes. Variations on such denials include claims that there have been multiple wearers of the shoes involved; that although the shoes have been found in the suspect's possession, they belong to someone else; that the shoes had been loaned to another person at the time the crime was taking place; or that the suspect is simply being framed for the crime by the police authorities through the deliberate planting of evidence on the shoes. Such situations can involve complex processes of footwear analysis to produce conclusions that would either support or refute such claims.

It is important to recognize that the forensic examination of footwear is a multidisciplinary activity, and it would not be usual for podiatrists to become involved in linking the shoe to the scene of crime because the knowledge base required for this task is solely that of a forensic footwear or a marks examiner. A forensic podiatrist usually becomes involved in cases involving footwear where the task is to consider possible links between the footwear and the suspected wearer, or where a complex question concerning ownership has arisen (Figure 5.1). Work undertaken within the International

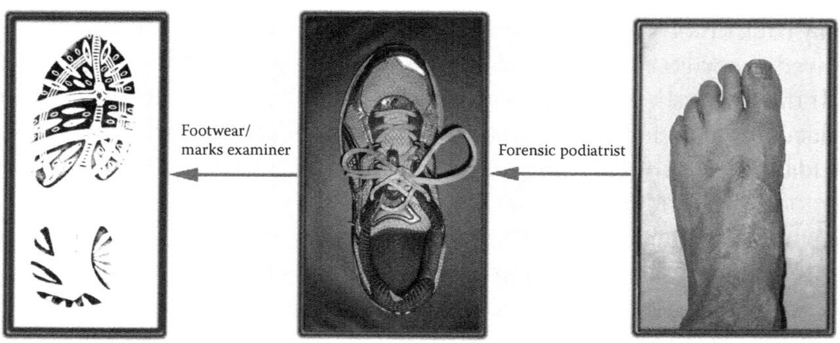

Figure 5.1 Positioning of podiatrists in footwear investigations.

Association for Identification has clarified this situation in detail, listing precisely what a forensic podiatrist does and does not do in this context (Vernon et al. 2009). A forensic podiatrist's involvement centers around the relationship between the foot and the shoe as represented by features related to fitting and wear.

Assistance in the process of identification from footwear has been a regularly performed area of forensic podiatry practice. Footwear examination and identification in such scenarios considered below.

5.2 Footwear Assessment: Initial Considerations

Initially, there is a need for personal protection to be considered before the footwear examination is carried out. Footwear items that have been associated with a crime scene can potentially represent a biohazard, and it is even possible for sharp items (e.g., needles) to be deliberately placed within the shoe to cause harm to anyone examining that shoe. A forensic podiatrist must therefore take reasonable precautions in this respect and wear protective gloves, facemasks, and general protective clothing, if required. Having made arrangements to ensure personal protection, the examining podiatrist would verify the parameters allowed on each particular case in relation to examination of the footwear evidence.

It is possible that at some point investigators could consider it necessary to examine footwear for the presence of DNA which could be used as evidence. Typically, considerations around the potential for DNA evidence from footwear take place before the footwear is sent to the forensic podiatrist for his or her input. An early decision is made as to whether to send the footwear to the DNA expert or forensic podiatrist with a view to evidence of one type or the other producing information useful in the identification or elimination of a suspected wearer. Which form of evidence is likely to be the most useful depends on the context of a particular case. For example, shoes associated with a crime may have been found later at a suspect's home, and the suspect may deny ownership of the shoes, stating perhaps that someone left the shoes there after a party. Given that the shoe was found in that person's home, DNA could be present on the shoes for innocent reasons arising from close domestic proximity and in itself not necessarily indicate personal involvement with that crime. As such, in this example, it may be more useful to have the shoes examined by the forensic podiatrist than the DNA expert. Conversely, in other situations, if the establishment of ownership is enough to prove involvement in the crime, it could make more sense for the shoe to be passed on to the DNA expert for examination, given the higher levels of certainty attainable through the use of DNA as opposed to podiatric evidence.

The situation is further complicated by the fact that attempts to obtain DNA evidence from footwear can be unsuccessful. Such attempts can involve intensive and destructive swabbing, the physical removal of materials from the footwear (e.g., sections of the insole), or both. Such unsuccessful attempts to obtain DNA evidence from the shoes can then adversely affect the potential for forensic podiatry approaches to be of assistance because the wear features of interest to the forensic podiatrist can be destroyed through this necessarily destructive analysis.

Within the shoe, the sites most likely to yield DNA include those where there has been good contact between the foot and the footwear materials: areas where the plantar surface of the toes, ball of foot, and heel have been in routine contact with the insole or sock liner. If it is possible that a forensic podiatry examination of the shoe could be requested after the DNA examination, the recommendation would be to consider taking such samples from the area of central heel wear on the insole or sock liner because the removal of materials from that specific site would be unlikely to compromise later forensic podiatry analysis, which is unlikely to focus on the central heel area. In any early discussions with the investigators, the forensic podiatrist should pass on appropriate advice covering this recommendation.

Where both DNA and forensic podiatry evidence are to be used in a footwear case, it is usual for the shoes to be examined by the DNA expert first. This order removes the necessity for additional precautions to be taken by the forensic podiatrist to guard against contamination or cross-contamination of the DNA evidence. It should never be assumed that this is the case however, and the forensic podiatrist should always check to determine whether the footwear might need to be examined later by a DNA expert. Although the investigators should be advised that it is preferable for all DNA work on the shoes to have been completed before the forensic podiatry examination, rarely the investigators can require both forms of analysis to be carried out, with the forensic podiatry analysis taking place first.

If this is the case, a range of precautions should be taken to avoid compromising the potential to use DNA evidence later. The U.S. National Institute of Justice provides basic information on how DNA evidence should be handled in casework and suggests that investigators and laboratory personnel should work together and take the following routine precautions (NIJ 1999):

- Keep the evidence dry and at room temperature.
- Maintain the chain of custody at all times.
- Avoid storing such evidence in plastic bags and in areas that can become hot.
- Wear gloves and change them often.

- Either use disposable instruments or clean any nondisposable instruments thoroughly before and after handling each sample.
- Avoid touching any area that may potentially contain DNA.
- Do not talk, cough, or sneeze over the evidence.
- Avoid touching one's own face, nose, and mouth when collecting and packaging evidence.
- Ensure that the evidence is dry before packaging.
- Use new paper bags and envelopes without staples for evidence containment.

All podiatrists are trained in surgical theater techniques, i.e., precautions that should be taken to avoid cross-contamination during surgery. Taking the same precautions is appropriate in relation to the avoidance of DNA cross-contamination. In addition, it can also be useful to double-glove before handling evidence that may later be subject to DNA analysis. Where there has been any accidental exposure to the DNA of the examining personnel, a sample of that person's DNA could be provided to the investigating officer for elimination/exclusion purposes, following the appropriate procedures in place within that jurisdiction.

Clarification should be specifically obtained over whether the questioned and reference shoes may be cut open and whether access to the suspect for examination purposes is possible. The equipment required for the examination should then be selected, and in addition to protective clothing, should include the following:

- Digital photography equipment (see Chapter 3)
- Shoe-sizing device
- Locking steel tape
- Sharp knives (multitools are particularly useful in this respect)
- Strong scissors
- Stiff card of square dimensions larger than the shoe outsole
- Impression foam box
- Inkless paper kit
- Clear acetate sheets
- Fine indelible marker pens
- Inspection mirror
- Adhesive tape
- Small frame (to support the shoe for photography purposes)
- General adjustable lighting source (e.g., angle poise lighting)
- Bright flashlight
- Forensic lighting kit with filters
- Portable computer with preloaded digital photography software
- Adhesive labels

- Adhesive tape
- Masking tape
- Notepaper and writing implements
- Large carrying case

The examination itself should be carried out in a suitable area, typically a workbench, such as found in a laboratory. This area should be secure so that unauthorized access throughout the examination is not possible. Having prepared for the footwear examination, the examining podiatrist must consider the chain of custody requirements in the evidence-handling process. The footwear evidence is usually sealed within heavy-duty labeled brown paper evidence bags, fastened securely with a locking cable tie or tape. Before opening the evidence bags, labels should be read carefully to verify that the contents are in fact the evidence to be examined. Assuming that this is the case, the cable tie or tape should then be cut away and the contained brown paper evidence bags removed to one side. It is essential that only one item of evidence is dealt with at a time. When ready to deal with a footwear item, the time of examination should be recorded in the examiner's notes and the detail on the label should be carefully recorded in these notes at the same time. The examiner should put his or her name on the label, sign the label, and record the date and time of opening. The evidence bag itself should be opened with care (preferably with scissors) to avoid damaging the contents. Where the bag has been opened and sealed previously, the bag should be accessed along the original opening, if possible, with the contained footwear article finally being removed for examination. It is good practice to photograph all steps before proceeding with the examination. After the examination, the shoes should be replaced in the bag, and the bag then carefully resealed and returned to the retaining authority.

The times that the evidence bag has been opened and closed should be recorded in the case notes before moving on to another item of evidence.

5.3 Footwear Assessment Phase 1

The examiner should initially observe the footwear item from all angles. Details of the style, indicated make (if known), shoe type, color, and marked size should be recorded, along with a subjective assessment of the general condition of the shoe. Descriptors of any wear, distortions, and crease lines of the upper should be made in the examiner's notes, as should the presence of any unusual features such as areas of deliberate damage and the style of lacing. The outsole is then examined for signs of wear and where such wear is present, it should be recorded. Although providing a written description of the outsole wear pattern is appropriate, a principle is available to assist

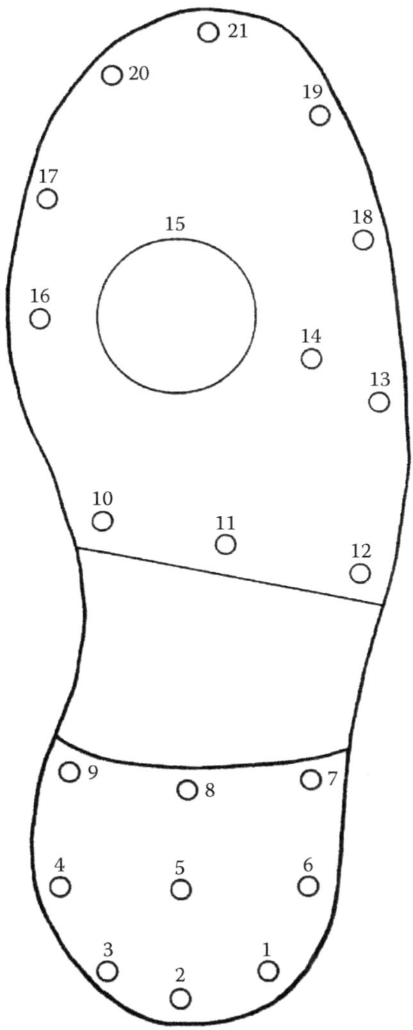

Figure 5.2 Focal point concept for assessment of outsole wear patterns.

with this task. The focal point "instrument" is a tool that considers the areas of the outsole from which each anatomically referenced component of wear spreads (Vernon et al. 1999). Each such area is described as a focal point (Figure 5.2). The focal point instrument is not a physical tool as such, but instead a means by which the examiner can describe the outsole wear for later comparison purposes. Figure 5.3 shows how the focal point approach would work in practice, with the examiner considering which focal point would be ascribed to each component of wear, leading to a combination of focal point code numbers that describe the wear pattern in its totality.

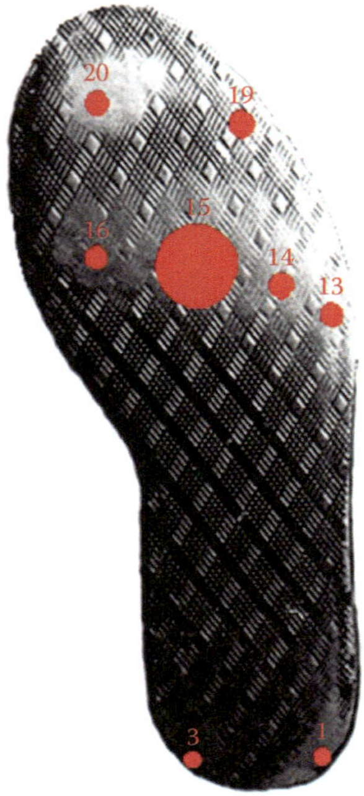

1/3/13/14/15/16/19/20

Figure 5.3 Use of the focal point concept in practice.

Shoe sizes vary in the footwear industry, with variations in the actual length of marked sizes occurring between shoe style and between manufacturers. These variations can lead to apparent discrepancies in shoe sizing. Size alone is therefore not an indication of correct shoe fit, with size being used instead to assist a shoe fitter and the purchaser of shoes by providing an initial guide as to the potential for a pair of shoes to fit the purchaser. This primary indication is not a definitive gauge of fit. In shoe fitting, this means that although the foot will be measured to give an indication of the correct shoe size for that foot, this does not automatically mean that a shoe marked with the size sought will fit appropriately. In addition, footwear is often purchased subjectively with many people selecting and wearing shoes that are incorrectly sized for their feet (Frey et al. 1993; McInnes et al. 2012; Nixon et al. 2006). Footwear marked or measured as being of a particular size therefore does not necessarily correlate with the owner's required shoe size. At best, shoe fitting is an ideal compromise in which the required length size will vary and where many other fitting variables serve to compound the problem of correct fitting. Thus, when examining a shoe as a forensic podiatrist, the marked shoe size should always be verified.

The usual method of verifying the length of a shoe involves the use of an internal shoe size gauge. Two types of gauge are available: a gauge that gives

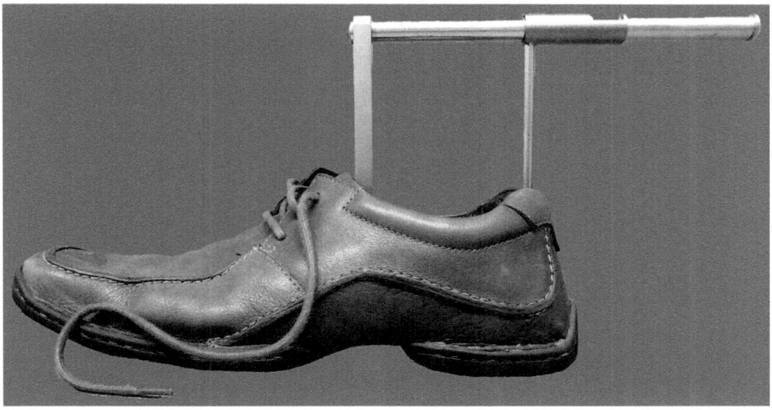

Figure 5.4 Use of an internal size gauge to indicate shoe size.

an indicated shoe size and a gauge that gives the internal length of the shoe in millimeters. Because of the lack of standardization in the footwear industry, the millimeter-scale device is preferred. With this version of the device, the indicated length can be checked where possible against each manufacturer's standards to give a more specific shoe size indication. Shoe-sizing systems also vary internationally, and the use of a millimeter scale allows a meaningful comparison with shoes from any country through the greater sensitivity to change offered by the millimeter scale.

Before inserting the gauge into the shoe, it is advisable to check the inside of the shoe as far as possible for the presence of any potentially harmful item within the interior of the shoe. In use, the internal shoe size gauge is inserted into the footwear item being examined, with the anterior edge of the device being placed carefully against the furthest aspect of the shoe toe box. With the anterior aspect of the device held securely in place, the rear component of the device is then slid backward until it just contacts with the internal heel area of the shoe. The indicated internal size of the shoe is then read off from a scale (Figure 5.4). In this way, the internal length of the shoe from front to rear (toe box to heel) can be confirmed (Lucock 1980). Where the examined shoes have a styled toe box, allowances need to be made for the greater internal length cause by that styling with the examiner by using an arbitrary line to judge where the most anterior aspect of the shoe would have been situated without the presence of the styling extension (Figure 5.5).

As an alternative to this specialist device, shoe length can also be indicated through the use of a locking steel tape measure. With this device, the front end of the measure is slid to the end of the toe box inside the shoe, and the body of the tape measure is extended until it makes a snug contact with the rear of the shoe (Figure 5.6). The tape is then locked, carefully removed, and the total internal length is given by the locked tape distance plus tape

Figure 5.5 Need to compensate for shoe styling when using an internal size gauge.

case length, which is often marked by the tape manufacturer on the side of the tape casing. The indicated shoe length is then checked against manufacturer's shoe length or other tables to allow this length to be converted into an indicative shoe size, with the measurements being recorded in the examiner's notes.

Having provided a written description and confirmation of the internal length of the footwear item to be examined, the footwear should be photographed from the upper, medial, lateral, anterior, posterior, and outsole aspects, following the principles advocated in Chapter 3. In addition, simple records of the upper crease marks and distortions of the shoe upper can be made. Place the shoe onto an item of stiff card, trace the outsole periphery of the shoe outsole onto the card, and mark the crease mark and upper distortion positions onto the card stock. The outline is then be carefully cut out and can be used later as necessary for preliminary comparison purposes.

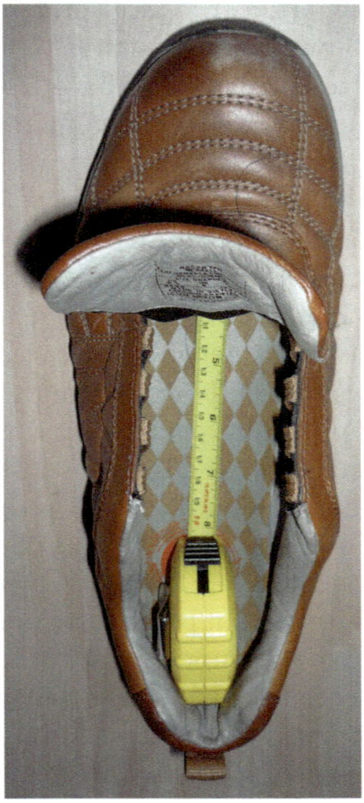

Figure 5.6 Use of a locking steel tape measure to indicate shoe size.

The card template should be carefully labeled to include the evidence code, shoe description, date, and an indication as to whether this template is of the right or left shoe. A more accurate template can be prepared later from a life-size printout of the photograph of the shoe upper; however, the cardboard template allows simple, early physical comparisons to be undertaken before that stage.

5.4 Footwear Assessment Phase 2

The next phase of the footwear examination requires the shoe to be examined internally. An inspection mirror and hand-light allow a simple inspection of the shoe interior to be undertaken with a particular focus on signs of wear. Where the shoe cannot be cut apart, the examiner needs to rely on the inspection mirror in conjunction with the simple palpation of wear (while wearing protective gloves as necessary) to determine the sites of wear within the shoe. In this scenario, it is also possible to photograph the images of reflected wear in the mirror with simple qualitative descriptions being provided to describe the internal wear features present. It must be stressed however that this approach is far from ideal, and permission to cut open the footwear should be sought wherever possible.

A "novel" approach presented by Nirenberg (2008) to inspect the interior of the shoe without cutting involves the use of an arthroscope (used by surgeons in, e.g., knee surgery), a fiber optic instrument that consists of a lens, a light source, and a focusing dial.

At this stage, the examiner would determine whether the shoe insole/sock liner could be detached. In some footwear items, this is a simple task with the insole/sock liner simply being placed and not adhered into position. In other cases, the insole/sock liner may have been fastened into position with an adhesive. It is worth gently attempting to remove the insole/sock liner, even if it has been glued into place because in some cases, the insole/sock liner can be detached from the adhesive within the shoe relatively easily. Care is required at this stage, however, to prevent tearing of the upper surface of the insole/sock liner. At the first signs of damage when attempting to remove the insole/sock liner, the examiner should cease the attempt to remove this material and proceed, if possible, to opening the shoe.

Regardless of whether the attempt to remove the insole has been successful, closer inspection is required, and if allowable (as is most often the case) the shoe should now be opened carefully. As a rule, in the United States, the shoe is cut open as a matter of routine protocol. If permission is required, then it is requested, and if there is a refusal, a court order can be requested to allow for such, because it is an integral part of the evaluation. That being said, the task is to separate most of the upper from the sole unit, leaving a section of material intact to act as a hinge on completion of the task (Figure 5.7). A sharp, strong knife is essential for separating the shoe upper from the sole unit, and this separation is often easiest to use on the sides of the shoe, where because of the design of the shoe, the material tends to be relatively soft, pliable, and not reinforced. To separate the heel and toe box areas, which may have been reinforced, a strong pair of scissors may be easier and safer to use. Once the shoe has been opened, if the insole/sock liner is still in place, a further attempt could be made to separate this material from the body of the sole unit, taking advantage of the improved access to this structure. The use of a blunt instrument could be useful to aid the separation process, but at the first indication of potential damage, the examiner should end the removal attempt and photograph the insole in situ instead. If it has been possible to remove the insole, the insole should be photographed separately using the techniques of lighting and photography advocated in Chapter 3. The purpose of making a recorded image of the insole/sock liner is to capture the foot impression and "shadow" image on that insole/sock liner in a manner that shows optimal detail of that impression for later comparison purposes. At the same time, it can also be useful to make a simple tracing of the outline of the insole/sock liner to show the position of the foot impression on the material surface.

Figure 5.7 Preparation of footwear for internal examination.

An acetate sheet can be placed into secure, close contact with the insole/sock liner, with the examiner palpating the impressions carefully to determine the extent and shape of the impression, tracing the outline carefully at the same time. The acetate sheet can then later be used to make a preliminary comparison of this foot impression with that present within other footwear items. A written description of the wear impression can also be provided, with particular emphasis on the presence or absence of particular toe impressions, unusual features of the imprint, and a preliminary assessment of the positions of the various features of the print relative to the periphery of the shoe as an early indication of shoe fit.

Having examined the shoe insole/sock liner as described, the next task is to consider the lining of the internal upper surface of the shoe. All sites of wear, distortion, and damage should be recorded using digital photography. Notes should also be made of the site and level of deformation/damage caused by the related anatomical features (e.g., the apex of the second toe, lateral aspect of the fifth metatarsophalangeal joint). Further comment can be made on any foot/shoe size match implications and any unusual features that may be apparent.

At this stage, the examination of the single footwear item is complete. A final check should be made to ensure that all required notes have been taken, that all digital photographic images have been captured, and that these images seem to be of the required quality. When the examiner is satisfied that this is the case, the footwear evidence that has been the subject of the examination should be put back together as far as practicable and returned to the relevant evidence bag. The bag should then immediately be resealed. The time of the resealing should be recorded and the evidence bag returned to its keeper. The described process is then repeated for all questioned and known items to be examined.

5.5 Footwear Owner Assessment

It can also be advantageous to examine the suspected owner of any of the footwear items involved in the investigation, and in the case of possible multiple wearers of shoes, the known wearer of any shoes that may have found their way into the suspected wearer's possession. This may not always be possible, particularly where the person concerned refuses to be examined (when a subject is uncooperative, in the United States a court order can be requested to allow for whatever the examiner needs). If examination of the suspected owner of the footwear is not possible, the comparison phase would proceed on the basis of footwear item comparisons alone. Where the owner, or suspected wearer, of any of the shoes is available and can be examined, inkless footprints should initially be captured using the protocols advocated in Chapter 4. In addition to acquiring foot molds, photographs, and other material as deemed necessary, the subject's feet should be measured using a standard foot measuring device. Although many such devices are available, one of the most common is the Brannock Device/Gauge®, which is available in child and adult versions. In forensic identification situations, the adult version is most frequently required.

The Brannock Device is used to measure overall length, heel-to-ball length, and ball width of the feet. The following procedure is recommended when using the Brannock Device:

1. Check that the Brannock Device to be used has the correct measurement scale for the population being considered. Brannock devices produced for United Kingdom use are to measure U.K. (adult) and U.K. children's feet, whereas in the United States, such devices are produced to measure U.S. men's, U.S. women's, and U.S. children's feet.
2. The width indicator of the device is placed on its widest setting, and the heel-to-ball indicator (referred to in the United States as the arch length indicator) should be slid back to facilitate positioning of the foot on the device.
3. The person whose feet are to be measured is asked to remove his or her shoes and stand in preparation for the Brannock Device to be used. Socks would normally be worn for this measurement; however,

experience has indicated that sometimes a suspect will attempt to hide the true length of the feet by wearing multiple pairs of socks. To guard against this possibility, the subject should be asked to remove the socks and the feet should be examined before measurement with the device while one pair of socks only is worn.

4. Taking the right foot first, the subject is asked to place the right heel into the right heel cup of the Brannock Device.
5. The heel should be firmly located against the heel cup of the device. To assist with this placement, the subject's ankle and the heel cup of the device should be grasped together while taking the foot measurement.
6. The subject is asked to stand with weight equally distributed between the right and left foot.
7. A second check of the socks is made to ensure that they are positioned optimally on the foot, i.e., not too tight and thus pulling the toes back, shortening the foot, or too slack potentially lengthening the foot.
8. Holding the toes flat against the Brannock Device scale, look straight down over the longest toe (whichever toe this may be) and read off the overall foot length measurement indicated. If necessary, a small, smooth wooden block can be gently placed against the end of the longest toe to help determine this position more accurately.
9. Ensure that the ankle is still soundly located in the heel cup of the device, and then use the thumb of the left hand to gently but firmly hold the first metatarsophalangeal joint of the foot across the very center of this joint while maintaining the position of the foot on the Brannock Device with the palm of the left hand.
10. With the right hand, slide the heel-to-ball (arch length) indicator to a position in which the medial side of the first metatarsophalangeal joint fits into the inner curve of this indicator. The two ridges in the center of this indicator should line up with the center of this joint. Ensure that the indicator does not rub against the ball of the foot while sliding it into place,
11. With the indicator and foot in this position, a central ridge now locates against the very center of the first metatarsophalangeal joint and this ridge also forms a pointer on the side scale of the Brannock Device. The scale number indicated by the pointer at this stage is that of the heel-to-ball (arch) length of the foot being measured.
12. Ideally, the overall foot length and heel-to-ball (arch) length measurements would show as the same length. However, these measurements often differ and generally, the larger of the two measurements (overall length or heel to ball) would indicate the overall shoe length required by the subject.
13. The Brannock Device is now used to measure the width of the foot.

14. Holding the foot in the position described above (heel firmly seated, heel-to-ball indicator in place), but now with the right hand, the left hand is used to slide the width indicator to a point where it is soundly located against the outside lateral edge of the foot.
15. For the indicated shoe length, read off required width as shown on the width indicator scale nearest the front of the foot being measured, i.e., the scale facing toward the examiner.
16. Where the relevant shoe length indicator lines up precisely with a particular width measurement shows the subject's indicative width. Where a "between-width" measurement is shown, the greater width measurement suggests the width fitting required for a "thicker" foot and the lesser width measurement for a "thinner" foot.
17. Using the procedures outlined above, the Brannock Device should then be used to measure the left foot.
18. Where, as is often the case, both feet are of different sizes, the indicative shoe size for the subject is that of the larger foot.
19. After use, the device should be wiped clean with a damp cloth according to the manufacturer's recommendations.

Having followed these procedures in the use of the Brannock Device, what has been obtained is a primary indication of the required shoe length and width only. Because of personal preference, manufacturer size variations, and the influences of style, the measurements indicated do not necessarily show the size of shoe that the subject wears routinely.

A full clinical examination of the suspect should then be undertaken and the presence of any foot pathologies recorded. Finally, a template of the suspect's foot outline should be made using the following technique:

- A standard box of foot impression foam is placed on a firm, flat, horizontal surface.
- The subject is asked to stand with the respective foot adjacent to the impression material, lightly supporting himself or herself, if required.
- The subject is asked to place the foot carefully in position over and just resting on the foam impression material and within the confines of that material.
- When the foot is positioned as described above, the subject is asked to force his or her foot vertically into the material. The examiner can gently press any of the dorsal aspects of the foot further into the material to ensure that an impression of adequate depth has been left of the foot.
- The subject is asked to carefully lift his or her foot vertically out of the impression material.

- The material and the contained box is labeled with the subject's name, the date and time that the impression was taken, and a code is ascribed to enable the item to be quickly and easily identified within the accompanying notes.
- The process is then repeated for the subject's alternate foot.

At a later stage, the impression taken in this way can be used to create an exact template of the peripheral border of the subject's foot. Placing a scale on the upper surface of the impression material and taking a digital image of the impression by using the photographic techniques described in Chapter 3 can make this template. The scale image is then printed out life size, and the peripheral template is cut out carefully to give the required template.

One might also consider a weight-bearing tracing of the foot to preclude the foam box technique. At least three tracings would be required to ensure reliability of the tracing. While this approach is unlikely to be as accurate as the foam box technique it will be quicker to perform, which may be advantageous depending on circumstances. The foam box technique may also allow a foot mold to be created that may help show foot fit in a shoe or on the sock liner.

5.6 Footwear Assessment Phase 3

Once phases 1 and 2 are completed, the foot impressions and other wear features from the examined footwear items, and features of interest noted from the subject, need to be considered further. At this stage, life-size foot impression images need to be created for comparison purposes by using the techniques described in Chapter 3. These life-size images can be printed out to allow the outlines of foot impressions within the shoes to be traced accurately onto clear acetate sheets for outline comparison. A second copy should then be made of the life-size electronic digital image. This image can then be used in electronic format to give accurate measurements of the foot impression by using either the Gunn or Reel method (see Chapter 4 on bare footprint examination). Such measurements can be made based on the basic Adobe Elements 9 software program's instructions, but the instructions can be adapted to use with other software packages such as Adobe Photoshop and GIMP by using the measurement tool associated with these programs as described in Chapter 3 for digital photographic techniques). The instructions are as follows:

- Use the Zoom tool to enlarge the image on screen to the maximum practical working size.
- Verify that the electronic image has been converted to life size.

- Select the pencil tool from the toolbox menu.
- Select an appropriate size for the pencil mark to be used (typically 10 pixels).
- To facilitate the accurate placing of the marks to follow, the grid function should be used on the software program and the image rotated so that the most posterior aspect of the heel print just contacts the adjacent horizontal line of the grid and the most lateral aspects of the footprint just touch an adjacent vertical line of the grid.
- Place pencil dots on the foot impression points to be used in the Gunn approach (basic measurements including rearmost aspect of the heel, tips of all toes, and medial and lateral aspects of the ball-of-foot areas).
- Select the Line tool from the software menu.
- Select an appropriate color for the line to be drawn from the Swatch menu (red is often particularly suitable, depending on the background color of the foot impression).
- Select an appropriate weight for the line width (typically 5 pixels).
- Use the line tool to place the cursor on the first foot impression point to be used in the measurement and drag and hold to the second point to be used.
- Continue until all required lines have been drawn.
- Flatten the image using the function Layer/Flatten Image (this step is essential to "lock" lines to be put in later with the foot impression image when the image is rotated).
- Place a grid across the image checking the function View/Grid.
- Select the function Image/Rotate/Free Rotate Layer.
- Place the cursor on one of the rotation points and then rotate the image until the first measurement is parallel with any of the grid lines.
- Select the Rectangular Marquee tool from the toolbox menu.
- Carefully place the cursor on one end of the first line to be considered and then drag and release to the opposite end of that line.
- Select Info from the menu.
- Read off and record the length (or for the cross ball of foot measurement, the width) of the line in centimeters to two decimal places.
- Deselect the Rectangular Marquee tool and go back to the function Image/Rotate/Free rotate layer.
- Complete the process for the measurement of all other lines involved.

This approach gives quantitative measurements taken from the footprint dimensions for later comparison using the Gunn method. If the optical center method is preferred (see Chapter 4), most examiners use manual approaches involving life-size printouts to determine and measure from the optical centers unless access to software that allows the creation and use of optical centers is available (e.g., AutoCAD®2010). In the manual approach devised by Kennedy,[2] an acetate-based "target" with a central pinhole is placed in the position of best fit over the morphological feature from which the measurement is to be taken, and then a mark is made through that center onto the foot impression image. Lines are then drawn as in the Gunn method to connect these marked points.

At this stage, the examiner will have measurements taken by either the Gunn or optical center approach, along with traced outlines of the foot impressions under consideration taken from the insole or sock liner. This information is used in the next task that involves the footwear comparison and evaluation phases.

5.7 Footwear Comparison and Evaluation

After examining all relevant footwear items, including the collection of descriptive and quantitative measurements, the next stage is to compare the detail present on both known and questioned footwear items. The comparison process can be considered as two separate but related phases: direct comparison and evaluation.

5.8 Direct Comparison

5.8.1 Marked Shoe Size

The first direct comparison to be undertaken is that of the marked and sized shoe lengths. The marked length is used to check for compatibility when the usual wearer of each compared shoe is being considered.

5.8.2 Sized Shoe Length

In the comparison of shoe length, as confirmed by the use of an internal measuring device, the measured internal length would need to be compared with the information provided by the manufacturer of that shoe to verify the shoe's size. This verification can be undertaken in two ways. First, the shoe may contain labeling that clearly states the internal length for that particular shoe in centimeters and also in size according to the length system used in various countries (e.g., U.K., U.S., or European size). Second, many manufacturers produce tables and these tables can be used to show the internal lengths used by that manufacturer for shoes of given sizes. These tables, where available, can also be used to confirm the size of that particular shoe. It behooves the

[2] Kennedy R., Personal communication, 1996.

podiatrist in clinical practice to evaluate patient's footwear at hand for wear, and especially the foot fit on the sock liner and the shadow image or impression produced. During a podiatrist's career, he or she can see hundreds of thousands of feet, offering an ideal opportunity to not only understand the foot and the shoe wear features in depth, but also to gain valuable insights into the relationship between the foot and shoe.

If a suspected wearer of these shoes is also available for examination, the overall length of that person's foot can also be compared with the marked and sized length of all shoes considered.

5.8.3 Upper Crease Marks

Next, the position and angle of the upper crease marks apparent between both known and questioned footwear items should be considered. The examiner is looking for similarities and differences in the placing and the measured angles of such marks (Figure 5.8).

If a suspected wearer of these shoes is also available for examination, the heel-to-ball length of the foot and any pathological features present in the suspect's feet that may have influenced the placing and angle of the upper crease marks can also be compared with these marks.

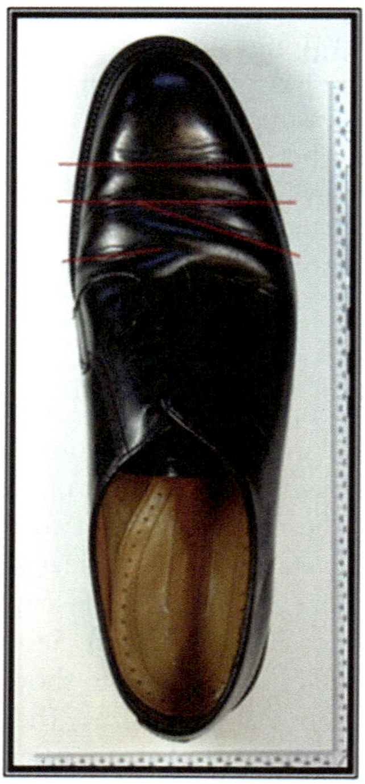

Figure 5.8 Position and angle of creasing of the shoe upper.

5.8.4 Upper Distortions and Inner Lining Wear

The upper surface of the examined shoes may show many wear features and distortions such as a general medial or lateral displacement of the upper (Figure 5.9a and b); bulging of the medial, lateral, or both aspects of the shoe in the shoe flex line region; and bulging of the toe box area, corresponding to the contained toes. The examined shoes can be compared for the presence or absence of such distortions. While considering distortions of the shoe upper, wear within the shoe or

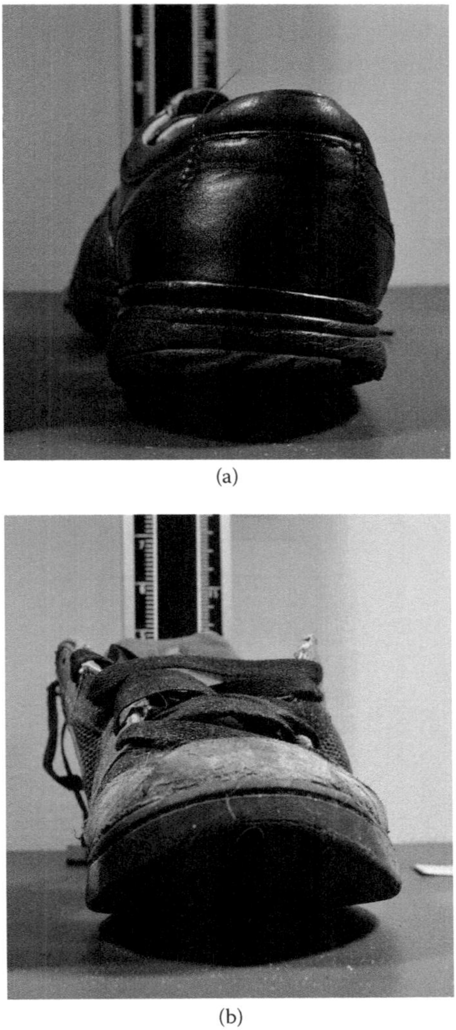

Figure 5.9 Distortions of the shoe upper. (a) Rear view of shoe showing lateral displacement of the rear aspects of the shoe upper, and (b) Front view of the shoe showing general medial displacement of the shoe upper.

the lining surface should also be taken into account. In considering these wear features and distortions, the examiner is looking for similarities and dissimilarities of wear features caused by foot function and relating this information to the fit of the medial and lateral aspects of the ball-of-foot area and around the heel.

If a suspected wearer of these shoes is also available for examination, the overall shape and function of the foot can be compared with any distortions apparent. To assist this comparison, templates can be prepared of the outline of that person's foot structure, and the features apparent within that outline can be compared to the wear features present within the shoe upper and lining, the ball of foot, and toe positions present within the examined shoe and with any distortions and wear of the shoe upper surface.

5.8.5 Toe Impressions

Inside the shoe, staining, impressions within the upper, or a wearing through of the lining of the upper may be found (Figure 5.10), all of which correspond with the positioning of the toes within the shoe. These wear features can be directly compared between the examined known and unknown shoes to determine similar and dissimilar placing of these particular features.

Again, if a suspected wearer of these shoes is also available for examination, the position, morphology, and any pathological states of the toes can also be compared with impressions and wear caused by the wearer's toes within the shoes. Creation of outline templates as suggested above also facilitates the comparison between the person's outline foot shape and toe impressions apparent within the shoe.

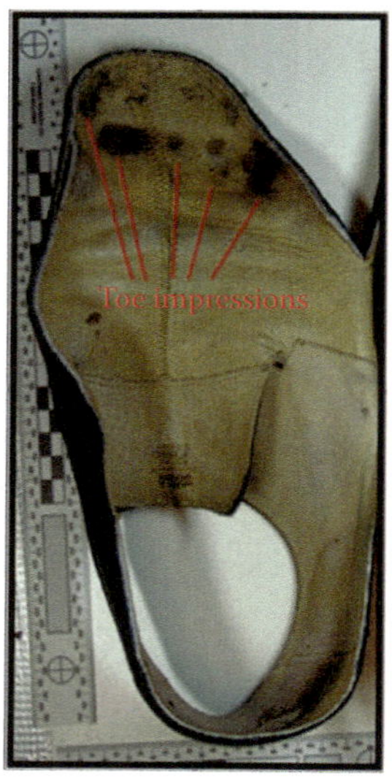

Figure 5.10 Toe impression wear features.

5.8.6 Foot Impressions (Image)

Central to comparisons involving footwear is the use of the plantar impressions taken from known and questioned footwear items. The comparisons undertaken follow the procedures detailed under bare footprint identification in Chapter 4; however, greater attention is needed when considering the additional variables in the relationship between the foot and the containing footwear. These variables need to be considered carefully in the evaluation phase.

The term "foot impression" implies a depth component, i.e., the plantar mark created by the foot is present in three dimensions. This can often be seen in footwear depending on the age of the shoe in combination with the materials of manufacture. It is however termed by some as a "foot (shadow) image." In addition, when a satisfactory impression is present, it is possible to create a thin casting of this feature if desired. This process damages the surface of the sock liner/insole but is a possibility under certain circumstances.

If a suspected wearer of these shoes is also available for examination, foot impressions can be taken and an outline template of that impression can be compared with foot impressions present within the examined shoes. This comparison may however not always be desirable. The bare footprint is, in effect, a snapshot in time in which the foot has briefly contacted the ground at the moment that the impression was created. Conversely, the foot impression within a shoe is in effect a history of the relationship between the contained foot and the shoe's sock liner or insole with which that foot has been in contact. As such, the form of the foot impression within the shoe may have been influenced by a whole range of activities together, e.g., walking, standing, running, turning, and sliding, and may therefore become quite different in shape and character. For this reason, the preferred comparison would be between separate footwear items that should also be like-with-like items where possible, i.e., training shoes should ideally be compared with training shoes, dress shoes with dress shoes. The reason for this like-with-like comparison is that many variables, including shoe style, can affect the foot when encased in a shoe. Removing as many of these variables as possible through the use of a like-with-like comparison facilitates a comparison in situations as closely matched as possible, thereby guarding against the potential for differences to be found that simply relate to the effect of different footwear on the contained foot as opposed to true differences between the feet of different wearers.

The use of exemplar bare footprints with foot outline collected from the suspected wearer of the shoe could however be a useful addition to this comparison process if unusual features of the foot impressions within the shoes are apparent.

5.8.7 Outsole Wear Patterns

Finally, the outsole wear patterns of footwear items that have been examined can be compared. The practical difficulty in this comparison is that of comparing the wear of older shoes with that of new shoes because the wear patterns can appear quite different in their spread across the outsole surface. The focal point concept mentioned herein (Figure 5.2) can assist with this comparison because it considers and compares the central positions from which each component of outsole wear spreads as opposed to considering the outer periphery of that wear. This allows worn new and old footwear items to be compared together irrespective of the amount of wear. In the comparison of outsole wear patterns, the examiner would again look for similarities and dissimilarities between the wear patterns of the outsoles being compared.

5.9 Evaluation (Interpretation)

Evaluation of the comparisons made as detailed in Section 5.7.1 requires interpretation of the comparison data. The significance of any apparent matches or mismatches in terms of identity is thus considered in the particular context created by the wearing of shoes. These shoes not only demonstrate wear features caused by the contained functioning foot but also introduce variable influences that may have affected the contained foot. The wear features in their own right and the effect of those external variable influences demand interpretation by the forensic podiatrist—a task that can be complex because of the many variables potentially involved.

5.9.1 Marked Shoe Size

Lucock (1980) considered that although differences in the sizes of shoes belonging to a single person commonly vary by a half or full size (United Kingdom), a person would be highly unlikely to wear footwear with length differences greater than 1½ sizes and our personal observations support this belief. Shoe sizing concerns can often be an integral part of the podiatrist's task in some cases. Close matching of shoe size could therefore be considered as a compatible class characteristic in footwear comparisons. But this consideration centers on the usual wearers of shoes and would not necessarily apply to situations in which footwear has been worn for a period of time by a second wearer for reasons of convenience, ignorance, socioeconomics, or a deliberate attempt to deceive. Here, major mismatches in shoe size are possible because factors other than normal purchasing habit may come into play; however, such mismatches would still usually be within the 1½ shoe-size range for the wearer. Size differentials may exist between shoe types worn by the same person and all these possible variables require the examiner to draw heavily on his or her expertise and experience. In the UK, podiatrists encounter shoe owners presenting for care while wearing shoes up to four sizes (UK) smaller than their measured foot length requires. There is however strong potential for shoes that are short for the wearer to show clear wear features demonstrating that an over-long foot has been worn within that shoe.

5.9.2 Sized Shoe Length

The comparison of sized shoe length is important for two reasons. First, confirming the marked size can be especially important if "fake" designer shoes are widely available and if such fakes may be incorrectly sized according to the true manufacturers' specifications. Second, if mismatches have occurred between foot length and shoe length, confirming the actual shoe length helps to determine the magnitude of such differences in terms of that manufacturer's shoe size and, in turn, helps the examiner to reach conclusions over the minimum length of the foot that has been contained within that shoe.

5.9.3 Upper Crease Marks

In compared shoes of approximately the same length, with common ownership the upper crease marks would be expected to share approximately the same position and angle. Where the position of these marks differs between known and unknown shoes being compared, further consideration would need to be given to the possibility of the shoe structure and design itself having influenced the position of the crease marks. For example, it is possible for the leading edge of the eyestay of the shoe to have influenced the upper crease mark position, requiring the crease to pass in front of as opposed to through this feature. It is also possible for the toe cap of the shoe to amend the crease position. Where such factors are believed to be present, they should be carefully documented as confounding factors. Where no influencing design features of the shoe are apparent, with common ownership, the crease marks would be expected in approximately the same position; conversely, different crease positions without any apparent footwear influence may indicate different wearers of the shoes being compared.

Similarly, upper crease marks would be expected to be positioned at similar angles where they share common ownership. Again, this conclusion would be dependent on the crease marks not having been influenced by the shoe design. Where no such design feature can be found that may have affected the crease mark angle and the crease marks of the compared shoes are found to be situated at different angles, the examined shoes may be considered to have different wearers. The angle of the crease mark may relate to the presence of foot pathologies that could have led to the formation of a mark at a more extreme angle than would normally be anticipated. This situation can particularly relate to a foot that has supinated toward the end of the stance phase of the gait cycle, such as typically seen in a foot that exhibits hallux rigidus or hallux limitus. The presence of such angled crease marks without apparent influence from the structure of the shoe may indicate the presence of such a condition. If it has been possible to examine the suspected wearer of the shoe and such a condition has also been observed in that person and brought into the comparison process, then that would be a further compatible class feature supporting the possibility of common ownership.

The crease mark plays a role in considering the implications of the shoe fit in terms of length. One of the most important foot measurements is the heel-to-ball measurement, or the distance from the rearmost aspect of the heel to the inner ball joint of the foot (Rossi 1992). The ball of the normal foot should flex during motion and simultaneously the shoe is designed to flex at a position related to this position, as represented by the heel-to-ball measurement of the foot. The shoe is designed to accommodate this function just anterior to the front edge of the shank of the shoe (Council of the Society of Shoefitters 1991; Rossi 1984, 96). For a shoe to fit correctly, the ball flex positions of foot and shoe should match. If there is a mismatch between the foot position and the shoe ball flex position, angle, or both, this mismatch can lead to friction in this area through the foot and shoe attempting to flex at different positions relative to each other, i.e., the shoe may crease in a position other than the point at which it was designed to flex. In the evaluation phase, the presence of such wear features away from the designed flex point of the shoe can indicate a mismatch of the foot versus shoe heel-to-ball length and can provide further evidence of a shoe having been worn by someone of either a larger or smaller foot size than the marked size of the shoe.

Also in relation to shoe length is the potential for an over-long shoe to show an additional crease mark toward the end of the shoe, where the foot has prepared for toe-off during walking with an additional length of shoe extending further forward than the shoe designer intended had the shoe has been correctly fitted (Figure 5.11). The shoe is then forced to bend as the toe-off takes place, leading to an additional anterior crease mark that is an indicator of a short foot being placed within that shoe. This indicator can, in turn, suggest size parameters for the contained foot, especially when considering additional wear features within the shoe (e.g., foot impression).

Crease marks can also indicate that more than one wearer has worn the shoe. In reaching such a conclusion, the crease marks would need to be considered in conjunction with other wear features of the shoe, particularly those relating to ball-of-foot positioning. A crease mark situated well behind the impressions caused by the ball of a foot that has been placed within a shoe that has fitted reasonably correctly would indicate the strong possibility that the shoe has experienced two different wearers, because the crease mark would then correspond with the metatarsal shaft positioning of the wearer who had created the ball-of-foot impressions (Figure 5.12).

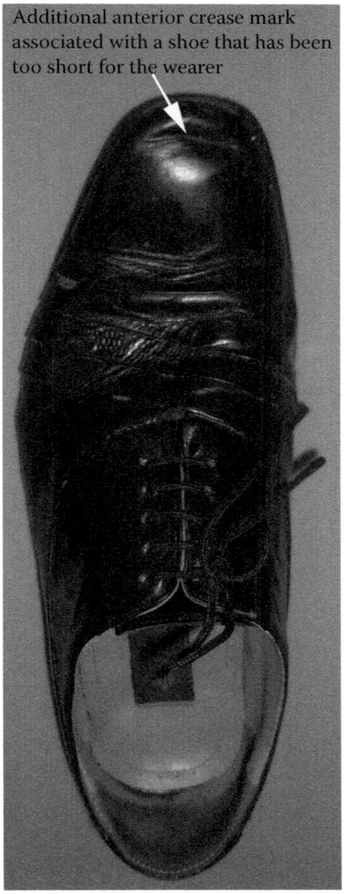

Figure 5.11 Additional anterior crease mark associated with a shoe that has been too short for the wearer.

5.9.4 Upper Distortions

Upper distortions involving a general medial or lateral displacement of the upper can either be related to function or to the fit of the foot that has been contained within that shoe. If these features have been noted in known and unknown footwear, further consideration is needed as to whether these features have arisen from common functional causes or from shoe-fitting problems. If differences as opposed to similarities exist between known and questioned shoes, further consideration should be given to whether these differences can be justified through factors such as different shoe fit, age, and design. For example, distortions that may be notable in soft upper material may not be apparent in comparison with a shoe manufactured to a much stiffer material specification.

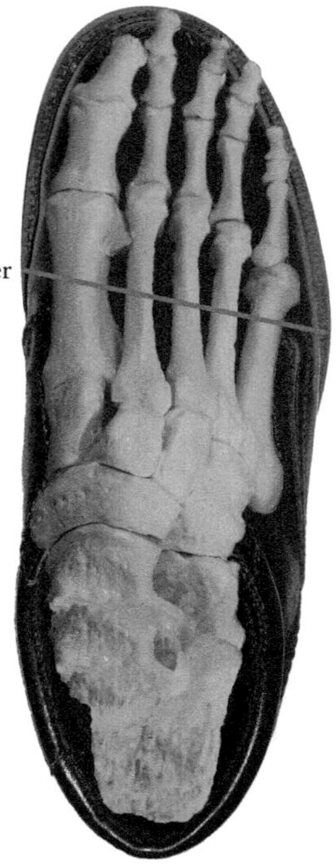

Figure 5.12 Conflicts between upper creasing of the shoe and functional anatomy of the foot seen in cases of multiple wearers of shoes.

At the end of this interpretive consideration, the examiner should be able to determine whether the cause or causes of such distortions relate to features suggesting common ownership, or whether the cause has been of unrelated fitting problems. When assessing such features, keep in mind that upper distortions of footwear may relate to other external causes, such as the placement of heavy weights on the top of the shoe, while being kept in storage.

If the suspected wearer of the shoes has been available for examination, features from that person or templates created from that person's foot outline can be brought into the evaluative considerations, further strengthening the evidential opinion.

5.9.5 Toe Impressions

Toe impressions formed within the shoe upper can indicate problems with the fit of the shoe, or alternately, the presence of toe pathologies that have affected the wearer of that shoe. Toe positions situated on or in proximity to the point at which the shoe upper meets the periphery of the sock liner or insole can indicate that the shoe has not correctly fitted the wearer, either in terms of available length or in toe box style.

Toe impressions apparent within the upper of the shoe can indicate the presence of pathologies such as hammer toe or mallet toe, hyperextension of the toes, and other similar problems. Referral to the prevalence data for these conditions shows the evidential value of the presence of such conditions across both known and unknown footwear items examined.

If it has been possible to examine the suspected wearer of the shoe and the recognized conditions have also been observed in that person and brought into the comparison process, this information would be a further compatible class feature indicating possible common ownership of the shoes in question.

5.9.6 Foot Impressions (Images)

The same features and considerations involved in the evaluation of bare footprints also come into play when considering foot impressions/images within footwear being examined. In dealing with a foot impression present within a footwear item as opposed to an impression created by the bare foot, additional considerations other than the effects of function on that impression need to be taken into account. These considerations include the potential for the plantar impression to have been modified from its natural position by the interaction taking place between the foot and the containing shoe; the effect of shoe fitting and shoe sizing on the impression; and the implications of additional wear features apparent in other areas of the examined footwear, when the shoe is considered in its entirety. The effects of function on the plantar impression were addressed in Chapter 4 on bare footprint identification. The additional factors to be considered in the evaluation are now discussed.

For example, it is possible for the plantar impression to be modified from its natural position by the interaction between the foot and the shoe. This factor is the main reason why like-with-like comparisons are highly preferable in footwear comparisons. There are many ways that a shoe can amend the form of a foot impression, and a like-with-like comparison can be invaluable for eliminating many of these variables. One of the most dramatic variations that can occur between compared foot impressions of the same person relates to the effect of the toe box shape on the contained foot, where a styled shoe can channel the toes into a position that they would not have naturally adopted (Figure 5.13).

An extreme manifestation of this variable can be seen in the effect that a court shoe has on the plantar impression. The possibility of a shoe channeling the toes away from their natural position in this way should be considered in plantar impression comparisons where measurements fall

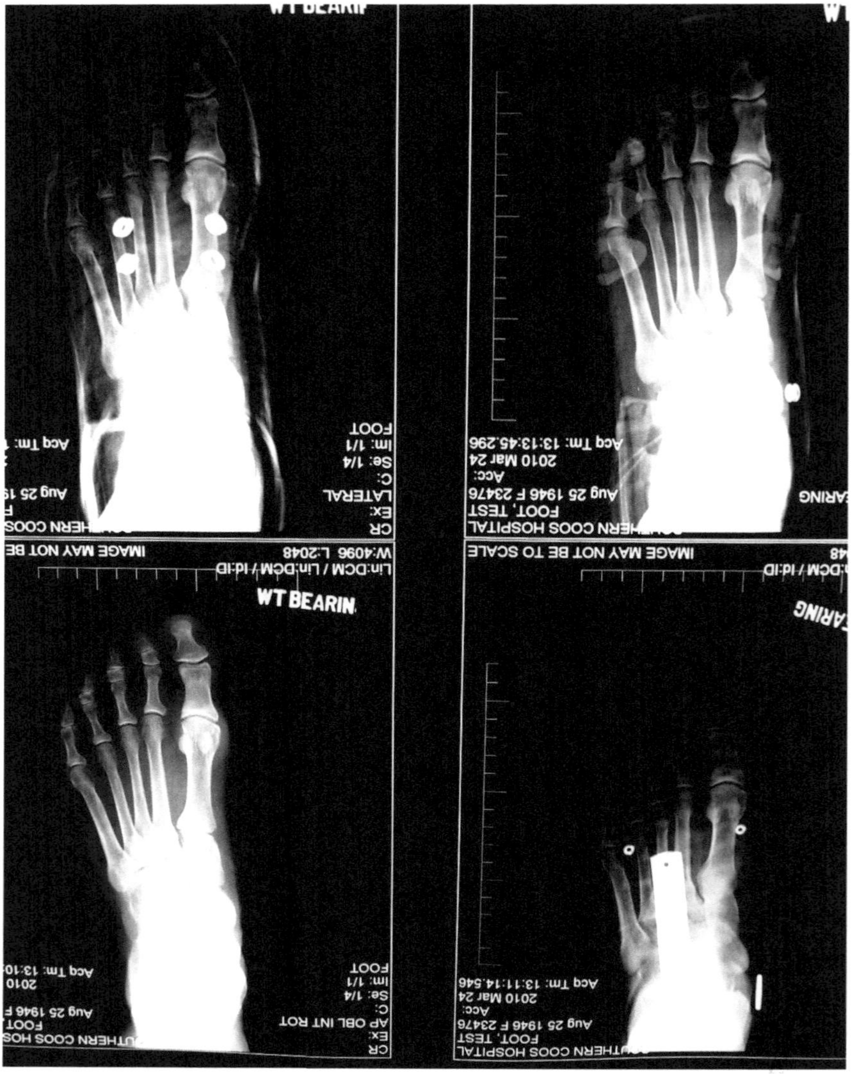

Figure 5.13 Clockwise from lower left (all standing): barefoot; running shoe (size 10); cross trainer (size 10); casual dress 2-in. heel (size 10).

outside the ±5-mm variation parameters and where the overlay/DiMaggio modified overlay approach demonstrates that toes fall out of line in their positioning. A careful evaluation may find that the toe box shape is the responsible factor. Although this factor may affect the general positioning of the toes through the forcing of the toes into proximity with each other, it might also mask the general morphology of the toes. This effect would be unlikely in and of itself to affect the heel-to-toe length of any impressions under consideration. In some examples of this form of restriction, the positions of just one, two, or three toes may be amended—typically, the fourth or fifth toes. If this situation is apparent through the shoe design and toe impression positions, it should be documented in the case notes as a possible cause of any variations observed. Indications that this may be a factor to be taken into account come from the shape of the toe box itself; distortions that are apparent in the toe box area of the upper surface of the shoe that relate to the toe positions; and wear, impressions within the shoe, or both that correspond to any toes that are believed to have been forced out of line.

Whether the shoes have fitted their usual wearer correctly can be an important fact to know when comparing shoes of different lengths. If a shoe is too long for the wearer, the foot could move about within the shoe creating a foot impression longer than expected for a foot of a particular size. This understanding can be relevant when shoes of different lengths are being compared and the wear features indicate that the longer pair of shoes has been too long for the wearer, whereas the short pair has been correctly sized. In such a scenario, where the longer shoes are found to contain a longer foot impression than the shorter shoes, the differences in foot impression length alone would therefore NOT preclude the shoes from having been worn by the same wearer (depending on the other wear features that are also apparent within these shoes).

Similarly, be aware of the possibility and effects of a shoe having been of inadequate width for its wearer, especially when considering the cross ball impression measurement. For example, the ball of the foot could have been compressed laterally, giving the impression that the cross ball length is less wide then it would be if allowed to adopt a more natural position. Consideration of the shoe in its entirety would provide support for this conclusion, particularly if corresponding distortions of the shoe upper are also apparent.

If the suspected owner of the shoe is available for examination, bare footprints from that person can be used in the comparison, as can any pathological features that may have manifested in the foot impressions being considered. Such features could include those that have amended the morphology of the foot (e.g., hallux valgus) and those that have had an effect on foot function (e.g., hyperpronation). Similarly, similar footwear of the suspect should be examined for sock liner images and transparency overlay comparisons to the questioned sock liner. One area of the image that we find very consistent between a person and his or her different footwear is the web space outline (Figure 5.14); therefore, comparing the dynamic in-shoe image of the foot is important in final analysis.

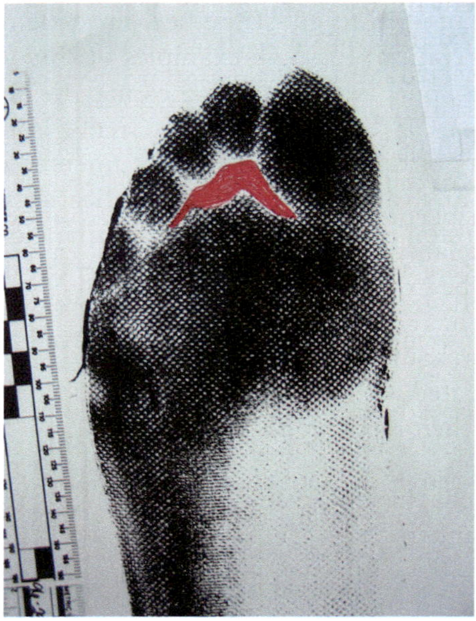

Figure 5.14 Web space outline.

5.9.7 Outsole Wear Patterns

The outsole wear patterns of footwear items that have been examined and compared should also be evaluated. Great caution is required when evaluating the comparisons between outsole wear patterns. Such patterns are not necessarily stable features, and it is known that they can be influenced by a multitude of variable factors (Vernon 2000; Vernon et al. 2004). Characteristic outsole wear patterns were previously considered to be created by known foot pathologies (Charlesworth 1961; Gibbard 1958a, 1958b; Gottlieb 1939; Hanby and Walker 1949; Lake 1943; Lucock 1980); however, it is now known that this is not the case (Vernon 2000; Vernon et al. 2003, 2004). A hierarchy of influence has now been constructed to show the factors that compete to influence the form of the outsole wear pattern of footwear (Vernon 2000; Vernon et al. 2004). This means that footwear belonging to the same person can, depending on circumstances, show quite different outsole wear patterns. Although this model is of clinical interest, its purpose in terms of identification involving shoe outsole wear patterns is to show that these features can be amended by three classes of variables, i.e., wear pattern differences observed between known and questioned footwear items do not necessarily mean that these shoes have different usual wearers. This can be problematic when attempting to use outsole wear patterns in human identification. They can however be used as another class indicator if identical patterns are observed across known and questioned footwear and if unusual wear patterns are repeated across known and questioned shoes, especially if a reason for such unusual wear patterns has been observed in a postulated wearer of these shoes. It is not possible, as previously thought, to examine the outsole wear pattern of a shoe in isolation and then name the causative pathology. To make such interpretations, a context is needed, such as may be provided by considering other wear features of the shoe, the history of that shoe, and the clinical features exhibited by the postulated wearer. If this context is available, then the evaluation of such wear features can become meaningful.

5.10 Conclusions

Footwear identification is a multidisciplinary process, but often the need to involve the podiatrist in this process is superfluous, particularly if the task is simply to link a shoe to a scene of crime. If the task is to associate or disassociate a person with shoes already linked to a crime (e.g., there is denial of ownership of shoes already linked to the crime scene), or there are differences between the wear features of compared shoes, then the very specialized knowledge of the podiatrist can be useful. For the footwear identification process to work smoothly, it is essential for each discipline specialist involved to understand and respect the contribution of other specialties and for podiatrists to recognize the strengths and limitations of their own highly specialized role in this task.

References

Charlesworth F. 1961. *Chiropody Theory and Practice.* London: Actinic Press Ltd.

Council of the Society of Shoe Fitters. 1991. *Fisher-George Memorial Student Membership Correspondence Course.* Norwich: The Society of Shoe Fitters.

Gibbard L.C. 1958a. The interpretation of wear marks on shoes as an aid to the diagnosis of foot troubles: Part 1. *British Chiropody Journal* 23: 231–3.

Gibbard L.C. 1958b. The interpretation of wear marks on shoes as an aid to the diagnosis of foot troubles: Part 2. *British Chiropody Journal* 23: 259–62.

Gottlieb A. 1939. The Foot in general practice. *The Chiropodist* 26: 316–23.

Hanby J.H. and Walker H.E. 1949. *The Principles of Chiropody.* London: Bailliere, Tindall and Cox.

Lake N.C. 1943. *The Foot.* 3rd ed. London: Bailliere, Tindall and Cox.

Lucock L.J. 1980. Identification from footwear. *The Chiropodist* 35: 343–50.

McInnes A.D., Hashmi F., Farndon L.J., Church A., Haley M., Sanger D.M. and Vernon W. 2012. Comparison of shoe-length fit between people with and without diabetic peripheral neuropathy: A case-control study. *Journal of Foot and Ankle Research* 5: 1–8. doi: 10.1186/1757-1146-5-9.

NIJ. 1999. National Commission on the future of DNA evidence. What every law enforcement office should know about DNA evidence. https://www.ncjrs.gov/nij/DNAbro/evi.html (Accessed December 9, 2015).

Nirenberg M. 2008. New method for examining the inside of footwear. *Journal of Forensic Identification* 58: 297–304.

Nixon B.P., Armstrong D.G., Wendell C., Vazquez J.R., Rabinovich Z., Kinbriel H.R., Rosales M.A. and Boulton A.J. 2006. Do US veterans wear appropriately sized shoes? The Veterans Affairs shoe size selection study. *Journal of the American Podiatric Medical Association* 96: 290–2.

Rossi W.A. 1992. Podometrics: A new methodology for foot typing. *Journal of Testing and Evaluation* 20: 301–311.

Rossi W.A. and Tennant R. 1984. *Professional Shoe Fitting.* New York: National Shoe Retailers Association.

Vernon W. 2000. The functional analysis of shoe wear patterns. PhD Diss., Sheffield Hallam University.

Vernon W., Brodie B., DiMaggio J., Gunn N., Kelly H., Nirenberg M., Reel S. and Walker J. 2009. *Forensic Podiatry: Role and Scope of Practice (In the Context of Forensic Human Identification).* International Association for Identification. http://www.theiai.org/disciplines/podiatry/podiatry_role_and_scope.pdf (Accessed March 26, 2010).

Vernon W., Parry A. and Potter M. 1999. Moving towards consensus: The first draft of an evaluative instrumental grid to interpret shoe wear patterns. *Journal of Forensic Identification* 49: 142–73.

Vernon W., Parry A. and Potter M. 2003. Consensus obtained in a Delphi study of shoe wear pattern experiences amongst podiatrists. *Journal of Forensic Identification* 53: 15–41.

Vernon W., Parry A. and Potter M. 2004. A theory of shoe wear pattern influence incorporating a new paradigm for the podiatric medical profession. *Journal of the American Podiatric Medical Association* 94: 261–8.

Forensic Gait Analysis

6

Forensic gait analysis involves the recognition and comparison of gait and features of gait, to assist the process of identification. The gait patterns and features of gait used in this process are usually those captured on closed-circuit television (CCTV) footage. This patterns and features then need to be examined in depth by the forensic podiatrist. As in other forensic identification processes, unknown (questioned) footage of the person of interest in relation to a crime scene is compared against known (reference) footage that has been made by a known person, usually a suspect. Conclusions are then made as to the value of the features, and they are concluded to either match or mismatch in this comparison. This chapter defines forensic gait analysis, describes the processes involved, and comments on cautions that should be adopted while performing this work.

6.1 Principles of Forensic Gait Analysis

Historically, practice in this area began in July 2000 when forensic gait analysis was first presented as evidence in a trial at the Central Criminal Court in the United Kingdom (Buncombe 2000). In this particular case, using his clinical expertise, Kelly, the podiatrist involved was able to recognize certain features of the gait of the perpetrator of a crime. By relating these features to the published literature, he was able to state that only 5% or less of the U.K. population would be expected to exhibit the gait features recognized (Buncombe 2000).

Forensic gait analysis has since continued to develop, mainly in the United Kingdom, but increasingly in many other countries where they are being developed within different legal systems. There are several definitions of forensic gait analysis, but to fully appreciate these meanings, it is first necessary to remember what is precisely meant by "gait" and "gait analysis" in their clinical context.

Gait itself is simply the manner of walking or stepping, or bearing or carriage while moving and is intended to propel the body in the desired direction, usually forward. Gait represents the most fundamental form of human movement (Watkins 2006). To achieve gait, a series of repetitive movements occur, producing sequences of steps and strides that produce forward motion and in their totality are described as the gait cycle. The gait cycle has two main phases: the stance phase, or that period in the gait cycle when the foot is in contact with the ground and the swing phase, when the foot is being swung forward and is not in contact with the ground (Decker and Albert 2002). During these phases, there is what is described as single- and double-support phases, when either one or both feet are in contact with the ground at a particular moment in the gait cycle. The swing phase, by definition, represents the single-support phase of the gait cycle; however, there is also a point within the gait cycle during which both feet together are in stance, and this is the period known as the double-support phase, and at that point lasts for just 10% of the gait cycle (Watkins 2006). These phases in the gait cycle can be broken down into considerably more detail to understand what is happening precisely at each and every point of the cycle.

The gait cycle as described in the literature (Decker and Albert 2002; Nixon et al. 2006; Watkins 2006) is usually considered from an ideal perspective, wherein normal gait has been explained as "A method of locomotion involving the use of the two legs, alternately, to provide both support and propulsion" (Whittle 2007). Where deviations occur from the norm, problems can occur, all of which are well known to podiatrists, physiotherapists, orthotists, orthopedic surgeons, and other professions who are concerned with problems of the functioning foot and lower limb. These deviations can be considered as functional anomalies within the gait cycle in which the anomalies themselves may be the direct cause of symptoms observed by the clinician, or as functional compensations that can be taking place in the presence of underlying pathologies. The work of podiatrists and some other clinicians involved in problems relating to the foot, the lower limb, and human movement is very much concerned with the recognition and management of such anomalies. The first phase of this work—recognition—involves gait analysis. Gait analysis is the process of quantification, interpretation, or both of human movement. There are two methods of gait analysis: qualitative and quantitative (Bartlett 1997).

Qualitative gait analysis is a nonnumerical evaluation of a movement and usually consists of a visual assessment of gait undertaken from the sides, front, and rear of the subject during walking (Perry 1990). The approach is routinely used by clinicians, particularly podiatrists who are taught first-level evaluation of gait during undergraduate and postgraduate education. In this clinical gait analysis, an examination of the subject's gait is made as he or she is walking and the gait features are then considered against a theoretical norm, thereby enabling any deviations from this norm to become apparent through observation. Subjective gait analysis is an experience-based skill that can be learned and improved with practice. As highlighted by Vernon (2000), caution is required in subjective gait analysis because such subjectivity can be prone to error. However, keeping this caution in mind, qualitative gait analysis is a valuable tool for clinicians to use in their evaluation of patients.

Quantitative gait analysis, in contrast, is a more in-depth form of gait analysis involving the collection and analysis of numerical data relating to the complex forces, pressures, and movements involved in gait. Such data are usually collected to allow movement to be studied and may include information such as linear and angular displacements, velocities, accelerations, forces, torques, energies, and powers (Bartlett 1997). This process is facilitated through the use of technology, such as computer-interfaced video cameras to measure patient motion, electrodes placed on the surface of the skin to appreciate muscle activity, and force platforms imbedded in a walkway to monitor the forces produced between the ambulatory subject and the ground.

Forensic gait analysis from the perspective of the podiatrist currently involves the recognition and comparison of nominal and some ordinal data and not the numerical (interval) forms of data that would be involved in objective or quantitative gait analysis. Kelly has however previously reported that "forensic gait analysis is undergoing quantitative development," which he has used in casework and in the development of an automated method of recognition,[1] although details are not currently available.

6.1.1 Definitions

Forensic gait analysis was first suggested by Kelly[2] to be "The identification of a person or persons by their gait or features of their gait, usually from closed circuit [sic] television (CCTV) footage and comparison to footage of a known individual." Forensic gait recognition was later defined by Grant (2006) as "the process of identifying people by the unique characteristics of their manner of walking," where "features are extracted from a person's gait in order to recognize them." This definition is currently somewhat optimistic; at the time of writing, the characteristics of walking and the features of a person's gait, as evaluated qualitatively, have not been demonstrated to be unique, although there is certainly class level distinction.

More recently, forensic gait analysis has begun to be used in the forensic examination and interpretation of footprint sequences found at scenes of crime, extending the techniques used beyond the analysis of recordings of gait captured on CCTV. Forensic gait analysis has been used to assist in cases involving forensic human identification in investigative and evidential capacities, including use by many security agencies as an investigational (intelligence) tool.[3]

[1] Kelly H.D., Personal communication, January 23, 2010.
[2] Kelly, H.D., Old Bailey Central Criminal Court London. R. v. Saunders, 2000.
[3] Kelly H.D., Personal communication, January 23, 2010.

For the purpose of this chapter, we would define forensic gait analysis as follows:

> The analysis, comparison, and evaluation of human gait including the components and features of gait, to assist the process of identification or to answer any other legal question concerning gait. This can involve the examination of recordings of moving images such as those captured by closed-circuit television (CCTV) and also sequences of foot and shoe prints that have been left at a site of interest.

Until recently, the practice of forensic gait analysis has been the exclusive domain of forensic podiatrists (Vernon et al. 2009, 11). Some other medically related professionals also have the background knowledge to be able to undertake this form of work, but with limited exceptions from a few particularly interested professionals, none have developed expertise in this area of practice. Academics in other specialized areas have however been considering the potential for the automated recognition of gait and thus have been attempting to develop biometric approaches to forensic gait analysis with this work being particularly investigated by computer engineers (Grant 2006; Nixon et al. 2006; Yun 2011). More work is required before this automated recognition technology can be used outside the laboratory; although a considerable amount of research has devoted to this area, the computational tasks required are still immense. As noted, however, Kelly has also reported that he is furthering the development of automatic gait recognition and publication of further detail is anticipated.

Forensic gait analysis as developed and practiced by podiatrists and the general biometric approach to automatic gait recognition both essentially look at a person's gait, although the methods used differ.

6.2 Methods of Comparison

One published biometric approach is an attempt to recognize gait by comparing repetitive patterns of a subject's gait cycle, with variations in this cycle being used to distinguish one gait pattern from another (Grant 2006). The biometric gait signature being worked on by Kelly[1] considers numerous aspects of gait in the gait recognition process. Forensic gait analysis as currently practiced by podiatrists is the recognition and comparison of particular forms or classes of gait, or of different class characteristics of the components of gait, by using known prevalence data, survey data, or personal experience to show how distinct the recognized features would be in the population being considered.

In practice, forensic podiatrists usually become involved in forensic gait analysis if the perpetrator(s) of a crime has been captured on CCTV recordings and his or her more obvious features, particularly facial identity, are obstructed or unclear. Forensic gait analysis is of particular use if the perpetrator(s) of a crime make deliberate attempts to cover up identity, e.g., by wearing hooded clothing or masks, or features are unclear because of image quality, shadow, or angle of view. Where such people are ambulant, this raises the potential for the analysis of gait, features of gait,[4] or both to assist in the identification process, when such features can be recognized. The focus for this work is on factors of podiatric importance, i.e., overall body movement during gait including foot and lower limb function anomalies recognizable within the speciality of podiatric biomechanics.

6.3 Methodology

At face level, the methods involved in forensic gait analysis seem to be relatively simple. The requirements are for questioned footage (also described as incident or unknown footage—recordings of the unknown perpetrator of the event in question) to be available as well as known footage (recordings made of a person suspected of being present in the questioned images) of acceptable quality. Both recordings would be examined sequentially (questioned footage followed by reference footage) by the podiatrist who would use his or her knowledge and skills in gait analysis when viewing and examining the recordings. The podiatrist would look for either the presence of common discriminating gait-related features in both sets of recordings that would show compatibility, or conversely any gait-related features that would demonstrate incompatibility. Although this process may seem simple, care is required in determining whether the images available can allow such comparisons to be made. It is usual for a preliminary examination to be made of all relevant recorded materials to determine whether forensic gait analysis is possible. If this preliminary examination determines that forensic gait analysis is possible, then forensic gait analysis could proceed to a full analysis, comparison, and evaluation of the recordings concerned. Ideally, the full analysis would be performed by another forensic gait analyst who has not been involved in the preliminary examination.

6.3.1 Requirements for Unknown and Known Footage to Be Submitted for Examination

When an initial inquiry is received to ask whether assistance can be provided in a particular case, it is important to ensure that the requesting person is aware that not all footage is appropriate or of acceptable quality for

[4] "The individual movements, positions and structures that collectively form the gait cycle" (Reidy 2015, adapted from draft Standard Operating Procedures document prepared by Vernon 2013).

forensic gait analysis. The submission of such inappropriate or poor-quality recordings may result in a considerable amount of time being wasted, first for the case investigators whose case may be negatively affected by unnecessary delays and second for the examining forensic gait analyst who may have agreed to provide the preliminary assessment free of charge to determine whether there would be any value in proceeding. To prevent this waste of time, the following information, which applies equally to unknown and known recordings, should be clearly communicated to the requesting person:

1. Before submitting recordings for preliminary examination, the referring person should check that all footage plays free of problems on any personal computer or laptop.
2. The footage to be submitted can often rely on proprietary software for playback. If this is the case, clear instructions as to how to use this software to play the footage should be submitted with the recordings. If the software is capable of playing the recordings at different speeds, backwards, or both as well as operating in normal playback mode, further operating details should be provided.
3. Footage submitted for preliminary assessment should only cover the relevant sections of the recordings, i.e., footage of the subject(s) of interest ambulating as opposed to standing.
4. All recordings submitted (unknown and known) should preferably be of a frame rate of at least 8 frames per second (fps) or higher.
5. Where more than one person is present in the recordings, short explanatory notes should be provided briefly describing the subject(s) of interest in the footage and the chronological points at which subject(s) appear [to enable the subject(s) to be recognized and distinguished from any other parties present].

6.3.2 Additional Requirements for Unknown Footage to Be Submitted for Examination

The requesting party should be advised that unknown footage should ideally meet several conditions to be useful for forensic gait analysis. These conditions should be communicated and are as follows:

1. Ideally, the subject's whole body should be in view for 10 or more steps. It may however still be possible to analyze footage with lower numbers of steps in view or when the whole body has not been captured, depending on the context of the recording.
2. The subject should be seen walking at what could be described as a reasonably normal pace.

3. The preferred viewpoints are from the front or side.
4. The subject's natural movement should preferably be unhindered (e.g., he or she should not carrying anything such as a heavy or bulky object that could interfere with the gait).
5. The subject's clothing should ideally allow a clear view of both foot and lower limb movement.
6. The frame rate should preferably be at least 8 fps or higher.
7. At some point in the recording, there should be a clear view of the subject walking.
8. The area where the subject is seen walking should be reasonably well lit, with minimal shadow and reflection interference (or adjustments have been made by the digital image analysts to compensate for such lighting problems).
9. The recordings should have reasonable resolution and ideally be contrasted well.
10. The subject should not be too distant from the camera.
11. Recordings or sections of recordings in which the subject is seen standing, fighting, or turning are of minimal or no use to forensic gait analysis.
12. Footage of the subject running is rarely of value unless he or she is displaying obvious gait anomalies.

6.3.3 Additional Requirements for the Collection of Known Footage

Although preexisting known footage is often already available for comparison with the questioned recording, this reference footage may not have been captured before the request for case assistance is received. Where this reference footage still needs to be taken, it can often be helpful to advise the instructing agencies as to how to collect this footage appropriately for comparative purposes. Where the recordings have already been taken, similar advice should be given covering conditions that should be met for that footage to be of use in forensic gait analysis. The intention is for the known and unknown recordings to be matched as closely as possible to eliminate as many variables as possible that could potentially affect the subject's gait. The requirements or advice to be given for the collection of reference footage are as follows:

1. The camera-to-subject angle in the known recordings should match the camera-to-subject angle in the unknown recordings as closely as possible.
2. As far as possible, the subject's walking speed in the known recordings should be matched closely to that of the unknown footage.

3. There should be a clear field of view between the camera and subject throughout.
4. The area from where the image is to be captured should be well lit, shadow free, and without interference from reflections.
5. The image should ideally be clear, not grainy, and contrasted well.
6. The whole of the body should ideally be in shot for 10 or more steps (although it may still be possible to analyze footage with lower numbers of steps in view depending on the context of the recording).
7. The subject should ideally be wearing clothing that allows a clear view of foot and lower limb movement.
8. As far as possible, the subject's natural movement should be unimpeded (e.g., free from handcuffs, not carrying any heavy objects that would interfere with gait), unless attempting to match a situation seen in the questioned footage.[5]

Although forensic podiatrists would provide advice over the collection of such recordings, it would be unusual for the podiatrist to become directly involved with this process. This role is usually left to those with expertise in carrying out covert recordings. Once this known footage has been collected and forwarded to the examining podiatrist, the recordings are subjected to the same initial checks as detailed above.

6.4 Assessment of Recordings

6.4.1 Quality Requirements

The key difference in dealing with CCTV images as opposed to image analysis in the clinical setting lies in the quality of the images, additional variables that the examiner has to deal with in the analysis, and the significance of these variables. In clinical settings, high-quality, high-resolution detailed images from standardized perspectives are used, whereas CCTV images are usually of much lower quality and resolution. CCTV images may also contain a significant number of variables that need to be taken into account through differences in positioning and context of the CCTV scenarios. Thus, the initial tasks of the examining podiatrist are to prepare for the appropriate examination of the images concerned and to determine whether the images are of sufficient quality to allow meaningful analysis. Although the

[5] Requirements for the submission of questioned and known (reference) recordings are adapted from a protocol prepared for use by the Forensic Podiatry Unit, Podiatry Service, Sheffield Teaching Hospitals.

instructions detailed above will have been provided to the authorities who are submitting footage for preliminary analysis, these instructions are only basic for the purposes of eliminating the worst examples of poor submitted recordings. The quality checks undertaken by the forensic gait analyst are more stringent and determine whether meaningful analysis and comparisons can be carried out.

Suitable equipment is required to allow meaningful examination of the recordings. Previously, in the United Kingdom, the Home Office listed recommended equipment for the examination and comparison of video recordings as evidence. However, with the wide availability and increasing quality of recording playback equipment, this list is no longer produced. The examiner should however ensure that there is either direct or indirect access to appropriate equipment, including

- Computer and high-quality DVD player with playback, pause, slow motion, and fast forward features
- High-quality videotape player (e.g., Super VHS) with playback, pause, slow motion, and fast forward features (becoming less of a requirement because with the increasing use of digital recordings, CCTV-associated videotape is now rare)
- High-resolution screen or monitor
- Video editing software
- CCTV video demultiplexing, recording, and enhancement software capable of extracting and displaying camera numbers, time, and date information on the examined images

After selecting the equipment to be used in the examination process and obtaining any known footage for comparison purposes, the next task is to ensure that the original/master recordings are available for viewing, whether DVD-based recordings or videotape. These originals, and not copies, are viewed to verify that any copies that are worked with are consistent with the original. Having viewed the original/master recordings and compared any copies provided against these original recordings for compatibility, it is acceptable to use the copies for analysis. With the continued improvement of technology and digital storage devices, copies in their original format (and copies where there is no data loss on transfer or conversion of the original format) taken from computer hard drives do not show loss of data. For forensic gait analysis, it is important that detail is not "lost" if compression of the data has been performed when copying from the original material. This loss is more likely to occur when the copying or conversion of the original footage involves compression of the images. Copying onto portable storage devices such as DVD is a convenient way in which to receive the material for analysis, and high-speed connections allow for video footage to be transferred more rapidly between organizations. However, if such electronic transfer is being considered, the preferred form of transfer needs to be agreed on by sending and receiving parties, with particular emphasis on security of the images. The online file hosting service Dropbox™ is regularly used for this purpose. This document storage and transfer facility can be used to securely send and receive files, images, and video recordings. Although such transfers are made securely with Dropbox, personal experience has suggested that not all organizations permit the use of this service because of concerns that security could be tighter. If an organization has such concerns, it may be necessary to transfer information by hand.

A preliminary analysis should now be made of the material provided (questioned footage first followed by the reference footage) to determine whether this footage is of suitable quality to allow meaningful analysis. This preliminary analysis is essential to help prevent errors being made that will not stand up to later scrutiny.

Birch et al. (2013) prepared and tested a tool for objectively assessing the quality of a recording in the context of evidence provision (Table 6.1). The tool is applied at the initial quality assessment stage of the examination. In working through the quality assessment, the examiner initially considers the picture itself. Others factors are also considered such as how the image varies between being very sharp or very blurred. The contrast in relation to the detail of interest would next be evaluated, as would the brightness of the image, i.e., whether the image is too bright, or too dark, or where the image lies on a continuum between these two extremes.

Having considered the picture overall, considerations over the suitability of the image are then made, and these considerations are limited to factors such as whether the lighting within the image is suitable and whether there is interference from shadows or reflections.

The direction from which the person within the recording is being viewed is also an important factor in considering and assessing the quality of the image from a forensic podiatrist's perspective. The person within the image could have been recorded from the side; front or back; or from the same plane, above, or below. Depending on what is of interest in the image, the positioning may or may not be detrimental to the quality of the recording in relation to the features of concern. The question that should also be considered is that of what information can be extracted from the footage or image(s) under examination.

In relation to the person of interest within the recording, another quality requirement is the detail of that person present within the recorded image(s). In podiatric gait analysis, whole body analysis should be considered as part of the evaluation. In forensic gait analysis, all aspects of the upper and lower body may not necessarily be available for viewing. The examiner must therefore consider whether all or part of the upper and lower body, respectively,

Table 6.1 Tool for Assessing the Quality of a Recording for Forensic Gait Analysis

Tool for assessing the quality of a recording for forensic gait analysis

Name of analyst:		
Date:		
Footage reference:		
Footage rating:		A = most suitable for use. E = least suitable for use

Picture						
very sharp	○	○	◉	○	○	very blurred
very good contrast	○	○	◉	○	○	very poor contrast
too bright	○	○	◉	○	○	too dark

Lighting						
very good lighting	○	○	◉	○	○	very bad lighting
no shadow interference	○	○	◉	○	○	significant shadow interference
no reflection interference	○	○	◉	○	○	significant reflection interference
direction of light source good	○	○	◉	○	○	direction of light source poor

Direction						
directly from the side	○	○	◉	○	○	directly from the front or back
from below the subject	○	○	◉	○	○	from above the subject

Frame rate						
continuous flow of image	○	○	◉	○	○	series of still images

Subject						
whole of upper body in shot	○	○	◉	○	○	none of upper body in shot
whole of lower body in shot	○	○	◉	○	○	none of the lower body in shot
moving very fast	○	○	◉	○	○	moving very slowly
10 steps or more in shot	○	○	◉	○	○	2 steps or less in shot
clothing good for gait analysis	○	○	◉	○	○	clothing poor for gait analysis

Distance of subject to camera						
Too close for gait to be viewed	○	○	◉	○	○	Too far for meaningful analysis

is in view and whether the detail available in its totality is adequate for forensic gait analysis.

Similarly, the effects of clothing need to be taken into account. In podiatric gait analysis, podiatrists are interested in the movement of the body, and the type of clothing worn can facilitate, impede, or even not

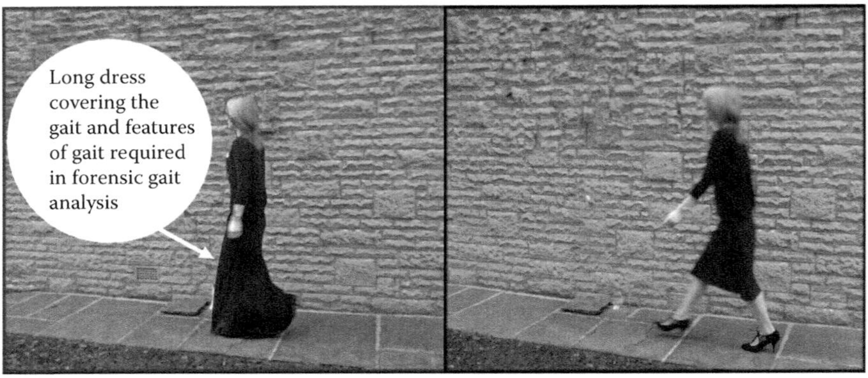

Figure 6.1 Comparison of clothing types that can affect the ability to perform forensic gait analysis.

affect the analysis. For example, if tight clothing is worn, the gait and features of gait may become more easily accessible to the observer than they would be in the presence of loose, or flowing clothing that may hide the features of interest (Figure 6.1).

Speed of motion must also be taken into account when determining whether the quality of the image is adequate for forensic gait analysis. For example, if the subject is moving very quickly, a meaningful analysis may be prevented both from the perspective of lost detail and from changed gait form, i.e., from walking to running, whereby like-for-like gait comparisons are not so easy to undertake and in many cases are simply not possible to obtain.

Consideration must also be given to frame rate when assessing the suitability of the recording for gait analysis. The greater the frequency of the recording measured in Hertz, the greater the amount of detail that can be seen. Recordings may however vary considerably, with digital video recordings typically recorded at 50 Hz, whereas many CCTV images are recorded at 2 Hz or less. In the interests of economy and practicality, low frame rate recordings are suitable for analysis, but when the gaps are more than 1 second between images, this information may be unreliable and whether the images can be useful to forensic gait analysis may depend on the amount of material available for examination. For example, a single frame being taken every 30 seconds would make true forensic gait analysis impossible, because this analysis requires assessment of the kinetic flow of gait as opposed to single, disconnected images many seconds apart. In such circumstances, it may be possible to recognize single features of the foot and lower limb that contribute to the gait form; however, these single features would need to be very obvious and noted to be repeated in the footage to guard against the possibility of these features being isolated variations from the normal repetitive gait cycle for the person under observation. The quality assessment as detailed above should be undertaken for both unknown and known recordings.

Birch et al. (2014) performed a study on the effect of frame rate on the ability of experienced gait analysts to identify characteristic of gait from CCTV recordings. In this study, a subject's lower limb was strapped tightly to produce a defined functional limitation of the lower limb on the side of interest. Various versions of the same footage seen at different frame rates were then produced and sent to participating gait analysis experts. The first version distributed was that at the lowest frame rate (one frame every four seconds) and the final distributed version was that at the highest frame rate (25 fps). Participants had to comment on what they could see within each version of the footage sent, and once these comments had been received from all participants, they were then given access the next round of recordings taken at a faster frame rate. This process continued until all versions of the footage had been examined and commented on by the gait analysis experts.

The study confirmed that frame rate affects the ability of forensic gait analysts to identify characteristics of gait captured on CCTV recordings. It also found that experts involved in the project could recognize some features of gait at low frame rates. The project conclusions recommended that footage should be taken at as high a frame rate as possible to help optimize the work of forensic gait analysts (Birch et al. 2014).

The Birch et al. (2013) study which lead to the production of a tool for objectively assessing the quality of a recording in the context of evidence provision (Table 6.1) was based on consensus among a small group of experts in forensic gait analysis. Although it was previously suggested that consensus techniques can become more reliable with larger panel sizes (Couper 1984; Fink et al. 1984), given the highly specialized nature of forensic gait analysis, the number of experts available to participate in such a project was extremely limited. Although consensus was achieved over factors to be considered to assess the quality of a recording for forensic gait analysis, later experience with the resultant template indicated that one other factor, namely, distance of the subject from the camera, should be considered. Where a subject is a considerable distance away from the camera, assessing gait and features of gait can become difficult, or even impossible. As such, although not included in the original template, forensic gait analysts are also advised to consider this additional factor as part of the initial quality checks to determine whether a recording is suitable for forensic gait analysis.

The template itself should be applied at the initial quality assessment stage of the examination. Where the quality of the image is deemed unsuitable for analysis, consideration should be given as to whether the image could be enhanced to improve the detail within the image. An appropriate laboratory specializing in digital technology assessment could consider the quality issue and where possible, adjust various aspects of the image to attempt to enable more meaningful analysis. Such adjustments would typically cover minor adjustments to lighting and contrast. It must be recognized, however, that laboratories, particularly those relating to sampling rate, angle of view, and clothing restrictions, cannot correct many problems, but if any noncorrectable problems exist with the known recordings, a request can be made for a further attempt to collect improved recordings.

Once the examiner is satisfied that the images are of such quality as to allow meaningful forensic gait analysis, assessment to consider the gait and features of gait are undertaken. For example, the examiner makes an in-depth assessment of the questioned and known recordings to determine and document any characteristic gaits or features of gait recognized in the footage. In making this assessment, the recordings are initially be viewed in their totality at normal and slowed speed, with the sections of interest being noted. The focus is then placed on these particular sections that would again be viewed repeatedly at normal speed, in slow motion, and frame by frame. Observations made should initially describe the overall context of the recordings, such as noted in the following example:

> Recording AB/1 consisted of one daytime color video recording of a male in a small yard. This person is seen to undergo a range of activities including standing, interrupted walking and push-up exercises in one corner of the enclosure.

The examiner would then comment on the sections of the recording that are of further interest, e.g., as follows:

> In the first recording, many of the low frequency frames were of poor quality with the feet being obscured, and therefore did not allow meaningful assessment to be made. However, in one section of the recording designated 15:30:16 to 15:30:24, the right foot of the male present within the image could be clearly viewed.

The examiner would then proceed to detail meaningful gait observations made for each frame that is to be considered further, as noted in the following examples:

1. Frame 15:30:16: Despite the image being somewhat poor, the right foot is forward, seen at heel strike and is abducted.
2. Frame 15:30:22: The right foot is forward and again abducted when compared to the pavement edge with the forefoot being situated much nearer to the pavement than the rearfoot.

Such observations should be made for both questioned and known recordings for later comparison and evaluation.

6.4.2 Observation Framework

The forensic gait analyst follows an approach similar to that used in clinical gait observation to describe the nature, position, and movement of the gait of the subject being observed. As such, the following considerations may be examined[6]:

- *Symmetry:* whether the left and right sides are symmetrical during gait or whether the gait itself is erratic and variable
- *Relationship between the head and torso:* any rolling movement of the head and torso; the relative position of the head to the midline of the torso in frontal and sagittal planes
- *Shoulder position and movement:* whether the shoulders are level or inclined to either left or right as well as any apparent dipping movement of the shoulders to either side during gait
- *Arm swing:* degree and nature of arm swing; whether there is absent or erratic arm swing movement on either side; relationship of arm swing to the torso in terms of degree of anterior and posterior movement and the degree of elbow flexion
- *Hips:* linear motion; presence and degree of circumduction
- *Knees:* temporal relationship between angle (flexion, extension, or hyperextension) and heel strike and heel lift
- *Base of gait:* width (i.e., whether very narrow, narrow, moderate, or wide) and any variability present
- *Feet:* orientation in relation to the midline of the body during the stance phase of gait (including any asymmetry between left and right)
- *Feet:* orientation in relation to the midline of the body during the swing phase of gait (including any asymmetry between left and right)
- *Feet:* relationship between forefoot position, degree of inversion/eversion, abduction/adduction, and heel strike; whether heel raise occurs at a relatively early stage; asymmetries between left and right

If possible, step and stride is also described in spatial terms, with asymmetries between left and right sides being noted. Cadence could also be described if relevant and particularly if enough footage is available to allow cadence to be determined.

It is important to record in the case notes if any of the above-mentioned considerations could not be determined along with the reasons (e.g., limited view, poor camera angle).

When providing such descriptions, terminology can be an issue because terms used to describe gait across the various disciplines involved in gait

[6] This list was adapted from Reidy, S. 2015. *Standard Operating Procedures for Forensic Gait Analysis: Version 1.* Sheffield Teaching Hospitals Internal document, referring to an unpublished checklist created and used by Birch.

analysis are diverse and often incorrectly used (Birch et al. 2015). As Birch et al. (2015) point out, the use of complex professional language is often encouraged in the wider professional field, but work undertaken within the criminal justice system also needs to be understood by nonexperts. As such, care should be taken to ensure that appropriate and accepted terms, where possible, avoid unnecessary complexity when used to describe gait and its components during initial note taking through subsequent written and verbal communications (including any resultant expert report) and subsequently in court documents. This clarity may require the use of glossary or footnote explanations throughout the work to assist the nonexpert reader (Birch et al. 2015).

6.4.3 Recognizable Features

Gait analysis performed under clinical or laboratory conditions allows a wide range of gait anomalies and characteristics to be more easily recognized and identified than those seen on CCTV footage using current technologies. Examples of the features and conditions that are apparent through such analysis tend to be the more obvious gait forms and features that could include, e.g., ataxic, calcaneal, hemiplegic, and asymmetric gait forms and ankle equinus, genu varum, genu valgum, and tibial varum gait features. The task of the examiner is to recognize and record the presence of these features where their presence is incontrovertible. If there is the possibility of such features having been affected by a known variable (e.g., standing or running as opposed to walking positions being viewed), other reasons for the identified features must be considered as appropriate to prevent erroneous conclusions.

6.5 Comparisons and Evaluation

Having worked through unknown and then known recordings in that order, the forensic podiatrist must then compare the detail recorded as being present in both sets of recordings. As in all forensic comparisons, the examiner must not only look for compatible features but also, with equal rigor, features that suggest incompatibility, i.e., the recordings could not have been of the same person. It is also important to take into account those features noted that may represent the same class of condition, but that may not necessarily relate to that particular person's usual gait form.

Having compared the gait and features of gait from unknown and then known recordings, the examiner must evaluate the significance of his or her findings. It is usual to consider compatible features from all compared recordings and to then determine their prevalence in the population of interest to judge what level of individuality a particular feature demonstrates.

The prevalence can be obtained from the literature, surveys, databases, or unpublished data. Where this does not exist, the examiner may need to undertake an additional item of work to quantify the prevalence within a given population for the purpose of the particular exercise. In this way, a numerical conclusion as to the significance of isolating the same feature or features in both known and questioned recordings can be made.

6.6 Cautions

Although forensic gait analysis is often relatively straightforward, it is frequently time-consuming. There are nevertheless several cautions that the examiner must be aware of during casework.

The need to always examine the questioned recordings before the reference recordings. In recent times the need to guard against bias and error in forensic practice has been given attention (Byrd 2006; Dror and Charlton 2006; Smith and Bond 2015), with the issue of confirmation bias[7] being of particular interest. Although several actions can be taken to reduce bias and error, one particular action relates to the need to always view the questioned recordings before the reference recordings. This approach helps prevent what has been described in another forensic discipline as the known item showing the examiner what they need to look for in the questioned item, i.e., giving the examiner information that would lead him or her to what may be seen as a preferred outcome (Byrd 2006), namely, a conclusion that the items examined match together through preconception.

Could the usual gait pattern have been amended in either or both of the recordings used for comparison? The examiner is interested in the compatibility of usual gait forms or features of gait and whether it is likely that these forms or features have been significantly affected to visibly alter the person's gait, features of gait, or both. It is possible for these features to be affected through the effects of external variables such as immediate effects of alcohol or drugs, temporary antalgic gait forms through the effects of short-term injury, and perhaps deliberate attempts to alter gait in the forensically aware criminal. Without maintaining an awareness of such possibilities, such affectations of the gait may potentially lead to either an incorrect conclusion

[7] "Confirmation bias is when people observe more, give extra emphasis to, or intentionally look for evidence that would validate their existing beliefs and expectations and are likely to excuse or completely ignore evidence that could reject their beliefs" (Byrd 2006).

of incompatibility, where a temporary state is present in one recording alone; or, alternately, to an incorrect conclusion of compatibility through the presence of a temporary class of gait/gait feature in one of the recordings, suggesting a compatibility that is not usually present.

Forensic gait analysis is a class-level identification technique. The features that can be recognized and used in forensic gait analysis are class-level features, i.e., features that demonstrate incontrovertible compatibility between similar items.[8] Thus, the conclusions that can be reached do not represent the unique levels of individuality afforded by true identifying characteristics. They do, however, afford a degree of discrimination that can either be used to discriminate between persons within a closed population, or alternately, in conjunction with other evidential features to strengthen conclusions in relation to individuality.

The forensic podiatrist undertaking forensic gait analysis must not comment on matters outside his or her expertise. Although this point seems obvious, it can nevertheless be misleadingly easy to deviate from areas requiring forensic podiatry expertise into those more appropriately covered by other disciplines. Examples of pitfalls to be avoided in this respect include not commenting on the particular characteristics of clothing (other than the fact that clothing has or has not impaired the ability to comment on specific aspects of the gait) and not providing an estimate of a person's height from the footage examined. A forensic podiatrist should only provide an opinion on such matters within his or her expertise or if with proven adequate training and experience in these specialty areas. An understanding of the fact that such factors can affect the gait is required (Vernon et al. 2009), but the forensic podiatrist should not extend his or her opinion to anything beyond that level of understanding.

The forensic podiatrist should not extend the opinion expressed in his or her reports beyond the point at which any competent forensic podiatrist would agree with the findings. The only safe way to practice forensic gait analysis is to adhere to agreed levels of understanding. Podiatric gait analysis has an abundance of competing "theories" and differences of opinion, few of which are truly research based. As with all areas of forensic expertise, the forensic podiatrist should confine his or her opinion within reports to the facts that, by definition, will be that level which is at that moment beyond dispute. This approach would avoid adopting any of the debated and disputed podiatric biomechanics theories that are yet to be validated. It is however also

[8] See earlier section on principles of forensic podiatry for a detailed explanation of the formal term "class characteristic".

important to note that when acting as an expert witness in court, any expert witness can be asked to give an opinion based on his or her expertise and experience. The point being made here, however, is that when reporting a case, this report should be mindful of the scientific basis of the profession.

Forensic gait analysis in the forensic examination and interpretation of footprint/footwear sequences

In addition to analyzing and comparing gait forms as captured on CCTV images, forensic podiatrists are also beginning to be asked to consider and, if possible, interpret sequences of footprints/footwear found at crime scenes. Requests of this nature can initially be made if such sequences are present at crime scenes and if an opinion is required for investigative purposes. This can include situations where leads are being sought as to what activities have taken place at a scene of crime or where a suspect has gait problems that the investigators hope may be apparent from the footprint/footwear sequences. Similarly the sequences of prints can be used to help determine or confirm whether there has been more than one person present at a scene, particularly where both people may have worn the same style and size of shoe. Here, the forensic footwear or marks examiners can also help determine such differences through their expertise in outsole wear and damage feature comparisons, which can be used to distinguish between different sets of footwear sequences. This is a situation where working together to address such considerations could be advantageous. Also, additional footprints or footwear marks may have been left by third parties legitimately present at the scene (e.g., the person who discovered the crime, emergency service personnel), and appropriate questioning should be used to determine this possibility.

Footprint/footwear sequencing for forensic gait analysis can be divided into two distinct phases before any comparisons are undertaken (if required).

The first phase involves determining the sequence of prints available for examination. There may be multiple prints from multiple people who each may have left multiple sequences of prints at the scene, and all of which at first view seem complex and confusing (Figure 6.2). From a podiatry perspective, techniques developed by the tracking community can be used. This is a stage of the work that may require multidisciplinary approaches. If the forensic podiatrist does not have training and experience in tracking techniques or if his or her experience is limited, it may be advisable to bring in someone experienced in tracking to undertake this work. Tracking is a highly skilled specialized discipline whose experts are experienced in interpreting the manifestations of human ambulation in all of its forms and in the presence of many variables; and in anything other than basic scenarios their involvement in determining a person's footprint/footwear sequence at a crime scene is highly recommended.

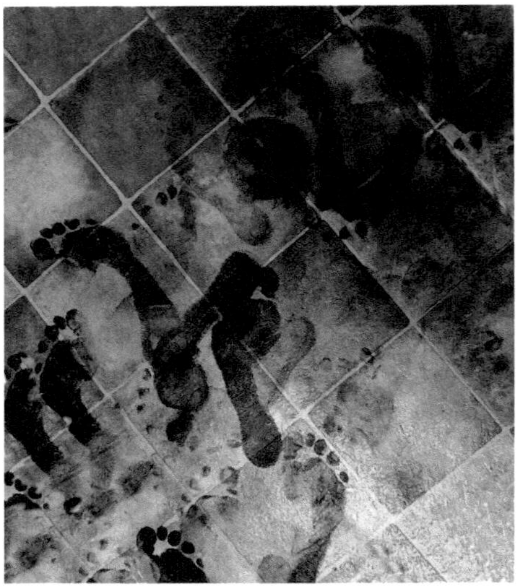

Figure 6.2 Multiple footprints at the crime scene.

Assuming that the situation in which footprint/footwear sequences are available is relatively simple to work through, the preliminary assessment is founded on the principle that the person who passed through the scene leaving a sequence of prints has a habitual gait form. As such, distances between steps and strides should be predictable and approximately the same during a walking sequence.

To use this knowledge, the following measurements would apply in attempting to determine a particular sequence of footprints at a crime scene:

- Overall footprint width and length
- Step length as measured from the back of heel
- Stride length as measured from the back of heel

The first task in determining a footprint sequence would be to find as clear an example as possible of two or more consecutive footprints within the sequence. The width and length of each print can be measured to show the dimension required for any print that is part of that sequence. Measurements of step, stride, or both show the approximate expected distances at which the next step in a particular sequence can be expected to be found. As such, the forensic gait analyst would use this knowledge to attempt to find the next step, stride, or both in a particular sequence. Although care is needed to manage situations where the person leaving the prints has slowed down or accelerated the gait pattern, this technique can be very successful in determining step and stride sequences and if single prints are missing, it can be used to find where the subsequent print in the sequence should be present to maintain continuity.

As noted above, the involvement of someone with tracking skills could be very useful at this stage of the analysis. In addition, once a sequence of prints seems to have been found, contact with a forensic marks or footwear examiner may be useful. This specialist can use knowledge relating to the level of blood or other substrates staining a shoe outsole. Given that as the person walks, materials from the outsole can be transferred to the ground and as such become less pronounced, this information can be used with someone with expertise in this field to show a footprint sequence. Working with a footwear or marks expert in this way has the potential to triangulate the findings and opinions of the forensic podiatrist by examining the footprints in such a different manner, and agreement between the podiatrist and footwear/marks examiner has been achieved.

Once a sequence of footprints has been determined, the next task is to analyze these footprints. The sequence can be used to determine step and stride length, base of gait, and angle of gait for both feet. This aspect of the work can indicate the habitual gait form of the person who left the footprint sequence as well as any variations from the expected norm (e.g., exaggerated angle of gait, wide or narrow base of gait, differences between left and right sides, and unexpected spatial variations between each step and stride sequence).

Within the clinical literature, criticism has previously been made of the fact that there have been several papers suggesting different means of determining landmarks of the foot and of measuring step, stride, and the angle and base of gait (Wilkinson et al. 1995). In addition to noting these different approaches, Wilkinson et al. (1995) also commented on there being a lack of precise definitions with regard to the landmarks selected when using these methods in measuring gait parameters from footprints. Through critical consideration of these various preexisting methods, Wilkinson et al. (1995) worked through the various perspectives on this subject area and suggested a preferred approach in the form of step-by-step guidance. Accepting the logic of this work in conjunction with a follow-up reliability study by two authors of the original paper (Wilkinson and Menz 1997) that demonstrated high reliability of the proposed methods, this has been our preferred approach to footprint analysis in forensic investigation situations to date. The approach and measurements advocated by Wilkinson et al. (1995) are as follows.

Creating a longitudinal bisecting line for each foot by adapting methods advocated by Shores (1980) (Figures 6.3–6.5)

1. The vertical lines of a grid are initially aligned with the medial border of the first toe and forefoot, whereas a horizontal grid line is aligned with the apex of the first toe (Figure 6.3). The horizontal lines of the

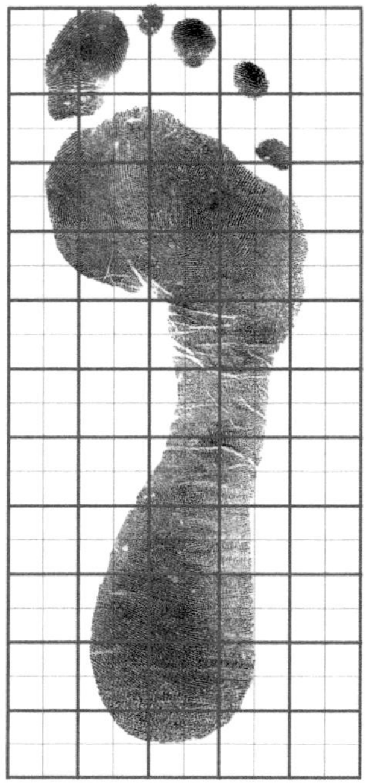

Figure 6.3 Creating a vertical bisecting line of the foot: initial grid placement.

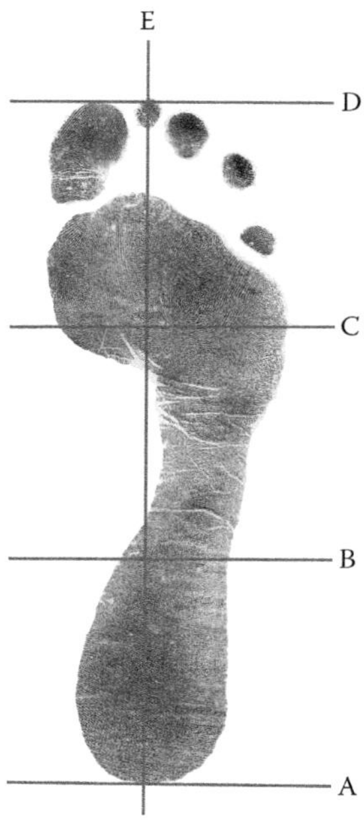

Figure 6.4 Creating a longitudinal bisecting line for each foot: dividing the foot into thirds longitudinally.

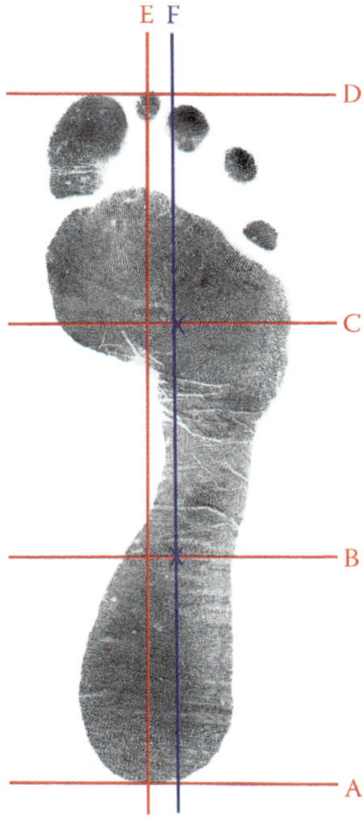

Figure 6.5 Creating a longitudinal bisecting line for each foot.

grid are used to locate and mark the rear of the heel (A) and most anterior aspect of the print (D) irrespective of whether this is the first toe. A longitudinal line (E) situated between these two points is then divided into three equal parts by drawing horizontal lines across the print at the one-third intervals. The posterior line (B) will cross the heel area of the foot and the anterior line (C) the ball of the foot (Figure 6.4).

2. Where lines B and C cross the foot, the center of that part of the foot is determined and connected by a longitudinal line (F) that runs through the length of the entire foot—the bisecting line of the foot (Figure 6.5).
3. The point at which line F crosses the rearmost line B is the reference point for the back of heel from which other reference lines are taken.
4. Where a shod footprint as opposed to a bare or socked footprint is being considered, the method would be adapted accordingly using outsole as opposed to bare footprint landmarks.

Determining the combined line of progression and angle of gait (Figure 6.6)

1. The approach of Wilkinson et al. (1995) describes the angle of gait as that angle formed between the bisecting line of the foot as determined above and the central line of progression of the whole body (Figure 6.6).

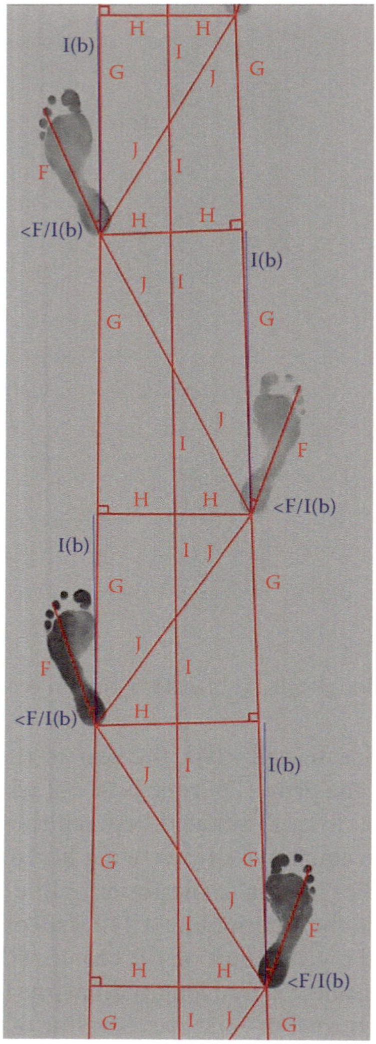

Figure 6.6 Gait evaluation from walking patterns. (F = bisecting line of the foot, G = ipsilateral line of progression/stride length, H = base of gait, I = central line of progression, J = step, I(b) = line drawn parallel to the central line of progression to assist in measuring angle of gait, <F/I(b) = angle of gait, GH intersection to next GH intersection = step measurement.)

2. A line (G) is drawn connecting the rearmost aspect of the heel of a print to the rearmost aspect of the heel on the following ipsilateral[9] print. This line represents the ipsilateral line of progression.

[9] Ipsilateral in this context refers to footprints on the same side (i.e., left to left or right to right) as opposed to footprints on opposite sides (i.e., left to right or right to left).

3. A line (H) is drawn from the rearmost aspect of the heel to meet the ipsilateral line of progression for the opposing footprints at right angles to that line.
4. The midpoint of line H is marked for each footprint and the midpoint all lines H are connected, giving line I—the central line of progression that may vary between steps and as such represents an approximated best fit.
5. The angle of gait [F/I (b)] can then be measured by comparing the bisecting line (F) of the footprint to a line drawn parallel to the central line of progression (I) for each and every footprint.

Determining the base of gait (Figure 6.6)
Although Wilkinson et al. (1995) recognized that determining the base of gait can be undertaken in many ways, they advocate the use of line H, as determined above, to represent the base of gait.

Determining step length (Figure 6.6)
Although steps are represented by lines (J) connecting the rearmost aspect of the heel of contralateral prints, Wilkinson et al. (1995) advocate that this is measured by considering the positioning of the back of each heel in relation to the ipsilateral lines of progression (G). As such, step length would be represented by the distance between the rearmost points of a particular footprint to the point where line H of the contralateral footprint meets the lien of progression of the earlier footprint.

Determining stride length (Figure 6.6)
Stride length is represented by the ipsilateral line of progression, line (G) connecting the rearmost aspect of the heel of ipsilateral prints.

Although these measurements can be used to describe the various parameters of sequences of footprints, in a forensic context they are best viewed as a means of clarifying and demonstrating observations in relation to the footprint sequences. It is also important to view the footprint descriptions so derived in context, i.e., taking into account the situation in which the print sequences have been left, with emphasis on variable factors that may have affected the form of the prints. As such, when looking for characteristics of the gait of someone who has left a sequence of footprints, account should be taken on whether the prints are midsequence, or instead are present at the start or end of a sequence where the person may have been accelerating from a starting point or slowing down at the end of the sequence. Similarly, account needs to be made for the potential for prints to have been amended by variables such as variations in terrain, inclination, declination, the need to negotiate obstacles, and nonlinear walking (e.g., walking in curves or around corners). There is also the possibility of the print sequence having been affected by the carrying of heavy weights and the excessive consumption of alcohol. In addition, whether or not the person has been walking should be considered and if not, how the alternative gait forms may have impacted on the characteristics of the footprint sequence should be noted. Such analyses may be more difficult to anticipate than CCTV analysis of gait, the latter of which provides additional contextual detail to show whether any such factors have been present. Taking all known variables into account, the examiner could use the gait features as determined above to show the habitual characteristics of the gait of the person who left a print sequence.

6.7 Conclusions

Although forensic gait analysis is the most recent area of forensic podiatry practice, it is the fastest growing subspecialty through the potential to help with identification from CCTV images where few other identifying features are apparent. Forensic gait analysis has also recently begun to be used in the analysis of footprint sequences found at crime scenes. There is the potential for forensic gait analysis to be developed much further through additional supportive research, improvements in technology, and developments in practice. Such further development could lead to forensic gait analysis becoming one of the most valuable tools that forensic podiatry can offer to the identification process.

References

Bartlett, R. 1997. *Introduction to Sports Biomechanics*. London: E & F.N. Spon.

Birch, I., Vernon, W., Burrow, G. and Walker, J. 2014. The effect of frame rate on the ability of experienced gait analysts to identify characteristics of gait from closed circuit television footage. *Science and Justice* 55: 159–163. http://www.scienceandjusticejournal.com/article/S1355-0306(13)00114-7/full text (Accessed January 7, 2016).

Birch, I., Vernon, W., Walker, J. and Saxelby, J. 2013. The development of a tool for assessing the quality of closed circuit camera footage for use in forensic gait analysis. *Journal of Forensic and Legal Medicine* 20: 915–917.

Birch, I., Vernon, W., Walker, J. and Young, M. 2015. Terminology and forensic gait analysis. *Science and Justice* 55: 279–284.

Buncombe, A. 2000. Gang leader is unmasked by his bandy-legged gait. *The Independent, London*, July 13.

Byrd, J.S. 2006. Confirmation bias, ethics and mistakes in forensics. *Journal of Forensic Identification* 56: 511–525.

Couper, M.R. 1984. The Delphi technique: Characteristics and sequence model. *Advances in Nursing Science* 7: 72–77.

Decker, W., and Albert, S. 2002. *Contemporary Pedorthics*. Seattle, WA: Elton-Wolf.

Dror, I.E. and Charlton, D. 2006. Why experts make errors. *Journal of Forensic Identification* 56: 600–616.
Fink, A., Kosecott, J., Chassin, M. and Brook, R.H. 1984. Consensus methods: Characteristics and guidelines for use. *American Journal of Public Health* 74: 979–983.
Grant, M.G. 2006. Gait. In: *Forensic Human Identification*, edited by T. Thompson and S. Black. pp. 343–362. London: CRC Press.
Nixon, M.S., Tan, T. and Chellappa, R. 2006. *Human Identification Based on Gait.* New York: Springer.
Perry, J. 1990. Pathologic gait. In: *Instructional Course Lectures*, 29 edited by W.D. Green. pp. 325–331. Rosemont, Il: American Academy of Orthopaedic Surgeons.
Shores, M. 1980. Footprint analysis in gait documentation. *Physical Therapy* 60: 1163–1167.
Smith, L. and Bond, J. 2015. *Criminal Justice and Forensic Science*. London: Palgrave.
Vernon, W. 2000. The functional analysis of shoe wear patterns: Theory and application. PhD diss., Sheffield Hallam University.
Vernon, W., Brodie, B., DiMaggio, J., Gunn, N., Kelly, H., Nirenberg, M., Reel, S. and Walker, J. 2009. *Forensic Podiatry: Role and Scope of Practice (In the Context of Forensic Human Identification).* International Association for Identification. http://www.theiai.org/disciplines/podiatry/podiatry_role_and_scope.pdf (Accessed January 6, 2016).
Watkins, J. 2006. Basic biomechanics of gait. In: *Neale's Disorders of the Foot.* 7th ed., edited by D. Lorimer, G. French, M. O'Donnell, J.G. Burrow, and B. Wall. pp. 425–440. Edinburgh: Churchill Livingstone.
Whittle, M.W. 2007. *Gait Analysis-An Introduction.* 4th ed. London: Elsevier.
Wilkinson, M.J. and Menz, H.B. 1997. Measurement of gait parameters from footprints: A reliability study. *The Foot* 7: 19–23.
Wilkinson, M.J., Menz, H.B. and Raspovic, A. 1995. The measurement of gait parameters from footprints. *The Foot* 5: 84–90.
Yun, J. 2011. User identification using gait patterns on UbifloorII. *Sensors* 11: 2611–2639. doi: http://dx.doi.org/10.3390/s110302611.

Identification from Podiatry Records

7

As a routine aspect of their practice, podiatrists are required to keep accurate and relevant records of their patients' foot conditions, associated diagnoses, and subsequent treatment. This recorded information has previously been demonstrated to have value in person identification. This chapter considers identification from podiatry records, presents an overview of the approaches that would be taken in this work, and considers potential sources of error that forensic podiatrists may encounter.

7.1 Introduction

As a clinical practice/governance requirement, podiatrists must keep records of their professional work, and such records include those pertaining to patient management, that is, the patient records. Podiatry patient records contain details of the patient whom the podiatrist has examined, treated, or both. These details include personal information, medical history, supervised medication, diagnosed foot and lower limb disorders, vascular and neurological status, foot lesions present, clinical investigation results, and any treatment methods undertaken. The possibility of using podiatry records to be able to help with person identification, specifically in mass disaster situations was originally suggested by Doney and Harris (1984). The potential of the use of podiatry records to identify unknown persons in forensic and mass disaster situations was tested successfully by Vernon (1994) and later by Sanger and Vernon (1997).

There are many techniques used in investigations pertaining to identification, some of which are more commonly used than others. Circumstances such as trauma, loss of body tissue, and decomposition can however limit the usefulness of all of these approaches. In doing so, the need to widen the "armory" of available identification techniques can be justified, even with the availability of the powerful DNA identification techniques now being used as evidence of identity.

Such records are available through public funded podiatry services (such as the National Health Service in the United Kingdom), clinical practices in the private and independent sectors, and schools of podiatry. Although it has been shown that the standards of such record keeping have been variable in the past (Idris-Evans and Pooke 1985; Vernon 1994), the demands for improved clinical governance arrangements in modern-day practice now require higher record keeping standards, and failure to keep appropriate records may lead to disciplinary action through professional regulatory arrangements (such as the Health and Care Professions Council in the United Kingdom), or the professional bodies to which podiatrists may be affiliated.

The possibility of podiatry chart/record card identification was first raised in 1984 by Dr. Ivor Doney, a police surgeon (Doney and Harris 1984). Doney highlighted the work of podiatrists and the potential of their records in identifying the deceased after disasters from features of their lower limbs. Podiatry records were seen by Doney as having particular value in situations in which only the foot is recognizable and also in dealing with the problem of the identification of headless murder victims. In disaster situations, the feet are well placed to survive trauma through being encased in shoes and socks, and they are often the last body part to be destroyed in fires. In such circumstances, this can leave the feet as the final possible means of identification. Doney noted that the fine details kept by podiatrists are not recorded by any other medical practitioners. At the time, podiatrists work predominantly focused on treatment of the elderly population, and Doney also argued that there was a preponderance of elderly persons at risk in disaster situations, adding further justification to the consideration of podiatry record card use in the identification process. Although the work of podiatrists now focuses on clinical need irrespective of age, the elderly remain high users of podiatry services (Garrow et al. 2000; Spink et al. 2008; Vernon et al. 2011). As such, Doney's comment on high numbers of elderly persons receiving podiatry treatment is still correct.

It was postulated that such identifications could be assisted through recognizing the use of individual styles of podiatry treatment, and through the antemortem recording of distinctive lesions (e.g., hemangioma, cysts, and pigmented nevi) that would be expected to be detailed in the podiatry records. The possibility of orthotic devices (such as those fitted by podiatrists into footwear) being marked with details such as the source of manufacture, a patient's personal details, or both, was also considered by Doney as an aid to identification. In addition, the American Navy was reported to be charting the feet of its crews for identification purposes in line with Doney's suggestions. This was because it was known that in deaths due to fire, very often the lower limbs protected by thick boots would be the last part of the body to be destroyed, leaving foot parts as the only means of identification (Filer 1983).

In the United Kingdom, research was then undertaken to consider the potential and the efficacy of podiatry record use in human identification (Vernon 1990, 1994). In this work, Doney's ideas were widened to consider all aspects of detail recorded in podiatry notes, e.g., foot type; local deformities (both major and minor); and the form, size, and pattern of podiatric lesions present. In the early stage of this research, using a stratified random selection of 300 podiatry record cards, patterns represented by combinations of foot lesions alone were considered and in this sample, only 18 distinct lesion patterns were found to have occurred more than once (Vernon 1990). The repeated patterns of lesions all represented the presence of very simple podiatric conditions and did not take both feet or nonpodiatric identifying features recorded on the podiatry records into consideration. Tests were also conducted to determine the value of podiatrist's clinical judgment in identifying a person from details recorded in their podiatry notes alone (Vernon 1994). Early testing required the participating podiatrists to compare the feet of an unknown person with the details recorded on an anonymous record card and to conclude simply whether the record card selected was that pertaining to the person being examined or not. The judgments expressed were based on consideration of the features present and knowledge of their expected frequency of occurrence. The test was crudely performed and simply required podiatrists to state whether the records under consideration related to a particular person under examination or not. As such, there was minimal potential within the test to deal with matters of uncertainty, e.g., where the podiatrist believed that it was possible that the card belonged to the person, but with no strong evidence being present to suggest that this was the case. Regardless, 85.65% of all judgments made by the participating podiatrists who had considered whether a record card related to an unidentified person were found to be correct. In later tests, a simple strength scale was introduced in which the participating podiatrists were allowed to state different levels of certainty in relation to their identification judgments (Sanger and Vernon 1997). Here, it was found that when podiatrists expressed an opinion that they were absolutely certain that a match between detail listed in the patient record card and that observed on the feet of the unidentified patient indicated that the records were of that subject, 100% of these judgments were correct. It was also noted that 56% of all judgments made by the participating podiatrists were made with such certainty. When considering the individuality of the human foot as expressed in podiatric records and the success demonstrated by podiatrists in testing their judgments in identification from such records, a strong potential for the use of such records in human identification was demonstrated.

7.2 Method of Identification

Identification from podiatry records is likely to be required for deceased persons, such as in cases where a single missing person is known to have received podiatry treatment and upon recovery of a body, the potential to use more conventional identification approaches is compromised or impossible to perform. This could be through the results of trauma, or loss of other evidential features, with the foot or feet being found relatively intact. Other situations requiring podiatry record identification include mass disaster investigations where multiple victim identification is required and use more traditional identification techniques may have been compromised as detailed above. It is likely that the identifying podiatrist in both circumstances would undertake such work in a mortuary. In mass disasters, the emergency field mortuary facility would be used and would thus require the podiatrist to have knowledge of, and adherence to, disaster team working protocols and a general prior understanding of the required procedures and working practices. Such contextual understandings are beyond the scope of this text, and it is recommended that anyone working in this field gain prior familiarity with the working protocols involved, such as considerations of accountability, procedure, recording, storage, cross-contamination, and infection control.

As part of the research undertaken to consider the potential of podiatry records in human identification, a protocol for the approach to be adopted was devised (Vernon 1990). Based on this protocol, the following approach to podiatric identification is recommended.

7.2.1 Assessment of the Unidentified Foot/Feet

Initially, a proforma should be prepared for the appropriate recording of information obtained from the foot examination process. This should be headed with the date, time, and place of assessment, and the coded reference (label) of the foot or feet to be examined. After this preparation, it is important to verify that the coding references (labels) of the foot or feet to be identified are those listed for this particular examination, and it should be recorded whether this is the examination of one foot or two feet. The condition of the foot or feet to be examined should be stated, and then the following information should be recorded as part of the examination process:

- Overall length of the foot from the rearmost aspect of the heel to the tip of the longest toe (using a foot measuring device)
- Heel-to-ball length of the foot being examined (using a foot measuring device)
- Width of the foot across the widest aspect of the ball (using a foot measuring device)
- Foot type if apparent
- Presence of minor structural toe deformities

- Presence of structural forefoot deformities
- Presence of midfoot/arch area deformities
- Presence of heel area deformities
- Presence of deformities at the rear of the heel/tendo-Achilles insertion

For each toe, the status of all nails should be recorded, including reference to any deformity, fungal affectation, discoloration, and length. Comments on the quality of nail care if apparent should also be made.

The presence of podiatric lesions (e.g., corns, callus), dermatological conditions, or skin blemishes (e.g., scars, nevi, pigmentation), and other marks should be recorded along with the site, type, and if relevant, the size of such lesions on the foot/feet under examination. Thus, the following situational order should be followed:

- Dorsal surfaces (toes/other areas)
- Apices of toes
- Interdigital areas
- Medial and lateral aspects of the foot
- Plantar metatarsal area
- Plantar midfoot area (inner longitudinal arch/lateral surface)
- Plantar calcaneal area
- Posterior heel area
- Medial and lateral malleoli

In addition to the use of a proforma, a diagrammatic representation of the human foot indicating its various anatomical areas has been created on which the exact location of lesions present on the foot can be marked (Figure 7.1). This diagrammatic representation can usefully supplement the written information on the proforma and create a more detailed record of the findings of the examination. The proforma can be further supplemented by the use of digital photography to show the foot from its various viewpoints (i.e., anterior, posterior, plantar, dorsal, medial, and lateral) and to provide close-up detail of any deformities or lesions present on the foot or feet in question. As in all photography of this nature, a scale situated in the same plane as the feature being recorded and parallel to the camera lens. Finally, if possible, a print of the plantar surface of the foot should be taken, preferably using an inkless paper system. However in the case of the deceased, this print is rarely successful because of the changed, nondynamic nature of the postmortem foot that when printed can produce a print of considerably different size than that of a reference print taken from the same person when alive.

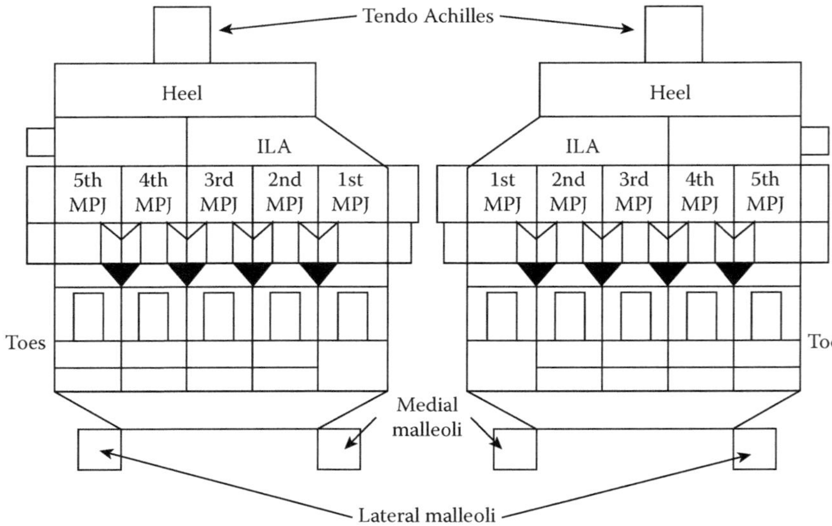

Figure 7.1 Diagrammatic representation of human feet designed for podiatry record card identification purposes.

7.2.2 Assessment of the Podiatric Records

The foot examination has little value in the identification process without the availability of antemortem records with which to compare the observational data obtained from the examined foot/feet. At this stage, podiatric records pertaining to missing persons should have been obtained for comparison, and these records should be carefully examined using the same category headings as in the foot examination process detailed above. The examiner should note all relevant antemortem data on another clearly labeled proforma. In labeling the proforma, it is especially important to clearly distinguish between the ante- and postmortem records and also to note the personal details of the subject to whom these records belong. It is possible that many such records will be considered in the identification process and because of this the potential for confusion can arise. Again, the notes can be supplemented through the use of the diagrammatic representation of the human foot (Figure 7.1) to record the site and type of any lesion detail apparent from these records.

7.3 Comparison

Finally, comparison should be made between the detail observed and recorded from the unknown foot or feet and that obtained from the known podiatry records, with the examining podiatrist reaching a conclusion as to the likelihood of a match. Here, the podiatrist should compare the features observed, in turn, under each category heading. Note should be taken of features that match and those that do not.

7.3.1 Matched Features

Where features match, consideration should be given to the following:

Stability: Stability refers to the potential permanence of the features noted. The stability of a feature is an important prerequisite for bodily features used in the identification process (Bernstein 1997). In reference to the foot, bony features such as hallux valgus, Tailor's bunion, and hammer toe deformity (Figure 7.2) are examples of permanent features, as are conditions such as onychogryphosis and the presence of nevi or other growths (Figure 7.3). Simple skin lesions (e.g., areas of minor callus) would not have such a degree of stability, being potentially able to be resolved through podiatric intervention and changes of function, footwear, or habit. Regardless, podiatry records may show that such lesions have been present over many years, suggesting a reasonable degree of stability for the feature being considered in the assessment process, thereby improving its value in identification. Consideration of the longevity of such lesions may therefore be an important factor in their assessment during the identification process.

Individuality: Some features can represent higher degrees of individuality than others. Scar tissue, especially when caused through trauma, would represent a highly individual "accidental" feature

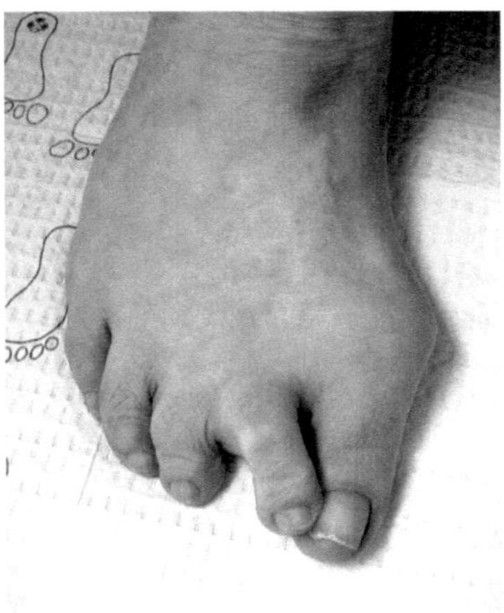

Figure 7.2 Bunion and hammer toe deformity.

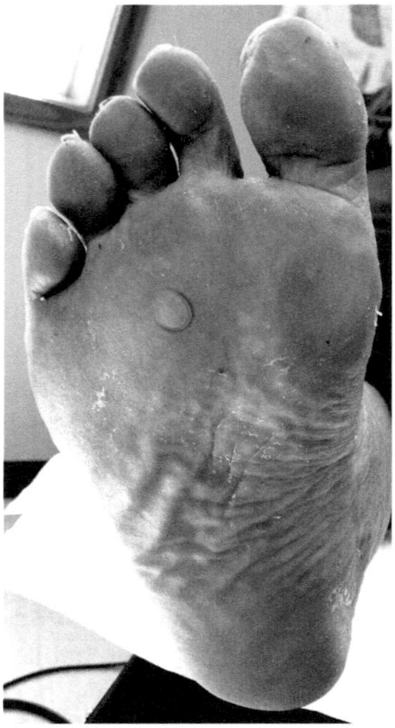

Figure 7.3 Skin "tag" growth.

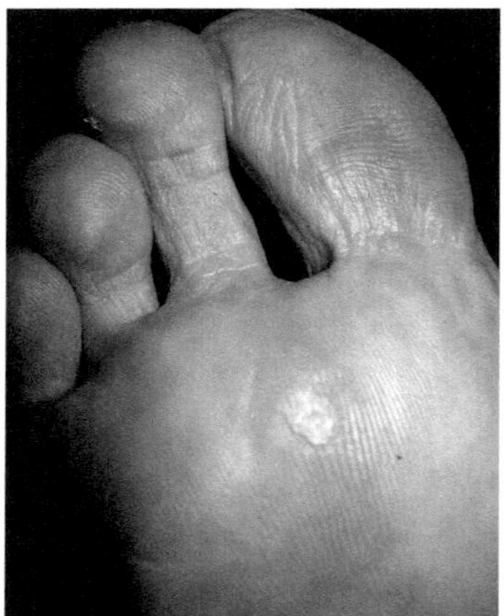

Figure 7.4 Residual keratosis after puncture wound.

and could be of great value in the identification process (Figure 7.4). Conversely, a single pressure point with a minor buildup of callus, e.g., on the dorsum of a fifth toe, would not represent such a high level of individuality; instead, it would suggest compatibility as opposed to uniqueness. Complications present within more common lesion forms can however increase the individuality represented by that lesion. For example, a multinucleate fibrous or vascular corn would be of greater identification value than a common heloma; however, it would be essential for these complications to have been recorded accurately in the antemortem records of the person concerned. A lesion may be a very common type (e.g., heloma durum), but the site of the lesion can be relevant to the level of individuality represented by that lesion. In the example above, a low level of individuality would be expressed by a single heloma durum corn situated on the dorsum of a fifth toe, because such lesions can be commonly found at this particular site (Figure 7.5). Conversely, a heloma durum lesion found to be present on the lateral aspect of the fifth styloid process would represent much stronger individuality because this site is a much less common position for the presence of such a lesion. In judging the level of individuality represented by any feature found to be present on the foot, the examining podiatrist uses both personal experience and theoretical understanding based on published knowledge. In this respect, familiarization with research papers on lesion topography would be recommended.

Mismatched features: Mismatches between the detail observed on the foot or feet under examination and the detail written in the person's record card may also be apparent during comparison. Depending on the nature of the mismatch, this mismatch may or may not preclude the possibility of a match between examined foot or feet and the records under consideration. Various situations that could lead to a mismatch and their implications in the identification process are considered below.

- **Resolution** A prerecorded foot type listed in the antemortem records would be a strong feature that would not be expected to

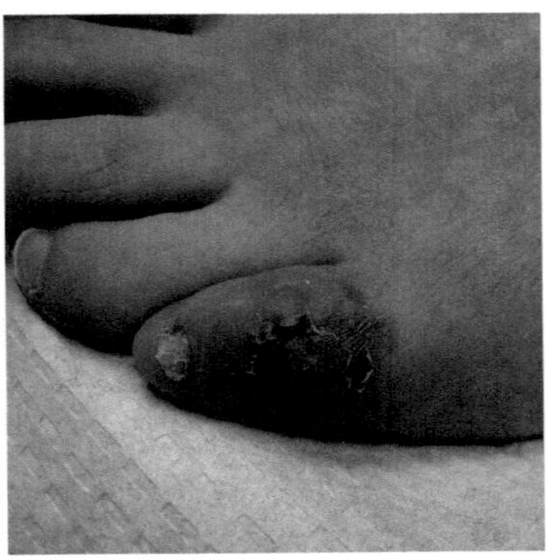

Figure 7.5 Heloma durum (corn) on fifth toe.

have resolved. If, e.g., the examined foot is of a pescavus type, and the records describe a pesplanus type foot, then subject to the absence of recording errors, a mismatch would be certain (Figure 7.6).

Other permanent bony features, such as hallux valgus or hammer toe, can be corrected by surgery. If such features have been listed in the antemortem records, yet are not present on the foot or feet being examined, the examiner should look for indications of surgery to preclude that possibility (Figure 7.7).

Similarly, skin lesions (e.g., nevi) can be removed through surgery. Although surgery to remove minor examples of such

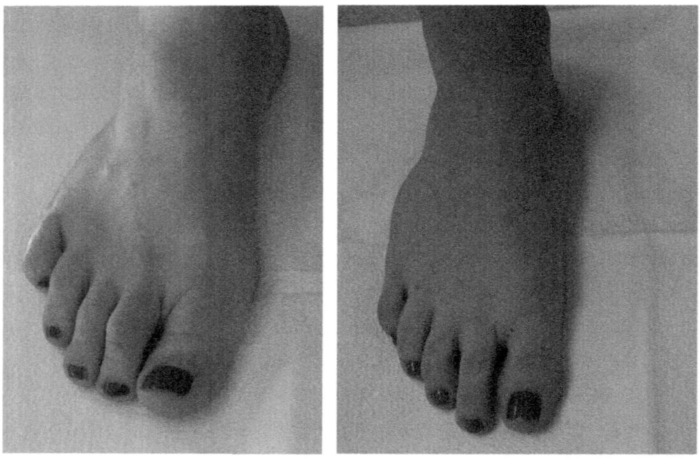

(a) (b)

Figure 7.6 Pescavus (high arch) (a) and pesplanus (low arch) (b) foot types.

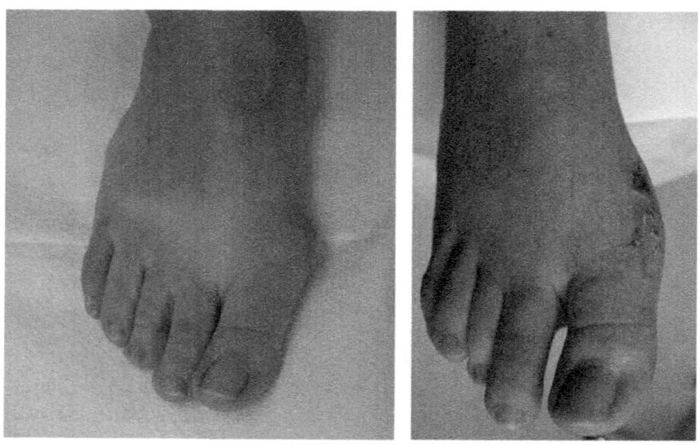

(a) (b)

Figure 7.7 (a and b) Scar indicating prior surgery.

lesions from the foot for cosmetic purposes is very unlikely, it is possible that surgery could have taken place for other reasons (e.g., biopsy). Where such a difference is apparent, the possibility of past surgical removal (i.e., the presence of scar tissue) on the foot in question should again be considered by the examiner. No postsurgical features present on the feet being examined suggest incompatibility, subject to the limits of antemortem record keeping accuracy.

As noted above, there is also the possibility that podiatric lesions may have resolved through treatment, functional change, or change of footwear or habit. If so, information present in podiatric records can be used to give an indication of the potential effectiveness of treatment, which has taken place previously. If, e.g., physical or chemical cautery has taken place, this may suggest the potential for the lesion to have been successfully removed. Indications may also be given through the recording of footwear advice being given and acted upon, which may suggest a positive change of footwear habit and anticipated improvement through such action. The notes may also record the use of orthotic devices or long-term functional changes that have been previously observed by the treating podiatrist. If so, then this may, in turn, indicate functional change and the potential for improvement and resolution of the associated lesions. When considering the potential for lesions to have resolved, the form of the lesion present should also be taken into account. A prerecorded fibrous heloma, e.g., would be unlikely to resolve with routine conservative treatment approaches alone and even if such treatment had led to localized improvements, complete resolution without leaving any trace of such a lesion being present is unlikely. The absence of long-standing significant lesions or the presence of several less or more significant lesions would suggest incompatibility between ante- and postmortem states, where such lesions have been previously recorded. Such conclusions would again require the availability of up-to-date and accurate podiatric records.

- **New lesions** In addition to the possibility of podiatric lesions having resolved, there is also the potential for new lesions to have developed since the last record entered on the antemortem records. Examples would include the formation of new pressure points, areas of callus, and helomata. Where such lesions are encountered on the foot or feet being examined, the nature and severity of these lesions should be taken into account by the examining podiatrist. Consideration should be given to the past lesion stability as shown on the antemortem records. The likelihood of the person having developed a new lesion to the level found within the time period since the last antemortem record entry should also be considered, as should any contextual information present in the antemortem records relating to the overall foot condition and potential to develop new lesions such as those observed. Such information may, e.g., be contained in a record card entry noting the purchase of new shoes with a particular identified issue (such as a toe box restriction). The presence of multiple lesions not recorded in the antemortem records would suggest a mismatch; however, the presence of single additional nonrecorded lesions should be considered cautiously in the comparison process and not necessarily lead to rejection of the potential for a match.

- **Change in nature/severity of a lesion** In the comparison phase of the examination process, lesions can be found to be present on the foot in places recorded in the antemortem records, but these lesions may be of a different nature or represent a mismatched level of severity. For example, the records may note the presence of an area of callus, whereas the foot being examined demonstrates a heloma durum on that particular area. Again, consideration should be given to the potential for the recorded lesion to have improved, and this would be indicated by lesion stability, severity, treatment carried out, and the time period elapsing since the last antemortem record was made, as indicated by those records. In this case, a subjective judgment needs to be made by the examining podiatrist that may impact on the strength of the resulting probability statement written into the identification report produced by that examiner.
- **Record keeping problems** Previous tests of podiatrist's judgments in human identification from podiatry records showed the potential for recording errors and other record keeping problems. Such issues can impair the identification process, with resulting failures of accurate identification/elimination (Vernon 1994). In many cases, notes used in the identification process in this study were found to be illegible (Figure 7.8). Where this is the case, unless the podiatrist who made the notes is available and can provide an explanation of these notes, the antemortem records may be useless and using these to help with identification will not then be possible. With partial illegibility, the notes may still be of value, depending on the level of detail still apparent. Another problem noted in the previous research related to the use of personal shorthand in clinical note keeping.

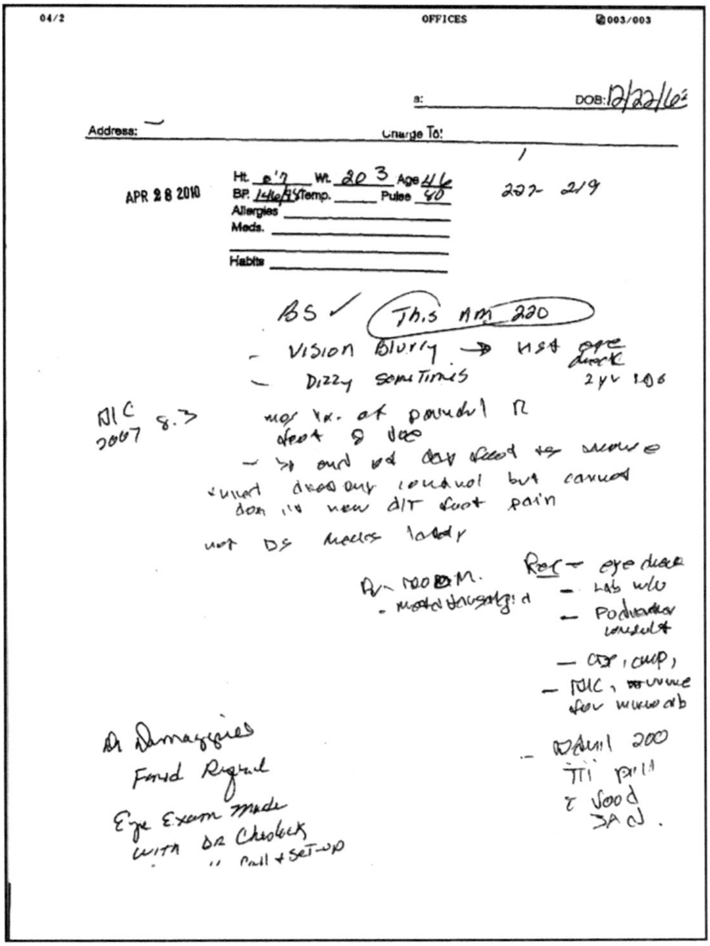
04/2 OFFICES 003/003

DOB: 12/22/62

Address: Charge To:

APR 28 2010

Ht. Wt. 203 Age 46
BP. Temp. Pulse
Allergies
Meds.
Habits

BS ✓ This AM 220
- Vision blurry → last eye check 2 yr ago
- Dizzy sometimes

Figure 7.8 Illegible notes.

Over many years, podiatrists use wide ranges of abbreviations in their records. Previously, different schools of podiatry have taught different systems of notation (Vernon 1990), and this has been complicated further by podiatrists developing their own personal forms of shorthand that may not be easily deciphered by other podiatrists. Although current recommendations are for note keeping to be made in full, the presence of multiple-taught systems in the past means that shorthand records can still be found and may cause problems in antemortem record card interpretation. Where this is the case, the podiatrist who wrote the original records should be contacted for an explanation, if possible, and failing that, other colleagues of that podiatrist may have knowledge of the shorthand system that has been used, and they should be contacted. Should such contact not be possible and should the system used be unclear, then the records in that case would be rendered useless in the identification process. With the advent of electronic medical records or other comparable terminology designating such, handwritten notes may soon become an obsolete notation system.

- **Incomplete records** Another problem encountered is where records required in the identification process are legible and accurate, but are incomplete. One example of such a problem is in the failure to record a podiatric diagnosis. The results of such failure can be catastrophic, e.g., when the task of the examiner may be to identify the owner of a lower limb where a gross feature such as pescavus, hallux valgus and the like has not been recorded in the clinical records. If the records have inadvertently been left blank in the section pertaining to the presence of that feature, then the question arises as to whether that feature has not been present on the person believed to be deceased or whether it was present, but had not been recorded. In such a case, the recording omission could leave the examiner unable to reach a conclusion of either compatibility or exclusion. If the features of the foot being examined are less obvious (e.g., the presence of a very mild example of hallux valgus or a partially overlapping toe) and have not been recorded, this omission would not be as serious; the examiner would be able to work with the other recorded information. In all cases of absent diagnoses, the examiner is advised to contact the practitioner or podiatry service from which the records had been obtained to determine whether any further information is available to confirm the presence or absence of the feature in question (e.g., older records, computer entries, referral letters that may inadvertently have not been attached to the case notes), or to seek knowledge of the involvement of any other agency in that person's care that may be able to provide additional information. For podiatric lesions, such agencies may typically include the patient's general practitioner, orthopedic surgeons, radiographers/radiologists, orthotists, and physiotherapists.

Similarly, the records of the known person being considered may have omissions in relation to the recorded treatment, or such treatments could have been recorded with detail that is inadequate for the purpose of assisting in the identification process. This situation can arise if the records have been made in busy clinical situations and the recording practitioner has rushed the note taking process. Recently, changes in clinical governance standards have improved this situation in recent years; previously, however, it was not uncommon to find whole treatment events written up as "B/F/op" (representing both feet general podiatric operating procedures), with no detail on the treatment process, the site and nature of lesions attended to, or other pertinent details (Idris-Evans and Pooke 1985). Although problems at this level are less likely to be encountered now, it is still probable that rushed notation may be encountered that contains omissions, inadequate details, or both of the current status of the feet being treated. In identification, when this occurs, the examiner should check back in earlier records for information that may be of value that was made on previous occasions. At the same time, the examiner needs to bear in mind that over time, soft tissue lesions could have improved or deteriorated, new lesions could have formed, or old lesions could have resolved. These situations would be especially problematic where detailed and accurate continuous records are not available. Omissions in the treatment notes create additional problems for the examiner, who is likely to be unaware of the omission, unlike the problem of inadequate note keeping that would be obvious on first reading. The possibility of an omission of detail is only likely to become apparent when a range of features have been noted as compatible on assessment, yet one or two additional features have been identified on the examined person that are not recorded in the patient notes. The level of problem that this causes for the examiner varies from situation to situation and may very well decrease the strength of certainty as to a match. If the apparently missing data relate to one small and insignificant lesion in the presence of several other compatible and possibly unusual features, then the problem to the examiner is minor. If, however, the missing feature was unusual and possibly one of few apparent features present on the examined foot, this situation would be unknown to the examiner and could lead to erroneous conclusions. It is therefore important for the identification examiner to be aware of the potential for recording omissions or inadequacies to be an issue and, where possible, the examiner should look for other features within the record-based information that may indicate that such a situation could have occurred (e.g., errors or incomplete recording of personal details, signs that the records have been rushed, missing signatures from the recording practitioner). Again, recording omissions or inadequacies may ultimately require the identification examiner to form the opinion that no conclusions can be reached over whether the records belong to the examined person. It is also possible that this type of recording error could lead the examiner to arrive at erroneous conclusions if the records have contained major omissions.

- **Inaccurate notes** The presence of inaccuracies within patient notes is one of the most frequent problems encountered when using podiatry records in the identification process. Such errors in record keeping most commonly relate to inadvertently mixing up right and left feet in the notes, or mistakenly recording a lesion observed or treated on the wrong toe. As in the above-mentioned consideration of recording omissions, such errors would not necessarily be apparent to the examining podiatrist in an identification situation and again could lead to erroneous conclusions being made. If, e.g., a unilateral hallux valgus with nail involution (incurvatus) and the presence of heloma durum on the medial side of the first metatarsophalangeal joint has been inadvertently recorded as being present on a right foot as opposed to a left foot and a single right foot being considered for identification purposes does not show these features, then the derived conclusions are likely to be incorrect. If such an error has been made within the records, it is more problematic if there has only been one clinical attendance recorded for the patient, or if the error has been copied through to subsequent appointments. Often, however, the mistake within the records can be of a one-off nature that becomes obvious when looking back through previous recorded entries. Sometimes, when looking through the sequence of treatment notes, references made to right and left sides change on several occasions through this error. Alternately, references can be made to, e.g., a particular toe being affected by a named deformity or lesion and the affected toe changes in the patient's notes, suggesting that this error has occurred on several occasions. To maintain an awareness of the possibility of this error, the examining podiatrist should pay particular attention to patterns of lesions and other pathological features that are present on the examined foot, yet recorded on the opposite side in record cards. If this situation is encountered, further work should be undertaken to seek confirmation of which side has been affected. This additional information could be elicited through notes and correspondence that could be available through other sources, such as related professional groups who may have also been involved in that same person's care.
- **Incorrect diagnosis** Incorrect diagnoses can arise in podiatry records used in the identification process because the records present a diagnosis of a foot condition that is simply wrong,

or disputable. Common examples of this type of error include the recording of hallux rigidus as opposed to hallux valgus, hammer toe as opposed to retracted toe, or excessive functional pronation as opposed to pesplanus; these are just a few simple examples of the many possibilities. The examining podiatrist should be aware of the potential for this error to occur. In the comparison process, where all other features have been found to be identical, and there remains just one source of incompatibility with the recorded lesions being similar in nature, this should suggest the potential for such a situation and where possible, work should be undertaken to investigate this further. As in previous examples of dealing with the possibility of erroneous podiatry records, such work could include contacting other disciplines that had been involved in the care of this person to determine the availability of other records that may be used to verify the exact nature of the lesion. It may also be possible to obtain footwear known to belong to the missing person, and the wear features of such footwear items may also be useful in determining the exact nature of the feature noted within the treatment records. It is again likely that such recording errors will compromise the level of certainty of any conclusion derived in the identification comparison process.

- **Mix-up of records** Occasionally, situations can occur in which the podiatry patient records have been inadvertently confused with those of another patient. In the identification process, this mix-up would simply be where records of a person other than the one under consideration have been forwarded inadvertently. This situation occurs from time to time in clinical situations, and it was through dealing with this occurrence in a real-life patient appointment situation that led to the research undertaken in the United Kingdom on identification from podiatry records. Although potentially problematic in identification situations, this possibility can be guarded against by the examining podiatrist through taking a protocol-based approach to this work that would demand careful checks of personal details on the record card, to verify that these notes are indeed the notes required for the comparison processes to take place.
- **Careless examination** A final source of error that could occur in identification from podiatry records is error that is entirely in the hands of the identifying podiatrist, i.e., the possibility of errors resulting from careless examination of the records or feet in question. Although this error was not the most commonly encountered error in the research undertaken on identification

from podiatry records, it did occur on four separate occasions, being responsible for 4 of the 199 failures in identification judgment that were encountered (Vernon 1996). These errors related to simple nonadherence to the protocols involved, the examiner forgetting to check through retrospective treatment records, and carelessness in not observing lesions present on the person's foot on examination. On other occasions, the information within the record card involved was misread, or the examining podiatrist mixed up the treatment notes and subsequently undertook the examination and comparison process with notes other than those that had been allocated. All of these sources of error can be minimized through the strict adherence to working protocols, through a verification process in which a second examiner independently works through the comparison and checks the work of the primary examiner. Such errors can also be minimized through the adoption of a methodological and careful approach to the work required.

7.4 Strength Scale

In the research undertaken in identification from podiatry records, the use of a strength scale was introduced to allow examining podiatrists to express degrees of certainty as to their strength of opinion in relation to a match/mismatch between examined records and the questioned feet. The strength scale used in this case was based on a scale in use within forensic odontology at the time and it allowed the following levels of certainty (Dailey 1987):

- Absolute certainty
- Most likely
- Possible
- Most unlikely

Work has since taken place to standardize the approaches to expressing degrees of certainty in dealing with forensic evidence. Newer methods, such as the "Levels of Certainty" (DiMaggio 2005, modified 2014), have been adopted. In Europe, work has been undertaken to standardize the approaches to expressing degrees of certainty in dealing with forensic evidence. The result is that the continued use of the above-mentioned scale as used in the earlier research on identification from podiatry records would not be recommended. Instead, the podiatry record card examiner would be advised to adopt current conventions when reaching conclusions in relation to his or her evidence. Detailed consideration of these approaches is presented in Chapter 4.

7.5 Conclusions

The examination of podiatry charts/records should be within the capability of all working podiatrists because by definition, podiatrists read and consider records relating to all the patients whom they treat in the course of their normal clinical work. As such, they are highly familiar with the problems encountered in the recording of patient diagnoses and treatments and in the management of these records. The main difference in considering such records for human identification is to consider these records within a different framework of rules. Gaining familiarity with this different context in a supervised environment is highly recommended before pursuing work of this nature to develop the necessary expertise required before undertaking casework involving identification from podiatry records.

References

Bernstein M. (1997). In: WG Eckert (ed.) *Introduction to Forensic Sciences*, 2nd edn. Forensic Odontology, pp. 295–342, CRC Press, Boca Raton, FL.

Dailey JC. (1987). Identification strength scale. *Journal of Forensic Science* 32(2): 317–318.

Doney IE and Harris PG. (1984). Mass disaster identification: Can chiropodists help? *The Police Surgeon* 25: 14–20.

Filer D. (1983). Clues in the News! GP, 14th October.

Garrow AP, Papageorgiou AC, Silman AJ, Thomas E, Jayson MIV, and Macfarlane GJ. (2000). Development and validation of a questionnaire to assess disabling foot pain. *Pain* 85: 107–113.

Idris-Evans D and Pooke MJ. (1985). *NHS Chiropody Services: National Chiropody Record System*. Northampton: ACCO.

Sanger D and Vernon W. (1997). The value of strength scales in identification from podiatry records. *Journal of Forensic Identification* 47(2): 162–170.

Spink MJ, Menz HB, and Lord SR. (2008). Efficacy of a multifaceted podiatry intervention to improve balance and prevent falls in older people: Study protocol for a randomised trial. *BMC Geriatrics* 8(30): 1–16. http://www.biomedcentral.com/1471-2318/8/30 (Accessed September 29, 2015).

Vernon W. (1990). The potential of chiropody records in forensic and mass disaster identification. Unpublished BSc (Hons) project, Brighton Polytechnic.

Vernon W. (1994). The use of chiropody/podiatry records in forensic and mass disaster identification. *Journal of Forensic Identification* 44(1): 26–40.

Vernon W, Borthwick A, and Walker J. (2011). The management of foot problems in the older person through podiatry services. *Reviews in Clinical Gerontology* 21(4): 331–339.

Medical Legal Concerns

III

Expert Witness

8

The work undertaken by expert witnesses in all forensic science and practice disciplines carries a high burden of responsibility. Expert reports are provided to help the criminal justice system find the truth in relation to whether someone is innocent or guilty of a crime for which they have been accused. The implications of presenting erroneous evidence in relation to this task are severe. A misleading or incorrect report can lead to a guilty person being found innocent, which depending on the nature of crime could place the public at risk where there is danger of repetition. Conversely, should someone innocent of a crime be wrongly found guilty, then they will unjustifiably be deprived of their freedom, and if they are convicted in a country or state that still exercises the use of the death penalty and the crime is serious enough, they will unjustifiably be deprived of their lives.

8.1 General Responsibilities of the Expert Witness

The forensic podiatrist's role is that of the expert witness. Operating in both civil and criminal courts, such witnesses provide expert evidence, that can include opinion evidence "on scientific and technological matters which are beyond the knowledge and experience or judges and juries" (EWI 2006). Definitions exist in both the United States and the United Kingdom to state precisely what it is that expert witnesses do. In the United States, the Federal Rules of Evidence (FRE) Rule 702 (US Govt. 2009) state the following:

> If scientific, technical, or other specialized knowledge will assist the trier of fact to understand the evidence or to determine a fact in issue, a witness qualified as an expert by knowledge, skill, experience, training, or education, may testify thereto in the form of an opinion or otherwise, if (1) the testimony is based upon sufficient facts or data, (2) the testimony is the product of reliable principles and methods, and (3) the witness has applied the principles and methods reliably to the facts of the case.

The Frye standard relates to the admissibility of expert testimony and was established by Frye v. the United States, 293 F. 1023 (LII 2016a).

This standard requires expert testimony to be based on science that has gained "general acceptance" in the relevant field. The Frye standard was used in federal courts until 1993 (Sacks 1995). At the time of this writing, the following states still adhere to this standard: California, Pennsylvania, Illinois, Maryland, Minnesota, New Jersey, New York, and Washington.

In 1993, U.S. Supreme Court case Daubert v. Merrell Dow Pharmaceutical Inc., 509 U.S. 579 (1993) established the Daubert standard (LII 2016b). In December 2000, FRE 702 was formally amended to reflect the implications of facts or data, the product of reliable principles and methods, and the witness must apply the principles and methods reliably to the facts of the case.[1]

In the United Kingdom, for civil cases, civil procedure rules (CPR), with practice directions, apply with CPR 35, CPR 49, and PD 35 (practice direction) being particularly relevant to the work of the expert witness (Civil Justice Council 2014). In criminal cases, the recently updated Crown prosecution rules apply (Ministry of Justice 2015). These rules state the role and responsibilities of the expert witness and describe an "expert" as follows:

> "... a person who is required to give or prepare expert evidence for the purpose of criminal proceedings, including evidence required to determine fitness to plead or for the purpose of sentencing"
>
> *[Ministry of Justice 2015: Section 19.1(2)].*

The rules continue to describe such an expert's duty to the court as follows:

"(1) An expert must help the court to achieve the overriding objective—
  (a) by giving opinion which is—
    (i) objective and unbiased, and
    (ii) within the expert's area or areas of expertise; and
  (b) by actively assisting the court in fulfilling its duty of case management under Rule 3.2, in particular by—
    (i) complying with directions made by the court, and
    (ii) at once informing the court of any significant failure (by the expert or another) to take any step required by such a direction.
(2) This duty overrides any obligation to the person from whom the expert receives instructions or by whom the expert is paid.
(3) This duty includes obligations—
  (a) to define the expert's area or areas of expertise—
    (i) in the expert's report, and
    (ii) when giving evidence in person;
  (b) when giving evidence in person, to draw the court's attention to any question to which the answer would be outside the expert's area or areas of expertise; and

[1] Written communication with the Arizona Identification Council 2009.

(c) to inform all parties and the court if the expert's opinion changes from that contained in a report served as evidence or given in a statement"

(Ministry of Justice 2015: Section 19.2).

Previous rules (Ministry of Justice 2010: Section 33.2) did not include the requirement for an expert's area of expertise to be defined and for the expert to draw attention to any area for which questioning would require an answer outside that expertise. These changes suggest that a greater focus is now being required by the court on the nature and boundaries of the expert knowledge used by the courts.

Although the rules in the United States and the United Kingdom are stated differently, they share many similarities, and it is within these rules that the forensic podiatrist must operate as an expert witness. These rules are however basic and only refer to expert witness obligations. In addition, those obligations of all who work within forensic context as forensic scientists and practitioners and those obligations of all health care professionals who must also work to the required standards of their core professional and regulatory bodies must be met. As such, in addition to their responsibilities as expert witnesses, many more standards and governance responsibilities apply to podiatrists working as forensic scientists and practitioners.

8.1.1 Scientific and Experienced-Based Expert Opinion in Forensic Podiatry

Podiatry was formally founded under a national body in the United States in 1895, with the first school of podiatry opening in 1911 (Weinstein 1968). In the United Kingdom, podiatry was established in 1912 (Dagnall 1987); it then sought full professional recognition with a specialist professional knowledge base for many years, only managing to achieve this status in relatively recent times. Larkin (1983) noted that chiropodists[2] needed to prove their worth and at the time of writing, they had not developed their own science. In his PhD study, Vernon (2000) noted that his work had revealed certain knowledge limitations amongst podiatrists. Professional groups have both a theoretical and a practical knowledge basis (Eraut 1994), with further tacit knowledge being developed through practical experience, wherein reflection on that experience is required (Mattingley and Fleming 1994). "Knowing how" has been previously described as the nonpropositional knowledge developed by

[2] In the United States up to the mid-1950s and in the United Kingdom up to 1983, chiropody was then the predominant title of the professional groups dealing with the health of the foot. The profession of podiatry developed from this basis, with both the term and practice of chiropody now fading into obsolescence.

practitioners through practice and experience, some of which may be tacit (Polyani 1967). Vernon (2000) speculated that such knowledge may not have previously developed to the level expected among podiatrists because of the immediate effects that many podiatry interventions are known to have and that, in turn, may have impaired the level of reflection otherwise anticipated. Since the time of Vernon's comments, the profession has adopted a more evidence-based approach to its work, with research now becoming commonplace to inform, direct, and develop practice (Lazzarini et al. 2013) and with high-quality dedicated journals being available to inform the practice of the profession (Landorf et al. 2013).

In common with many other professions, the knowledge available to podiatrists is therefore not only that with a scientific basis but also that which can be described as "prescientific," or that concerned with everyday practice (Frolov 1984). Given this scenario, in the practice of forensic podiatry there must be a clear differentiation between the podiatrist's knowledge that is scientific and robust and the knowledge that is tacit and experience based.

Although the ideal is for the knowledge used in forensic podiatry practice to be scientific, an appeal court ruling in the United Kingdom confirmed that professional experience that is not perceived as scientific knowledge also has a place in the forensic expert opinion (R. v. Otway 2011). In the R. v. Otway case involving forensic gait analysis, the defense suggested that the forensic podiatrist who presented evidence in support of the prosecution position in this case relied on an area that had not been fully developed as a science and thus represented no more than subjective opinion. The appeal court rejected these arguments, stating that "The proposition that evidence of a comparison cannot be admitted if its evaluation is expressed in terms subjective experience is simply wrong in law." (R. v. Otway: Section 19). The court further noted, "Expert evidence of opinion is, … one of the exceptions to the rule that opinion evidence is inadmissible" and considered that in the absence of contradiction; the evidence established the existence of science or expertise, witness proficiency in this area, and a foundation for the witness opinion.

In another appeal court ruling in the United Kingdom, forensic gait analysis was again challenged by the defense team (R. v. Ferdinand and others 2014). The challenge was made on several grounds, including considerations around the poor-quality images that had been the subject of the expert examination and the fact that opinion had been expressed on such poor-quality images. Comment was made by the defense team that the expert had been unable to "specify in scientific terms how he had made allowances for an imperfect image," which their appeal suggested rendered the expert's opinion unreliable or unsafe.

The appeal court did not accept this position, noting that although "care is required to ensure that features are reliably demonstrated," the fact that an expert could not state scientifically how allowances had been made for dealing with imperfect images did not make that expert's opinion "unreliable or unsafe." A key point made was that either the "features (of gait) could be seen by the jury or they could not," and in the original trial the jury had been directed that they could only act on the presence of such features if they themselves could also observe these features. The appeal court continued to note that the judge had been in a good position to assess whether the evidence was safe, as he had seen "exactly what the jury saw" (R. v. Ferdinand and others 2014). The appeal court noted the relative infancy of forensic podiatry techniques with research continuing to take place to establish national standards, and the need for careful scrutiny of (forensic gait analysis) evidence with rigorous examination of image quality and expert opinion was stated. At the same time, the appeal court again described the foundation of the discipline as being one of "science and expertise" and noted that an essential element was for the expert to be able to demonstrate features observed to the jury.

The judgment in this case supports the role of professional experience as opposed to solely scientific approaches to forensic podiatry practice. Particular points leading to this conclusion are the acceptance of the appeal court that research into the establishment of national standards was continuing (and therefore not complete), the comment relating to expertise as well as science being a foundation for the discipline and the key point that determining the presence of gait features is an observational task that a lay jury could appreciate themselves when such features are shown by the expert.

In another important successful appeal case in the United Kingdom (R. v. T 2010), this time in relation to work of another forensic discipline, among several issues raised was criticism of the inappropriate use of the word science in the presentation of evidence. The judgement specifically stated that in relation to the word "scientific" that "if that phrase is put before the jury, it is likely to give an impression to the jury of a degree of precision and objectivity which may not necessarily be present in an area of expertise" (R. v. T 2010). The judgement continued to note that an expert report should make it clear where a view is expressed that is subjective and based on experience (R. v. T 2010).

Considering these cases in their totality, it is clear that the expert is permitted to provide an expert opinion based on experience and not science in addition to an opinion that is based wholly on science or indeed a combination of experience and science. The critical condition seems to be that the expert must make it explicitly clear whether his or her opinion is founded on science or opinion, thereby allowing a jury to judge the value of that evidence and therefore how much weight to place on that evidence in subsequent deliberations.

8.1.2 Reliability in Relation to Expert Opinion

In the United States, Daubert hearings are used to determine the general acceptance of reliability of expert scientific testimony when evidence is presented (Daubert v. Merrell Dow Pharmaceuticals 1993). The criteria used in such hearings to determine whether the court should accept the evidence are as follows:

- To briefly name the technique or techniques employed in the work
- To consider whether the scientific technique or theory used can be tested
- To ensure that the technique or theory has been subject to peer review and publication
- To consider the potential rate of error of the technique
- To note the standards used for controlling the operation of the technique
- To find information to support the scientific theory or method being accepted within a relevant scientific community

These considerations link to the earlier principle that forensic podiatry practice should ideally be scientific. If the work undertaken by forensic podiatrists meets the criteria for scientific classification, it should then by definition also be capable of meeting Daubert, or similar criteria. In a recent trial in the United States, forensic podiatry approaches to bare footprint identification were tested against the Daubert requirements where they were accepted as meeting all of the required criteria[3] (see Chapter 10 for details).

There is not yet an equivalent process in the United Kingdom, although this has previously been considered (The Law Commission 2009). The principles involved in Daubert hearings do seem to be eminently sensible, and practicing forensic podiatrists could usefully consider their work in relation to the factors seen as pertinent to Daubert. There have been two relatively recent developments in the United Kingdom to improve the reliability of expert opinion. First, the forensic regulator for the United Kingdom has produced codes of conduct and practice (recently updated) (UKFSR 2016) in which expectations of practice are listed that are intended to improve the general reliability of forensic science and practice. Although the document is wide ranging and covers many aspects of practice, of particular note is the specified need to routinely validate the methods that will be used in forensic practice (UKFSR 2016).

The second development, concerns amendments to Criminal Procedure Rules Part 33 in place in the United Kingdom (Ministry of Justice 2014).

[3] Michael, N., Personal communication, December 2, 2015.

These changes provide guidance to courts on factors to consider for determining the reliability of expert opinion to be provided to the court (UKFSR 2014):

- Extent and quality of data to be presented
- Validity of the method used by the expert
- Whether the opinion expressed by the expert properly explains how safe or unsafe any inference made by that expert is
- Accuracy of the methods presented (e.g., estimations of uncertainty in relation to a measurement)
- Extent to which any material upon which the expert's opinion is based has been reviewed by others
- Range of expertise of the expert
- Completeness of information available to the expert
- Whether there is a range of expert opinion on the matter in question
- Whether the expert has diverged from established practice in any way

Forensic podiatrists should be familiar with all of these requirements to practice safely, effectively and within the expectations of the field of forensic work.

8.1.3 Expert Witness Background and Qualifications

Personal credibility is necessary for the forensic podiatrist acting as an expert witness. This fundamental principle cannot be overstated. There are two types of witness: lay and expert. The expert witness has knowledge, skills, or both derived through education, experience, or a combination that qualify that individual to take a set of facts and reach conclusions not attainable by the average person (including the judge and the jury) (Siegel 2007). This expertise can be qualification based, but it can also relate to people with very specific experience in a particular area. In forensic podiatry work, the expertise is more likely to be established by both education and experience in this area of work. In court, attorneys (barristers in the United Kingdom) usually take a considerable amount of time and effort to establish the credibility of an expert at the start of his or her questioning, and it is essential that the forensic podiatrist's background justify his or her presence as an expert in court. Typical factors that demonstrate the expertise required include the following:

- Higher educational qualifications (e.g., PhD, Professional Doctorate, Master's degree) if relevant to the casework undertaken.
- Postgraduate qualifications, e.g., courses that provide specific training in the area of consideration. In this respect, a Master's degree course specifically in forensic podiatry has now been developed in the

United Kingdom.[4] A course in forensic human identification is also available in the United Kingdom through the Faculty of Forensic & Legal Medicine of the Royal College of Physicians.[5] This course is aimed at "graduates who are engaged in medico-legal work involving the investigation of a crime or the action of a legal procedure to identify either the living or the dead" (Faculty of Forensic & Legal Medicine of the Royal College of Physicians 2015, 3), and podiatrists have also been successfully involved in this course.
- Forensic case experience, i.e., not only the number of cases undertaken but also the length of time that the expert has practiced in this area.
- Relevant clinical podiatry experience in terms of patient numbers and the length of time in practice.
- Experience of specialty footwear work (if relevant), including a specific interest in and focus on footwear work in practice.
- Relevant research in which the expert has personally been involved.
- Personal peer-reviewed publications.
- The number, type, and level of court presentations made.
- Membership of relevant professional bodies (both podiatric and forensic).
- Distinction through award or position of esteem (if relevant).

Importantly, credibility is only enhanced by factors relevant to the work undertaken (e.g., possession of a PhD in the sociological history of podiatry does not demonstrate expertise in footwear examination).

8.2 Reporting

8.2.1 Standard Report

The CRFP[6] identified 10 essential elements for the competent practice of forensic podiatry, irrespective of subspecialty. These elements dictate the approach to casework, note taking that should accompany casework, and the format of the subsequent forensic podiatry report. The 10 elements state that the forensic podiatrist should

- Understand the requested instruction or task
- Describe the exhibits, items, and material examined

[4] The University of Huddersfield offers a part time MSc in forensic podiatry. At the time of writing details are available through the University of Huddersfield web site, currently via the link: https://www.hud.ac.uk/courses/part-time/postgraduate/forensic-podiatry-msc/

[5] At the time of writing, further information is available at link http://fflm.ac.uk/exams/dipfhid/.

[6] CRFP. 2006. *Notes for Assessors and Process Verifiers: Forensic Podiatry*. CRFP.

- Establish that the exhibits, items, or materials submitted were of suitable quality for the requirements of the case
- Confirm the correct type of examinations and procedures have been selected
- Confirm the examinations and procedures selected have been carried out competently
- Record the findings, the interpretation of the evidence, and any range of opinion (if relevant) and make reasoned objective conclusions
- Refer to others involved in the investigation and what tasks they performed; recommend, refer, or both to other specialties where appropriate
- Present a clear, methodical, and logical report that only includes details that fall within the reporting officer's area of expertise; the content of this report is presented orally in court where required
- Ensure that the report is fit for purpose (including verification)
- Provide evidence of continuing education/training (in addition to qualifications, experience, and expertise) in the report

These elements considered separately and in detail below.

Understand the requested instruction or task: When writing a case report, the forensic podiatrist needs to provide evidence that he or she has understood the given instruction or task. Thus, it is important to obtain clear and precise instructions from the party requesting forensic podiatry assistance. These instructions should then be carefully stated in the subsequent written report for the benefit of other parties. In addition to *stating* the questions to be addressed, the forensic podiatrist must also show that he or she *understands* these critical questions in the context of the situation. Having established that the task has been understood, the reason for the examination and how it addresses the questions posed should be clear within the report.

Describe the exhibits, items, and the material examined: The forensic podiatrist describes the evidential items made available for examination. The report should contain a full list of these items, including any designator codes and a brief physical description of each item.

Establish that the exhibits, items, or materials submitted were of suitable quality for the requirements of the case: This requirement is, in effect, a preliminary quality check to determine whether examination and evaluation of the material is going to be possible. The conclusions arising from these considerations should be carefully documented in the case notes and in the final report, with any reasons for rejecting items as unsuitable also being recorded. This process is used to determine which of the evidential items available are critical to the case in question. In addition to considering the physical quality of the evidence made available, this check should take care to confirm that all available evidential materials have been received for examination. The items received should be checked to determine "as far as is reasonably practicable" whether there has been any potential for the evidence to have been compromised before receipt. An example of such a problem could be where the chain of custody, for the evidence in question, has not been maintained.

Confirm the correct type of examinations and procedures have been selected: The next task is to select the correct type of examination and procedure to use for the assessment and comparison of the selected items. In the subsequent report, this task usually requires some background information to be given indicating the justification for the chosen method in the context of the particular case and provides a brief explanation of the methods. The methods involved should have proven validity. They would also be those appropriately required in the podiatric assessment of records, the foot, bare footprints, footwear, and images of gait, covering the assessment and comparison of both unknown (questioned) and known (reference) material. In justifying the selected approach, the forensic podiatrist must show in the report that he or she understands the type of information that can be determined from each different approach to examination. In addition, the work should be carried out using appropriate equipment and materials, and details of this information should be available within the case notes.

Confirm the examinations and procedures selected have been carried out competently: In addition to *selecting* appropriate techniques and procedures, they also need to be *used* competently. Thus, the forensic podiatrist must be able to demonstrate this competence in the casework to enable others to determine whether the work has been appropriately and correctly carried out. In practice, this demonstration should be made apparent through a combination of information written into the subsequent report and supplemented by detail available within the supporting case notes. As noted, confirmation of the competent working of the case material can be indicated (although not proven) by making notes on the handling and recording of evidential material made available, and standards relating to general forensic practice and specific forensic podiatry practice should be adhered to throughout and documented as required.

Record the findings, the interpretation of the evidence, and any range of opinion (where relevant) and make reasoned objective conclusions: In the analysis, comparison, and evaluation process, fully detailed contemporaneous notes are required at all stages to demonstrate to others (if required) exactly what was undertaken and how. Such notes must be clear, accurate, legible, and comprehensible. They should also report all findings comprehensively and in an unbiased and impartial manner. The purpose of the notes is to provide a record that would allow (if required) "another forensic practitioner competent in the same area of work to review your work independently".[7]

The critical area of the forensic case report is that of the evaluation phase, where the examining practitioner has completed the assessment and comparison of evidential items and uses reasoned and informed judgment to reach a conclusion. The process of reaching this judgment should be demonstrated in the case notes and report combined, where the objective and critical assessment process leading to a balanced judgment should be apparent to the reader. This process should also clearly relate to the examined evidence.

In reaching the conclusions of the report, due consideration should be given to preexisting research reports. Where a range of opinion is required, "all relevant explanations should be listed" within the report.[8] These relevant explanations should be considered, in turn, with reasons being given for rejecting alternative explanations. Everything should be logically explained, and sound justification should being given for the selection of the most acceptable explanation, where a range of opinion has been apparent.

Refer to others involved in the investigation and what tasks they performed; recommend, refer, both to other specialties where appropriate: This requirement recognizes the responsibility of the forensic podiatrist to work within the boundaries of his or her own specific role and scope of practice at all times. These boundaries have been clearly defined in the International Association for Identification role and scope of practice document (see Chapter 9, Section 9.2.4.1) (Vernon et al. 2009), and in being careful not to encroach on the work of others, forensic podiatrists should be aware of the potential to recommend the input of specialists including forensic footwear examiners, DNA analysts, and fiber analysts. In casework where items of potential interest to other forensic specialties are apparent, the report should note the apparent presence of such items and recommend referring these to the appropriate specialty as required. In no circumstances should the report continue to present an analysis of such an item unless the author of the report possesses and has received the necessary training and development to do so competently.

[7] CRFP. 2006. *Notes for Assessors and Process Verifiers: Forensic Podiatry.* CRFP.
[8] CRFP. 2006. *Notes for Assessors and Process Verifiers: Forensic Podiatry.* CRFP.

Where a referral has been made or recommended to other specialties, the forensic podiatrist must make it clear in the report that he or she has noticed the possible presence of particular details that may be of interest and note that the commissioner of the work may want to investigate/pursue this further.

Present a clear, methodical, and logical report that only includes details that fall within the reporting officer's area of expertise; the content of this report is presented orally in court where required: The final report on the case should be well structured, well written, clear, and concise, yet comprehensive and impartial. Although case notes do not form part of the submitted report, these notes can be requested in relation to the work. As such, they should also be legible, accurate, clear, and impartial. The structure of the final report should cover the following areas:

- Information about the reporting expert. This information should include the name and title of the expert and a summary of his or her relevant qualifications and experience. An up-to-date curriculum vitae (CV) should be appended to the report. If the reporting expert or verifier has any conflicting interests, these conflicts should be declared in this section of the report. Such interests could include relationships or previous involvement with anyone involved in the case, no matter how limited.
- Terms of reference and the source of the instructions given. The instructions, details, and facts of the case over which an opinion is being sought should be clearly stated.
- Material upon which the author's assessment, comparison, evaluation, and conclusions have been based. It may be relevant to provide a list of such material with designated identification/code numbers where applicable.
- Summary of the report, including the results and conclusions.
- Limitations of the report. This requirement addresses areas that may have affected the quality of the conclusions, e.g., access restrictions (refusal, or limited time allowed to examine a subject, any refusal for a request to cut footwear apart, financial limitations, and the like).
- Reference to any required standards or protocols that have applied to the work being reported. These references can include the professional standards of the forensic podiatrist, or alternately, requirements stated by the requesting party, or by the court.
- The expert's opinion/conclusions. The opinion expressed should be grounded in any available relevant research; known literature; and where relevant, personal experience. The conclusions of the report should carefully balance the findings of the analysis,

comparison, and evaluation to produce an evidential statement in which the strength of conclusion is shown.

- Declaration of truth. The declaration of truth is in effect a statement of integrity, with the reporting expert confirming that the report is a genuine attempt to be truthful and that the responsibilities of producing such a report are fully understood and accepted by the author. The wording of this declaration can be prescribed [e.g., in the United Kingdom, in Criminal Procedure Rules Part 19 (Ministry of Justice 2015)], but would be signed by the author of the report.
- Verification. The report verification is, in effect, an independent working through of the case materials by a peer practitioner to answer the questions required by those commissioning the report and a final check of the report for errors. The verification results would be expected to match those of the report author. If any differences of opinion occur, these differences should be recorded and worked through with the reporting expert. If differences cannot be resolved, they should be recorded and a third party peer practitioner should work through the materials independently, with the majority view predominating.
- Relevant reference list as required. In producing a scientifically grounded report, references are likely to be required. It cannot be assumed that a science is simply accepted by the courts; therefore, the use of appropriate references should be carefully considered.
- Appendices. In addition to the need to reference the report appropriately, other appendices may be required. These appendices could include relevant tables, diagrams, and photographic images.

Ensure that the report is fit for purpose (including verification): The report, along with any associated notes, should provide evidence that the work is fit for purpose, meaning that all aspects of the report have contributed toward achieving what has been requested. This task includes competently addressing the question posed, using acceptable methods and techniques as part of the examinations and procedures followed, without bias and in a manner that can be understood by the intended audience. Following the approach and structure advocated will go a long way toward achieving this requirement.

In addition, in determining whether a report is fit for purpose, the report should always be verified. Verification is an attempt to reduce the effects of the natural human tendency to introduce cognitive bias, or favoring of evidence that supports a previous belief, in forensic casework (Smith and Bond 2015). Thus, it has been suggested that by preference, blind verification should be undertaken (Kassin et al. 2013) wherein the verifier has no knowledge of the opinions and prior conclusions of the previous examiners. Kassin et al. (2013) suggested that, ideally, the verifier should not know the identity of the original examiner. However, at the time of writing, there are limited numbers of practicing forensic podiatrists available and as such, this recommendation may sometimes be difficult to implement. Irrespective, the need for verification is overtly enshrined in many of the generic standards documents described in this chapter for forensic science and practice (ASCLD 2013; IAI 2011; NOS 805; Skills for Justice 2013; UKFSR 2016) and is therefore clearly expected (preferably as blind verification) as an essential aspect of the forensic expert report, irrespective of the forensic discipline concerned.

Provide evidence of continuing education/training (in addition to qualifications, experience, and expertise) in the report: Within the report (specifically through the CV), the expert should demonstrate that her or she has undertaken appropriate and timely education relevant to an area of podiatry practice. Education and training can cover a wide range of activities in addition to those presented by formal learning experiences. Alternative forms can include professional reading; research; publications and presentations; conference, seminar, and workshop attendance; and mentoring or being mentored.

A suggested draft generic template for the report is shown in Figure 8.1. In reality, the reporting format can vary slightly according to need, particularly in relation to large and complex casework.

8.2.2 Streamlined Reporting

In addition to the standard reporting format, streamlined reporting is now used from time to time in forensic casework in the United Kingdom where the Crown Prosecution Service provides guidance. Streamlined reporting is an arrangement that has been agreed to manage avoidable delays in the preparation of criminal cases and reduce costs, while ensuring that the requirements of the criminal procedure rules are still met (CPS 2016a). The first stage of the process [streamlined forensic reporting (SFR) SFR 1] involves the summary of the key evidence upon which the prosecution intends to rely (CPS 2016b). This summary allows any issues to be identified at an early stage of the case, and if such issues are identified the process would proceed to a second stage (SFR 2) where a report is provided identifying these issues (CPS 2016b). Expert witness appointed by both sides (prosecution and defense) can then work through these issues together at the earliest opportunity (CPS 2016b).

TITLE

REPORT BY

Author and designation

Date

For

Figure 8.1 Report template. *(Continued)*

1. **NAME:** The report author's name
    - **1.1 RELEVANT QUALIFICATIONS:** Summary of the report authors relevant qualifications
    - **1.2 EXPERIENCE:** Summary of the report author's relevant experience, including scientific/forensic experience
2. **REQUESTED TASK:** The task or instructions given would be stated here.
3. **EXHIBITS AND EXAMINATIONS:** Here, all items of evidence that have been provided with for examination purposes would be listed.
4. **EXAMINATION AND COMPARISON:** A brief summary of the area of examination and comparison (e.g., bare footprints) would be written with references being given where appropriate.
5. **THE EXAMINATION OF ....** Here, a brief description of the examination and findings would be provided, separately for each item.
6. **COMPARISONS AND EVALUATION:** The comparisons undertaken between the above items (usually known and unknown or questioned) would now be evaluated. The report would consider what was been found. It is important that the experts that they have looked hard for features that would indicate both a match and a mismatch
7. **CONCLUSIONS:** The conclusions would be written at the end of the comparison process, using a conclusions scale to show the strength of the evidential opinion (e.g., a likelihood ratio scale or equivalent where appropriate).
8. **REFERENCES CITED:** Any references cited in the report would be listed here.
9. **DECLARATIONS[1]: (Applicable to the UK)** It is often the case that various declarations must be made on conclusion of the work. These declarations are non-negotiable and serve to show that the report author has complied with the Court's requirements, that the report has been declared to be true and that any known limitations have been stated. In the UK, at the time of writing, according to CrPR Criminal Practice Direction 19.4 (2015), the declarations should contain the following:

> Such information as the court may need to decide whether the expert's opinion is sufficiently reliable to be admissible as evidence (Although not expressly stated in CrPR 19, this could be seen as suggesting a need for the expert's qualifications/expertise to be referred to).
>
> A statement that the expert understands an expert's duty to the court, and has complied and will continue to comply with that duty
>
> The same declaration of truth as a witness statement.

It is also a mandatory requirement by CrPR 19(1)[e] (2015) to declare any examinations etc. relied upon by the expert that had been carried out by another person. If this has been the case, the other person should be named and details of their qualifications, supervisory arrangements and whether the findings of these examinations were being relied upon by the reporting expert.

Signed by:	Authors name
Dated:	Date of conclusion
Verified by:	Verifiers name
Dated:	Date of verification

[1] UK requirements listed. These requirements will vary according to the country in which the report is being presented.

Figure 8.1 (Continued) Report template.

Three forms are used in the SFR process (Beckwith 2014):

1. MG22 (a) Initial forensic investigation report
2. MG22 (b) Stage 1 forensic result (requiring a defense response)
3. MG22 (c) Stage 2 forensic issues (addressing issues where feasible)

At the time of writing, there have been no known examples of forensic podiatrists in the United Kingdom being asked to participate in the SFR process, and to date, this arrangement has not included forensic podiatry. It is possible, however, that such an approach may be agreed/requested in the future. As such, should that time come, those working in the field of forensic podiatry are recommended to familiarize themselves with the requirements of SFR, e.g., by reading the CPS SFR guidance and toolkit document (CPS 2016a) in case this approach is requested.

8.3 Experts Conclusions

After the analysis, comparison, examination, and verification, the expert needs to finish the process with a conclusion. This task may seem straightforward or obvious, but it is often not. Other than areas where a positive identification is more readily accepted as such, primarily DNA evidence and fingerprint identification (although these areas have been more scrutinized over the past several years), most disciplines must struggle to use terminology that is often confusing or nondecisive.

The likelihood (Bayesian) ratio approaches were discussed in Chapter 2 and seem to be reasonable methods, although no method is perfect and evolves and adapts over time to better meet the needs of the legal system.

Please note that the information below was accurate at the time of this writing, but it may be changed or modified in the future.

8.3.1 Review of Past and Current Terminology in General Use

Earlier Terminology from United States and Abroad

In the affirmative: Possible, very possible, probable, very probable, with certainty
Question remains open: Nonconclusive
In the negative: Possible non-ID, probable non-ID, non-ID

More Recent to Current Examination Results

Non-ID
Probable non-ID

Insufficient detail for meaningful examination
Probable association
Identification

Recommended Report Conclusions for Footwear Examiners in the United States

Although we do not deal with outsole evaluations for identification purposes, as a general rule, similarities exist than can be modified or adapted to pedal casework.

Individualization: The questioned footwear impression corresponds with the combined class characteristics of the known footwear impression.

In addition, there are numerous accidental/individual characteristics noted. Based on the numerous class and individual characteristics found in agreement between the questioned impression and the known impression, the questioned impression has been individualized as having been made by the known impression and could not have been made by any other footwear.

Elimination
Inconclusive

Association: The questioned footwear impression corresponds in combined class characteristics, wear, and individual characteristics of limited quality and or quantity with the known footwear. Therefore, the likelihood exists that the known footwear made the questioned impression.

Association: The questioned footwear impression corresponds in combined class characteristics and general wear with the known footwear. Because of the absence of individual characteristics, the questioned impression could have been made by this footwear or by another footwear that exhibits the same combined class characteristics and general wear.

Association: The questioned footwear impression shares similar design features with the known footwear. However, because of the lack of sufficient detail, proper scale, or both, a more conclusive association was not made.

Scales in Use in Australia and New Zealand (JFI 2015) Relative to Footwear Examiners

This information is reprinted with permission from an article by Raymond and Sheldon (2015) in the *Journal of Forensic Identification.*

Their final (new) recommendations follow below—number 4.

1. Version of European "harmonized" scale
   a. Identification
   b. Strong support for hypothesis
   c. Support for hypothesis
   d. Inconclusive
   e. Support for alternate hypothesis
   f. Exclusion
2. "Traditionalist" scale
   a. Identification
   b. Probably made
   c. Could have made
   d. Inconclusive
   e. Probably did not make
   f. Elimination
   g. Unsuitable
3. "Capable of" scale
   a. Identification
   b. Capable of
   c. Exclusion
   d. Inconclusive
4. Recommended conclusion scale (refer to article by Raymond and Sheldon)
   a. Lacks sufficient detail
      In the opinion of the examiner, insufficient detail was present in the questioned impression for a meaningful comparison with the known footwear or tire.
   b. Exclusion
      This is the highest degree of nonassociation expressed in footwear and tire impression examinations. Sufficient differences were noted in the comparison between characteristics in the questioned impression and the known footwear or tire.
   c. Indications of nonassociation
      In the opinion of the examiner, the questioned impression exhibits dissimilarities compared to the known footwear or tire; however, certain details or features were not sufficiently clear to permit an exclusion.
   d. Limited association of class characteristics
      Some similar class characteristics were present; however, there were significant limiting factors in the questioned impression that did not permit a stronger association between the questioned

impression and the known footwear or tire. These factors may include, but were not limited to, insufficient detail, lack of scale, improper position of scale, improper photographic techniques, distortion, or significant lengths of time between the date of the occurrence and when the footwear or tires were recovered that could account for a different degree of general wear. No confirmable differences were observed that could exclude the footwear or tire.

e. Association of class characteristics
The class characteristics of both pattern and physical size must correspond between the questioned impression and the known footwear or tire. Correspondence of general wear may also be present.

f. High degree of association
The questioned impression and known footwear or tire must correspond in the observable class characteristics of the pattern, physical size, and general wear. For this degree of association, there must also exist (1) wear that by virtue of its specific location, degree, and orientation makes it unusual; (2) one or more randomly acquired characteristics; or both (1) and (2).

g. Identification
This is the highest degree of association expressed by a footwear and tire impression examiner. The questioned impression and the known footwear or tire share agreement of class and randomly acquired characteristics of sufficient quality and quantity.

8.3.2 Levels of Certainty (DiMaggio 2005, Modified 2014)

Reasoning for this system:

1. Confusion with many different terms generally used.
2. More understandable by jury, judiciary, and attorneys.
3. The system (methodology) is actually a confirmation of evaluation findings.

Level I:
The first question asked by the investigator is whether it is a footprint?

- Is there sufficient quantity or quality to continue in the evaluation process?
- If the answer is in the affirmative, then proceed to the next level; otherwise, it is inconclusive or an exclusion (Figure 8.2).

Level I

Is it a footprint?

Is there sufficient quality?

Quantity?

Continue to Level II??

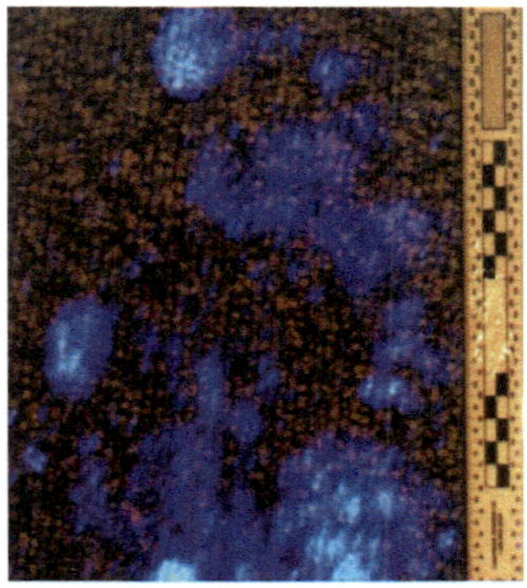

Figure 8.2 Level I findings.

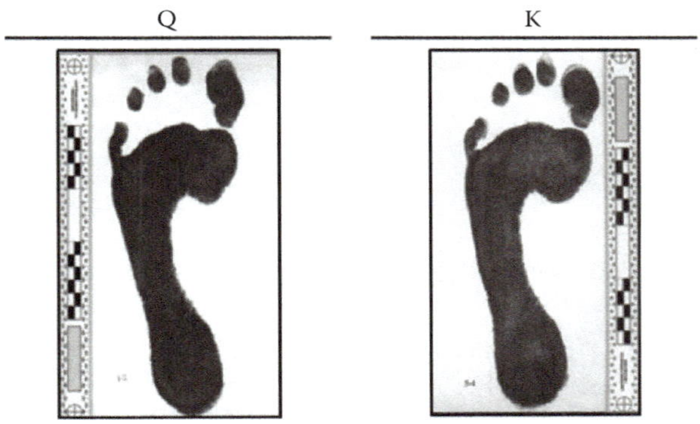

Figure 8.3 Level II agreement.

Level II: General Agreement
Is there a general agreement in size, shape, and position of the digits? If the answer is in the affirmative, proceed to level III (Figure 8.3).

Level III: Identification Lines/Foot Zones
Is there sufficient agreement of the web ridge line, arch line, lateral foot line, heel line, and web space outline? If the answer is in the affirmative, proceed to the level IV (Figure 8.4).

Toe positions
Shape
Size
Foot zones—Overall foot size/shape
ID lines—web ridge line, web space outline, arch line, heel line, lateral line

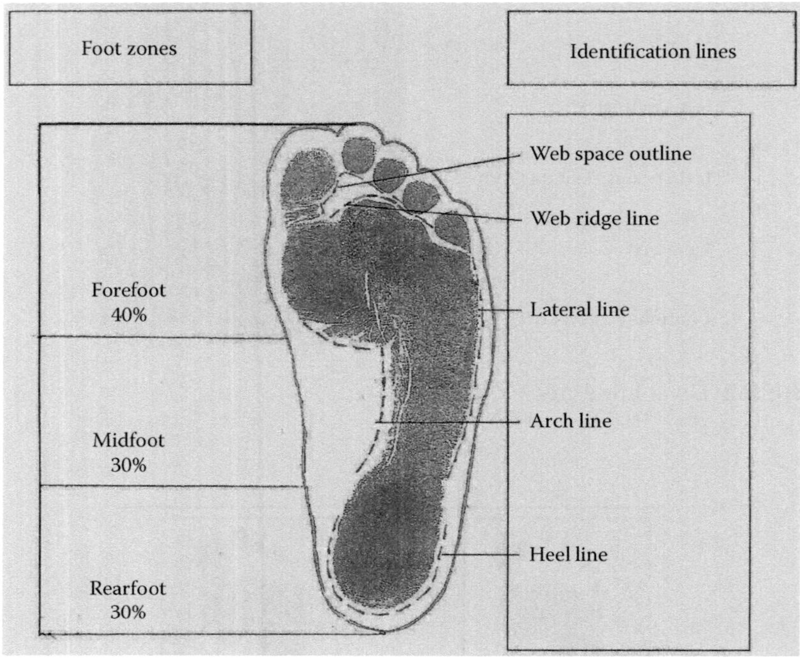

Figure 8.4 DiMaggio morphological identification lines and foot zones.

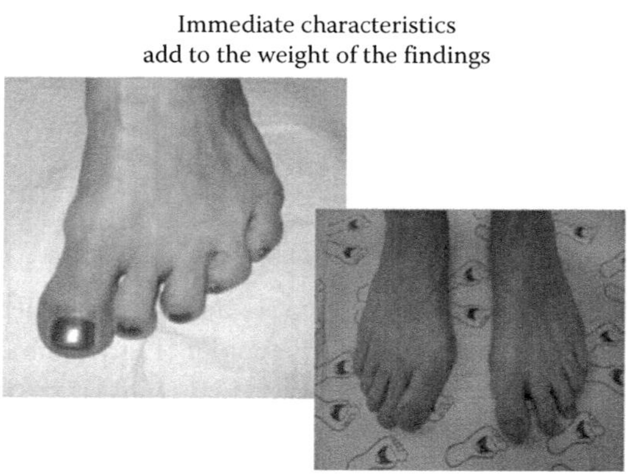

Figure 8.5 Level IV findings.

Level IV: Intermediate Class Characteristics

Level IV where the clinical expertise and knowledge of the medical practitioner regarding pathological, morphological, and biomechanical imbalances or deviations are used (Figure 8.5).

These characteristics add to the weight of the findings in the absence of unique/accidental characteristics.

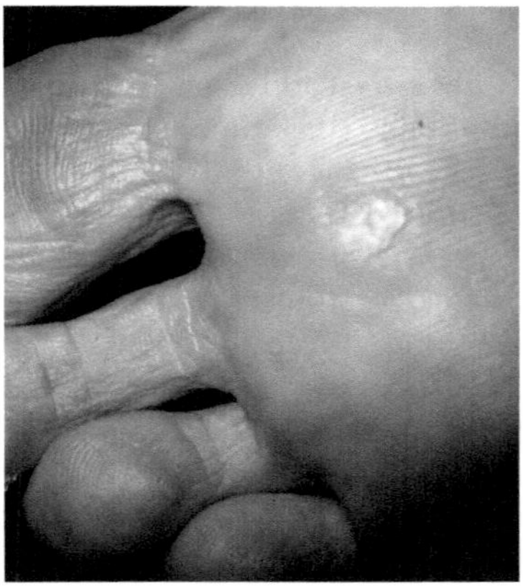

Figure 8.6 Level V findings: puncture (accidental) wound keratosis.

Level V: Unique/Accidental Characteristics

Scar
Foreign body puncture keratosis (Figure 8.6)
Other

8.3.3 Comments

There are various options open to the expert regarding appropriate terminology for conclusions. It is up to the examining practitioner to choose the system that best suits his or her needs. The levels of certainty are only of use in strictly bare footprint cases or sock liner image cases. Obviously, level V use is the exception. Presenting to the court, however, results defined as level III or IV out of five levels seems to add more objectivity to the process, but there is certainly other valid terminology in use, and maybe one day there will be a consensus in the forensic community as to what is best.

8.4 Courtroom (Expert) Testimony

Courtroom testimony is an extremely important responsibility of the expert witness. Courtroom testimony is a broad area, with many books dedicated to the subject. It is a skill that must be learned and practiced, often via workshops and conferences that are readily available through professional organizations, e.g., American Academy of Forensic Sciences and the International Association for Identification.

References

ASCLD (American Society of Crime Laboratory Directors). 2013. Guiding Principles of Professional Responsibility for Crime Laboratories and Forensic Scientists. http://www.ascld-lab.org/wp-content/uploads/2013/04/AL-PD-1014.pdf (Accessed March 3, 2016).

Beckwith J. 2014. *Digital Forensic Specialist Group Streamlined Forensic Reporting.* UKFSR. https://www.gov.uk/government/uploads/system/uploads/attachment_data/file/365452/SFRpresentation23Sep14.pdf (Accessed March 4, 2016).

Civil Justice Council. 2014. Guidance for the instruction of experts in civil claims. https://www.judiciary.gov.uk/wp-content/uploads/2014/08/experts-guidance-cjc-aug-2014-amended-dec-8.pdf (Accessed October 4, 2016).

CPS (Crown Prosecution Service). 2016a. Streamlined Forensic Reporting Guidance and Toolkit. http://www.cps.gov.uk/legal/s_to_u/scientific_evidence/sfr_guidance_and_toolkit/ (Accessed February 23, 2016).

CPS (Crown Prosecution Service). 2016b. *National Streamlined Forensic Reporting Guidance—Section 1—Supporting Information Version 3.0*, CPS.

Dagnall JC. 1987. The start, 75 years ago, of British chiropodial professional organization: The foundation of the National Society of Chiropodists in 1912. *The Chiropodist* 42: 417–426.

Daubert v. Merrell Dow Pharmaceutical Inc., 1993. 509 U.S. 579.

Daubert v. Merrell Dow Pharmaceuticals. 1993. 509 U.S. 579. 92. United States Court Of Appeals for the Ninth Circuit.

DiMaggio J.A. 2005. The role of feet and footwear in medico legal investigations. In *Forensic Medicine of the Lower Extremity*, edited by J. Rich, D.E. Dean, and R.H. Powers. pp. 375–400. Totawa, NJ: Humana Press.

Eraut M. 1994. *Developing Professional Knowledge and Competence.* London: The Falmer Press.

EWI (Expert Witness Institute). 2006. *Experts in the Civil Courts*, edited by L. Blom-Cooper. Oxford: Oxford University Press.

Faculty of Forensic & Legal Medicine of the Royal College of Physicians. 2015. Diploma in Forensic Human Identification (DipFHID) Regulations, Syllabus and Information for Candidates. http://fflm.ac.uk/wp-content/uploads/2014/06/DipFHID-Regulations-November-2015.pdf (Accessed February 5, 2016).

Frolov IT, ed. 1984. *Dictionary of Philosophy*. Moscow: Progress Publishers.

IAI (International Association for Forensic Identification). 2011. Code of Ethics and Standards of Professional Conduct. https://www.theiai.org/about/code_of_ethics.pdf (Accessed February 17, 2016).

Kassin SM, Itiel ED, and Kukucka J. 2013. The forensic confirmation bias: Problems, perspectives and proposed solutions. *Journal of Applied Research in Memory and Cognition* 2: 42–52.

Landorf KB, Menz HB, Borthwick AM, Potter MJ, Munteanu SE, and Bowen CJ. 2013. JFAR's role in publishing believable research findings. *Journal of Foot and Ankle Research* 6: 49.

Larkin G. 1983. *Occupational Monopoly and Modern Medicine.* London: Tavistock Publications.

Lazzarini PA, Geraghty J, Kinnear EM, Butterwirth M, and Ward D. 2013. Research capacity and culture in podiatry: Early observations within Queensland Health. *Journal of Foot and Ankle Research* 6: 1–11.
LII (Legal Information Institute). 2016a. Frye Standard. https://www.law.cornell.edu/wex/Frye_standard (Accessed March 4, 2016).
LII (Legal Information Institute). 2016b. Daubert Standard. https://www.law.cornell.edu/wex/daubert_standard (Accessed March 4, 2016).
Mattingley C, and Fleming MH. 1994. *Clinical Reasoning: Forms of Enquiry in a Therapeutic Practice*: Philadelphia: F. A. Davis Co.
Ministry of Justice. 2010. Criminal Procedure Rules. http://www.justice.gov.uk (Accessed March 26, 2010).
Ministry of Justice. 2014. *Criminal Procedure Rules Part 33*. London: Ministry of Justice.
Ministry of Justice. 2015. *The Criminal Procedure Rules. The Criminal Practice Directions*. October 2015 Edition. http://www.justice.gov.uk/courts/procedure-rules/criminal/rulesmenu-2015 (Accessed March 2, 2016).
Polyani M. 1967. *The Tacit Dimension*. London: Routledge.
R v Ferdinand and others. 2014. EWCA Crim 1234. 1 The Court of Appeal (Criminal Division) on Appeal from the Central Criminal Court.
R v Otway. 2011. (R v Otway: Section 19). EWCA Crim 3. 1 The High Court of Justice Court of Appeal (Criminal Division) on Appeal from Manchester Crown Court.
R v T. 2010. EWCA Crim 2439. 1 The High Court of Justice Court of Appeal (Criminal Division) on Appeal from the Crown Court.
Raymond J and Sheldon P. 2015. Standardizing shoemark evidence—An Australian and New Zealand collaborative trial. *Journal of Forensic Identification* 65(5): 868–883.
Sacks ME. 1995. *A Guide for Testifying and Consulting Experts*. Danvers, MA: LRP Publications.
Siegel JA. 2007. *Introduction to Forensic Science*. Boca Raton, FL: CRC Press.
Skills for Justice. 2013. National Occupational Standards. http://www.sfjuk.com/national-occupational-standards/ (Accessed March 3, 2016).
Smith L and Bond J. 2015. *Criminal Justice and Forensic Science*. New York: Palgrave.
The Law Commission. 2009. *The Admissibility of Expert Evidence in Criminal Proceedings in England and Wales: A New Approach to the Determination of Evidentiary Reliability*. Consultation Paper No 190. UK: The Law Commission.
UKFSR (UK Forensic Science Regulator). 2014. *Codes of Practice and Conduct for Forensic Science Providers and Practitioners in the Criminal Justice System. Version 2.0*. Birmingham: Office of the Forensic Science Regulator, Home Office.
UKFSR (UK Forensic Science Regulator). 2016. *Codes of Practice and Conduct for Forensic Science Providers and Practitioners in the Criminal Justice System. Version 3.0*. Birmingham: Office of the Forensic Science Regulator, Home Office.
US Govt. 2009. *Federal Rules of Evidence*. U.S. Government Printing, Washington D.C.
Vernon W. 2000. The functional analysis of shoe wear patterns. PhD diss., Sheffield Hallam University.

Vernon W, Brodie B, DiMaggio J, Gunn N, Kelly H, Nirenberg M, Reel S, and Walker J. 2009. *Forensic Podiatry: Role and Scope of Practice (In the Context of Forensic Human Identification)*. International Association for Identification. http://www.theiai.org (Accessed March 26, 2010).

Weinstein F. 1968. *Principles and Practice of Podiatry*. Philadelphia, PA: Lea and Febiger.

Standards of Practice, Governance, and Standard Operating Procedures

9

The forensic podiatrist is an expert witness whose overriding duties are to the court. In performing these duties, the forensic podiatrist must live and work to high professional standards and within strong governance arrangements during practice, where he or she should operate to defined standard operating procedures. This chapter provides an explanation of the generic and discipline-specific standards and governance requirements. Adherence to these requirements helps to prevent errors while working as a forensic podiatrist.

9.1 Overview

9.1.1 Importance of Governance and Standards in Forensic Science and Practice

Forensic science and practice has been the subject of criticism in recent times. In the United States, at the behest of Congress, the highly influential National Academy of Sciences produced a report in which the need for improvement was highlighted (NRC 2009). The report succinctly summarized the consistent message heard from those who provided testimony and evidence as follows:

> The forensic science system, encompassing both research and practice, has serious problems that can only be addressed by a national commitment to overhaul the current structure that supports the forensic science community in this country. This can only be done with effective leadership at the highest levels of both federal and state governments, pursuant to national standards, and with a significant infusion of federal funds.
>
> *NRC 2009, xx preface*

The report provided many recommendations as to how these criticisms could be addressed, including suggested improvements in the adoption and use of standards, governance, and standard operating procedures (SOPs).

Similarly, in the United Kingdom, the fundamental need for quality standards in relation to forensic science and practice is recognized at the highest level (House of Commons Science and Technology Committee 2013), and there have been high-level demands for improved standards in relation to forensic science and practice (House of Commons Science and Technology Committee 2005; Law Commission 2011; Rozenberg 2014). A past report by the Law Commission (2011) expressed concerns about the reliability of some forms of expert evidence being presented to the courts, and the need for "a full range of forensic services of the required quality standards" was also raised in a U.K. government report on forensic science (House of Commons Science and Technology Committee 2005). More recently, the current U.K. forensic science regulator prioritized the need for a risk assessment of forensic science quality (UKFSR 2015) and a newly publicized Home Office Forensic Science Strategy (2016) reinforces the need for consistent quality management and enhanced governance. These recent publications emphasize the importance of standards and governance in relation to forensic science and practice. In addition to expert comment on the importance of, and need for improvements in standards of forensic science and practice, there is a public perception that standards need to be improved in this area of work (Robinson 2015). Whether such opinions are right or wrong, the need for appropriate high standards to be maintained is shown by the presentation of such perspectives.

Multiple standards have emerged in relation to forensic science and practice at varying levels (international, national, generic, professional body, and discipline specific). Although the development and use of standards can and should generally be considered good, Vernon (2014) has pointed out that the presence of many and varying standards can be confusing, despite the potential for these standards to overlap. As such, the purpose of this chapter is to consider the various standards that can be relevant to forensic podiatry practice, along with relevant detail and suitable governance framework to guide the forensic podiatry practitioner through this complex, but very essential area.

9.2 Standards in General Forensic Science and Practice

Standards for forensic science and practice have been prescribed at various levels. These standards include internationally recognized standards (ISO/IEC 2005), standards applicable on a national level (NIST 2015a; Skills for Justice 2013; UKFSR 2016), generic standards written by various professional bodies in forensic science (AAFS 2016a; ANZFSS 2014; ASFLD 2005, 2013; CSFS 2016a; IAI 2011), discipline-specific standards approved by forensic science and dedicated professional organizations (Vernon and Kelly 2006; Vernon et al. 2009) and regulatory bodies (HCPC 2013, 2016). As in the case of rules for expert witnesses, several common factors are apparent within these standards. A brief description is provided below of the standards that forensic podiatrists need to be aware of in their practice.

9.2.1 International/Generic Standards

9.2.1.1 ISO 17025

This highly influential international standard was developed for practice in testing and calibration laboratories and was seen as directly applicable to the work of forensic scientists. It is recognized worldwide as representing the gold standard for laboratory[1]-based forensic science work (ISO/IEC 2005). The International Organization for Standardization (ISO) develops international standards through technical committees that deal with particular fields of activity (ISO/IEC 2005). The standard would then be used by accreditation bodies (ISO/IEC 2005) as the basis of their work of assessing and recognizing competence in a particular field of practice. Standard ISO 17025 considers laboratory management systems, technical competence, and the ability to generate technically valid results (ISO/IEC 2005). In relation to management system aspects of the standard, ISO 17025 has been aligned with ISO 9001:2000 that specifies requirements for a quality management system, focusing on product consistency and customer satisfaction (including continual improvement and the provision of customer assurance) (ISO 2015). This reflects the need for sound management and consumer sensitivity in addition to technical competence in relation to scientific practice.

ISO 17025 is a detailed and complex document covering management processes and controls on all aspects of practice. Customer services relationship standards are covered as are contractual aspects of such relationships, and where applicable subcontractor processes. Where the standards relate to practice, ISO 17025 states the requirements for the testing and calibration of methods and equipment used, including monitoring and corrective actions that should be taken where problems have been identified. There is an expectation that methods used will be validated. Standards are also stated in relation to data control, record keeping, and records management. The need for personnel competence and proficiency to be regularly tested, with interlaboratory comparisons being made, is also covered in the standard. In relation to casework, materials handling, quality assurance in the context of test results, and opinions and interpretations are explicitly considered. Final sections of the standards specified in ISO 17025 cover the expectations in relation to reporting and the electronic transmission of results.

The ISO has an expectation that the widespread adoption of this standard among relevant organizations would lead to improvements in cooperation, information exchange, and ultimately harmonization of working practices (ISO 17025).

[1] The term "laboratory" in the forensic context is interpreted as the place of work of persons working in forensic science, whether this be a laboratory in the literal sense, or any other workplace in which forensic science is practiced (UKFSR 2010, Personal communication).

Organizations can achieve ISO 17025 accreditation through formally recognized/appointed accreditation bodies that would undertake such assessments against the standards of ISO 17025. In the United Kingdom, the United Kingdom Accreditation Service (UKAS) has been appointed as the only national accrediting body that can assess against such "internationally agreed standards" and grant the appropriate recognition symbol to compliant organizations (UKAS 2016).

From a forensic podiatry perspective, ISO 17025 is so wide ranging that not all aspects covered are relevant. It is also the case that the standards of ISO 17025 do not cover everything required of a forensic podiatry practitioner, whose professional allegiances extend much wider than calibration and testing processes. The cost of accreditation is known to be high, and a considerable amount of effort is required to pull together the necessary evidence to demonstrate that ISO requirements have been met. As has been pointed out previously, these factors may be problematic to sole practitioners working full or part-time as forensic practitioners, including forensic podiatrists.[2]

Whether achieving ISO 17025 accreditation is possible for organizations or businesses providing forensic podiatry services, those working in the field need to be aware of the requirements of this important international standard and take measures to align relevant aspects of their business and practices with this standard. Where a decision is made not to seek ISO 17025 accreditation, the organization/business concerned should make alternative arrangements to ensure and demonstrate that appropriate standards of practice are in place.

9.2.2 National Standards

In additional to the international standard ISO 17025, many national-level standards also exist for those working in forensic science and practice. Such standards can be created by organizations that have responsibilities for developing and maintaining generic standards in nationally recognized areas of occupation (e.g., health, the criminal justice sector) (Skills for Justice 2016). These standards can also be created by professional bodies including those generic to forensic science/practice and others related specifically to forensic podiatry or by regulatory organizations that cover the practice of the forensic podiatry professional (e.g., Health and Care Professions Council in the United Kingdom).

[2] Vernon et al. (2009): CIFP Business Model July 2009. Unpublished document presented to UKFSR.

9.2.2.1 Forensic Science Regulator Codes of Practice and Conduct for Forensic Science Providers and Practitioners in the Criminal Justice System Version 3.0 (UKFSR 2016)

The U.K. forensic science regulator (UKFSR) has published this document to communicate the standards expected of those who practice forensic science in the United Kingdom. The document is now in its third version and is overtly written "to assist organizations with understanding and interpreting the requirements of the standards, particularly BS/EN ISO/IEC 17025" to which the document is closely linked and simultaneously refers to "the 2015 Criminal Procedure Rules, 2015 Criminal Practice Directions and relevant standards and guidance documents" (UKFSR 2016). Covered in the codes of practice and conduct are the accreditation requirements for all forensic science service providers, and as in ISO 17025 the document covers all areas of service management and delivery, not just the requirements of forensic casework (UKFSR 2016). The document is intended to show clearly to forensic service providers and practitioners, customers, and the public alike the values and ideals of the forensic practice disciplines and what those dealing with such organizations/practitioners "have a right to expect" (UKFSR 2016, 11). It is made explicitly clear that all forensic practitioners are expected to comply with the principles of the code of conduct contained within the document with the exception of those disciplines that do not have crime scene or laboratory elements to their work. Forensic podiatry is specifically mentioned in the document where it is noted that a stand-alone code of practice applies to any forensic science activity of the discipline.[3] "Occasional experts" for whom the delivery of forensic science services is not their core business are sometimes required to provide evidence. Although allowances can be made for these practitioners, the UKFSR codes of practice and conduct make it explicitly clear that such experts should nevertheless be "bound by, the code of conduct as a minimum" (UKFSR 2016, 14). This is a significant shift from the more lenient approach to the appointment and use of experts that has been criticized on the grounds that expert opinion evidence of insufficient reliability was being admitted to the courts (Law Commission 2011, 1.8).

Also considered in the document is the need to avoided conflicts of interest and threats to impartiality, highlighting the neutral approach with the freedom from bias (as far as is possible to achieve) that is required by all forensic practitioners.

One key area covered under a section considering the control of records is the need for forensic science providers to have systems for checking and reviewing their work, including critical findings of that work (UKFSR 2016).

[3] At the time of writing, this document is being prepared. Its publication is anticipated in the near future.

The policies and procedures for this process are expected to be documented, and where applicable, the level of independence of such checking procedures should be defined organizationally and shown through documentation (UKFSR 2016).

The document also notes that evidence of "proper training and formal assessment" of forensic practitioners should be kept by forensic service providers, with various broad examples being given to indicate the types of training, education, development, and practice-based learning that would be acceptable, with the need for regular assessments of competence to be made routinely (UKFSR 2016, 22). Implicit here is the understanding that demonstrable education and continuing professional development/medical education appropriate to forensic practice must be undertaken by all those working as forensic practitioners.

Standards to approaches used in casework are also covered, with requirements for the demonstrable control and care of materials being specified along with risk assessment requirements, not only in relation to the handling of potentially hazardous materials but also in relation to the management of factors that may adversely affect the chain of custody (e.g., compromised packaging, incorrect labeling of items of evidence), when these are found to have occurred.

As with ISO 17025, the UKFSR codes of practice and conduct also place considerable emphasis on the need for methods used by forensic scientists to have been validated, explained as "The process of providing objective evidence that a method, process or device is fit for the specific purpose intended" (UKFSR 2016, 57). The essential requirement is that the methods used in forensic practice have been independently demonstrated as being fit for the purpose for which the method is being used and that any parameters of use are understood. In other words, this requirement is for practice to be evidence based as supported by, e.g., published research, technical reports, reference collections, and databases (UKFSR 2016). In relation to this requirement for methods validation, the codes of practice and conduct make a clear distinction between measurement and interpretive methods. At the time of writing, much of the work of forensic podiatrists is interpretive, involving competent, expert knowledge of the field of practice as opposed to the physical measurement and comparison of evidential items. The codes of practice and conduct acknowledge that although there is still the need for interpretive methods used to be validated, the process for the validation of their "functional and performance requirements" is less prescriptive (UKFSR 2016, 30). The focus here is on the competence of the practitioner and how different practitioners can demonstrate that they can "provide consistent, reproducible, valid and reliable results" (UKFSR 2016, 32).

Four ways of achieving consistent, reproducible, valid, and reliable results are stated by the regulator (UKFSR 2016, 32):

1. Independent confirmation of results/opinions by another competent examiner (i.e., without prior knowledge of the first result/opinion provided)
2. Participation in interlaboratory comparisons (collaborative exercises or proficiency tests)
3. External recognition with a recognized and relevant professional body
4. Design frequent in-house assessment into the process by using positive and negative competence tests

It is critical that practicing forensic podiatrists understand and comply with these requirements to avoid errors in practice and avoidable challenge when presenting their evidence. The first requirement is the need for casework to be verified independently by a peer practitioner. This verification is in effect a working through of the same case materials without prior knowledge of the reporting forensic podiatrist's opinions. Given that the point of methods validation is to provide quality assurance and to ensure that different practitioners can reach the same conclusions when addressing the same question in relation to a given set of evidential materials, this approach is in effect a form of data triangulation—an approach commonly used in qualitative research designs in which different data collection techniques or sources are used to enhance the quality and credibility of the work (Patton 1990).

The second and third requirements (interlaboratory comparisons, collaborative exercises or proficiency tests and external recognition with a recognized professional body) can, in practice, be combined. It is possible for proficiency testing to be wide enough to recognize fitness to practice, education, and competence in the same exercise. Subject to individual practitioners being able to demonstrate that they can meet the required standards of practice through such proficiency testing, the results of such tests could be recognized by an appropriate professional body, such as the competency testing scheme leading to accredited forensic practitioner status for various groups of forensic practitioners, including forensic podiatrists, that is operated by the Chartered Society of Forensic Sciences (CSFS) (CSFS 2016b).

The final requirement can be met through the adoption of regular in-house mock casework under test conditions to confirm that the practitioners are working to the same framework in their approach and are able to achieve the same (correct) interpretations in practice, where the correct conclusion is already known by the internal examiner and the accuracy of the practitioner's interpretive conclusions can therefore be confirmed.

The consideration and handling of uncertainty is noted in many areas of the codes of practice and conduct (UKFSR 2016). Although this management is generally in relation to measurement uncertainty, the appropriate management of uncertainty is also central to interpretive approaches.

Forensic science and practice is undertaken in real-world situations where the consideration and management of variables are often required. Vernon and Nirenberg (2016) noted that the work of the forensic scientist involves reaching conclusions under conditions of uncertainty in the presence of these variables. Where interpretive methods are required, the need is for that interpretation to be made within context, where all uncertainties and variables known to be present are taken into consideration when determining the weight that should appropriately be placed on the evidential conclusion derived through the examination undertaken.

The UKFSR (2016) codes of practice and conduct cover several other areas in broad terms, including reporting and requirements in relation to the disclosure of work, including any "unused material." Disclosure requirements are covered in other documents (ACPO/CPS 2010; CPS 2016) and seem to be included in the codes of practice and conduct document to remind practitioners and providers of the importance of adhering to these requirements as required.

The UKFSR codes of practice and conduct are essential reading for all forensic science and practice providers in the United Kingdom. It is also useful reading for those practicing in other countries, particularly given the close links between this document and the requirements stated in ISO 17025. Although the requirements stated in the UKFRS codes of practice and conduct have not been made statutory at the time of writing, it is possible that they will be in the future. Meanwhile, it would be unwise for a forensic practitioner to ignore the demands the UKFSR has stated in the document because they are widely understood and viewed as essential baseline standards for practice in forensics.

9.2.2.2 NIST Forensic Science Standards Board: OSAC (2015)

In 2009 in the United States, the National Academy of Sciences, Committee on Identifying the Needs of the Forensic Sciences Community published a highly critical report on the state of forensic science in the United States (NRC 2009). The report made several recommendations that it was believed should address the criticisms highlighted in the report. After publication of the report, a joint initiative commenced between the National Institute of Standards and Technology (NIST) and the Department of Justice. In this initiative, a governing Forensic Standards Board was created to oversee the activities of a new body, the Organization of Scientific Area Committees (OSAC) (NIST 2014). The OSAC was created in February 2014 as a collaborative body "to strengthen the nation's use of forensic science by supporting the development and promulgation of forensic science consensus documentary standards and guidelines, determining each forensic discipline's research and measurement standards needs, and ensuring that a sufficient scientific basis exists for each discipline" (NIST 2016). As such, the focus of OSAC is on the development of national standards and guidelines for forensic science and practice in the United States. Before NIST, in the United States, standards and guidelines were created and agreed on through a scientific working group (SWG). With the formation of the OSAC, the work of many SWGs has been discontinued, with the intention to transfer work of the SWGs into the OSAC (SWGTREAD 2014). Until the transfer has been successfully transitioned, the work on standards and guidelines has been retained and is available for scrutiny on the SWG website "until comparable OSAC documents become available" (SWGTREAD 2014).

In performing its function, the OSAC has five scientific area committees: Biology/DNA, Chemistry/Instrumental Analysis, Physics/Pattern Interpretation, Crime Scene/Death Investigation, and Digital/Multimedia (NIST 2015). Twenty-four discipline specific subcommittees are responsible for the creation of standards, guidelines, and codes of practice that are approved by the overarching SACs and governing Forensic Standards Board (NIST 2015b).

At the time of writing, there is no OSAC subcommittee for forensic podiatry and therefore no specific national standards in the United States for practice in this discipline. Regardless, practicing forensic podiatrists are advised to familiarize themselves with the standards expected of similar or related forensic disciplines to raise awareness of the type of national standards expected and to consider which of these standards could apply directly to forensic podiatry practice. Through such familiarization, applicable standards could be adopted by the forensic podiatrist in his or her own practice in the form of working protocols until such time that the OSAC finds it appropriate to create a subcommittee specifically for forensic podiatry.

9.2.2.3 Skills for Justice NOS for Forensic Science

In the United Kingdom, a detailed range of relevant National Occupational Standards (NOS) have been created by the Skills for Justice, the Sector Skills Council, and Standards Setting Body specifically for the Justice sector. Skills for Justice is an employer-lead organization that is part of a joint venture company, Universal Skills, and is in place to provide better links between "employees, government and education" (Skills for Justice 2016). The organization aims to help employers to "develop and sustain a skilled workforce" fit for the purpose of the business of that organization. One of the means by which the aims of Skills for Justice are to be achieved is through the creation and use of the NOS that, according to Skills for Justice, "help specify the knowledge, skills and understanding needed in particular roles for most jobs in the UK" (Skills for Justice 2013). Such standards describe competent performance in terms of outcomes of a forensic practitioner's work and the knowledge and skills they need to perform effectively. They allow a clear assessment of competence against nationally agreed standards of performance, across a range of workplace circumstances (Skills for Justice 2013). A subset of NOS has been developed by Skills for Justice for the practice of forensic science. The NOS are wide ranging and consider all aspects of forensic science from the start of an investigation through to communicating the findings on conclusion of the work to "relevant stakeholders," which includes presentation of the evidence in court.

The NOS that apply directly to forensic podiatry practice in the United Kingdom cover the preliminary, middle, and concluding phases of the work undertaken that require forensic podiatry input. The preliminary phase includes NOS for the planning and preparation for the specific aspects of the investigation to be undertaken by the forensic podiatrist, visual record creation, and the safe handling and processing of evidential items. Occasionally, the forensic podiatrist may be required to visit the scene of crime in which case the NOS relating to safe and appropriate scene attendance should be understood and followed. The middle phase of the work includes the selection of appropriate methods for examination and the execution of that examination according to the method chosen, with analysis and comparison leading through evaluation of the significance of the findings to the production of objectives and unbiased conclusions in which alternative propositions are considered. This middle phase concludes with the independent review and verification of these conclusions for which further NOS are specified. The final phase of the work for which NOS are specified is that of the communication of the findings of the work undertaken along with the significance of those findings in such a way that they can be understood by all who need to understand these including various stakeholders with little or no specialist knowledge of the language and practice of the specialist area involved.

Not all of the areas specified in the NOS are relevant to the practice of forensic podiatry, which provides a limited specialist function within the overall framework of the investigation. However, the forensic podiatrist should be aware of NOS areas that could apply to his or her work and would be recommended to follow the requirements of these areas at all times. For forensic podiatrists practicing in countries other than the United Kingdom, the NOS can still be seen as providing good advice on standards of practice, and as such following the requirements of NOS should be helpful, if not essential. At the time of writing, the NOS can only be accessed directly by member organizations; therefore, linking with or joining such an organization is required to have access the required documents. As with many of the standards applicable to the practice of forensic science, there is overlap between the requirements of the NOS created by Skills for Justice and other standards of forensic science and practice. These standards are revised periodically; therefore, regular scrutiny is recommended once access to these standards has been gained.

9.2.3 Professional Body Standards

In addition to there being international and national standards for forensic science and practice, standards have also been stated by various professional bodies in forensic practice and human identification. Forensic podiatrists who are members of any of these organizations need to be aware of the obligations to live and work to the standards of each respective organization. Examples of such organizations and a brief consideration of their associated standards follow.

9.2.3.1 The Chartered Society of Forensic Sciences

Although based in the United Kingdom, the CSFS has ~3000 members situated across 60 countries (CSFS 2016c). The CSFS has a Standards Committee that defines, develops, tests, and monitors standards in forensic education and practice. The standards of the CSFS are extensive and are linked to an accreditation scheme for courses in forensic science, the CSFS continuing professional development and certificate of professional competence schemes (CSFS 2016), thereby ensuring that standards in both education and practice are in agreement. The CSFS maintains an awareness of available external standards, thereby ensuring that there are no discrepancies between its own standards and those set by other organizations/bodies.

9.2.3.2 The International Association for Identification

The International Association for Identification (IAI) is the oldest and largest professional organization in the world for those involved in scientific forensic identification (IAI 2016a). The IAI has a code of ethics and standards of professional conduct covering professionalism, competency, and proficiency and clear communications to which all members are expected to adhere (IAI 2011). Many broad themes are inherent within these standards and cover the requirement for unbiased and impartial approaches to practice, freedom from inappropriate external influence, confidentiality, honesty, and professional behavior. Also explicit in the codes of the IAI is the need to practice safely using sound and reliable methods with controls and standards, including review and verification underpinned by clear and comprehensive records and appropriate and up-to-date training and development. Examination of these standards shows links and overlap with the standards of other organizations/bodies.

9.2.3.3 American Academy of Forensic Sciences

The American Academy of Forensic Sciences (AAFS), based in the United States, describes itself as "a multi-disciplinary professional organization that provides leadership to advance science and its application to the legal system. The objectives of the Academy are to promote professionalism, integrity, competency, education, foster research, improve practice, and encourage collaboration in the forensic sciences" (AAFS 2016b). The AAFS is involved in developing standards for forensic science and practice through an Academy Standards Board (ASB) that is tasked with creating documented standards for forensic science and practice (AAFS 2016c). The ASB is expected to work closely with the Forensic Science Standards Board of NIST and its OSACs to match its activities with work being undertaken nationally in the United States on forensic standards development. In addition to the work of this ASB, seen as an involvement with the creation of national as opposed to internal standards, the AAFS also has its own code of ethics and conduct (AAFS 2016). These obligations placed on AAFS members are stated in broad terms and essentially state the requirement for members to exercise professionalism, honesty, integrity, and competency in all areas of their practice.

9.2.3.4 The European Network of Forensic Science Institutes

The European Network of Forensic Science Institutes (ENFSI), by definition, is a European-wide organization. Its stated purpose is "to share knowledge, exchange experiences and come to mutual agreements in the field of forensic science" (ENFSI 2013a). To meet this requirement, among its overall aims, ENFSI states that it will "encourage all ENFSI laboratories to comply with best practice and international standards for quality and competence assurance" (ENFSI 2013). Although a European-wide organization, ENFSI has been listed under the professional body standards section of this chapter as opposed to the national or international body standards sections due to the nature of ENFSI, i.e., a member based organization with its members representing the specific forensic laboratories within which they work (ENFSI 2013b).

Much of the work of ENFSI concerns the sharing of knowledge and experience and reaching mutual agreements across the laboratory-based membership, with several influential projects being undertaken as part of this remit. The work of ENFSI also encourages its member laboratories to "comply with best practice and international standards for quality and competence assurance" (ENFSI 2013). As such, ENFSI does have a role in encouraging the adoption and maintenance of quality standards in forensic science and practice. Although to date ENFSI does not have forensic podiatry representation, as in the case of the U.S.-based OSACs, forensic podiatrists practicing in Europe would be recommended to be mindful of the work of ENFSI and be prepared to adopt any relevant recommendations concerning standards in their working practices and protocols.

9.2.3.5 *American Society of Crime Laboratory Directors*

The American Society of Crime Laboratory Directors (ACLD) is a membership-based Society for managers of forensic science laboratories in the United States. The organization has various purposes, one of which is "to promote, encourage and maintain the highest standards of practice in the field" (ASCLD 2016). To assist with this aim, the ASCLD has a code of ethics that places some obligations on its members (ASCLD 2005) such as the need to maintain appropriate personal conduct at all times, honesty, the avoidance of misrepresentation of expertise, qualifications and in relation to technical matters in relation to technical matters, and the requirement for casework conclusions to be supported by scientific data. Because the ASCLD is an organization for managers, the code of ethics also includes managerial standards that are placed in broad terms.

The ASCLD has also written "Guiding Principles of Professional Responsibility for Crime Laboratories and Forensic Scientists" (ASCLD 2013). Here, the ASCLD overtly declare that "these principles have been drawn from other professional codes and suggestions made by leaders in the forensic community" thereby guaranteeing overlap with other standards for forensic scientific practice. It is therefore no surprise that the principles cover requirements for honesty; impartiality; working within one's expertise; use of appropriate, proven methods; maintenance of practice competence; verification of casework conclusions; and clear communication.

At the time of writing, most forensic podiatrists work as sole trader practitioners as opposed to operating in teams within laboratories, although it is possible that this will change in that there is at least one forensic podiatry unit that employs several forensic podiatry specialists overseen by a senior forensic podiatrist manager. Should this model of practice develop further, those involved in the management of such a unit would be advised to be aware of the ASCLD requirements for forensic laboratory management, even if they are not members of the ASCLD themselves. Given the overlap between the ASCLD guiding principles of professional responsibility and the standards of other organizations, forensic podiatrists are advised to be aware of these requirements that through this overlap, by definition, are widely expected.

9.2.3.6 *Australian and New Zealand Forensic Science Society*

The Australian and New Zealand Forensic Science Society (ANZFSS) is a professional organization primarily aimed at those based in Australia and New Zealand. Its purposes are to encourage the advancement of forensic science, and membership is open to "those with a professional or active interest in forensic science" (ANZFSS 2016). The ANZFSS has a code of professional practice that applies to all members; this code replaced a previous code of ethics that was in place until September 2014 (ANZFSS 2014).

The ANZFSS Code of Professional Practice is wide ranging. It not only summarizes the professional role and responsibilities (including those responsibilities to one's employers) of forensic practitioners but also covers external obligations to society in general, to clients, and to the justice system, although for the latter category, members are referred to the rules of the jurisdiction in which they work (ANZFSS 2014).

Under these codes, members are expected to be honest and truthful and to avoid misrepresentation of any aspect of their work and position, avoid conflicts of interest, and be mindful of their duty to the court (ANZFSS 2014). In relation to their professional work, the obligations of members to the court are addressed and include the need to adhere to the rules of disclosure, to adhere to methods that are fit for purpose, and to validate and document their work throughout. The code of practice also notes that members are expected to undertake lifelong learning, and those working in a supervisory capacity should be appropriately knowledgeable and accept full professional responsibility and control of those being supervised in such a manner as to enable their service to meet relevant standards (ANZFSS 2014).

The ANZFSS code of professional practice acknowledges that it has been based on a similar code devised for engineers in Queensland. In doing so, it serves as a reminder that the requirement for professional members to have and adhere to such codes of ethics and professional practice is not unique to forensic practice, but instead is an obligation expected of professional practice in general.

The codes of professional practice are presented in broad terms and show similar characteristics to those of professional forensic organizations in other countries. Although they would only apply directly to forensic podiatrists who are also members of the ANZFSS, the requirements are so similar to those of other organizations that even nonmember forensic podiatrists should be familiar with their broad intent and build such thinking into their professional life and practices.

9.2.4 Forensic Podiatry–Specific Standards

In addition to the international, national, generic, and professional body standards for forensic science and practice of which forensic podiatrists need to be aware and comply with as appropriate, there are also standards and guidelines written specifically for forensic podiatry practice. These forensic podiatry–specific standards are considered below.

9.2.4.1 IAI Role and Scope of Practice for Forensic Podiatrists

In 2009, as part of the work to establish forensic podiatry within the IAI through the creation of a science and practice committee for the discipline, a document detailing the role and scope of practice of forensic podiatrists was created (Vernon et al. 2009). The overriding purpose of this document was to provide clarity regarding forensic podiatry in general terms and in doing so, prevent misunderstandings and provide reassurance as to what the discipline involves. The document provided a basic model for training and development; defined the tasks involved in each area of forensic podiatry practice; and defined the boundaries of forensic podiatry practice, with particular emphasis on what the discipline did and did not cover. Of particular importance was the consideration of areas of practice covered by forensic podiatry and other forensic disciplines. The document explicitly stated what fell within the scope of practice of the forensic podiatrist, and what did not. Should a forensic podiatrist wish to practice in one of these additional areas, he or she would need to undertake additional specialist training and development that is accepted for qualification as an expert witness in the additional discipline(s). For example, it was noted that forensic podiatrists

- Would not usually be required to recover evidence from crime scenes, this being the task of the crime scene investigators
- Would not concern themselves with ridge detail assessment of bare footprints, this falling under the auspices of a ridge detail analysis specialist
- Would focus on features relating to wear and fit when undertaking examination of footwear (this contrasts with the role of the marks or footwear examiners who assess footwear manufacturing characteristics and features of accidental damage)
- Would focus their analysis on gait/features of gait when undertaking forensic gait analysis and would leave considerations of features such as clothing characteristics and height estimation to those with appropriate expertise in these areas

The role and scope of the practice document represented an important start to considering standards in forensic podiatry by providing definitions and boundaries relating to practice. It also provided a means of benchmarking the practice of forensic podiatrists in the United States and elsewhere.

9.2.4.2 CRFP: Legacy Standards

In the United Kingdom, the standards for forensic practice for all subspecialties of forensic podiatry were defined by a previously existing body, the Council for the Registration of Forensic Practitioners (CRFP), in October 2006 (Vernon and Kelly 2006). Three forensic podiatrists—Vernon, Kelly, and Walker—worked closely with the CRFP to develop these standards that were later formally used to regulate the practice of podiatrists wishing to voluntarily register with the CRFP. This program was tailored to the needs of the forensic podiatry discipline and allowed registered podiatrists to benchmark the quality of their work and demonstrate that their standards complied with a broad generic framework used across all registered specialities. The CRFP is no longer in existence as a regulatory body in the United Kingdom; and on cessation of their activities, a gap existed in the formal regulatory arrangements for sole forensic traders, including forensic podiatrists in that country. Through the Forensic Science Society (now the CSFS), this gap was filled by the development of a competency testing scheme for forensic podiatrists as part of the requirement to become an accredited forensic practitioner (AcFP) within the CSFS. The standards written by the CRFP for forensic podiatry practice were taken and developed further through the competency testing scheme as they were found to still apply to forensic podiatry practice. As such, the legacy of the CRFP standards remains within the CSFS competency testing scheme; and although the CRFP no longer exists, the standards created within that organization are still applicable. The competency testing scheme developed by the CSFS for forensic podiatrists has now been developed further and forms part of the CSFS AcFP scheme (CSFS 2016d) that is available for scientists and practitioners in other fields recognized by the CSFS.

At the time of writing, the United States does not have an equivalent competency testing or certification scheme that could be used to formally regulate practice in forensic podiatry, although the CSFS scheme is available for podiatrists from countries outside the United Kingdom, and interest has been expressed in completing the competency test by some non-U.K.-based podiatrists.

Although created in the United Kingdom, these standards represent reasonable expectations of forensic podiatrists working in this field and should therefore be applicable to practice in other countries. The author from the United States ascribes to the standards of practice developed through the CRFP and CSFS schemes, and the considerations described below are relative to such. The framework described in this section is that developed within the CRFP, with some of this framework having an organization-wide basis that was later translated to the requirements applicable to forensic podiatrists by Vernon, Kelly, and Walker. As such, this section is mainly reporting the standards developed within that organization that believed that not only was it "undesirable to try to protect these legally," but that it was also "fine to promulgate the guidance" with due reference being given to this having been created within the CRFP.[4] Because the CRFP has now ceased to operate as a regulatory body, the source of reference to the work (i.e., CRFP website) no longer exists; however, what is being reported are those standards that were in place within the CRFP and were being used for the regulation of those disciplines that fell under the auspices of the CRFP until April 1, 2009, and that now continue through the CSFS competency testing scheme for forensic podiatrists.

[4] Personal communication with Dr. Kate Horne, January 28, 2010, past Chief Executive of CRFP.

As in other areas, overlap can be seen with other sources of standards for forensic science and practice. Despite this overlap, forensic podiatrists should not view these discipline standards in isolation and should also maintain a constant awareness of and compliance with all relevant generic standards for forensic science and practice.

As with all branches of forensic science, the professional status of forensic podiatrists carries with it a range of specific professional responsibilities. In forensic podiatry practice, these responsibilities cover maintaining professional conduct in personal life and professional practice; maintaining fitness to practice; safeguarding confidentiality where required; and working to the high standards required of this discipline, which includes not extending professional opinions beyond those that the individual practitioner is qualified to provide. The standards for specific professional responsibilities are considered in more detail below.

Personal and professional conduct: Forensic practice requires practitioners to operate to the highest standards at all times, whether acting in a professional working capacity or in one's personal life. The practitioner must act with honesty and integrity and must comply with the code of conduct of the professional body or bodies of which he or she is a member. To do otherwise would compromise the personal integrity required in this area of work and would also have the potential to bring the speciality into disrepute. Practitioners are also expected not to discriminate against people or groups who enjoy legal protection against such discrimination.

Professional practice: The primary duty of the forensic podiatrist is to the court. When working as a forensic podiatrist, the first principle of professional practice is that the podiatrist's overriding duty is to the court and not to the agency that has asked for his or her expert opinion. This means that work must be carried out fairly and impartially and presented at all times in that same fair and impartial manner. In this respect, if the forensic podiatrist is aware of anything that may be seen as a conflict of interest when working on a particular case, this should be declared at the first opportunity and where this has been an issue, should only act further with the explicit written consent of those who asked for forensic involvement.

Professional competence: Forensic podiatrists have a responsibility to ensure their professional competence in the area(s) within which they specialize. This competence would extend to participating in continuing education/development activity, thus allowing competence to be maintained in line with developments in that particular field and thereby ensuring that their practice remains of high quality and current. This continuing education/development activity does not need to be formal education, although it could count as such and could include professional reading, mentorship, conference, or seminar attendance or the preparation of conference presentation materials. What is essential however is a learning diary or log that is kept by the practitioner as evidence of such development.

Linked to the need to ensure professional competence in the area of practice is a need to work exclusively within the area(s) of professional competence within which the forensic podiatrist has been properly trained as addressed in the IAI role and scope of practice document (Vernon et al. 2009; see Section 9.2.4.1).

The other element that relates to ensuring professional competence is fitness to practice on health grounds. It is possible to be unable to practice safely as a result of illness and in line with medical practice. It is incumbent on the practitioner to not practice when medically unfit to do so.

Miscarriage of justice: When providing expert witness reports in a legal context, there is always the potential that the forensic podiatrist can come across information that, if it remains undeclared, may lead to a miscarriage of justice. Miscarriage of justice can occur in situations where reports have been provided that are clearly erroneous, or alternately where an error has later been revealed in one's own work. Although the latter should not happen if appropriate care has been taken in casework, it is nevertheless possible. Whenever such errors surface, they should be reported confidentially, if appropriate, to what was described by the CRFP as "a suitable person or authority," with, in most cases, this being the authority that has approved or requested the expert's involvement.

Quality assurance: Quality assurance processes are expected to be followed by large forensic laboratories, and it has been stated that similar standards should be practiced by all providers of forensic science services "regardless of their size or the scope of their examinations" (UKFSR 2009). As noted in Section 9.2.2.1, although it is recognized that "occasion experts" can be required to provide opinions occasionally, in the United Kingdom the UKFSR codes of conduct and practice applies to all experts providing services to the criminal justice system (UKFSR 2016), and competency testing has been developed for such "sole trader" practitioners who work outside the large laboratory systems (CSFS 2016b). Whether working inside or outside a large laboratory, there is a clear obligation to provide an acceptable level of quality assurance in the approach to and the outcomes of the work provided. Thus, forensic podiatrists are advised to work to SOPs, including strict working protocols, and to ensure that their work is checked and verified by a peer practitioner.

Full responsibility for all work: The forensic podiatrist must recognize that by undertaking forensic podiatry work and subsequently providing a legal report for the court, he or she is accepting full responsibility for everything (i.e., work either undertaken or participated in) within that report. There is also a level of responsibility on the part of those verifying such reports and by counter-signing the report, the verifier must be prepared to answer questions related to the verification. This does not, however, remove the fact that the report author has full ownership of, and responsibility for, the report produced.

Being prepared to change an opinion in the presence of new developments, information, or research findings: The forensic podiatrist should be prepared to change an opinion in the presence of new developments, information, or research findings. The task of all forensic practitioners, including the forensic podiatrist, is to help the courts to come to a truthful conclusion. Thus, the practitioner should adopt and maintain a mature, reflective, open, and unbiased approach at all times. This means that if new information surfaces at any time that suggests that the conclusions of the report provided may be incorrect because of such information, the practitioner must be prepared to declare this and, if necessary, amend such conclusions. The authority that requested the work should then be informed of such reinterpretation at the earliest opportunity.

Confidentiality: Although podiatrists are used to working in situations of confidentiality, there is a major difference between working in clinical situations and the work of a forensic podiatrist who is also obliged to work confidentially. This difference relates to the fact that when a forensic podiatry report has been prepared, it is entirely possible that this report will need to be exchanged with the other party involved in the case (either the defense or prosecution). Once this exchange has taken place, it is also possible that the exchanged information will be presented and challenged in an open court of law. As such, any aspect of the report that has been covered in court will therefore normally be available within the public domain from that point onward. Nevertheless, confidentiality should be preserved until authorization has been given to disclose the information, such as when the client requests this information, via court orders, via legal obligations, or the information is demanded by the overriding duty to the court or the administration of justice.

In relation to confidentiality, the issue of preserving legal privilege must also be considered. Legal privilege is in effect "an enforceable duty of confidence" in a legal context (Gillhams 2010). Such a duty applies to all communications between professional legal advisers and their clients and also between those advisers and expert witnesses involved in the case. Forensic practitioners are obliged to preserve these privileges unless the client waives this right.

9.2.5 Forensic Podiatry Responsibilities to Other Professional Bodies

Forensic podiatry is an area of specialized practice of what is predominantly a health care profession. As in the case of other professionals who work in areas other than the criminal justice system, forensic podiatrists have obligations to professional bodies that they have membership with and to the regulatory bodies that govern their general standards of practice and personal conduct. The relevant organizations and agencies vary according to the countries within which the practicing forensic podiatrist is based. The additional standards required of forensic podiatrists do not replace the practitioner's obligations to these other organizations, but instead represent additional requirements of working in the forensic arena.

9.2.6 Anticipated Standards for Forensic Podiatrists Practicing in the United Kingdom

Since 2013, discussions have been taking place between the College of Podiatrists and the office of the UKFSR with a view to create a comprehensive single document covering the standards required of forensic podiatrists practicing in the United Kingdom. Once completed, the forensic regulator will approve this document. In line with these discussions, various developing drafts have been prepared of a stand-alone code of practice, ethics and professional standards in forensic podiatry. It is anticipated that a final version of this document will be produced in the near future. After a period of consultation with those working in forensic podiatry, this document will be published by the forensic regulator, who will then expect compliance with these standards from all working in this field in the United Kingdom.

9.2.7 Standards Summary

There are many sources of standards—international, generic, professional, and national—of which those working in forensic podiatry need to be aware of and comply with as required. The bodies responsible for their creation and maintenance revisit these standards regularly, and as such, forensic podiatrists should keep abreast of and adopt their practice accordingly when any changes occur.

9.3 Governance

Standards of forensic podiatry practice can be seen as one requirement falling under the wider theme of governance in forensic practice. Although it has been suggested that at the highest level the concept of governance is complex and accompanied by confused discussion, at governmental level, an offered definition of governance includes the "ability to make and enforce rules, and to deliver services" (Fukuyama 2013). In other words, while standards of practice relate to practice expected by individual and collective practitioners, governance reflects an all-encompassing corporate responsibility for the successful delivery of a service within a framework of rules. Some aspects of governance can be see as representing an elaboration of the standards required of individual practitioners with governance responsibilities covering the wider requirements, and processes by which the standards, business delivery, and outputs of organizations will be met. Some key areas of governance in relation to the practice of forensic podiatry are considered below. They address the requirements stated in standards of forensic science and practice applicable to forensic podiatrists and also cover organizational processes devised to ensure quality of service delivery, standardization, clarity, and the avoidance of errors.

9.3.1 Education

Given that many of the standards covering forensic science and practice require appropriate training and education as well as demonstrable and appropriate education and development, the education of forensic podiatrists is an important aspect of governance in forensic podiatry. The IAI document "Forensic Podiatry: Role and Scope of Practice" (Vernon et al. 2009) broadly states three requirements for the training and education of those intending to work in forensic podiatry.

To practice in forensic podiatry, the first requirement is to be qualified as a podiatrist in the country in which you are to be based. It is however important to note that this is a requirement for those who would *describe* themselves as a "forensic podiatrist." Some professionals who are not podiatrists may have the knowledge, experience, and expertise to cover some areas of work undertaken by forensic podiatrists. This consideration particularly arises in the practice of forensic gait analysis, where other nonpodiatric disciplines legitimately provide expert reports. In this instance, a title such as "Forensic Gait Analyst" may be used. Although it is incumbent on such experts to be able to demonstrate to the courts that their qualifications and expertise are appropriate for the evidence that they are presenting, only those purporting to be forensic podiatrists need to be qualified as podiatrists. It is also important to note that a podiatrist not practicing in all areas of forensic podiatry should be cautious when using the term "forensic podiatrist" because others may assume expertise in all four areas of current practice. As such, although someone may be entitled to describe themselves as a forensic podiatrist, they would also be recommended to qualify that title by making it explicit the areas of forensic podiatry practice in which they specialize (e.g., bare footprints, forensic gait analysis).

The second stated requirement in the IAI document (Vernon et al. 2009) is for forensic podiatrists to have gained postgraduate knowledge of specific relevance to the practice of forensic podiatry. This knowledge could include relevant M or MS (Master's) level qualifications in forensic podiatry, forensic science, or forensic identification.[5] Such knowledge also could be gained through research in an appropriate area, or demonstrable experience, through supervised participation in forensic podiatry work. At the time of writing, two Master's level courses are of particular relevance for this developmental requirement. The first of these is the Diploma in Forensic Human Identification offered by the Faculty of Forensic and Legal Medicine of the Royal College of Physicians in the United Kingdom and administered by the Academy of Forensic Medical Sciences (AFMS 2016). This course aims to "deliver core knowledge in the field of Forensic Human Identification so that those attending will have a better understanding of the principles involved in the various specialist areas as well as an awareness of the broad scope of the field" and is described as being suitable for several professional groups, including health care professionals (AFMS 2016). The second course of particular relevance is the availability of a Master of Science (M.Sc.) degree in forensic podiatry through the University of Huddersfield in the United Kingdom. Believed to the only course currently available specifically in forensic podiatry in the United Kingdom and possibly in the world, its aim is to help develop expertise in this field (University of Huddersfield 2016) in preparation for practice.

Although other courses have been made available in the past and the availability of additional courses is being discussed and considered, the above-mentioned courses currently seem to be the most applicable to those interested in working as forensic podiatrists and who wish to develop the theoretical understandings required.

The third stated requirement in the IAI document (Vernon et al. 2009) is for those intending to work as forensic podiatrists to gain competence as forensic practitioners. This is the phase of development in which those training and developing as forensic podiatrists would gain the practical expertise necessary for this work. No one means of achieving this goal was considered in the role and scope of practice document; instead, it was suggested that this

[5] Some individuals may also have first degrees in forensic science as well as podiatry qualifications that would be acceptable.

practical expertise could be achieved through a combination of activities, such as attending or being involved in various training events; undertaking mock casework; being mentored; and importantly, acting as a supervised assistant in forensic podiatry casework. At the time of writing of the first edition of *Forensic Podiatry: Principles and Methods* (DiMaggio and Vernon 2011), there were limited opportunities for acting as an assistant to practicing forensic podiatrists; however, the amount of casework involving forensic podiatrists has increased to the level that greater opportunities for such participation now exist and would be recommended as the preferred way forward in this phase of development.

9.3.2 Competency Testing/Certification

In isolation, the presence and adoption of standards is not enough to ensure consistency and quality of practice. Benchmarking and monitoring processes are also required to ensure these standards are being applied and in effect to "calibrate" practitioners. Many different mechanisms are available for the assessment, accreditation, certification, and approval of practice and the management of forensic practice. At the time of writing, not all of these methods are used to assess forensic podiatrists. Furthermore, they may not be applicable in the context of current practice where sole trader practitioners and small units still predominate as opposed to forensic podiatry services being provided via large forensic laboratories. These available mechanisms are considered below, along with comment on their current applicability and use.

9.3.2.1 CSFS Competency Testing Scheme

As noted in Section 9.2.4.2, after the CRFP ceased to operate in 2009, a competency testing scheme was developed for forensic podiatrists by the CSFS with the regulator's approval (UKFSR 2011). This test of forensic podiatrists' competence built on and addressed the limitations of the CRFP model. The three phases of this process are discussed below.

Stage 1: *Face level evidence of the practitioner's competence in the chosen specialty (either bare footprints/footwear or forensic gait analysis).* In this first stage, the applicant would provide details of his or her relevant qualifications, publications, recent continuing education/training activity, and forensic podiatry casework (including preliminary assessments, one's own cases, and verifications of other experts' reports). In addition, the applicant would make a declaration of fitness to practice (covering matters relating to health, workplace disciplinary issues, and criminal convictions) and agree to adhere to the CSFS code of conduct while being subjected to the competency testing. The submission is scrutinized by two appropriate experts who would also examine one or two recent cases worked by the applicant (at preliminary, main reporting officer, and verification levels). This process aims to identify provisional evidence of competence by comparing the case reports against the standards for forensic podiatry reporting.

Stage 2: *MCQ with general forensic practice and speciality-specific sections.* Should the applicant successfully pass through stage 1, his or her general forensic knowledge (legal and procedural issues and evidence interpretation) and theoretical specialist knowledge would be assessed by multiple-choice questionnaire (MCQ) examination. If the candidate passes this examination, he or she would proceed to the final phase of assessment. If the candidate fails the generalist section only, he or she would still proceed to the final phase of assessment and later re-sit (i.e., a second and normally final attempt to pass) the failed section. However, if the specialist section or both the general and specialist sections are failed, the practitioner would not proceed to the final phase until successfully re-sitting the MCQ examination.

Stage 3: *Supervised mock casework, with the candidate producing preliminary findings and interpretation.* The CRFP scheme was criticized on the grounds that the assessment of the applicant's work was restricted to his or her case reports and if required, accompanying materials only. The current scheme incorporates this final phase in which applicants are given the opportunity to demonstrate acceptable skill levels in their specialty, working on case materials for 2.5 hours, while under supervision (to ensure that the work undertaken is the candidate's own). During this time, a mock case would be worked using provided materials and writing case notes covering the analysis, comparison, evaluation, and preliminary conclusions, all of which would be produced by the applicant for later marking against predetermined criteria.

When the applicant has successfully passed all three stages of the competency testing, he or she would be eligible to receive the AcFP status of the CSFS and to be placed on a register of practitioners competent in that field.

The scheme commenced in 2010, and those practitioners who successfully passed the competency test were retested 4 years later in line with requirements of the scheme. The scheme has since been extended to other forensic disciplines, and there have been requests to make the tests available to more disciplines in the near future (CSFS 2016e).

This scheme is the only known practical competency test designed specifically for forensic podiatrists that is currently available. Consideration has been given to the development of a forensic podiatry certification scheme in the United States. To date, such as certification scheme has not yet been developed, although preliminary discussions have taken place to explore the potential for such a scheme in the near future and/or possible recognition of the CSFS scheme as an acceptable alternative.[6]

The CSFS scheme is, however, intended to be available for forensic podiatrists in countries other than those in the United Kingdom, and at least one U.S.-based forensic podiatrist is known to have joined the CSFS with the intention of undertaking this test.[7]

9.3.2.2 Certification in the United States

In the United States, the established means of assessing and demonstrating forensic practitioner competence has been via certification programs that are available through the IAI (IAI 2015). Although certification is not legally required in most states, this nationwide certification is anticipated in the future (Lautenbach 2016). Requirements for certification cover the following areas.

1. General qualifications would be for the applicant to work within that discipline with good moral character, repute, and integrity and high ethical and professional standing and meet the standards of their discipline. Demonstrable relevant forensic science work experience is also required.
2. Education and experience as approved by the relevant Certification Board.
3. Satisfactory completion of a specified training program developed by the relevant certification board.

The process involves written MCQs, practical problem testing, and retesting after 5 years (IAI 2016b). As such, this process is similar to that of the CSFS competency testing with application form.

9.4 Standard Operating Procedures

In the context of forensic practice, SOPs have been described as documents "containing a detailed description of the equipment, apparatus, and methods employed in a specific analysis or procedure in a laboratory. SOPs are core documents that provide step-by-step guidance for specific procedures that everybody trained to perform the task will be able to follow.

[6] Vernon, Wesley. A proposed certification scheme for forensic podiatrists: presentation and subsequent discussion at IAI board meeting, Providence, August 4, 2013.

[7] Anon., Personal communication, December 11, 2015.

This is essential … in order to ensure the analysis and results presented are consistent and repeatable" (University of Florida 2016). They are "Detailed, written instructions to achieve uniformity of the performance of a specific function" (ICH 2016). Such instructions will define expectations and enable practice to be carried out in line with expected industry and internal business quality standards and relevant laws (Vernon 2015).

It is only relatively recently that forensic podiatrists have begun to consider/develop SOPs relevant to their practice. This is for two reasons. First, formally organized forensic podiatry practice is relatively new; therefore, the focus was on the creation of standards, an essential phase that must be completed before the developed of SOPs to enable the SOPs to be based in part upon those standards. Second, forensic podiatry casework has increased dramatically (Vernon 2015); therefore, forensic podiatrists can no longer be considered as "occasional experts" and as such they have responsibilities at the same level as regularly practicing forensic practitioners.

SOPs are wide ranging and are intended to cover the entire process of the management of forensic casework from initial contact by the requesting party to conclusion of that case, with archiving or safe return of any evidentiary materials. In the context of forensic practice, the presence and use of SOPs has many advantages. They can show that an organization/practitioner has recognized the external standards expected of the work. They can demonstrate that the chain of custody has been secure throughout management of each case and that the security of materials and personnel has been optimized as far as possible. This allows a healthy and safe work environment to be defined and maintained. The SOPs can be used to show that the work carried out in each area of practice has been fit for purpose and has been produced at reasonable cost. Through the stated processes and methods involved, SOPs can show that the findings of the experts involved are as far as possible error-free, consistent, and reliable, thereby ensuring scientific reproducibility. Their adoption provides a mechanism for resolving conflicts between experts where conflicting opinions may occur. For example, the work of individual experts can be benchmarked against expected approaches and differences of opinion can be managed through a stated framework. The SOP document provides a framework for monitoring, audit, and inspection, and through the explicit documentation of all procedures and processes it provides clarity within the practice/organization to show what is expected at all stages of work and externally to reassure commissioners of the service that their work will be handled competently and in line with expectation. Adopting SOPs and monitoring work against stated requirements could help protect the organization from claims of incompetence and liability, should these issues arise. Thus, although the adoption and use of SOPs is not mandated, their creation and use is recommended to practices/organizations providing forensic podiatry services.

9.4.1 Setting Up SOPs

Assuming that a practice/organization has not used SOPs for forensic podiatry practice before, an appropriate lead with extensive knowledge of practice and experience should be tasked with the responsibility of writing the SOP document. Although this is likely to be undertaken by a quality manager, extensive liaison with the forensic practitioners to whom the SOPs apply would be required. All key documents stating standards for forensic practice and other relevant publications covering the science and practice relevant to forensic podiatry should be obtained and scrutinized, and any sections of direct relevance should be listed. Preexisting processes and practices can then being documented in detail and checked against these standards/requirements for the entire process from initial contact from a potential casework commissioner through to conclusion and archive/return of materials. Through this process, if any gaps or mismatches between practice and expectation are identified, they can be addressed by making necessary written adjustments in the new procedures. The initial draft of the SOP document would then be passed to all forensic podiatry practitioners within the organization for comment and to check for further errors, omissions, or both. In a smaller practice, those involved in undertaking preliminary case assessments, verifying an expert's report, or both would be suitable persons to undertake this checking of the initial draft. Any required amendments are then discussed and written into the procedures as necessary and finalized. In a larger organization, the draft SOP can be passed on to an appropriate senior manager or management team for approval. For a smaller organization, the senior practitioner or practice partner would approve the document.

9.4.2 Content of SOPs

Given that organizational forms can differ considerably and that forensic podiatry is practiced in many countries, it is not possible or desirable to provide a single detailed SOP document that applies directly to all organizations or practices providing forensic podiatry services. The SOP document should however cover the following areas, with each practice showing in detail how its own procedures match the standards and requirements of forensic science and practice.

- A general introduction to forensic podiatry and the unit from which the forensic podiatry services are provided.
- Duties and responsibilities of forensic podiatrists.
- Practitioner ethics and conduct.

- Professional standards and competence required for each level of work (assisting, preliminary, verifying, and full reporting expert levels), including the minimum training and development requirements that will be undertaken by those working at each level.
- SOPs for casework detailing the entire process from initial client or authority contact through to courtroom exhibits preparation. Generic procedures irrespective of subspecialty will be stated and these should include the appropriate use and maintenance and use of equipment required by the practitioner or service and health and safety consideration.
- For each respective area of forensic podiatry practice (e.g., records, bare footprints, footwear, forensic gait analysis),
  - Materials storage, management, analysis, comparison, and evaluation
  - Exhibit handling
  - Involvement of other specialists
  - Additional considerations that may be specific to each area of practice.
- Expert report including report structure and production processes, including report verification.
- Case conferences and subsequent actions following such conferences.
- Court attendance.
- Reference section (the document should be comprehensively referenced and linked to relevant standards and other appropriate published documents throughout.

Table 9.1 presents a suggested outline for the SOP document, with a short summary of the requirements of each section of the work.

The document should present each procedure in detail in such a manner that there is no potential for misinterpretation or ambiguity. As noted, a single SOP document cannot be produced that applies to every organization or practice providing forensic podiatry services, but an example of the level of detail required is given in Figure 9.1, in this case considering the handling of an initial contact from a potential client or casework authority.

9.4.3 SOPs Summary

There have been many demands for improved clarity and governance in relation to forensic science and practice (Law Commission 2011; NRC 2009; Robinson 2015; Rozenberg 2014). Although many of these demands are justified, some seem to be based on misunderstanding (Robinson 2015; Vernon and Nirenberg 2016). Regardless, the adoption and use of SOPs show how an

Table 9.1 Suggested Generic Template for the Standard Operating Procedures (SOPs) for a Forensic Podiatry Unit/Practice

1. Introduction	A basic explanation of forensic podiatry and the unit/practice to which the SOPs apply
2. Duties and responsibilities	The role of forensic podiatrists and their broad responsibilities in addressing the tasks involved in fulfilling that role.
3. Ethics and conduct	Ethical behavior according to regulatory, professional and advisory bodies covering obligations as both forensic and health practitioner (podiatrist).
4. Professional standards and competence	A statement of the purpose and scope of professional standards and levels of competence. The minimum requirements for standards and competence stated with sources for these assertions being referenced as applicable.
5. Standard operating procedures: general	Detailed procedures covering the following stages of the casework: • Initial police or legal contact and response • The preliminary assessment • Ensuring health and safety • The casework analysis comparison and evaluation • Casework verification • Exhibits • Productions • Equipment • Exhibits/Productions
6. The expert witness report	Guidance and detailed requirements for the production of a standard expert report. The required approach is stated for all sections of the report, namely: • Introduction • Background • Methods • Results (Analysis, comparison, evaluation) • Supplementary analysis (if required) • Discussion and Conclusions • Final check/Verification (who provides this, the process and actions required where differences of opinion which cannot be resolved.) • Time of submission of the report • Disclosure of information • Case Review Report
7. Bare footprint case procedures	Equipment (type, use and management) Procedures for: • Storage of bare footprint case materials • Preparation of materials • Preliminary assessment • Advice on the involvement of other specialists • Examination and Analysis • Comparison and evaluation

(Continued)

Table 9.1 ***(Continued)*** **Suggested Generic Template for the Standard Operating Procedures (SOPs) for a Forensic Podiatry Unit/Practice**

8. Footwear case procedures	Equipment (type, use and management) Procedures for: • Storage of footwear case materials • Preparation of materials • Preliminary assessment • Advice on the involvement of other specialists • Examination and Analysis • Comparison and evaluation
9. Forensic gait analysis case procedures	Equipment (type, use and management) Procedures for: • Storage of materials • Preparation of materials • Preliminary assessment • Advice on the involvement of other specialists • Examination and Analysis • Comparison and evaluation
10. Record card identification case procedures	At the Mortuary (complying with the procedures of other organizations) Disaster Victim Identification (DVI) (complying with the procedures of other organizations) Equipment (type, use and management) Procedures for: • Storage of materials • Preparation of materials • Preliminary assessment • Advice on the involvement of other specialists • Examination and Analysis • Comparison and evaluation
11. Archive storage	Arrangements for the return and/or archive storage of: • Reports and case notes • Materials (documents, electronic and hard copy) • Materials (physical)
12. Conferences and other subsequent action	Standards required Guidance
13. Attendance at court	Standards required Guidance
14. References	A listing of all reference documents upon which the SOP has been based and any other relevant publications which have been referred to in the document
15. Membership of author group	A listing of the designated SOP author and all other contributors

Source: Adapted from the Sheffield Podiatry Service draft Forensic Podiatry Operating Standard Procedures, September 2014.

- If the first line initial contact is received by a general administrative staff member of the forensic podiatry unit (typically by telephone) the following actions should be undertaken by that staff member:
- Note in writing:
  - The time and date that the phone call was received.
  - The enquirers name, rank, organization and contact details (telephone number and/or mobile telephone number, e-mail contact details and address)
  - Who the enquirer is trying to contact with their enquiry.
  - The basic nature of their enquiry (i.e., whether this is a forensic gait analysis, footwear, bare footprint or podiatry records case).
  - Whether the enquiry is an urgent one and if so the timelines involved.
  - Any additional notes made in conversation that fall outside the above.
- Advise the enquirer who the enquiry will be passed on to (i.e., which forensic podiatry expert) and if this is not passed on immediately through forwarding of the telephone call to that expert, advise when they can expect a response and how they prefer this response to be made (i.e., whether by e-mail, telephone or other means and if by telephone, their preferred number)
  - Immediately pass on the enquiry to the lead for the area of expertise involved or in their absence, their nominated deputy.
  - Should neither the lead expert nor their nominated deputy be available, the enquiry should be passed on to the most senior member of the forensic podiatry team who can provide a timely response.
  - The staff member who has received the initial contact should document who the enquiry was passed on to for further action and the request made of that person.

Figure 9.1 The level of detail required in Standard Operating Procedures for a Forensic Podiatry Practice/Unit – Initial contact from a potential client/casework commissioner. (Adapted from the Sheffield Podiatry Service draft Forensic Podiatry Operating Standard Procedures, September 2014.)

organization or practice is performing to the high standards required in forensic science and practice and in doing so can help prevent misunderstandings. The creation and maintenance of SOPs represent a large piece of work for any organization to undertake. However, there are sound arguments to suggest this is not about the creation of an unnecessary bureaucratic burden. SOPs instead are about the demonstrable use of appropriate standards and procedures that will bear scrutiny and transparently show that the practice of an organization has been acceptable in the case of an enquiry or external challenge.

Detailed SOPs, grounded in the required standards of forensic science and practice, are not enough to ensure quality and standardization of practice in isolation. In addition, regular monitoring needs to take place to ensure standards involved in the forensic podiatry processes of that organization are being met. The standards should also be reviewed frequently considering changes to external standards and policy requirements. As noted, although SOPs are intended to ensure standardization, their exact form will be context specific to each organization creating and using the SOPs.

9.5 Conclusions

Although there are many standards required of forensic science and practice, they are not simply bureaucratic burdens. They are necessary to ensure that work undertaken in this arena is fit for the purpose, particularly where that purpose carries such a high level of responsibility as that of work in the criminal justice system. The purpose and relevance of standards need to be understood by practitioners, lawyers, report commissioners, and the lay public (who can be called for jury service) alike. These standards can represent the minimum requirements for safe practice, average or typical practice, and best practice. The considerations in relation to standards presented in this chapter represent what should be the minimum requirements for safe practice, although on occasions it is possible that these have previously been interpreted as best practice. Because forensic science and practice have been placed under scrutiny, and through this scrutiny subjected to criticism in recent times, it is paramount that practitioners recognize the need to work to, and demonstrate compliance with these standards. It is the responsibility of the individual practitioner and the organization providing forensic podiatry services to work through the many sources of standards to determine which apply to their own area of practice. However, this chapter has attempted to indicate which sources are applicable and the key areas within such sources that are likely to be relevant to forensic podiatry practice. It is hoped that this information will help to guide forensic podiatry practitioners to the standards they require in their own practice by streamlining the task of finding these applicable standards.

In addition to the adoption of appropriate standards, compliance with these standards should be demonstrable. Forensic podiatry practitioners are strongly advised to consider the suggestions made in this chapter for appropriate governance arrangements in relation to their practice. The dangers linked to noncompliance are those relating to the potential for miscarriages of justice, with implications for the individual lives of those concerned. Where there has been ignominious failure due to unsafe working practices as represented by standards and associated governance frameworks, there are also adverse implications for the forensic discipline concerned and the individual practitioner who has failed to recognize his or her responsibilities in this regard. By being aware of the various standards that apply to forensic podiatry practiced in a given area, and by ensuring that these standards are followed at all times, such problems can be avoided.

References

AAFS (American Academy of Forensic Sciences). 2016a. Article ii. Code of Ethics and Conduct. http://www.aafs.org/about-aafs/aafs-bylaws/article-ii-code-of-ethics-and-conduct/ (Accessed March 3, 2016).

AAFS (American Academy of Forensic Sciences). 2016b. American Academy of Forensic Sciences. http://www.aafs.org/ (Accessed February 17, 2016).

AAFS (American Academy of Forensic Sciences). 2016c. About the Academy Standards Board. http://asb.aafs.org/about-the-aafs-standards-board/ (Accessed February 17, 2016).

ACPO/CPS. 2010. Guidance Booklet for Experts Disclosure: Experts' Evidence, Case Management and Unused Material May 2010. https://www.google.co.uk/search?q=Guidance+Booklet+for+Experts%2C+Disclosure&oq=Guidance+Booklet+for+Experts%2C+Disclosure&aqs=chrome..69i57j0.271j0j4&sourceid=chrome&es_sm=93&ie=UTF-8 (Accessed March 3, 2016).

AFMS (Academy of Forensic Medical Sciences). 2016. Diploma Course in Forensic Human Identification. http://afms.org.uk/diploma-course-in-forensic-human-identification/ (Accessed February 25, 2016).

ANZFSS (Australia and New Zealand Forensic Science Society). 2014. Code of Professional Practice for Members of the ANZFSS Version 1, 11 August 2014. http://anzfss.org/wp-content/uploads/2012/05/ANZFSS-Code-of-Professional-Practice-Final.pdf (Accessed March 3, 2016).

ANZFSS (Australia and New Zealand Forensic Science Society). 2016. Membership. http://anzfss.org/act/branch-membership/ (Accessed February 19, 2016).

ASCLD (American Society of Crime Laboratory Directors). 2005. ASCLD Code of Ethics. http://www.ascld.org/wp-content/uploads/2014/08/Code-of-Ethics.pdf. (Accessed March 3, 2016).

ASCLD (American Society of Crime Laboratory Directors). 2013. Guiding Principles of Professional Responsibility for Crime Laboratories and Forensic Scientists. http://www.ascld-lab.org/wp-content/uploads/2013/04/AL-PD-1014.pdf. (Accessed March 3, 2016).

ASCLD (American Society of Crime Laboratory Directors). 2016. Our History. http://www.ascld.org/about-us/our-history/ (Accessed February 19, 2016).

CPS (Crown Prosecution Service). 2016. Chapter 36: Expert Witnesses – Prosecution Disclosure Obligations. http://www.cps.gov.uk/legal/d_to_g/disclosure_manual/disclosure_manual_chapter_36/ (Accessed March 3, 2016). https://www.gov.uk/government/uploads/system/uploads/attachment_data/file/365452/SFRpresentation23Sep14.pdf (Accessed March 4, 2016).

CSFS (Chartered Society of Forensic Sciences). 2016a. Standards. http://www.csofs.org/Standards (Accessed March 3, 2016).

CSFS (Chartered Society of Forensic Sciences). 2016b. Certificate of Professional Competence. http://www.csofs.org/Training/CPC (Accessed March 3, 2016).

CSFS (Chartered Society of Forensic Sciences). 2016c. Join the Society of Forensic Sciences. http://www.csofs.org/ (Accessed February 17, 2016).

CSFS (Chartered Society of Forensic Sciences). 2016d. Accredited Forensic Practitioner. http://www.csofs.org/Accredited-Forensic-Practioner (Accessed February 23, 2016).

CSFS (Chartered Society of Forensic Sciences). 2016e. CPC Business Development. http://www.csofs.org/CPC-Business-Development (Accessed March 3, 2016).

DiMaggio J. and Vernon W. 2011. *Forensic Podiatry: Principles and Methods*. New York: Humana Press.

ENFSI. 2013a. About ENFSI. http://www.enfsi.eu/about-enfsi (Accessed February 17, 2016).

ENFSI. 2013b. Members. http://www.enfsi.eu/about-enfsi/members (Accessed February 18, 2016).

Fukuyama F. 2013. What is Governance? *Governance: An International Policy Journal of Policy, Administration and Institutions* 26: 347–368.

Gillhams Solicitors. 2010. *LLP Term: Legal Professional Privilege*. http://www.gillhams.com/dictionary/345.cfm (Accessed January 28, 2010).

HCPC (Health and Care Professions Council). 2013. Standards of Proficiency—Chiropodists/Podiatrists. http://www.hcpc-uk.org/assets/documents/10000DBBStandards_of_Proficiency_Chiropodists.pdf (Accessed March 3, 2016).

HCPC (Health and Care Professions Council). 2016. Standards of Conduct, Performance and Ethics. http://www.hcpc-uk.org/assets/documenFStandardsofconduct,performanceandethics.pdf (Accessed March 3, 2016).

Home Office. 2016. *Forensic Science Strategy: A National Approach to Forensic Science Delivery in the Criminal Justice System*. London: The Williams Lea Group on behalf of the Controller of the HMSO.

House of Commons Science and Technology Committee. 2005. *Forensic Science on Trial: 7th Report of session* 2004–5. London: The Stationery Office Ltd.

House of Commons Science and Technology Committee. 2013. *Forensic Science: 2nd Report of session 2013–14*. London: The Stationery Office Ltd.

IAI (International Association for Forensic Identification). 2015. Certification Program Operations Manual. https://www.theiai.org/certifications/certification_manual_20150717.pdf (Accessed March 4, 2016).

IAI (International Association for Forensic Identification). 2016a. About the IAI: IAI Mission Statement. https://www.theiai.org/about/index.php (Accessed March 3, 2016).

IAI (International Association for Forensic Identification). 2016b. Footwear Certification Process. https://www.theiai.org/certifications/footwear/process.php (Accessed March 4, 2016).

ICH (International Conference on Harmonisation of technical requirements for registration of pharmaceuticals for human use). 2016. Good Clinical Practice: Glossary. http://ichgcp.net/1-glossary (Accessed March 4, 2016).

ISO (International Organisation for Standardisation). 2015. *ISO 9001:2000. Quality Management Systems—Requirements*. Switzerland: ISO Copyright Office. http://www.iso.org/iso/catalogue_detail?csnumber=21823 (Accessed March 3, 2016).

ISO/IEC (International Organisation for Standardisation/International Electrotechnical Commission). 2005. *International Standard ISO/IEC17025: General Requirements for the Competence of Testing and Calibration Laboratories*. Switzerland: ISO Copyright Office, Geneva.

Lautenbach R. 2016. The value of certification—A laboratory directors perspective. *Identification News* 46: 10.

Law Commission. 2011. *Expert Evidence in Criminal Proceedings in England and Wales*. London: The Stationery Office Ltd.

NIST. 2014. Organization of Scientific Area Committees. http://www.nist.gov/forensics/osac/index.cfm (Accessed February 17, 2016).
NIST. 2015a. Scientific Area Committees. http://www.nist.gov/forensics/osac/sacs.cfm (Accessed March 3, 2016).
NIST. 2015b. OSAC Subcommittees. http://www.nist.gov/forensics/osac/subs.cfm http://www.nist.gov/forensics/osac/sacs.cfm (Accessed March 3, 2016).
NIST. 2016. NIST Organization of Scientific Area Committees Roles and Responsibilities. http://www.nist.gov/forensics/osacroles.cfm#O (Accessed March 3, 2016).
NRC (National Research Council). 2009. *Strengthening Forensic Science in the United States—A Path Forward*. Washington DC: The National Academies Press.
Patton M.Q. 1990. Enhancing quality and credibility. In *Qualitative Evaluation and Research Methods*. pp. 460–494. Newbury Park: Sage.
Robinson N.J. 2015. Forensic Pseudoscience: The unheralded crisis of criminal justice. *Boston Review*, November 16. https://bostonreview.net/books-ideas/nathan-robinson-forensic-pseudoscience-criminal-justice (Accessed March 4, 2016).
Rozenberg J. 2014. Are juries being blinded by science? Lord chief justice says jurors should not be expected to understand complex scientific concepts from expert witnesses. *The Guardian*, October 15. https://www.theguardian.com/law/2014/oct/15/juries-blinded-science-lord-chief-justice-primers. (Accessed October 4, 2016).
Skills for Justice. 2013. National Occupational Standards. http://www.sfjuk.com/national-occupational-standards/ (Accessed March 3, 2016).
Skills for Justice. 2016. Who we are. http://www.sfjuk.com/about/who-we-are/ (Accessed March 3, 2016).
SWGTREAD (Scientific Working Group for Shoeprint and Tire Tread Evidence). 2014. SGTREAD Transitions to OSAC Footwear and Tire Subcommittee. http://www.swgtread.org/about-us/mission-history-and-funding (Accessed February 18, 2016).
UKAS. 2016. Our Role. https://www.ukas.com/about/our-role/ (Accessed March 3, 2016).
UKFSR (United Kingdom Forensic Science Regulator). 2009. *Quality Standards for Forensic Science Services, Consultation Document*. London: Forensic Science Regulation Unit, Home Office.
UKFSR (United Kingdom Forensic Science Regulator). 2011. *Newsletter No. 17*. London: Forensic Science Regulation Unit, Home Office.
UKFSR (United Kingdom Forensic Science Regulator). 2015. *Newsletter No. 25*. Birmingham: Office of the Forensic Science Regulator, Home Office.
University of Florida. 2016. *Standard Operating Procedures: Laboratory Quality Assurance (QA) and Quality Control (QC) Introduction*. College of Pharmacy, University of Florida. https://ufl.instructure.com/courses/313181/pages/standard-operating-procedures (Accessed February 27, 2016).
University of Huddersfield. 2016. Forensic Podiatry MSc 2016–2017. https://www.hud.ac.uk/courses/part-time/postgraduate/forensic-podiatry-msc/ (Accessed February 25, 2016).
Vernon W. 2014. Quality Standards in Forensic Science and Practice. *Police Oracle*. http://www.policeoracle.com/news/Investigation/2014/Mar/14/Quality-standards-in-forensic-science-and-practice_79699.html (Accessed March 4, 2016).

Vernon W. 2015. Developing Standard Operating Procedures for a Forensic Podiatry Unit. Paper presented at the 100th Educational Conference of the IAI, Sacramento, August 2–8. 2015.
Vernon W. and Kelly H. 2006. New specialties: Forensic podiatry registration—The first eight weeks. *CRFP Newsletter* 18: 10.
Vernon W. and Nirenberg M. 2016. Should we trust forensic science? Forensic experts respond to Nathan J. Robinson. *Boston Review*. https://bostonreview.net/books-ideas/vernon-nirenberg-respond-robinson-forensic-pseudoscience (Accessed March 3, 2016).

Frye Test and Daubert Standard[1] 10

This chapter presents to the U.S. Supreme Court's standard of admissibility of forensic evidence and testimony at trial, with a focus on how this information is applicable to forensic podiatry.

A podiatrist serving as forensic expert is a recent development, with Dr. Norman Gunn being the first to partner with law enforcement in the analysis of footprint evidence and to provide court testimony in the 1970s. Since that time, podiatrists have played a significant role in interpreting foot-related evidence in criminal proceedings (DiMaggio 2005; Vernon 2006).

With the increased awareness of this specialty and the use of podiatry as a forensic tool, it is important for U.S. forensic podiatrists to understand that expert testimony at trial is required to follow the court's procedural and evidentiary rules (Vernon 2010). Although this chapter discusses forensic podiatry expert testimony in the United States, the standards for experts are similar in other countries.

10.1 Legal History

Forensic testimony can be extremely beneficial to the trier of fact—the judge or jury—in providing greater insight when deciding a criminal case. Before the enactment of the uniform Federal Rules of Evidence (FRE) (Federal Rules of Evidence 2015) judges had broad discretion on whether to admit testimony into evidence in a case. The FRE created parameters around which judges were required to base their evidentiary decisions, but before 1975, judges relied on the reasoning of a federal court of appeals decision from the D.C. Circuit. Rule 702 of the FRE provides that a witness who is qualified as an expert by knowledge, skill, experience, training, or education may give an expert opinion if the following four criteria (Fed. R. Evid.) are satisfied:

1. Expert's specialized knowledge will help the trier of fact understand the evidence or to better decide an issue.
2. Testimony is based on sufficient facts or data.
3. Testimony is produced from reliable principles and methods.
4. Expert has reliably applied the principles and methods to the facts of the case.

[1] Contributed by Michael J. Nirenberg, DPM Crown Point, IN.

10.2 Frye Test

The initial standard used to determine the admissibility of an expert's scientific testimony was established in 1923 in Frye v. United States (Frye v. United States 1923). In this case, the court of appeals was asked to examine the issue of judicial error by the district court in refusing to a systolic blood pressure test, a forerunner of today's polygraph test.

Judge Van Orsdel, who authored the D.C. Circuit opinion, established a guideline for admissibility of scientific expert testimony by opining "... the thing from which the deduction is made must be sufficiently established to have gained general acceptance in the particular field in which it belongs" (Frye v. United States 1923). Known as the "Frye Standard," this opinion was accepted by all federal courts (and many state courts) as authority for nearly 50 years. It held that if the expert's theories and methods had "gained general acceptance" in the relevant scientific community, the testimony would be admissible.

The Frye court noted that although courts will effort to admit experimental testimony deduced from a well-recognized scientific principle or discovery, the seed from which the deduction has been geminated must be adequately established to have general acceptance in the particular scientific field. Given the application and acceptance of the Frye standard, courts were then tasked with deciding whether the relevant scientific community generally accepted the procedure, technique, or principle at issue (Frye v. United States 1923).

An increase in the use of scientific evidence in court proceedings as well as a more diluted reading of FRE 702 (Fed. R. Evid.) in the 1970s hastened the admission of expert testimony, which could "assist the trier of fact." This caused Frye's "general acceptance" test to also become less rigid and more open to liberal interpretation.

The 1980s saw opponents of growing litigation and of the role of scientific testimony and evidence call out the widespread use of scientific testimony as a crutch to aid otherwise unsupported claims. Considering such objections and before the U.S. Supreme Court's decision in Daubert (Daubert v. Merrell Dow Pharmaceuticals 1993), judges used more thought to their role as gatekeepers of evidence to keep juries from hearing expert testimony that might be suspect. In addition, the advance of scientific evidence in the courtroom has caused unease from judges in making such admissibility rulings, and the image of experts holding themselves out as "hired guns."

The Frye standard was in effect until the U.S. Supreme Court heard Daubert v. Merrell Dow Pharmaceuticals, Inc. in 1993. Daubert superseded the Frye standard and set out a test more in line with contemporary thought.

Frye's somewhat straightforward "if-then" standard (Frye v. United States 1923). allowed courts to easily decide a question of admissibility of expert testimony: IF the expert's methods were *generally accepted in the relevant scientific community*, THEN the evidence was admitted. Questions as to the strength of the underlying science or the expert's qualifications were given to the jury to evaluate the weight of such testimony.

Summing up Frye (Frye v. United States 1923), the Third Circuit explained that courts' preliminary determination was aided by other evidence, including expert testimony, concerning the following (United States v. Downing 1985):

1. Status of the scientific principle underlying the tendered novel evidence in the relevant scientific community
2. Technique applying the scientific principle
3. Application of the technique as to the circumstances of the proffered testimony

Although the "general acceptance" standard in Frye was the prevailing view within the federal courts when the FRE were considered and adopted, some thought Frye was too general and vague, was conducive to excluding possibly valuable evidence, and was not absolute in all situations. The Frye standard also received criticism for its ultra-Orthodox approach, causing caused undue delay in the admissibility of potentially reliable evidence, and for directing attention away from the issue of whether the expert applied the proper testing procedure as the groundwork for his or her opinion (Klein 2006).

For example, the Second Circuit long criticized the Frye test (United States v. Jakobetz 1992) and held that issues as to the admissibility of scientific evidence should be determined under the FRE. Professor Charles McCormick in his treatise *McCormick on Evidence* stated that

> General scientific acceptance is a proper condition for taking judicial notice of scientific facts, but it is not a suitable criterion for the admissibility of scientific evidence. Any relevant conclusions supported by a qualified expert witness should be received unless there are distinct reasons for exclusion. These reasons are the familiar ones of prejudicing or misleading the jury or consuming undue amounts of time.
>
> *(McCormick on Evidence 1984)*

Scholars have noted that as sciences advances, the efficacy of the Frye standard runs aground in its logic (Hedger 2004; Kaye 2001; Murphy 1990). As is the case with forensic podiatry, just because a science is new does not make it fallible, nor does it make it "junk science." This argument is particularly true when using forensic evidence—a field of science that has catapulted into the mainstream of criminal procedure.

At the time of this writing, the following states continue to use the Frye test: California, Pennsylvania, Illinois, Maryland, New York, New Jersey, Minnesota, and Virginia.

10.3 Daubert Standard

The Supreme Court explained in Daubert that evidence is admissible under FRE 702 if "it rests on a reliable foundation and is relevant." Because "expert witnesses have the potential to be both powerful and quite misleading," courts must "ensure that any and all [expert] testimony ... is not only relevant, but reliable," the court stated, citing cases from the Fourth Circuit (Daubert v. Merrell Dow Pharmaceuticals 1993). The court identified five nondispositive factors for evaluating the reliability of proposed expert testimony (Daubert v. Merrell Dow Pharmaceuticals 1993):

1. Whether the particular scientific theory "can be (and has been) tested"
2. Whether the theory "has been subjected to peer review and publication"
3. "Known or potential rate of error"
4. "Existence and maintenance of standards controlling the technique's operation"
5. Whether the technique has achieved "general acceptance" in the relevant scientific or expert community

These factors do not constitute a definitive checklist or test. The real difference in Daubert as compared to Frye is flexibility. As the Fourth Circuit explained, "rather than providing a definitive or exhaustive list, Daubert merely illustrates the types of factors that will bear on the inquiry" (United States v. Prince-Oyibo 2003). In determining whether proffered testimony is adequately reliable, the judge has "broad latitude to consider whatever factors bearing on validity that the court finds to be useful" (Westberry v. Gislaved Gummi AB 1999), and these factors are based upon the unique circumstances of the expert testimony involved.

After Daubert, a trial judge must initially decide, pursuant to the FRE, if the expert is "proposing to testify to (Vernon 2006) scientific knowledge that (DiMaggio 2005) will assist the trier of fact to understand or determine a fact in issue" (Frye v. United States 1923). Daubert held that the FRE and specifically FRE 702 displaced Frye's "general acceptance" test, making the FRE controlling in all federal courts.

Daubert stressed that the admissibility of the expert's testimony is to be based only on a review of the expert's "principles and methodology," rather than "on the conclusions that they generate" (Daubert v. Merrell Dow Pharmaceuticals 1993). On the issue of scientific certainty, the court stated, "... it would be unreasonable to conclude that the subject of scientific testimony must be known to a certainty; arguably, there are no certainties in science" (Daubert v. Merrell Dow Pharmaceuticals 1993). The Daubert court explained that scientific testimony "must be supported by appropriate validation—i.e., good grounds, based on what is known" (Daubert v. Merrell Dow Pharmaceuticals 1993).

The majority of the U.S. Supreme Court saw their decision in Daubert as encouraging debate of expert testimony in an effort to ferret out evidence not based on science. Justice Blackmun wrote in the majority opinion, "Vigorous cross examination, presentation of contrary evidence, and careful instruction on the burden of proof are the traditional and appropriate means of attacking shaky but admissible evidence" (Daubert v. Merrell Dow Pharmaceuticals 1993).

In explaining how the decision complimented the FRE, Blackmun said, "'General acceptance' is not a necessary precondition to the admissibility of scientific evidence under the Federal Rules of Evidence …" (Daubert v. Merrell Dow Pharmaceuticals 1993). However, FRE 702 requires that the trial judge ensure that an expert's testimony "both rests on a reliable foundation and is relevant to the task at hand." Pertinent evidence that is "based on scientifically valid principles" would be adequate to meet those demands, the Daubert court reasoned (Daubert v. Merrell Dow Pharmaceuticals 1993).

The U.S. Supreme Court explained that trial judges are the "gatekeepers" of what scientific or technical testimony is admissible in court. Judges were required to use sound discretion in determining whether to admit such expert testimony. For such scientific testimony to be admissible, the trial judge must find the following criteria present:

Relevancy: The expert's testimony is relevant to helping the fact-finder (i.e., the jury or judge) determine the facts of the case.

Reliability: It is more likely than not that the expert's methods are reliable and were reliably applied in the particular case. "In a case involving scientific evidence, *evidentiary reliability* will be based upon *scientific validity*." As far as tests of reliability of an expert's opinion, the U.S. Supreme Court held that "the expert's opinion will have a reliable basis in the knowledge and experience of his discipline."

Scientific knowledge: The scientific testimony to be given by an expert witness must indeed be based in scientific knowledge. The U.S. Supreme Court advised that the trial judge must find that the scientific testimony comes from the scientific method or "scientific methodology." This is "based on generating hypotheses and testing them to see if they can be falsified; indeed, this methodology is what distinguishes science from other fields of human inquiry." (Daubert v. Merrell Dow Pharmaceuticals 1993)

Some states had concerns that the Daubert test was too permissive. Although in most states, the Frye standard has been superseded by Daubert, Illinois, Maryland, Minnesota, New Jersey, New York, Pennsylvania, Washington, and the District of Columbia still adhere to the Frye standard (New Jersey Courts 2015).

10.4 Daubert "Trilogy"

Since the Daubert decision, the U.S. Supreme Court has decided two cases that have refined the legal doctrine on the admissibility of expert testimony. The so-called Daubert Trilogy of cases represents Daubert and subsequent distinctions and explanations.

In General Electric Co. v. Joiner (General Electric Co. v. Joiner 1997), the U.S. Supreme Court provided clarity to the Daubert standard. Here, an expert's testimony was ruled inadmissible because the expert did not respond—most likely in nonscientific layman's terms—to objections from the defense. The district court in Joiner had the discretion to hold that the statements of the plaintiff's experts on causation were only speculation. The U.S. Supreme Court stated that the plaintiff did not explain, "how and why the experts could have extrapolated their opinions" from the studies far removed from the circumstances.

The majority also said that the district court's decision that the studies on which the plaintiff relied were an inadequate foundation for the experts' opinions (General Electric Co. v. Joiner 1997). The plaintiff claimed that the studies demonstrated causation—provided all of the studies' results were grouped together and that this type of weight-of-the-evidence methodology was reliable. The plaintiff contended that the district court did abuse its discretion by excluding testimony that was based on a scientifically reliable methodology.

The Joiner court examined whether the experts' opinions were sufficiently supported by the scientific studies that they relied upon in offering their opinions. The U.S. Supreme Court found that the studies offered by the plaintiff's experts here were so antithetical to the facts presented that the district court was correct in rejecting the experts' reliance on them; the ipse dixit, of the expert—unsupported statements resting solely on the authority of the expert who makes it—was insufficient support for admission. The U.S. Supreme Court explained,

> Conclusions and methodology are not entirely distinct from one another. Trained experts commonly extrapolate from existing data. But nothing in either Daubert or the Federal Rules of Evidence requires a district court to admit opinion evidence, which is connected, to existing data only by the *ipse dixit* of the expert. A court may conclude that there is simply too great an analytical gap between the data and the opinion proffered.
>
> *(General Electric Co. v. Joiner 1997)*

The discretion of the trial court has become critical to admission of expert scientific testimony. The judge's decision on whether to allow testimony, such as forensic podiatry, would be presumed to be valid, absent some very clear circumstances that called for reversal.

The U.S. Supreme Court did not address the type of inquiry trial courts should implement, concentrating instead on Daubert's requirement that an expert opinion needs to adhere to a scientific methodology and must include scientific reasoning. In Joiner, the plaintiff's experts did not give any additional rationale to support their conclusions. The U.S. Supreme Court held that there was no mandate that required a court "to admit opinion evidence which is connected to existing data only by the *ipse dixit* of the expert," (General Electric Co. v. Joiner 1997) or only because the expert himself said it was so. If the gap is too wide, the trial court is within its authority to rule the expert testimony inadmissible.

In Kumho Tire Co. v. Carmichael (Kumho Tire Co. v. Carmichael 1999) the U.S. Supreme Court ruled that Daubert was applicable to testimony based on "technical" and "other specialized" knowledge, in addition to testimony based on "scientific" knowledge—here it was engineers. Quoting Daubert, Justice Breyer, writing for the majority in 1999, stated that the test of reliability is "flexible." Daubert's list of specific factors, he said, "neither necessarily nor exclusively applies to all experts or in every case" (Kumho Tire Co. v. Carmichael 1999). Instead, a court has "the same broad latitude when it decides how to determine reliability as it enjoys in respect to its ultimate reliability determination" (Kumho Tire Co. v. Carmichael 1999).

The U.S. Supreme Court held that FRE 702 grants a judge the discretionary authority "... to determine reliability in light of the particular facts and circumstances of the particular case" (Kumho Tire Co. v. Carmichael 1999). Kumho stated that the trial judge as gatekeeper may also recognize the role of professional experience. This is an aspect that forensic podiatrists who also practice in podiatry may bring to their forensic analysis. The court explained,

> To say this is not to deny the importance of Daubert's gatekeeping requirement. The objective of that requirement is to ensure the reliability and relevancy of expert testimony. It is to make certain that an expert, whether basing testimony upon professional studies or personal experience, employs in the courtroom the same level of intellectual rigor that characterizes the practice of an expert in the relevant field.
>
> *(Kumho Tire Co. v. Carmichael 1999)*

Thus, an expert may be qualified to render opinions based on experience alone. If so, he or she "must explain how that experience leads to the conclusion reached, why that experience is a sufficient basis for the opinion, and how that experience is reliably applied to the facts" (Kumho Tire Co. v. Carmichael 1999). This further expands the parameters for a judge's determination of the admissibility of the expert testimony. Indeed, the U.S. Supreme Court said the judge has "considerable leeway in deciding in a particular case how to go about determining whether particular expert testimony is reliable."

The court also held that a judge was free to consider one or more of the more specific factors provided in Daubert. Thus, Daubert was expanded to both apply to different types of experts beyond science and affirm the discretion of the trial court to make determinations as to these experts' admissibility.

Federal courts have interpreted the Daubert Trilogy to hold that the proponent need not prove to the judge that the expert's testimony is correct, but to prove by a preponderance of the evidence that the expert's testimony is reliable.

The Fifth Circuit noted that Kumho's permissive language does not "grant open season" on the admission of expert testimony by allowing courts discretionarily to disavow the Daubert factors. Black v. Food Lion (Black v. Food Lion, Inc., 1999) in 1999 stated "*Kumho* thus does not require district courts to reinvent the wheel every time expert testimony is offered in court. Just as the U.S. Supreme Court relied on the *Daubert* factors in *KumhoTire*, those factors may be used as a starting-point for analysis in the usual case" (Black v. Food Lion, Inc. 1999). Two years earlier, that Circuit advised that not every Daubert factor will necessarily apply to expert testimony; however, a judge's "preliminary assessment of whether the reasoning or methodology underlying the testimony is scientifically valid is important" (Daubert v. Merrell Dow Pharmaceuticals 1993). The Circuit said that in most cases, the district court should initially decide whether the Daubert factors are appropriate, then it can consider whether other factors not mentioned in Daubert are relevant (Watkins v. Telsmith, Inc. 1997).

Although Daubert initially was viewed as reforming the admissibility of expert evidence—particularly novel scientific evidence like forensic podiatry—the cases that followed the decision demonstrate that the rejection of expert testimony is the exception rather than the rule. Daubert did not work a "seachange over federal evidence law," and "the trial court's role as gatekeeper is not intended to serve as a replacement for the adversary system," the advisory committee on the FRE noted when it codified Daubert in FRE 702 in December 2000 (Fed. R. Evid. 702, 2000).

The Daubert factors—and others added by the courts—may not always be applicable in every circumstance as to scientific testimony. Decisions before and after Daubert have indicated additional factors deemed to be germane in determining whether expert testimony is sufficiently reliable to be considered by the trier of fact (Jaurequil v. Carter Mfg. Co. 1999; United States v. Natson 2007; Wagner v. Hesston Corp., 2006; Watkins v. Telsmith, Inc. 1997).

The First Circuit in its 2002 decision, U.S. v. Mooney (U.S. v. Mooney 2002), found that the expert's testimony and his ultimate opinion were "inevitably linked because they were based on the same methodology." The Circuit also commented that FRE 702 "specifically allows qualified experts to offer their opinions, a testimonial latitude generally unavailable to other witnesses" (U.S. v. Mooney 2002). The Court also held that "once a trial judge determines the reliability of the proffered expert's methodology and the validity of his reasoning, the expert should be permitted to testify as to the inferences and conclusions he draws from it, and any flaws in his opinion may be exposed through cross-examination or competing expert testimony" (U.S. v. Mooney 2002). This has been played out many times in courts where a party objects to the admissibility of an expert witness, but the judge allows the testimony with the reminder that cross-examination is the vehicle for probing the weight of the evidence.

The FRE were revised in 2000 in response to Daubert (Daubert v. Merrell Dow Pharmaceuticals 1993) and Kumho (Kumho Tire Co. v. Carmichael 1999). The notes by the federal advisory committee declared that if the expert is relying primarily on his or her own experience in arriving at a conclusion in testifying, the expert "must explain how that experience leads to the conclusion reached, why that experience is a sufficient basis for the opinion, and how that experience is reliably applied to the facts" (Fed. R. Evid. 702, 2000). FRE 702 was updated (Fed. R. Evid. 702, 2000) so that a witness who is qualified as an expert by knowledge, skill, experience, training, or education may testify in the form of an opinion or otherwise if

1. The expert's scientific, technical, or other specialized knowledge will help the trier of fact to understand the evidence or to determine a fact in issue.
2. The testimony is based on sufficient facts or data.
3. The testimony is the product of reliable principles and methods.
4. The expert has reliably applied the principles and methods to the facts of the case. (Fed. R. Evid. 702, 2000)

As part of a project to reword the Rules of Evidence to make them more easy to understand and consistent, FRE 702 was amended again in 2011 (Fed. R. Evid. 702, 2011). In its explanation of the changes, the advisory committee said that Rule 702 "recognizes that an expert on the stand may give a dissertation or exposition of scientific or other principles relevant to the case, leaving the trier of fact to apply them to the facts" (Fed. R. Evid. 702, 2011). They noted that the use of opinions would still be permissible, "for the experts to take the further step of suggesting the inference which should be drawn from applying the specialized knowledge to the facts" (Fed. R. Evid. 702, 2011).

Because the majority of litigation in the United States occurs in state courts, it is more likely that a forensic podiatry expert witness will testify there. Therefore, it is important to understand that each court is regulated by its own specific procedural and evidentiary rules, and its own precedential case decisions. A potential forensic podiatry expert should understand that the general principles of Frye and Daubert impact the manner in which he or she will be treated in most courts.

10.5 Case Study

Forensic podiatrists participating in Daubert or Daubert-type hearings should realize that the factors outlined in Daubert are guidelines—they are flexible, and based on the facts of the case and the testimony offered, not every factor will be included or required. One other issue in a Daubert hearing often is the determination as to whether the expert is qualified to testify. The trial judge will base this decision on a review of the expert's knowledge, skill, experience, education, and training. As a result, the forensic podiatrist should be prepared to explain how forensic podiatry, in the context of the case in question, meets the admissibility standard.

The U.S. legal system is adversarial with the use of cross-examination. Opposing counsel will likely attack the forensic podiatrist's opinions on these issues and should be expected to question the expert's testimony as to its reliability, arguing that it should not be admitted. Typically, opposing counsel is afforded wide latitude in its inquiries in a Daubert hearing, many times going beyond questions about the qualifications of the forensic podiatrist, the science of forensic podiatry, and the methods used in the case. Because forensic podiatry is a relatively new forensic science, the forensic podiatrist may expect face questions on the scope and origins of the specialty. He or she should be prepared to answer questions concerning the techniques used and the results and to stress the scientific reliability and validity of the underlying science.

An illustration of a Daubert hearing to exclude the admissibility forensic podiatry expert testimony is State of Wisconsin v. Travis L. Petersen (State of Wisconsin v. Travis L. Petersen 2015), a case in which the author worked with law enforcement to analyze footprint evidence.

Robert Kasun was found murdered in a hotel room in Waushara County, Wisconsin with a fractured skull, broken ribs, and a severed aorta. Near the body, investigators identified blood on the floor. Chemical enhancement with luminol revealed footprints made in the blood. Based on this and other evidence, police arrested Travis Petersen, who was staying in the room next door, charging him with first-degree intentional homicide.

Investigators asked the author, a forensic podiatrist, for his expert opinion as to whether Petersen could have made (or not made) the bloody footprints, or whether the evidence was inconclusive. After the author conducted a forensic podiatry analysis and submitted a report showing commonality between Petersen's foot and the bloody footprint, Peterson's attorney made a motion for a Daubert hearing to exclude the admissibility of the author's report and his testimony at trial.

The Daubert hearing is similar to a trial, and is sometime called "a trial within a trial." As an expert witness for the state, the prosecution questioned the author first, followed by the defendant's cross-examination. A redirect questioning is permitted by the state, and then each side gives a closing argument prior to the ruling by the judge.

Before the Daubert hearing, the author gave the judge and the defense peer-reviewed journal articles and material from forensic textbooks on forensic podiatry and footprint evidence (Barker 1998; Blinka 2011; Bodziak 1999; Kaufman 2006; Kennedy 1996; Kennedy 2003; Kennedy 2005; Krishan 2007; Laskowski 1988; Qamra 1980; Reel 2010; Rich 2005; Smerecki 1984; Thompson 2007; Vernon 1994). The author recommends that forensic podiatrists distributing such materials need to possess an extremely well-versed knowledge of the materials supplied to the court. In this case, one of the articles provided was on a study of bare footprints. The author was asked to explain how the study's sample population was obtained, and he was able to do based on his research and readings.

As this chapter notes, the questioning during a Daubert hearing will not be a verbatim recitation of the Daubert factors (Daubert v. Merrell Dow Pharmaceuticals 1993), as the U.S. Supreme Court has held it to be a flexible standard. Nonetheless, the line of questioning in the Petersen hearing corresponded to the overall Daubert standard. This case study highlights several interesting passages within the hearing which when transcribed ran more than 100 pages.

The questioning of the author at the Daubert hearing focused on forensic podiatry as it relates to footprint analysis—the evidence at issue in the Petersen case.

Prosecutors for the state of Wisconsin questioned the author about podiatry and forensic podiatry in general. Their questions concerned forensic podiatry's definition, scope, and history. Forensic podiatry principles and the research underlying those principles was discussed, along with the specialty's general acceptance, whether forensic podiatry has been subject to peer review, the methodology of forensic podiatry, the potential error rate and reliability in footprint analysis, and the methods used in this case. That encompassed the linear objective measurement method and the overlay method of footprint analysis, and how the forensic principles of class and individual characteristics relate to footprints.

The state subsequently asked about the specifics of this case, and also about the author's qualifications—his background, experience, and training with regard to podiatry and forensic podiatry.

The defense's cross-examination focused on the principles and methodology of forensic podiatry in general and also with respect to the Petersen case. A lack of questioning about the author's training and credentials was unusual; forensic podiatrists need to be prepared for this on cross-examination, as case law shows regular objections to expert qualifications in the initial round of an attack. In this case, the author's training and credentials were provided to defense counsel before the hearing. The defense seemed to be satisfied with the author's expertise in forensic podiatry.

The defense counsel questioned the author about the process of analyzing footprints and about whether a footprint found at the crime scene was of adequate quality to have evidentiary value. This led to specific questions about a sock-clad footprint—as opposed to a bare footprint—as was the situation at hand. The defense claimed that research on footprints to a great extent concerned only bare footprints, rather than those clad with socks. As a result, the defense counsel argued that forensic podiatry testimony should be inadmissible. Of significance to the sock-clad argument was the defense's attempt to establish differences between a sock-clad footprint and bare footprint. Defense counsel then asked the author, "Is it your belief or is it your opinion that a bare foot would make a different impression than a foot covered with a sock?" (State of Wisconsin v. Travis L. Petersen 2015)

In a Daubert hearing, the expert testifies to support a judge's decision to allow him or her take the stand and testify at trial. Thus, the expert should clarify his or her answers so as not to confuse or mislead the judge. Whereas the answer to the question posed by defense counsel above might easily be answered "Yes," that answer by itself would not allow the judge to appreciate the more granular permutations of sock-clad and bare footprints. By adding such detail, the author explained that sock-clad and bare footprint impressions are different. He then explained their similarities. This question on cross gave the author the chance to bolster the state's case by explaining that the linking a sock-clad footprint at the crime scene to the suspect's sock-clad footprint increased the chance for variation between the footprints because the type of socks that the criminal wore at the crime scene was not known. Socks were given to Petersen to wear to make a set of his footprints that were used for comparison with a footprint found at the crime scene. The author explained to the court:

> … The interesting thing is that the police are guessing at or they are doing an educated guess in some cases on what kind of sock to put on the suspect when they do the barefoot impressions; so there is a higher likelihood of difference when you are dealing with a sock footprint to sock footprint. And when you have a degree of matching … that is in some ways stronger, because we do not know with certainty what kind of sock he was wearing when he made his footprint.
>
> *(State of Wisconsin v. Travis L. Petersen 2015)*

On redirect examination on this "sock-clad versus bare footprint" issue, the prosecutor used a similar tactic by giving the court additional relevant information within its question, while cuing the expert witness expound on that information (State of Wisconsin v. Travis L. Petersen 2015). Directing the author to recall a chapter on foot impression evidence that he submitted as part of the materials to the court before the Daubert hearing from the textbook *Footwear Impression Evidence: Detection, Recovery and Examination*, Second Edition, the prosecutor asked:

> … On page 389 of that [textbook], there is some suggestion that, quote, The study also noted that the foot leads [sic] a two-dimensional impression that is

> repeatedly consistent in its size, shape, contour, and proportional features which can be used to distinguish one foot from another. This is also true for sock-clad impressions, which leave an impression very similar to the bare foot....
>
> *(Bodziak 1999)*

In addition, the state questioned the author on the findings of other scientific research from the materials supplied to the judge that addressed what the state coined as the "morphological reliability" of sock-clad footprints. As a part of this discussion, the author relayed a quote in his answer, saying, and "... The article by Smerecki and Lovejoy says... '... footprints made through socks or stockings can leave an anatomical morphology that can be examined to yield a high degree of identification'" (Smerecki 1984).

During its closing argument, the state commented on the science of forensic podiatry:

> You are not talking about a theoretical science here. You are not talking about amorphous theory or a fact pattern that involves PTSD, or psychology, or the nature of addictions. In this case, what you are dealing with is what I would call the classical hard science, if you will, or very close to them. [...] You are dealing with something like a print. It is tangible, okay? You can see it. You can photograph it. You can trace it. You can luminol it. You can replicate it to scale, and then you can measure it to scale. You can measure its width, its length, its depth—and this is—and then apply math, just simple math. You can split it into hemispheres ... and then measure it form static points in various fields.
>
> *(State of Wisconsin v. Travis L. Petersen 2015)*

In contrast, the defense's closing argument emphasized that forensic podiatry is not science and does not meet the Daubert standard:

> I find it odd that we, "we" being the defense, weren't able to find any scholarly articles or any experts who refute this information that Dr. Nirenberg has presented. And the fact that we haven't found any doesn't mean that the Court can't rule in our favor, because what it tells me Judge, is that this is a field that's still emerging and hasn't been fully vetted as a reliable scientific field ... Let's use fingerprint and tool mark, for example. Those are the most comparable scientific fields because those two, along with this forensic podiatry field, all involve identifying crime-scene evidence to the suspect. And those fields have been fully vetted. And there is a lot of criticism in those fields, and that criticism continues. And how forensic podiatry has sort of escaped being fully vetted is beyond me.
>
> *(State of Wisconsin v. Travis L. Petersen 2015)*

The scientific literature on forensic podiatry and footprint evidence provided to the judge by the author prior to the Daubert hearing undermined this argument.

The judge drafted an 11-page decision on the matter of forensic podiatry evidence. In part, he stated:

> I do recognize that we are working through what is not necessarily a novel area, but one with which we have a collective degree of ignorance among the counsel that are participating, in this case. I know I've never seen a situation involving the use of forensic podiatry … I believe it's probable that the reason for that is that you don't very often have a footprint, barefoot or sock-clad, left at the scene of a crime the same way that you would expect fingerprints to come into the picture. We don't touch things with our feet the way we do with our hands. It's a simple, common, understood way about how humans interact with one another and their environment.
>
> *(State of Wisconsin v. Travis L. Petersen 2015)*

With regard to the Daubert "relevancy" issue, the judge explained:

> When the Court is addressing a challenge of this nature, I, first of all, must determine whether or not the evidence is relevant. I find it highly relevant in this instance. It matters, in this case … It places an identification of a latent footprint left at the scene of a crime. And any information tending to assign ownership to that footprint is, by definition, relevant and will be immensely helpful to the trier of fact in determining the identity, if you will, of the perpetrator of the offense….
>
> *(State of Wisconsin v. Travis L. Petersen 2015)*

As far as reliability, the judge noted:

> The Court next has to address the reliability of the information that is being evaluated, and that's where much of the criticism has been offered here. Recognizing this is not an area that has been subjected to the same degree of peer scrutiny, perhaps, as other areas of forensic science, we, nonetheless, in the Court's judgment, have substantial reliability that's been established. The series of articles that were produced in advance of the hearing and which were referred to during the course of Dr. Nirenberg's testimony provide a great deal of guidance in that regard … all of which I've read, indicative of the process through which this method of identification has evolved and the scientific principles that are applied to it.
>
> *(State of Wisconsin v. Travis L. Petersen 2015)*

The defense's argument was predicated on the claim that research using bare footprints was not applicable because the bloody footprint was made from a sock-clad foot, not bare. The judge addressed this assertion:

> I believe the issue is very clearly addressed to the Court's satisfaction, first of all, by the two Treatises, which directly address it … both of which indicate the

> relationship and direct nexus between studies that have been done on bare feet and podiatric analysis and the studies that have been done on feet that have been in socks. [...] And then after Dr. Nirenberg explained the similarity to me and why that nexus can be directly drawn, I understood it much better ... The foot leaves specific impressions when the owner of the foot walks upon it, does so in a manner, which, essentially, if not nullifying, greatly mitigate the necessity of having any of the types of skin surface to imprint surface transition normally affiliated with a fingerprint, which, from a lay perspective, had troubled me to a certain extent. And it's very clearly understood to this Court now why it is that the relationship between the science applied in a barefoot podiatric analysis translates without any type of interruption to a circumstance where the foot leaving the impression was clad with a sock.
>
> *(State of Wisconsin v. Travis L. Petersen 2015)*

The judge also spoke to the concept of the expert accounting for "obvious alternative explanations," stating:

> Critical also, in the Court's judgment, there were at least three or four times in his testimony where Dr. Nirenberg indicated what he is really trying to do, more than finding similarities between the latent print and exemplar, is to find distinguishing features to try and eliminate, rather than include. I derived a very clear understanding from his analytical approach that the thrust of what he is trying to do is to find something that doesn't match, to find something inconsistent or that excludes.
>
> *(State of Wisconsin v. Travis L. Petersen 2015)*

In summary, the judge concluded the Daubert hearing by ruling that the author would be permitted to give forensic podiatry testimony (State of Wisconsin v. Travis L. Petersen 2015).

The author subsequently testified at the Petersen trial. To add to the forensic podiatry evidence linking of suspect's footprint to the crime scene, investigators also discovered the victim's blood in Petersen's residence, along with other evidence. Petersen was found guilty sentenced to life in prison without parole.

The arguments raised by defense counsel challenging the admissibility of forensic podiatry evidence in the Petersen case were as follows:

1. A lack of scientific criticism against forensic podiatry, and a dearth of reliability
2. The fact that most scientific research concerning forensic footprint analysis used bare footprints rather than sock-clad footprints, as was the case with footprints found at the crime scene
3. A podiatrist was unnecessary to compare the suspect's footprint to that found at the crime-scene footprint, which could be conducted by a layperson—intimating that forensic podiatry is not science.

Arguments in response to the challenge by the prosecution included the following:

1. The existence of sufficient published and peer-reviewed research on forensic footprint analysis, which established forensic podiatry's reliability
2. The understanding of the manner in which a sock-clad footprint translates to a surface, maintaining pertinent footprint morphology, along with published research on sock-clad footprint evidence, thereby establishing the forensic value of sock-clad footprint evidence
3. The need for podiatrist's expertise to comprehend complex interactions of the foot, influenced by motion, anatomy, pathology, body weight, and other factors, when interpreting a footprint

This case study illustrates the importance and applicability of forensic podiatry evidence and testimony as to footprint evidence in a criminal case. Daubert challenges to forensic podiatry testimony may well increase, as this specialty is better known. Forensic podiatrists should anticipate the potential for a Daubert hearing at some point, and if opposing counsel does not request a Daubert hearing before trial, the forensic podiatrist should prepare for Daubert-type questions like those experienced by the author when giving expert testimony in court.

In preparation for a Daubert hearing, forensic podiatrists need to be well versed with current relevant research and scientific advances. They should be familiar with the Daubert standard, the factors it employs. Finally, potential experts should stay abreast of significant legal rulings and evidence rule changes which could affect forensic podiatry testimony. Forensic podiatry practitioners also must remain steadfast to examine and incorporate theories, methodologies, and techniques to maintain the highest legal and scientific standards.

References

Barker SL, Scheuer JL. Predictive value of human footprints in a forensic context. *Med Sci Law* 1998; 38(4): 341–6.

Black v. Food Lion, Inc., 171 F. 3d 308, 311 (5th Cir. 1999).

Blinka DD. The Daubert standard in Wisconsin: A primer. *Wisconsin Lawyer* 2011; 84: 14–9, 60–62.

Bodziak WJ. *Footwear Impression Evidence: Detection, Recovery and Examination.* 2nd ed. Boca Raton: CRC Press, 1999; 381–411.

Daubert v. Merrell Dow Pharmaceuticals, 509 U.S. 579, 598 (1993).

DiMaggio J.A. 2005. The role of feet and footwear in medico legal investigations. In *Forensic Medicine of the Lower Extremity*, edited by J. Rich, D.E. Dean, and R.H. Powers. pp. 375–400. Totawa, NJ: Humana Press.

Fed. R. Evid. 702 Advisory Committee note amendment (2011).
Fed. R. Evid. 702 Advisory Committee Note on Rules – 2000 Amendment (2000).
Fed. R. Evid. 702.
Federal Rules of Evidence, as amended to December 1, 2015.
Frye v. United States, 293 F. 1013, 1014 (1923).
General Electric Co. v. Joiner, 522 U.S. 136, 146 (1997).
Hedger C. Daubert and the States: A Critical Analysis of Emerging Trends, 49 St. Louis U. L.J. 177, 179–182 (2004).
Jaurequi v. Carter Mfg. Co., 173 F.3d 1076, 1083 (8th Cir. 1999).
Kaufman MS and Atlantic Legal Foundation. *The Status of Daubert in State Courts.* New York City: Atlantic Legal Foundation, March 31, 2006: 31.
Kaye D.H. Choice and Boundary Problems in Logerquist, Hummert, and Kumho Tire, 33 Ariz. St. L.J. 41, 63 (2001).
Kennedy RB, Pressman IS, Chen S, Pressman AE, Petersen PH. Statistical analysis of barefoot impressions. *J Forensic Sci* 2003; 48(1): 55–63.
Kennedy RB, Sanping C, Pressman IS, Petersen PH, Pressman AE. A large-scale statistical analysis of barefoot impressions. *J Forensic Sci* 2005; 50(5): 1071–80.
Kennedy RB. Uniqueness of barefeet and its use as a possible means of identification. *Forensic Sci Int* 1996; 82: 81–7.
Klein R, Lott L, & Rojas J. Expert Witnesses: When are They Necessary and Does Daubert/Kumho Make a Difference? SM017 American Law Institute—American Bar Association Continuing Legal Education 135 (2006): 5.
Krishan K. Individualizing characteristics of footprints in Gujjars of North India—Forensic aspects. *Forensic Sci Int* 2007; 169(2): 137–44.
Kumho Tire Co. v. Carmichael, 526 U.S. 137, 141 (1999).
Laskowski GE, Kyle VL. Barefoot impressions—A preliminary study of identification characteristics and population frequency of their morphological features. *J Forensic Sci* 1988; 33(2): 378–88.
McCormick on Evidence § 203 (3d ed. 1984).
Murphy T. The admissibility of scientific evidence in Illinois, 21 Loy. U. Chi. L.J. 935, 972 (1990).
New Jersey Courts, 2013–2015 report of the Supreme Court Committee on the Rules of Evidence, Part II, Evidence Rule 702 Project: Current State Approaches to Admission of Expert Testimony (Excluding NJ) (2015): 18–43.
Qamra SR, Sharma BR, Kaila P. Naked footmarks—A preliminary study of identification factors. *Forensic Sci Int* 1980; 16(2): 145–52.
Reel S, Rouse S, Vernon W, Doherty P. Reliability of a two-dimensional footprint measurement approach. *Sci Justice* 2010; 50: 113–18.
Rich J, Dorothy DE, Powers RH, editors. *Forensic Medicine of the Lower Extremity.* Totowa: Humana Press, 2005: 375–400.
Smerecki CJ, Lovejoy CO. Identification via pedal morphology. *The Police Chief* 1984; 51(4): 52–4.
State of Wisconsin v. Travis L. Petersen, No. 13-CF-38, (Waushara Cnty Ct. January 8, 2015).
State of Wisconsin v. Travis L. Petersen, No. 13-CF-38, (Waushara Cnty Ct. January 8, 2015), at 81–82 (testimony of MS Nirenberg).
State of Wisconsin v. Travis L. Petersen, No. 13-CF-38, (Waushara Cnty Ct. January 8, 2015), at 61–62 (testimony of MS Nirenberg).

State of Wisconsin v. Travis L. Petersen, No. 13-CF-38, (Waushara Cnty Ct. January 8, 2015), at 88 (testimony of SC Blader).
State of Wisconsin v. Travis L. Petersen, No. 13-CF-38, (Waushara Cnty Ct. January 8, 2015), at 80 (testimony of SC Blader).
State of Wisconsin v. Travis L. Petersen, No. 13-CF-38, (Waushara Cnty Ct. January 8, 2015), at 92–93 (testimony of TL Nielsen).
State of Wisconsin v. Travis L. Petersen, No. 13-CF-38, (Waushara Cnty Ct. January 8, 2015), Case No. 13-CF-38, at 97 (Order, Judge Guy Dutcher).
State of Wisconsin v. Travis L. Petersen, No. 13-CF-38, (Waushara Cnty Ct. January 8, 2015), Case No. 13-CF-38, at 98 (Order, Judge Guy Dutcher).
State of Wisconsin v. Travis L. Petersen, No. 13-CF-38, (Waushara Cnty Ct. January 8, 2015), Case No. 13-CF-38, at 97 (Order, Judge Guy Dutcher).
State of Wisconsin v. Travis L. Petersen, No. 13-CF-38, (Waushara Cnty Ct. January 8, 2015), at 107–108 (Order, Judge Guy Dutcher).
State of Wisconsin v. Travis L. Petersen, No. 13-CF-38, (Waushara Cnty Ct. January 8, 2015), at 108 (Order, Judge Guy Dutcher).
State of Wisconsin v. Travis L. Petersen, No. 13-CF-38, (Waushara Cnty Ct. January 8, 2015), at 108 (Order, Judge Guy Dutcher).
Thompson T, Black S, editors. *Forensic Human Identification—An Introduction.* British Association for Human Identification. Boca Raton: CRC Press, 2007: 14.
U.S. v. Mooney, 315 F.3d 54, 63 (1st Cir. 2002).
United States v. Downing, 753 F.2d 1224, 1231 (3d Cir. 1985).
United States v. Jakobetz, 955 F.2d 786, 796–798 (2d Cir. 1992).
United States v. Natson, 469 F. Supp. 2d 1253, 1258 (M.D. Ga. 2007)
United States v. Prince-Oyibo, 320 F.3d 494, 498 (4th Cir. 2003).
Vernon W, Brodie B, DiMaggio J, Gunn N, Kelly H, Nirenberg M, Reel S, & Walker J. Forensic podiatry: Role and scope of practice (in the context of forensic human identification). Identifications News 2010; 40: 22–24.
Vernon W. The development and practice of forensic podiatry. *J Clin Forensic Med* 2006; 13: 284–7.
Vernon W. The use of chiropody/podiatry records in forensic and mass disaster identification. *J Forensic Ident* 1994; 44: 26–40.
Wagner v. Hesston Corp., 450 F.3d 756, 758 (8th Cir. 2006).
Watkins v. Telsmith, Inc., 121 F.3d 984, 989 (5th Cir. 1997).
Westberry v. Gislaved Gummi AB, 178 F.3d 257, 261 (4th Cir. 1999).

Case Readings IV

Case Readings in Forensic Podiatry

11

11.1 Bare Footprint Case Reading (Crown v. Clarke 2005)

Case Scenario: The suspect in this case, Michael Clarke, was a young man of 21 years, who lived with his parents. One evening, he went out with friends to attend a rock concert. His friends had called for him that day and on leaving his home, he asked his friends to wait because he had forgotten something, returning to his home for a few minutes to collect the item he had left behind. Upon returning home that evening after the music concert, the young man telephoned the police to advise that on arriving at his home, he had found both his parents dead. On attending the scene, the police found that Clarke's parents had been stabbed to death in what seemed to be a very expert manner. Suspicion soon fell on Clarke who was known to be a practitioner of Eskrima, a Filipino stick-and-knife fighting form of martial art. Although there had been a period of less than 10 minutes when Clarke had returned home on his way out for the evening, the police believed that his expertise and fitness were such that he could have had time to slay his parents, change, and return to his friends within that window of opportunity.

Circumstantial evidence mounted against Clarke and consisted of material on Clarke's computer indicating that he had been developing a forensic awareness and closed-circuit television (CCTV) film at the concert venue Clarke had attended. This seemed to show Clarke entering a men's restroom with what appeared to be a full sports bag and later leaving with the same bag now looking apparently empty. The suggestion here was that Clarke may have been disposing of incriminating evidence such as bloodstained clothing and the murder weapon. During the investigation of the crime scene, several bare footprints were found using luminol enhancement, and the situation of these prints indicated that they were in fact associated with the crime.

Opinion Required: A request was received from the police to collect footprints from Clarke and compare these prints with the luminol-enhanced footprints captured at the crime scene to determine whether the known (reference) and unknown (questioned) sets of prints has been formed by the same person.

Analysis, comparison, and evaluation: An appointment was made to examine Clarke, who was being held in police custody. Because the exact circumstances under which the prints had been left were not known, at this appointment, footprints were collected from the suspect under a variety of conditions: barefoot, socked, standing, walking, light running, and on both hard surface and carpet. Clarke made inked prints on the carpet, and the inkless paper method was used to collect all other prints from him. During collection of the prints, paired observations were made by two observing podiatrists as well as video recordings being made from posterior and lateral viewpoints of every step that left a print. This was with a view to ensuring that no attempts were being made to purposely amend each print formed.

The best-quality known prints collected from the suspect were compared with the best-quality questioned prints found at the crime scene (Figure11.1). The methods used for this comparison were the Gunn and overlay methods as described in Chapter 4. In the comparison between known and questioned footprints, the Gunn lines closely matched all but one of the measurements taken (Figure 11.2). In addition, the morphological outlines of known and questioned prints closely matched in terms of both position and form. Considering the Gunn lines, the heel-to-third toe measurements between known and unknown prints was 4 mm different in length, but from close examination of the unknown print, it was apparent that this was a partial toe print only; hence, there was an explanation for this difference. A difference of 10 mm was however apparent between the heel-to-fifth toe measurements of known and questioned prints. Closer examination revealed that on the questioned print, the fifth toe print was partial and also that the position of this toe print was in line with the fourth metatarsophalangeal joint position, suggesting that a some torsional movement had taken place that would further have amended the placement of this toe. Again, an explanation for this difference was apparent.

The close matching of measurements as described above also suggested that the known and questioned prints had been made by feet requiring the same size shoe. It was also apparent that both known and unknown prints had been formed by someone who exhibited a "Greek Ideal"—a state in which the second toe is the longest toe of the foot (Figure 11.3).

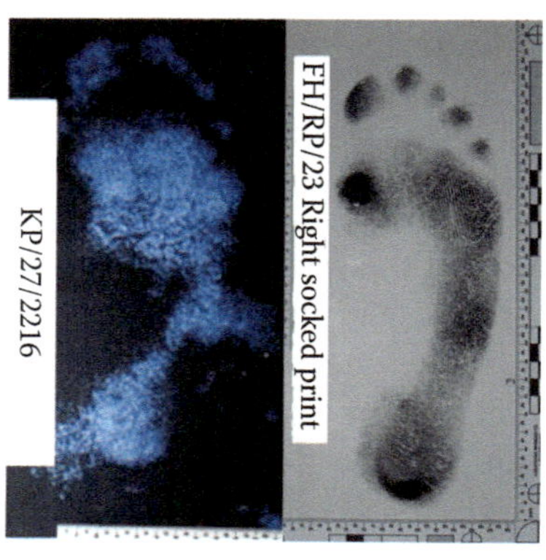

Figure 11.1 Known and questioned footprints in the Crown v. Clarke 2005 case.

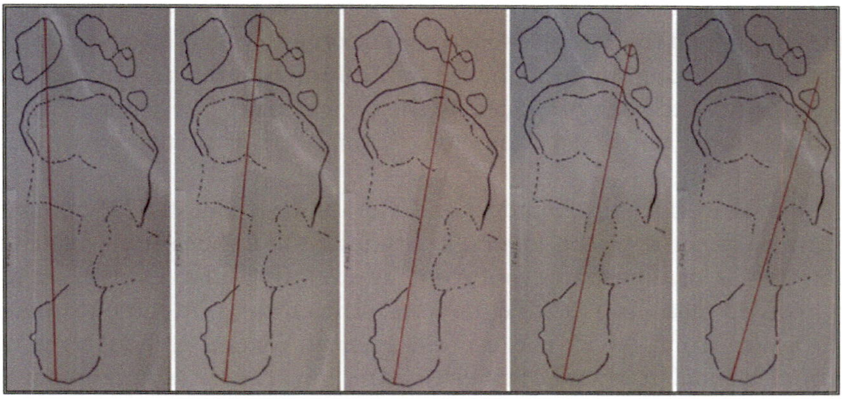

Measurement	Known footprint	Questioned footprint	+/– mm
Heel to 1st toe	250 mm	250 mm	0 mm
Heel to 2nd toe	255 mm	253 mm	2 mm
Heel to 3rd toe	244 mm	240 mm	4 mm
Heel to 4th toe	233 mm	232 mm	1 mm
Heel to 5th toe	216 mm	206 mm	10 mm
Cross ball	97 mm	95 mm	2 mm

Figure 11.2 Crown v. Clarke 2005: Comparison of known and questioned bare footprints. Black out line = questioned bare footprint; red line = Guinn line measurements taken from known bare footprint.

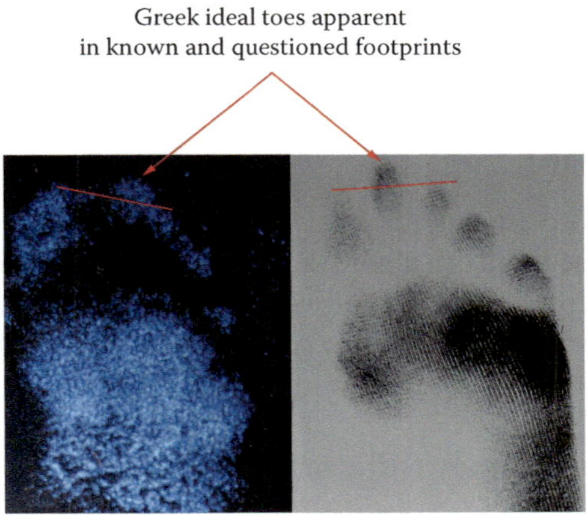

Figure 11.3 Greek Ideal toe prints in case comparators.

The known and questioned prints were also examined for the presence of features that would have suggested that different persons had made the prints. No such differences could be found other than those for which an explanation could be provided to show how these prints could still have been formed by the same person.

In the evaluation, the common features of known and questioned prints suggested that in European convention terms, there was at the time "moderately strong support" for the proposition that the known and questioned prints had been produced by the same person. The report was verified by another podiatrist competent in this work and duly submitted in statement form.

Several weeks later, an additional report was requested. The luminol testing had been repeated to a higher standard and the request made that photographs of the clearer footprints be examined and a further report be provided regarding the likelihood of a match between these prints and the known prints, which had been taken from Clarke. Although the new luminol test had produced obviously clearer images for examination, it was also apparent that these images had been taken without the use of a scale within the image. Such a scale had been provided with the images of the original tested prints, and this scale is essential in the assessment process because it is only by the use of a scale that the size and overall dimensions of the print can be determined. In the absence of such a scale, the possible conclusions that could be derived were limited and were in fact restricted to the presence of the Greek Ideal—the only feature apparent that was not dependent on the overall dimensions of the print being known for a conclusion to be made. Because of the absence of a scale, in this second report it was only possible to produce conclusions at the "moderate" level of support for the proposition that the same person had formed both the known and the clearer questioned prints; therefore, the findings of the original report remained stronger. The fact that a lower level of certainty was derived from the clearer prints demonstrated the need to use a scale in all evidence-quality images.

Outcome: The footprint evidence was presented in court and having chosen not to use a defense report that considered the footprint evidence, in oral evidence Clarke accepted that the footprints were his and changed his evidence in an attempt to provide a different explanation as to how his prints had been left in the position in which they were found, without being responsible for his parents' murder.

Clarke was found guilty of the murder of his parents and was sentenced to 29 years in prison.

Key Points: The case provides a typical illustration of how podiatrists approach bare footprint casework. The recognition of features of the foot supported by survey data related to such features is shown, as is the need to consider the potential for the bare footprint to be amended by function. The case also illustrates the need for a scale to be included in evidence-quality images submitted for examination.

11.2 Footwear Case Reading (Crown v. Chester-Nash 2006)

Case Scenario: A woman was found murdered in her home and later that day, transport police arrested a man who was about to board a train after stealing sandwiches from a sandwich shop at the railway station. Police noticed spots of blood on this person's shoes and investigated further, finding that the person that they had arrested, one Gary Chester-Nash, was well known to the criminal justice system. When the bloodstained shoes being worn by Chester-Nash were later examined, they were linked through DNA to the murder victim. Chester-Nash provided an explanation as to how the blood had found its way onto his shoes. He stated that he had been living in a squat with a Russian gentleman, who had a complicated name he could not remember. On the morning in question, the Russian man had borrowed Chester-Nash's clothing, including his shoes; left, and returned 1.5 hours later, leaving the clothing with Chester Nash; and departed again. Chester-Nash then commented that under these circumstances, it must have been the Russian man and not he who had committed the murder and that this was how the blood had found its way onto his shoes.

The police were concerned because implausible as it was, the story provided by Chester-Nash could have adversely affected the need to prove guilt beyond all reasonable doubt, thereby introducing an element of doubt to their case that potentially could have resulted in Chester-Nash's acquittal.

Opinion Required: Contact was made by the police, who asked whether the questioned footwear could be examined for signs of multiple wearers as claimed by Chester-Nash, or whether the shoes did really seem to have been worn by only one person. An additional piece of work was also suggested to the police, namely, the testing of identical shoes to those questioned to determine their susceptibility to wear and the effect of a second wearer. This latter item of work was suggested in view of the known different susceptibilities of shoes to wear. Although Kennedy (1995) presented images showing footwear containing a clear foot impression after just 15 minutes of wear and we had personal experience of footwear showing clear wear features after just 2 hours, experiences reported in the Nike project (Keereweer 1998) were that the training shoes used in that project needed to be worn for at least 44 hours before foot impressions were exhibited and in some cases required up to 155 hours of wear before these features became apparent. This variation suggested that the propensity of the shoes in question to demonstrate wear should be investigated to determine whether these shoes could in fact show wear within a period of just 1.5 hours.

Analysis, comparison, and evaluation: An appointment was initially arranged to examine the questioned footwear (Figure 11.4) and a comparator

Figure 11.4 Footwear in Chester-Nash case.

pair of shoes that had been seized from the suspect. On examination, the questioned and known footwear items were found to exhibit a clear foot impression of the same form and size. The questioned footwear items were examined in much closer detail to reveal any signs that more than one wearer had worn these shoes. These shoes were examined using the Crime-lite® 80S range with various filters, followed by a multiple waveband forensic light source to maximize contrast and highlight the wear features apparent within the shoe (Figure 11.5). Throughout the examination, no wear features were apparent to suggest that the shoes had been worn by anyone other than one wearer. From the experience of the investigating podiatrist, where more than one person has worn footwear, it would usually be expected that some wear features of the different wearers should be apparent. The conclusions reached at this stage of the investigation were that there was "limited support" for the proposition that the questioned footwear items had only been worn by one wearer.

Two separate and new pairs of the same make, type, and size (9 UK) of the questioned footwear items were then obtained and forwarded for wear testing. In this task, the shoes were subject to wear that would have closely matched that of the questioned shoes that were known to have been worn for one week by the suspect, who had then claimed that they had also been worn by the Russian man for 1.5 hours. Each pair of shoes was first worn for 1 week by separate people, and the shoes were photographed at intervals of 30 minutes, one hour, 1.5 hours, two hours, and then daily to determine their susceptibility to wear from a single wearer. After one week, separate and different wearers were found for each shoe, and these wearers wore the shoes for 1.5 hours, i.e., the time that Chester-Nash claimed that the Russian man had worn the shoes. Because little was known of the claimed missing Russian man, the test of these shoes was made as difficult as possible. The shoes were

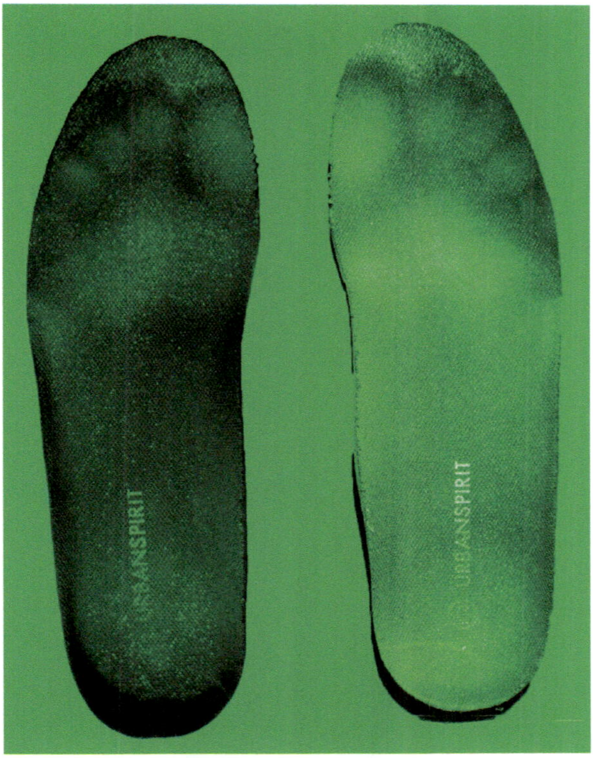

Figure 11.5 Contrasted foot impressions in questioned shoes.

therefore worn by size UK 9 wearers for the first week, followed by size UK 9 wearers for the second week. This would have prevented any explicitly obvious differences from becoming apparent in the shoe wear through mismatches in sizing between the feet involved and through the shoes being worn by someone with an incorrect foot length for that shoe. It was however probable that size differences could have occurred in a situation in which footwear was being borrowed and without proper fitting.

For the first wearer of each pair of shoes, a clear and permanent foot impression was apparent at the first photographing of the shoe after just 30 minutes of wear (with the shoes being left overnight for 16 hours before the photograph being taken) (Figure 11.6). This impression became more and more pronounced through the week of their being worn. The conclusions derived at this point were that the shoes were capable of demonstrating permanent wear features after just 30 minutes of wear.

The second wearer then wore the shoes for the required 1.5 hours, and the shoes were then left overnight and photographed once more 16 hours later. At this point, all shoes exhibited clear additional toe impressions from

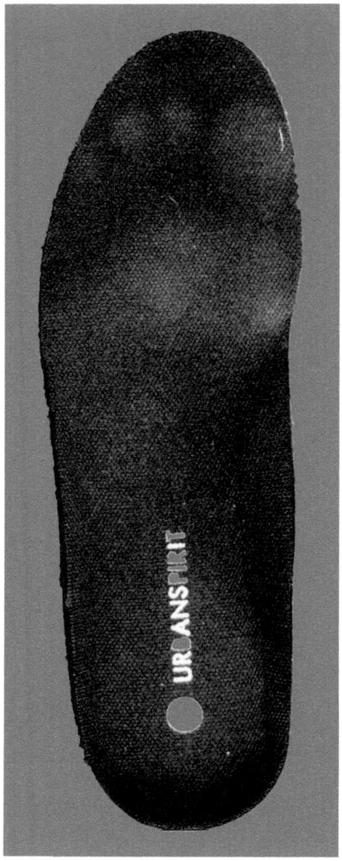

Figure 11.6 Foot impressions in test shoes after 30 minutes of wear.

the second wearer—impressions that could not have been created by a single wearer of the shoes (Figure 11.7). The conclusions derived at this stage were that the shoes were capable of clearly showing the effects of a second wearer within just 1.5 hours of wear from that additional wearer.

Outcome: The report stating the conclusions derived at each stage of this work were then shown to Chester-Nash. At this point, Chester-Nash changed his story, advising that the shoes had not in fact been worn by the Russian man, and that he had actually been at the scene of crime, hence the blood being present on these shoes. However, he held out that it was still the Russian man who had committed the murder and that he had simply been present. Because Chester-Nash had now admitted that he had been the only wearer of the questioned shoes, this evidence was not required to be presented in court; however, the fact that the story had changed in the manner described contributed to the jury being convinced that Chester-Nash

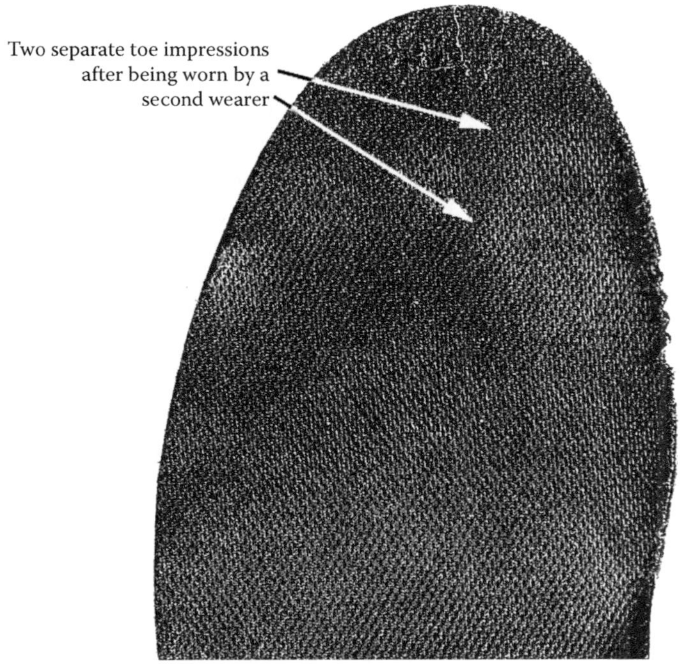

Figure 11.7 Effects of a second wearer on the foot impression present on the shoe insole after 1.5 hours.

was guilty of the murder, and he was sentenced to serve a minimum sentence of 30 years in prison.

Key Points: The potential for shoes to wear at different rates was central to the thinking in this case and served as a reminder that such considerations can be important in shaping the casework strategy. The case also showed that different wearers can leave different wear features within shoes, even when their feet are closely matched in terms of required shoe size.

11.3 Footwear Case Reading (2002)

Case Scenario: A murder had been committed in which a man had been kicked to death, and the following day police recovered a pair of blood-stained training shoes from elsewhere in the district in which the crime had been committed. Forensic examination of the training shoes determined that the blood staining the shoes was that of the victim. The police already had a suspect and seized another pair of training shoes from this person for direct comparison with the questioned training shoes associated with the crime scene. The questioned training shoes were of the Reebok brand and the training shoes seized from the suspect were Adidas. Both pairs of shoes were marked as size UK 8. The shoes were duly examined by a forensic marks examiner who focused on the foot impressions within both pairs of shoes. The forensic marks examiner noted several closely matched features between the foot impressions of both shoes, particularly the shape of the anterior ball of foot area and the shape of each of the toes. The examiner did however note that despite the close matching of these features, the foot impression present within the questioned Reebok training shoes was noticeably longer than that present within the known Adidas footwear items. Because of this difference, for which the marks examiner did not have an immediate explanation, the report provided noted in European convention terms that there was "moderate support" for the proposition that both known and questioned footwear items had been worn regularly by the same person.

Opinion Required: A podiatric opinion was sought, and it was believed that the podiatrist's viewpoint might be able to introduce additional factors to improve the strength of the evidence and to hopefully provide an explanation for the differences apparent between the lengths of two sets of foot impressions.

Analysis, comparison, and evaluation: An appointment was arranged to view the shoes at the laboratory. At the assessment, it was noted that both footwear items were indeed marked as size 8 UK. The sizes were checked in both pairs of shoes with an internal sizing device. This check indicated that the questioned Reebok training shoes were indeed an indicative size 8 UK in length; however, the known Adidas training shoes were an indicative size 7 UK. A difference of one shoe size in length terms was therefore apparent between these and the questioned Reebok shoes.

Examination of the wear features of the questioned Reebok training shoes indicated that these shoes had been too long for their usual wearer. Features of note in this respect were a turning up of the leading edge of the insoles in these shoes where the foot had not been in contact with the insole during walking, causing the leading edge to curl upward during toe-off and creating an additional anterior crease mark of the shoe upper, where toe-off had taken place during walking in a more posterior position than the design of the shoe allowed (Figure 11.8).

Examination of the wear features of the known Adidas training shoes did not elicit any wear features that suggested that these shoes has been similarly over-long for their usual wearer, but to the contrary, appeared from those wear features present to have fitted the owner reasonably well in length terms.

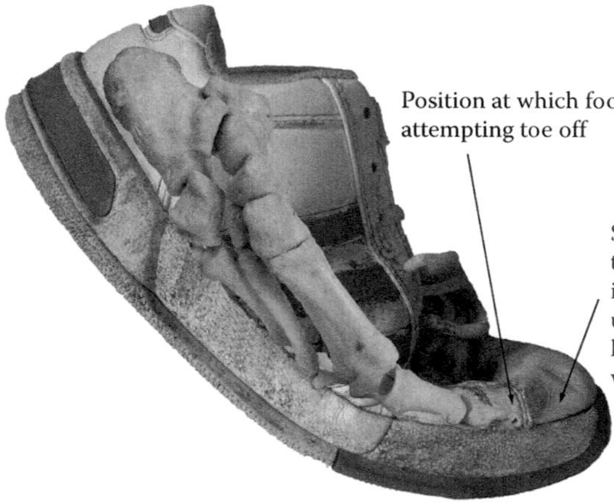

Figure 11.8 Effects the contained foot being shorter than the shoe being worn.

When the foot impressions present in both known and questioned training shoes were examined, it was noted that those impressions present within the questioned Reebok training shoes were longer than those present within the Adidas shoes. Both sets of impressions were measured, and it was found that the heel-to-toe measurements (measuring from the rearmost aspect of the insole to the anterior aspect of each toe) were exactly 1/3 inch longer in the Reebok shoes than in the Adidas for each and every toe impression. One-third inch is the exact difference between shoe sizes in the United Kingdom.

The scenario thus determined was one in which the foot of the usual wearer of the longer Reebok shoes had been able to slide forward during gait because of the excessive length of these shoes. In sliding forward, the toes would have reached the anterior position in relation to the shoe that they would have adopted if the owner had been wearing the correctly sized shoes for his foot length (Figure 11.9).

Outcome: Given the close similarity of the other wear features of the foot impression, having provided an explanation for the foot impression length differences based on the intrashoe function that would have taken place when wearing a shoe of excessive length, it was then possible to increase the strength of the conclusion to that of "moderately strong support" for the proposition that both footwear items had the same usual wearer.

Key Points: The case illustrated the value of multidisciplinary working in the forensic examination of footwear. The lack of shoe length standardization in the footwear industry was demonstrated along with the importance of considering the true internal length of a shoe when allowing for and interpreting the wear features of that shoe.

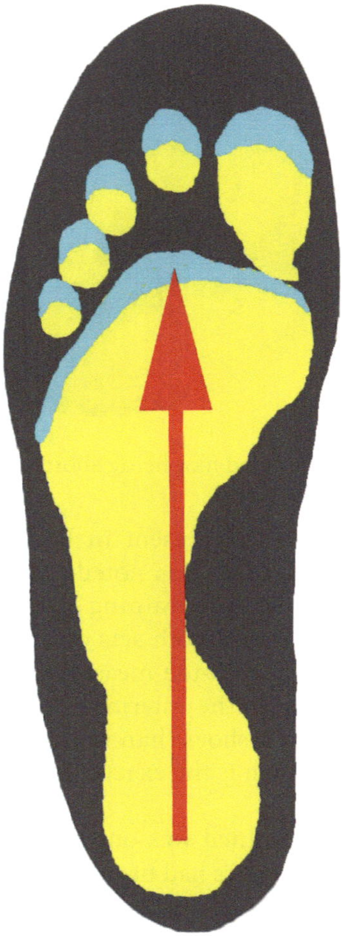

Figure 11.9 Lengthening of the foot impression in shoes that have been too long for the wearer.

11.4 Footwear Case Reading (2007)

Case Scenario: A series of burglaries had taken place, and shoe impressions had been found at each scene. Forensic marks examiners determined that these shoe impressions were all made by the same pair of shoes, being of the same make and type, and with the same accidental damage features present on the outsole impressions. The police arrested a suspect and seized two pairs of shoes from his home for comparison with the outsole prints found at the crime scenes. The marks examiners determined that these were the same shoes that had produced the foot impressions found at the crime scenes.

The suspect however denied ownership of the shoes, stating that many people visited and stayed at his home and that these shoes must have been left there by one of these many visitors.

Opinion Required and Limitations: This scenario presented the need to determine whether the suspect could be linked with these shoes in any way, or whether the story was genuine and the suspect had not in fact worn the questioned footwear items. A second pair of training shoes was taken from the suspect with a view to comparing the wear features of these with wear features of the questioned training shoes. This comparison was to determine whether any of the wear features would associate or disassociate the suspected wearer and the questioned shoes.

Analysis, comparison, and evaluation: Both pairs of shoes were collected from the police headquarters where the shoes were being held for examination. Both known and questioned training shoes were of the Nike brand and of the Air Max style. In the known training shoes, the Nike insole had been replaced with a Reebok brand insole, and the insole present within the left questioned training shoe had missing upper covering material. This left a firm closed cell rubber construction that did not present a foot impression of the wearer, meaning that comparison of the left foot impressions was not possible. The focus of the comparison was therefore on the right training shoes, although factors relating to the left shoes were also considered as far as possible.

In the comparison process, it was noted that the known training shoes were size 7 UK and the questioned training shoes were size 8 UK. Although one size different, this difference fell within the observations noted by Lucock, and supported by the author's experience, that single people commonly purchase and wear shoes of a full size-length difference, although they would be highly unlikely to purchase shoes with length differences greater than 1.5 sizes (Lucock 1980). The two pairs of shoes examined therefore fell within the expected tolerance for common ownership. Known and questioned footwear items also exhibited some common wear features. In relation to wear of the outsole, unusually heavy wear was noted at the posterior-lateral aspect of the heel and also at sites corresponding with the medial and lateral aspects of the ball-of-foot area. The uppers of both shoes demonstrated wear corresponding with the apex of the first toe, whereby the toe had worn completely through the lining at that point, due to the shoes being too short for the wearer at that position. Because of the missing left insole, foot impression comparisons were restricted to the right insoles only (Figure 11.10). The right foot impressions were closely matched in terms of overall length (measured from the rearmost aspect of the insoles, toe position and shape, and the contour of the anterior ball-of-foot impression). The similarities could be demonstrated clearly by

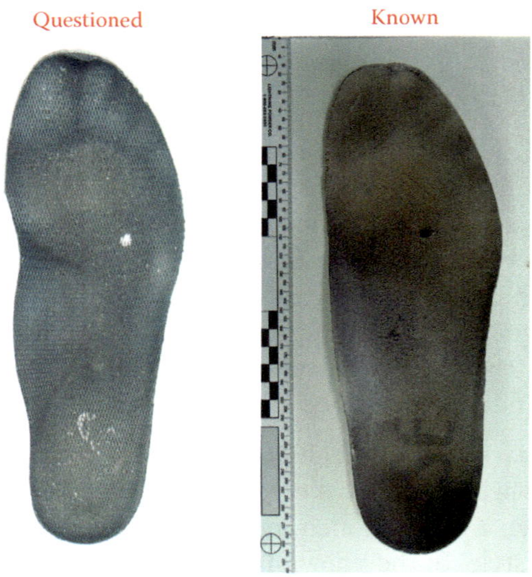

Figure 11.10 Known and questioned insoles for comparison.

taking a series of cross sections of each impression and matching them together, showing that irrespective of where the cross section was taken, the features being compared between questioned and known shoes lined up perfectly (Figure 11.11a–c).

An additional feature was apparent on the right insole of the questioned shoes, namely, an extra set of toe prints, situated some way behind the first set. The overall wear features of the shoes did not suggest any reason relating to function, fit, or habit, as to how this additional set of toe prints could have belonged to the wearer of the right known shoe whose foot impression had lined up so well with the overall foot impressions present within the right known and questioned shoes. No features could be found suggesting that the same wearer had not worn the questioned and known shoes. The following were therefore concluded:

1. There was "moderately strong support" for the proposition that both shoes had been worn by the same person (using the European scale of convention).
2. There was "strong support" for the proposition that the questioned trainer had also been worn by another person with a shorter foot length than the other wearer.

The recommendation was made that an examination be carried out of the wearer of the known shoes to tighten the conclusions reached above and also to confirm whether there were any functional reasons for the same

(a) (b) (c)

Figure 11.11 (a–c) Known and unknown foot impressions superimposed.

person to have created two different sets of toe impressions in this particular case. This recommendation was not however taken up because of time and resource restrictions.

Outcome: Upon being shown the report, the suspect then remembered that he did in fact own the shoes in question. Although the defense expert agreed with the findings of the report, a conviction did not result from the trial. This was because in the presence of "strong support" for the proposition that there had been two wearers of the questioned shoe, it could not be proved that the suspect was the actual wearer of the shoes when the burglaries in question had been carried out.

Key Points: The fact that people do not always purchase and wear shoes of the same marked size was shown in this case as was the understanding that despite such differences, the range of sizes bought and worn by a single person is limited. That two sets of toe prints present within a shoe cannot always be attributed to the shoe having been worn by multiple wearers came into consideration. The case also served as a reminder that just because ownership of a shoe can be suggested or admitted, depending on the case context, this does not necessarily in itself imply guilt, with the context presented by the case scenario being critical to such considerations.

11.5 Phoenix Arizona Homicide Case Reading (1996)

Crime: Homicide

Date of Incident: November 19, 1996, Phoenix, Arizona

Case Facts: In the early morning hours, four young friends took a drive around Caesar Chavez Park in Phoenix, Arizona, that ended in murder.

One of the girls is on trial for the murder facing charges that she twice tried to strangle her 19-year-old roommate. CM took one of the other girls' purses and started to strangle DB, who was driving, when the strap broke. The car started to swerve, and DB pulled on the emergency brake. When the car stopped, DB got out and started to run but CM caught her. CM started choking DB again, but the strap broke a second time. All the time DB was screaming for help. That's when CM grabbed a large rock that required two hands to hold and repeatedly crushed DB's head with it. These are the facts as described by the other two suspects who agreed to testify against CM to avoid murder charges.

Autopsy findings included stab wounds and bite marks on the body. The girls put DB's body in the trunk then drove to the West Valley and dumped it in a pond at a sand and gravel pit.

CM is accused of ordering her roommate from their apartment to kill her and forcing the other two girls who were 14 and 16 into helping her dump the body. CM was 18 and pregnant at the time of the incident. If she is found guilty she could get the death penalty.

The victim was DB, an Ahwatukee (residential area of Phoenix) girl who graduated from Mountain Pointe High School and was living in her own apartment and owned a car.

Two different footwear impressions were discovered and photographed at the crime scene.

The three females were arrested driving the victim's vehicle on November 20, 1996, and the shoes (500K, 501K, 502K) they were wearing were recovered.

On November 21, 1996, four pairs of shoes (304K, 305K, 306K, and 313K) were recovered from the victim's apartment.

On November 22, 1996, two pairs of shoes (419Q and 420Q) were recovered from the trunk of the victim's vehicle with other clothing items. The outsoles of the shoes were similar to the impressions discovered at the scene, but they could not be positively identified or excluded by the crime laboratory; however, one pair because of its proximity to the body was considered to most likely be the shoes worn by the perpetrator.

Subsequently, two pairs (914K and 915K) of the victim's shoes were given to the police by her parents to be used for purposes of the evaluation.

What Was the Forensic Podiatrist's Objective?

Can it be determined whether (1) the suspects most likely wore the questioned shoes and (2) who was the predominant wearer of each?

Initial contact was by the case detective stating that they were interested in retaining me for a case involving footprint evidence. They advised they had discovered footwear impression(s) at the crime scene. The laboratory evaluated them, but could not reach a definitive conclusion. They wanted my input relative to examining some questioned footwear. I examined several photographs and the two pairs of questioned shoes. I felt confident there was adequate quality and quantity of data to make a determination, one way or the other. I was not privy to any of the details of the crime by my own request. The initial facts are transcribed to a case determination form (Figure 11.12).

(*Casework comment:* It is very important to isolate oneself from the emotions of a case. One's opinion whose intent is to be totally objective will always have some subjective component, albeit very small. For example, knowledge that a 3-year-old child was brutally murdered and aware of all the facts of that gruesome act before the trial can affect one's opinion. Alternatively, having no prior knowledge does not allow anyone to imply that you had made up your mind because of this and may possibly use this against one, at times, in their testimony).

The evidence was hand delivered to my office. Chain of custody was maintained and logged appropriately.

(*Casework comment:* Your laboratory or in most cases a room in your residence or office dedicated to casework should have a door that can be secured and restricted to entry).

I received the shoes appropriately sealed with evidence tape in paper bags and identified as to its content. The evidence was removed from the paper bags, logging each item with appropriate identifiers (Figure 11.13).

(*Casework comment:* It is a good idea to photograph everything as received initially and after removing from packages. It is also important to confirm that the lab has examined, e.g., a pair of shoes for trace evidence so there is no concern of contamination or loss of evidence if there is a need to cut the shoe open, which in many cases is required.)

The methodology used is the ACE-V (analysis, comparison, and evaluation of the evidence with independent peer verification) paradigm. Analysis (The questioned evidence is examined first).

Questioned footwear (unknown) #419Q was a pair of canvas sneakers (Figure 11.14) size 5.5 US.

FORENSIC PODIATRY INITIAL CASE INQUIRY FORM:

CONTACTED BY:

AGENCY:

DATE:

TIME:

REQUEST (OBJECTIVE):

PHONE:

E-MAIL:

BRIEF SYNOPSIS: TYPE OF CRIME:

CASE NUMBER:

DATE OF OCCURRENCE:

SUSPECT (S):

STATUS: ____IN CUSTODY ____OTHER

PHYSICAL EVIDENCE RECOVERED:

COURT STATUS:

EVIDENCE REQUESTED FOR INITIAL REVIEW:

____ORIGINAL PHOTOGRAPHS

____FOOTWEAR

____BARE FOOTPRINT EXEMPLARS

____OTHER, I.E., PLASTER MOLDS

REFERRAL SOURCE:

DISPOSITION:

Figure 11.12 Example of initial case inquiry form.

Questioned footwear (unknown) #420 was a pair of designer athletic shoes size 5.0 left and size 5.5 right (Figure 11.15).

Each shoe is analyzed, including the upper, outsole, and sock liner/insole (see Chapter 5).

At the time of the arrest of the three suspects, their shoes were removed and placed into evidence. Suspect #1 (CM) was wearing item #500, a pair fashion

ID#	Questioned (Q)/ Known (K)	Make	Size	Description
419	Q	Nike®	5 ½	canvas off court casual sneaker *black*
420	Q	Kani®	5L 5 ½ R	designer athletic thick outsole *white*
500	K	Ellemenno®	8	canvas lace fashion sneaker *white*
501	K	Fila®	9	canvas off court casual sneaker *blue*
502	K	Nike®	8	Air running shoe Pegasus *white*
304	K	Highlights®	10	dress lace slip-on mule *tan*
305	K	Reebok®	7	cross trainer *black*
306	K	TFL®	5	lace up ankle boot *black*
313	K	Nike®	9	canvas off court casual sneaker *white*
914	K	Fila®	10	high top court shoe *white*
915	K	Asics®	9 ½	running shoe gel *white*

Figure 11.13 Inventory of footwear.

canvas sneakers size 8. Suspect #2 (YE) was only wearing a left shoe, item #501, a canvas casual sneaker size 9. She had injured her right foot/ankle a couple of weeks before and wore a cast on her right side. Suspect #3 (TS) was wearing a pair of running shoes item #502 size 8. Several other shoes, items #304, 305, 306, and 313, were recovered from the victim's apartment. It might be assumed these were the victim's shoes, but suspect #1 (CM) was also residing there at the time. Items #914 (size 10) and #915 (size 10.5) were supplied by the victim's parents of known shoes that the victim had worn. The suspects were examined

Figure 11.14 #419Q.

at the jail infirmary. Each suspect was evaluated, including photographs, inked footprints in a weight-bearing position, foam impressions, and a biomechanical evaluation (both static and dynamic). Foot measurements were also taken using two separate devices to equate them to shoe size. The data were then transferred onto a forensic foot evaluation sheets for further study.

Appropriate standards (exemplars; see Chapter 4) were constructed, including dental stone cast molds of each foot and appropriate transparencies from the inked footprints and photographs. The laboratory supplied examination-quality photographs of the sock liners of each shoe as requested (Figures 11.16 and 11.17).

All standards were verified for accuracy before any comparison evaluation.

(*Casework comment:* If the original photographs were not received, then it must be verified that what was received was accurate, although every attempt should be made to receive originals. This also includes photocopies of bare footprints, e.g., for accurate size reproduction.)

Comparison (known to questioned item): The modified overlay technique (DiMaggio 2005; Figure 11.18) was used. Other methods should also be used to confirm or corroborate findings. Direct overlay of the sock liner is performed as well as using the foot casts for it. At this time, suspect #2 (YE) was

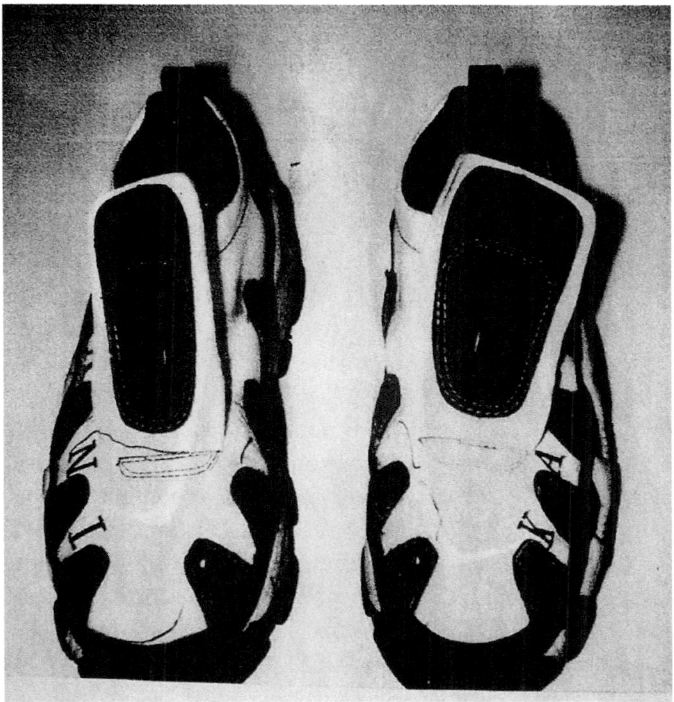

Figure 11.15 #420Q.

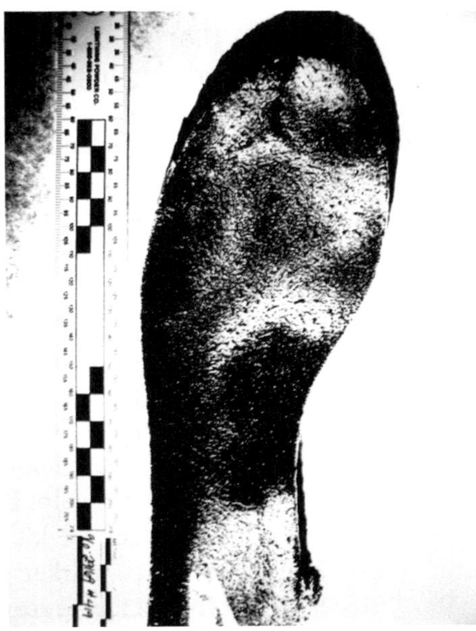

Figure 11.16 Sock liner image 419Q.

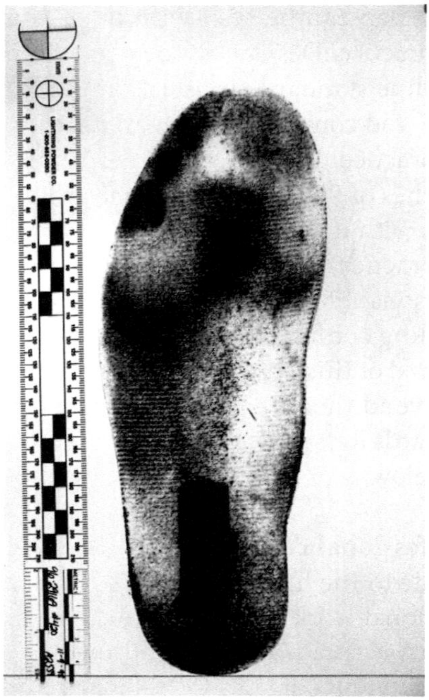

Figure 11.17 Sock liner image 420Q.

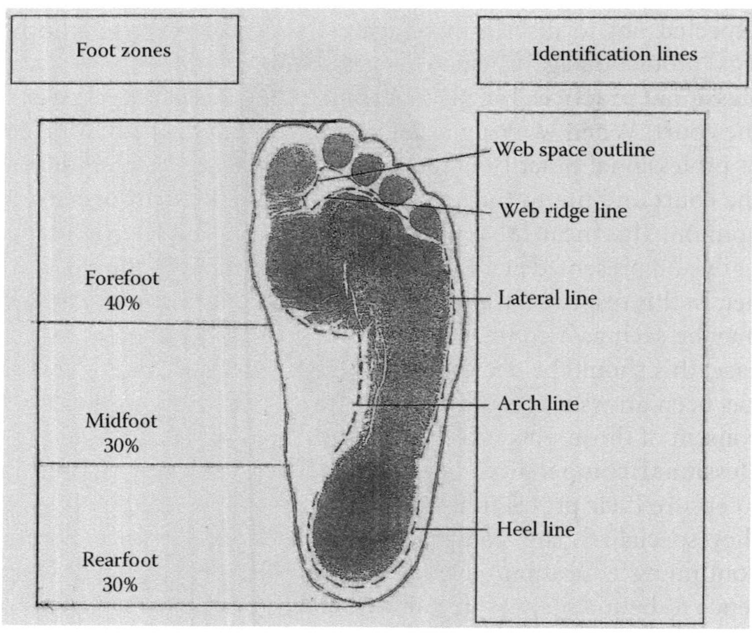

Figure 11.18 DiMaggio morphological identification lines and foot zones.

excluded because of a considerable size differential. She had a larger foot size than the two other suspects and would not have been an appropriate wearer of either of the questioned footwear. Suspect #1 (CM) (Figures 11.19 and 11.20) and suspect #3 (TS) were then used for comparison purposes against the questioned shoes and the known shoes.

Examination: The examination stage consists of correlating findings to determine the strength of the evidentiary findings on the affirmative side or the negative side.

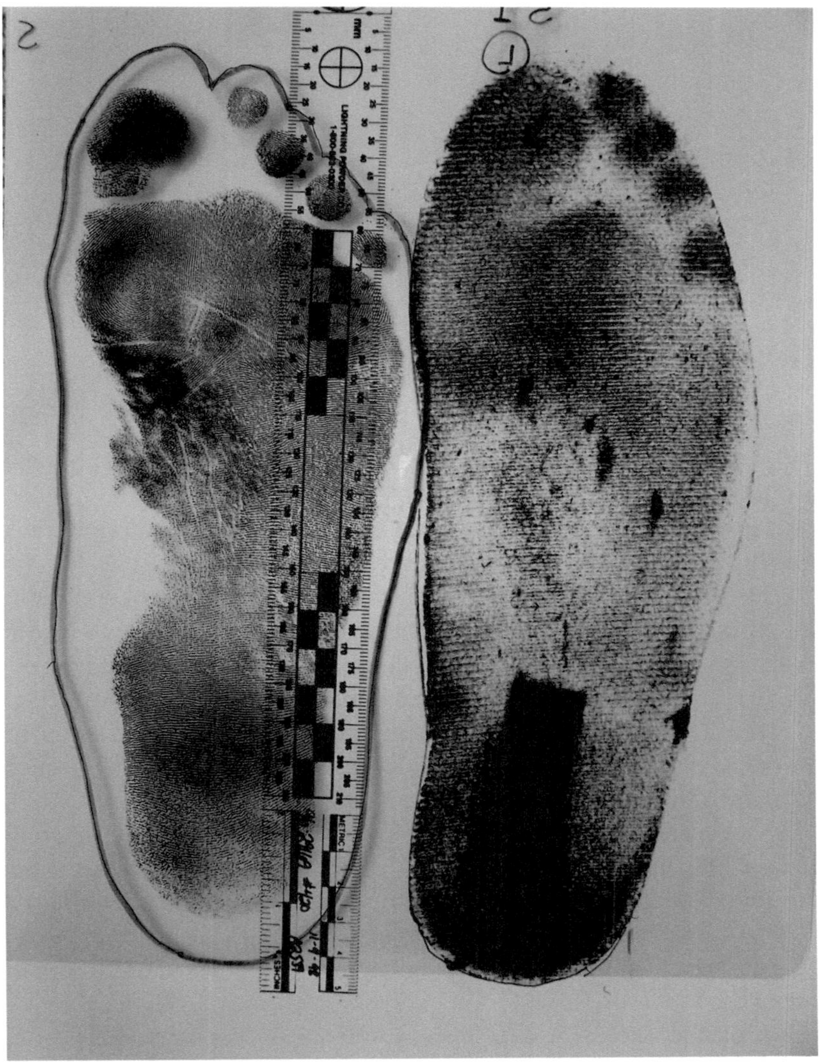

Figure 11.19 Side-by-side CM to 420Q.

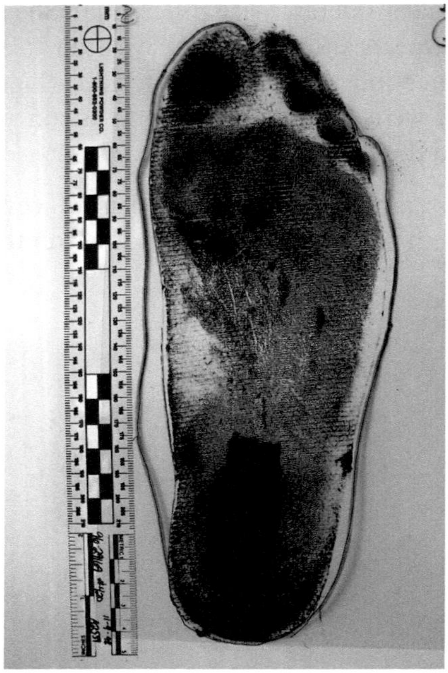

Figure 11.20 Overlay CM to 420Q.

The bases of opinions are the cumulative findings from each phase of the case study.

Because of the large number of footwear and suspects there were some interesting components that needed investigation.

I consulted with a footwear examiner for information on the questioned shoes. Also, a query was made to a computer database available to research a particular shoe. In this case, however, shoes #420 were somewhat unique and required as in some cases, personal investigation. It was determined these were part of a new African-American line of designer clothes and shoes. Shoes #500K were determined to be a popular brand of shoes sold by a midlevel department store common to the Phoenix area.

The sock liners in the questioned shoes #419Q posed a minor problem. Because of the black nylon cover, it was difficult to see a good shadow image of the foot. The crime laboratory of the Maricopa County Sheriffs Office spent considerable time to test different wavelengths, and other features, using a forensic light source to enhance the image to a more usable form (Figure 11.16).

One of the most important components of the sock liner analysis includes the web space outline (Figure 11.21). This feature usually exhibits

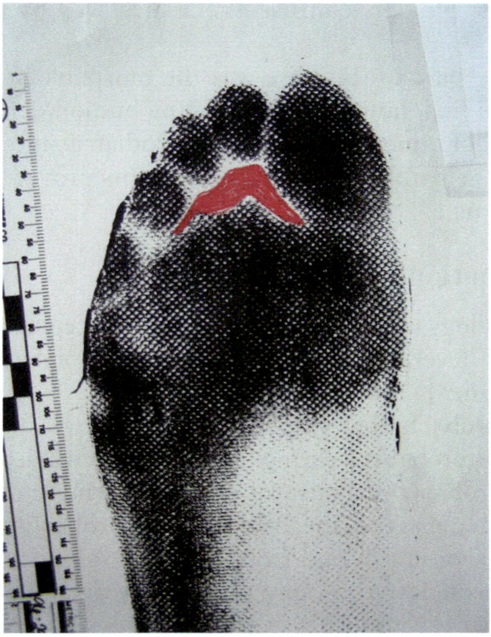

Figure 11.21 Web space area.

the best clarity and detail for comparison and seems to be fairly constant for one person, although other lines may exhibit similar findings.

The sheer number of shoes involved made this case interesting as well as the size variations. #420Q was in different sizes per foot? Were they mismatched at the time of purchase?

Suspect #1 (CM) when arrested was wearing a size 8 fashion (dress) style shoe, but her size measured 5–6. The questioned shoes #419 (size 5.5) sock liner was the same length as that in the size 8 dress shoe.

(*Casework comment:* The knowledge of how feet actually fit shoes properly is something that still needs clarification and for the most part in this author's opinion, at best highly inaccurate. An appraisal of the foot to sock liner can be more accurate, and these are things the podiatrist is trained to understand. The foot–shoe combination is evaluated from a static point of view, but one must consider and be aware of dynamic influences that may affect the foot placement. Considering this evaluation a "simple" physical comparison does not consider the knowledge acquired from evaluating and treating many hundreds of thousands of feet. The end results to these cases, often involving someone's life, are too important to allow less qualified persons from making such determinations.

It was also interesting considering they left their shoes in the trunk and two of the suspects (YE and TS) seemed to be wearing the victims shoes.

The apparent ploy to confuse the issues was by planning or just happenstance?

A challenging part to this case was the morphologic similarity of the suspect's feet. CM had, however, a developing bunion deformity and a long second toe with hammer toe deformity. Podiatric interpretation of the pathologies and their influence on certain factors proved highly significant to the final outcome.

Final Determination

Note: The terminology used for "conclusions" was accepted as such at the time of this case. (The "levels of certainty" would be the preferred method of use today by an examiner.)

It was very probable that suspect #1 wore footwear #419Q. It was also concluded she was probably wearing her own shoes when arrested.

It was very probable that suspect #3 was wearing footwear #420Q. The shoes she was wearing at the time of arrest were probably the victims.

Two pairs of shoes recovered from the victim's apartment were the victims. One was inconclusive because of severe wear and obliteration of any detail and the other was probably suspect #1's shoes.

Note: As mentioned, because of shoeprint placement at the crime scene, the outsole pattern of suspect #1 (419Q) was considered to be that of the perpetrator, which was corroborated by the podiatry determination.

(*Casework comment:* Another component of the ACE-V methodology is the V (verification) component. This is like a "second" opinion in medicine and is always a good idea. It is suggested that this component be fulfilled whenever possible).

Disposition: The jury deliberated on all the evidence and came back with a guilty verdict.

Final Comments: The pedal evidence was just one component (a piece of the puzzle) of the physical evidence presented at trial. The ultimate responsibility of the expert is to present his or her findings objectively and allow the court to make the final determination as far as guilt or innocence.

11.6 Footwear Case Reading: The State of Western Australia v. Rayney (2012)

Case Scenario: This high-profile case from Western Australia related to a murder that had occurred in 2007. The victim's husband had been charged with the crime, and the case came to trial in 2012. The prosecution alleged that the accused had either planned in advance to kill his wife or killed her during an argument that took place on the evening of August 7, 2007. That evening, the victim had attended a boot scooting (line dancing) class after which she left the class to drive home. The victim was not seen alive again and was later found buried in parkland some distance away from her home. In attempting to prove that the accused unlawfully killed the deceased, the state relied upon circumstantial evidence, with an attempt to support it with various material items.

Prosecution Theory: One theory that the state attempted to prove in this case suggested that the victim had arrived home after the boot scooting class still wearing the cowboy boots used for this activity. It was proposed by the state that after arriving home, the victim was attacked by the accused, her body was subsequently dragged from the house across a brickwork path with the boots still situated on her feet, and she was placed into her own vehicle that was then driven to the gravesite by the accused. To support this theory, the boots had been considered by the state. The presence of mineral materials within worn areas of the boots was said by the state to link the boots to the driveway in this postulated scenario. Similarly, it was the state's assertion that various wear features of the boots concerned could only have been caused by the wearer being dragged while supine and with the feet having dropped to the left side during this dragging event. A test carried out later suggested that such a dragging event would have taken between ~16 and 20 seconds.

Opinion Required and Limitations: The defense team in this case asked for an expert opinion to be provided in relation to the postulated scenario based on consideration of the wear features of the boots concerned. Although any considerations in relation to the mineral materials embedded within worn areas of the boots were outside the scope of forensic podiatry practice, providing an opinion on causes of the wear features of the boots was not and as such it was possible to proceed with the requested work.

The work was carried out with two notable limitations. First, the case was Australian, but the forensic podiatrist undertaking the examination on behalf of the defense team and report verifier were both based in the United Kingdom. As such, despite a request being made, the boots could not be provided for direct examination. Instead, a significant collection of photographs was made available for examination. These photos showed the site where it was alleged that the victim had been dragged out of the house into her car and the boots involved. The boots had been photographed at various distances and from many different angles to show the wear features, where these features were situated on the boots, and the close-up detail of these features (Figure 11.22). Second, other footwear known to have belonged to the deceased and that could have the potential to show wear features typical of, or usual to, the owner of these shoes had not been made available for

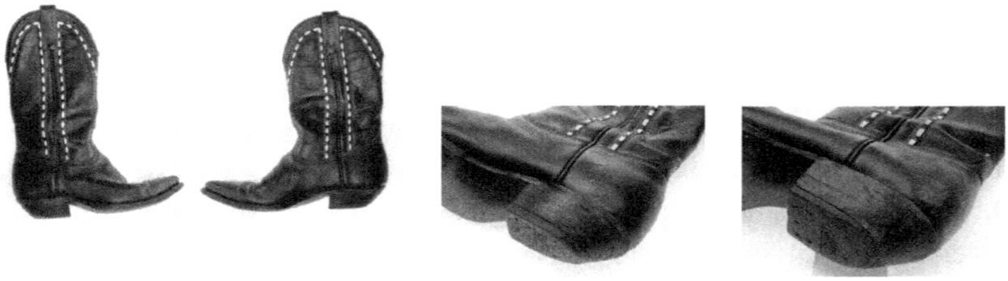

(a) (b) (c)

Figure 11.22 Questioned boots (a) including wear detail on right boot (b) and left boot (c).

examination (although the subsequent report recommended that examination of such footwear items could have been useful).

Boots-Analysis: Analysis of the images provided of the boots concerned determined the style of the boots and the site and nature of wear features of these boots. The boots were a pair of patterned black leather cowboy style boots with styled toe box, exaggerated toe spring, and moderate-height heels heavily tapered at the rear (i.e., Cuban heel style) (Figure 11.22).

Considerable general wear was apparent on left and right boots, with markings that had been used to support the prosecution position being present in the following areas:

Right boot—Wear and scoring at the rear, upper aspect of the heel unit and some wear damage of the upper slightly above that position. Some scoring at the inner rear aspect of the upper (Figure 11.22).

Left boot—Scoring at the outer aspect of the rear of the upper, the outer aspect and the inner and outer tip of the heel unit, and angled scoring of the inner heel area (Figure 11.22).

Comparison: In this particular case, a conventional physical comparison between questioned and reference footwear was not required. What was needed instead in this phase of the work was in effect a comparison between the wear features of these shoes, in particular, with wear features occurring in footwear of a similar design and of similar age, the knowledge for which had been acquired through long-term experience and research study.

In this sense, two key comments could be made. First, the wear features of the boots concerned were features often seen on footwear with heels (Figure 11.23). Second, the amount of wear present on the rear upper and heels of the boots was too great to have occurred in the single postulated dragging event lasting ~16–21 seconds and compared more closely with features arising through longer term repetitive damage. Although the dragging test carried out later used new and not old boots, the differences in the degree

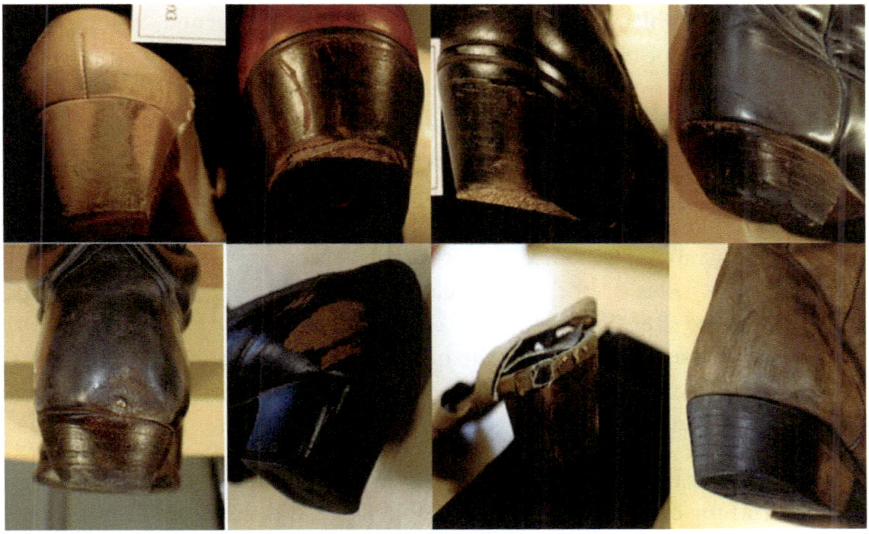

Figure 11.23 Wear of heel area seen in other footwear items.

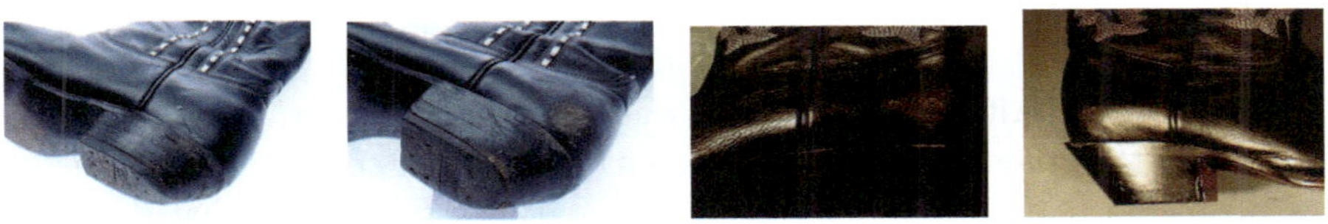

(a) (b) (c) (d)

Figure 11.24 Wear of test boots (a and b) compared with questioned boots (c and d).

of wear occurring in this test and that on the boots under consideration was considerable (Figure 11.24).

Evaluation: After considering the above wear feature comparisons, the significance of these comparisons was considered. Of fundamental importance was the need to carry out any interpretation within a relevant context. It is known that the interpretation of shoe wear patterns requires a full contextual understanding of a shoe's history and the physical status of the wearer (Vernon 2000). The boots in this case were well worn, far from new, and the understandings required to state what had caused the wear patterns concerned was not available. Although it remained possible for some of the wear features of the boots to have been produced through the postulated dragging event, the key point here is that such features are seen regularly in well-used, heeled footwear worn by the general population. The context for the creation of these wear patterns had therefore not been set by the short dragging event, but instead by the lifetime of the shoe, during which many normal everyday activities could have been responsible for creating the wear patterns concerned. Such activities would include the potential of the shoe heel and nearby upper surfaces to experience general trauma in which the heel area catches and abrades against hard objects during daily activity. Of particular note is the potential for the heels of footwear to catch against the risers when descending stairways. It is the case that when descending stairs, people will not necessarily descend with the feet pointing straight forward (Figure 11.25), especially when wearing a shoe with a relatively unstable heel. Such strategies for descending stairs exposes either the left or right sides of both heel areas together to the risk of wear through abrasion at these sites. Such everyday occurrences could have easily led to the wear seen in these same areas of the questioned boots, especially in the presence of the Cuban heel design, which would have rendered the rear of such boots especially vulnerable to this form of damage.

Conclusion: Without further understanding of the history of the boots and the potential for circumstances to have been present that could have created the wear features observed, it was concluded that although it was possible that some of the wear could have been caused by the event postulated by the state, it was equally possible that such wear could have been caused by unrelated, everyday events.

Case Outcome: Although shoe wear was not the only material evidence presented by the state in this case, the court was convinced by the arguments presented in relation to the boots, particularly in suggesting that the wear features present on the boots are commonly encountered in footwear of this type. The prosecution theory was rejected by the judge in the trial, which was a judge-only case, and the work undertaken contributed to the accused being found not guilty by the court.

Figure 11.25 Same direction deviations of feet from midline when descending stairs in heels.

Key Points: The case is of interest for three reasons. First, the work was undertaken on behalf of the defense, serving to remind podiatrists that their work, which should remain unbiased, can be required by all sides in a case. Second, the case involved considerations of the external wear patterns of footwear including those of and affecting the outsole, and cases of this type are relatively unusual. Third, the case served showed that where the work carried out requires scientific interpretation, such interpretation should be carried out within context; the context in this case being set by the entire life of the boots, not the 16–21-second parameters of any postulated dragging event.

11.7 Footwear Case Reading Involving Unusual Foot Pathology (2008)

This reported case was highly unusual for two reasons. First, the task required was to consider possible link between the victim of the crime and the questioned footwear involved as opposed to considering such possibilities in relation to a suspect. Second, the feet of the victim were highly unusual, leading to the possibility that the strength of the evidential conclusion in the case could be much higher than that usually associated with forensic podiatry evidence.

Case Scenario: In this case, a female with severe head injuries had been found unclothed and unconscious. When she returned to consciousness, she was found to have extreme memory loss. Her injuries were initially thought to have been the result of a vehicle hit-and-run incident. Clothing and shoes were discovered near to the site where the victim had been found, and examination of these items lead the police to concluded that they may be dealing with a serious and violent sexual assault as opposed to a road traffic accident.

Evidence was recovered from the clothing but because of memory loss, the victim was unable to identify either the clothing or the shoes as her own. In addition, although the perpetrator's DNA was present on the clothing, traces of the victim's DNA could not be successfully collected from either the clothing or the shoes. This represented a gap in the scenario that the police were putting together and one that the perpetrator could potentially exploit in the defense to suggest that although perpetrator DNA was present on the clothing, it could not be determined that the found clothing and shoes belonged to the victim. The police were therefore seeking another means of determining whether the clothing, shoes, or both could have been those belonging to the victim. It was at that point that the investigating officer noticed that the victim had unusual feet; therefore, a forensic podiatry opinion was sought.

Opinion Required, Materials and Information Available, and Limitations: A forensic podiatry opinion was required on whether the questioned footwear could have belonged to the victim and on the level of certainty for that opinion.

To consider and address the questions asked, the following materials and information were made available:

1. The questioned footwear (one pair of high heeled, styled court shoes)
2. Reference footwear known to belong to the victim (as confirmed by the victim's father)
3. Access to the victim for assessment of the victim's feet and her current footwear

The work was carried out in the presence of certain limitations. The victim was no longer able to walk unaided and for mobility purposes was now wheelchair bound. In addition, she no longer wore the styled court shoes that had been her footwear preference and was restricted to wearing comfortable, loose-fitting training shoes that her caregiver could place on and remove from her feet with ease. Given the significant change of mobility and footwear style worn, the ideal like-for-like comparisons were no longer possible in relation to the victim's feet and current footwear (although like-for-like comparisons were possible in relation to the court-style footwear previously worn regularly by the victim).

Feet Analysis: As noted above, the investigating officer had noticed that the victim had unusual feet. The scenario that was determined through questioning was that when carrying the victim during pregnancy, the victim's mother had been prescribed thalidomide to help with morning sickness problems. Thalidomide was later found to cause birth defects, including phocomelia (among other deficiencies) (Learning Radiology 2015), leading to tighter drug regulation and control in many countries (Bhattacharya et al. 2014, p. 245). In this case, the victim has been born with foot deformities caused by, but not typical of, problems associated with thalidomide. Features of the victim's deformities resulting from the use of thalidomide included left foot toe absence (complete absence of second–fourth toes and partial absence of the first and fifth toes), short toes of the right foot (particularly the third and fourth toes), and the relatively small size (size 3 UK) of the victim's feet (Figure 11.26).

Footwear—Analysis and comparisons (interfootwear and feet/shoes): All shoes examined, whether questioned or reference, showed the same features of wear and fit. All shoes were size 3. In the left shoes, absence of internal wear sock liner, insole, and upper anterior ball

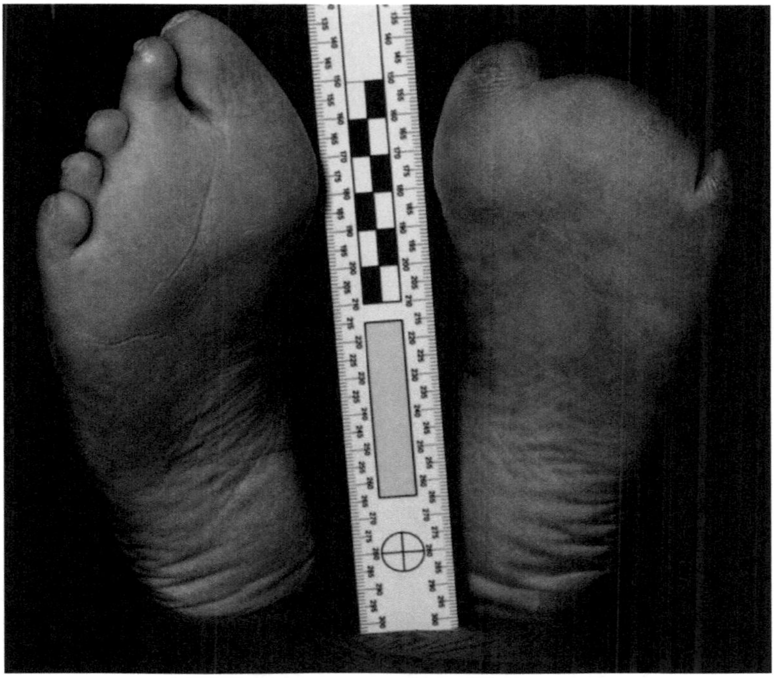

Figure 11.26 Victim's feet.

position, and matched anterior ball position and morphology were observed (Figure 11.27). In the right shoes, measurements taken from the rear of the heel to the tips of the toe impressions all fell within ±3 mm of each other (Figure 11.28). When questioned and reference shoes were compared to the victim's feet, the left foot anterior ball morphology and position closely correlated with the insole/sock liner impressions of the left shoes and the absence of left toes also concurred with the anterior absence of wear within the left shoes. The victim's foot size (size 3 UK) matched the size of all shoes examined (also size 3 UK), and the victim's foot and toe size and shape closely matched the foot and toe impressions on the sock liner of the right shoes examined.

Evaluation and conclusion: The close matching of the unusual features of shoes and feet suggested that the questioned shoes had been worn by the usual wearer of the victim's known shoes and that the victim had been the wearer of these questioned shoes. No features could be found that would have precluded this possibility or that suggested an alternative hypothesis regarding shoe ownership. As part of the considerations to determine the weight of evidence that the close matching of these features represented, the proportion

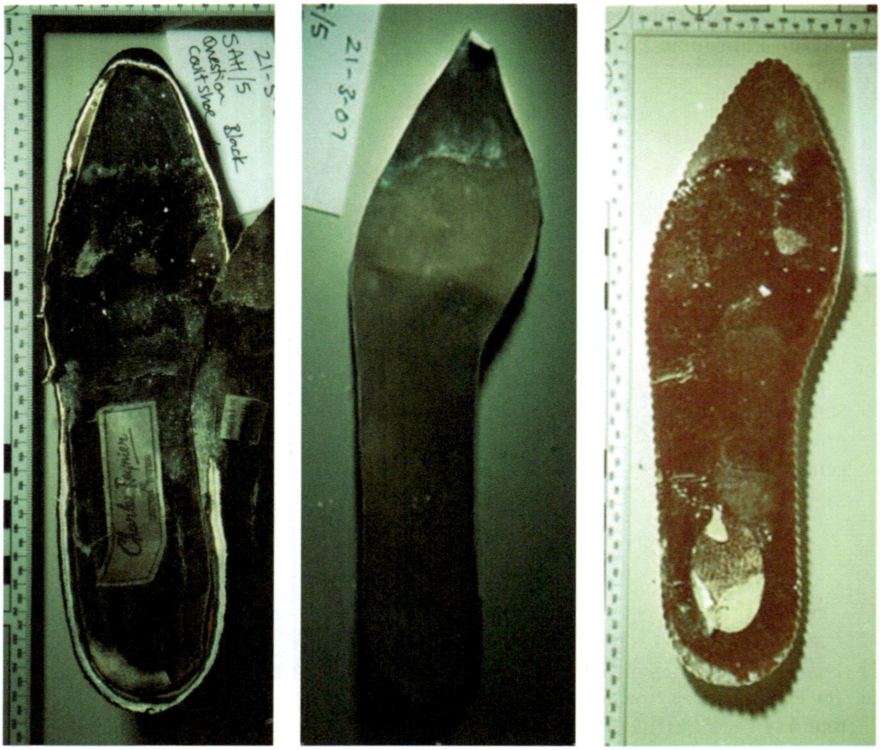

(a) (b) (c)

Figure 11.27 Comparison of left footwear. (a) Questioned sock liner, (b) reference sock liner 1, and (c) reference sock liner 2.

of females wearing size 3 shoes in the United Kingdom was considered (1:30) as was affectation by a rare causal pathology (thalidomide-related affectation of the feet), where at the time of working the case 1:150,000 of the general population were believed to be thalidomide tragedy survivors. However, there was a need to consider reasons for such extensive toe loss or apparent toes loss other than thalidomide in the patient group being considered. Such causes include ectrodactyly, surgical amputation, frostbite, gangrene, and traumatic amputation of the toes, and it was suggested that the thalidomide situation represented just 1 in 10 reasons for such extensive toe loss in the U.K. population. The overall conclusion was that there was extremely strong support for the proposition that the known and questioned shoes had the same usual wearer.

Case Outcome: The report submitted was not challenged by the defense team. In time, the suspect was extradited from another country to which he had fled, charged and ultimately convicted of this crime

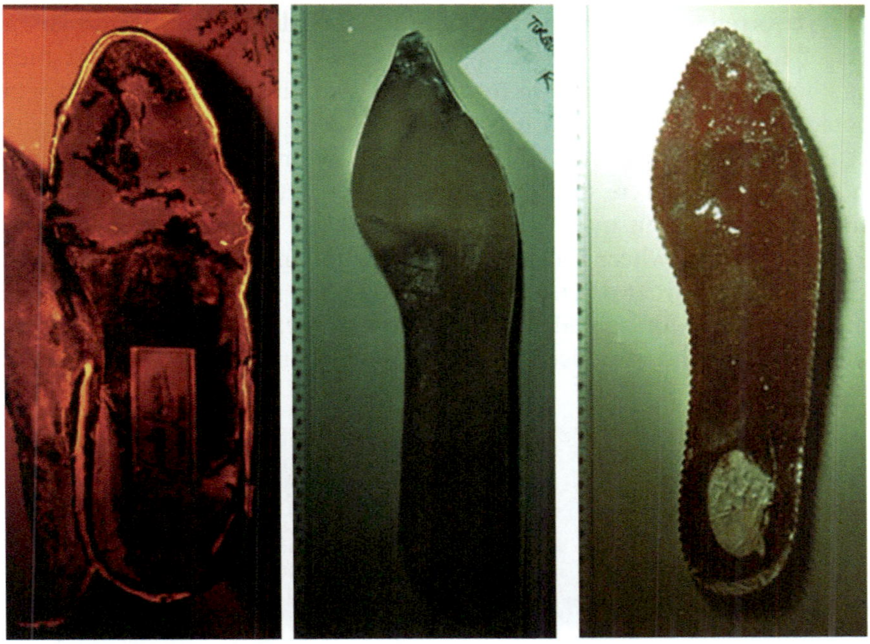

(a) (b) (c)

Figure 11.28 Comparison of right footwear. (a) Questioned sock liner, (b) reference sock liner 1, and (c) reference sock liner 2.

Key Points: As noted above, this case was unusual because of the request to look into the potential for a match of the questioned shoes with the victim's shoes and feet and because of the highly individual nature of the features of the worn shoes and the victim's feet. The high strength of the conclusion reached (extremely strong support) was only made possible through the interpretive approach to the casework in which causal pathology was considered in addition to considerations of foot/foot impression morphology alone.

11.8 Forensic Gait Analysis: Case Reading (2015)

Case Scenario: The case concerned a series of serious sexual assaults on women of all ages. The police had identified a suspect, and the forensic podiatry team at Sheffield Teaching Hospitals NHS Foundation Trust was contacted with a view to undertaking forensic gait analysis using CCTV footage associated with the events in question. Forensic gait analysis was one of several techniques that were being used by the investigating team to assemble evidence to enable the identification of the perpetrator.

Task required, materials and information available, and limitations: Two sets of footage were submitted by the police for preliminary assessment, together with brief instruction to compare the figure seen in the first set of footage with the figure seen in the second set of footage. In this case, the recordings submitted were not identified as being questioned and reference footage, they were simply two sets of footage (Figures 11.29 and 11.30). Although this is unusual, it is not unknown, and casework had previously been undertaken where the instruction was to simply compare the gait of the figures seen in two sets of footage. As noted in Chapter 6, in forensic gait analysis it is considered good practice to analyze the questioned footage before viewing the reference footage to ensure that assumptions of the guilt

Figure 11.29 Reference footage A.

Figure 11.30 Reference footage B.

of the subject seen in the reference footage do not introduce cognitive bias into the analysis of the questioned footage. Such assumptions can occur, e.g., when reference footage is captured in a police station or custody suite, where the presence of the subject could be interpreted as implying guilt. However, in this case, both sets of footage had been captured in public places, with no indication of which footage was questioned and which was reference, other than slightly suspicious behavior being seen in the first set of footage listed on the instruction, and as such would have attenuated any factors relating to cognitive bias through such assumptions of quilt.

Analysis, comparison, and evaluation: Preliminary quality assessment was undertaken in line with the processes detailed in Chapter 6. The first set of footage (Figure 11.30) was quality rated as B by using the Birch et al. (2013) methodology, and second footage (Figure 11.29) was rated as A. This member of the team, who undertook the preliminary assessment, played no further role in the case, again in line with best practice recommendations detailed in Chapter 6. After the preliminary assessment, it was determined that there would be value in proceeding with a full analysis and comparison of the two sets of recordings. Thus, the footage and instructions were sent to a designated lead analyst for full analysis.

In line with convention, an ACE-V strategy was used for the core of the work. The first set of footage listed on the instruction was analyzed initially and comprehensive notes were made. The set of footage listed second on the instruction was then analyzed and notes were taken. Next, a comparison was undertaken of the features of gait exhibited by the figures in the two sets of footage by using only the detail recorded in the notes (Table 11.1). An exceptionally close match was found between the two sets of features of gait. Only one feature seen on the first set of footage could not be matched between the two sets of recordings. As a result of this evaluation, it was concluded that, in the opinion of the analyst, forensic gait analysis provided strong evidence for the proposition that the figures seen in the two sets of footage were from the same person. The report and the footages were then forwarded to another member of the Sheffield team for independent verification. The verifier concurred with both matched features of gait and the conclusion reached, with the report then being submitted to the commissioning agency.

Some months later, a request was received from the same police force for three additional sets of footage to be analyzed and compared to the first of the two sets of footage originally submitted (Figures 11.31–11.34). Again, a preliminary quality assessment of the three sets of footage was undertaken, and the footage was rated as B, D, and E, respectively, according to Birch et al., (2013) methodology. The footage was sent to the lead analyst, and analysis, comparison, and evaluation were undertaken as described above. It was concluded that, in the opinion of the analyst, forensic gait analysis provided

Table 11.1 Features of Gait Observed

✓ feature observed; m marked; ss on some steps; R right side only; sl slight; mos on the majority of steps; L left side only	Original Questioned Footage	Additional Questioned Footage 1	Additional Questioned Footage 2	Additional Questioned Footage 3	Reference Footage
Asymmetrical gait[1]	✓	✓			✓
Erratic gait				✓	
Symmetry of gait could not be determined			✓	✓	
Rolling of the head and torso[2]			✓	✓	
Rolling of the head and torso, more to the left on left steps than to the right on right steps	✓m	✓m			✓m
Noticeable vertical movement of the head and torso on each step	✓	✓			✓
Head held approximately in line with the midline of the torso in the frontal plane[3]	✓	✓			✓
Frontal plane alignment of the head could not be determined			✓	✓	
Head held approximately in line with the midline of the torso in the sagittal plane[4]	✓				
Head held forwards of the midline of the torso in the sagittal plane		✓sl			
Sagittal plane alignment of the head could not be determined			✓	✓	✓
Left shoulder lower than the right shoulder	✓				✓
Relative height of the shoulders could not be determined		✓	✓	✓	
No right arm swings are visible			✓		
More arm swing movement anterior of the torso than posterior of the torso	✓				✓
Arm swing movement anterior and posterior of the torso approximately equal					

(Continued)

Table 11.1 *(Continued)* Features of Gait Observed

✓ feature observed; m marked; ss on some steps; R right side only; sl slight; mos on the majority of steps; L left side only	Original Questioned Footage	Additional Questioned Footage 1	Additional Questioned Footage 2	Additional Questioned Footage 3	Reference Footage
Oblique path of motion of the hands, passing across slightly in front of the torso at their most anterior point	✓	✓		✓	✓
Elbows remain flexed throughout arm swing					
Flexion at the elbow increasing during the forward motion of the arm	✓	✓			✓
A reliable assessment of arm swing could not be made			✓L		
Largely linear motion occurring at right hip[5]		✓ss			
Largely linear motion occurring at left hip		✓ss			
Circumduction occurring at right hip[6]	✓	✓mos		✓	✓
Circumduction occurring at left hip	✓	✓mos		✓	✓
Nature of the movement occurring at the hips could not be determined			✓		
During the early part of the stance phase of gait, the thigh of both lower limbs appears slightly inverted[7]	✓	✓			✓
Right knee points forwards approximately in line with the direction of travel at feet adjacent during swing	✓	✓	✓	✓	✓
Left knee points forwards approximately in line with the direction of travel at feet adjacent during swing	✓	✓	✓	✓	✓
Right knee reaches a position of full or close to full extension at or close to heel strike	✓	✓			✓

(Continued)

Table 11.1 ***(Continued)*** **Features of Gait Observed**

✓ feature observed · m marked · ss on some steps · R right side only · sl slight · mos on the majority of steps · L left side only	Original Questioned Footage	Additional Questioned Footage 1	Additional Questioned Footage 2	Additional Questioned Footage 3	Reference Footage
Left knee reaches a position of full or close to full extension at or close to heel strike	✓	✓			✓
Angulation of the knees at or close to heel strike could not be determined			✓	✓	
Right knee reaches a position of full or close to full extension prior to heel rise	✓	✓	✓		✓
Left knee reaches a position of full or close to full extension prior to heel rise	✓	✓	✓		✓
Angulation of the knees prior to heel rise could not be determined				✓	
Base of gait is very narrow[8]	✓	✓	✓	✓	✓
Base of gait is narrow				✓	
Base of gait is variable				✓	
Right foot points outwards, away from the midline of the body, when weight bearing during stance	✓	✓	✓	✓	✓
Left foot points outwards, away from the midline of the body, when weight bearing during stance	✓	✓	✓	✓	✓
Right foot points outwards, away from the midline of the body, at feet adjacent during swing	✓m	✓m			✓m

(Continued)

Table 11.1 ***(Continued)*** **Features of Gait Observed**

✓ feature observed; m marked; ss on some steps; R right side only; sl slight; mos on the majority of steps; L left side only	Original Questioned Footage	Additional Questioned Footage 1	Additional Questioned Footage 2	Additional Questioned Footage 3	Reference Footage
Left foot points outwards, away from the midline of the body, at feet adjacent during swing	✓	✓			✓
Orientation of the feet, at feet adjacent during the swing, could not be determined			✓	✓	

1 An asymmetrical gait is the one in which the gross movement of the head and torso to the right is different to the gross movement to the left.

2 Rolling of the head and torso is a rotation that would be best seen from the front or back.

3 The frontal plane is the plane of body movements which are best seen from the front or rear of the body.

4 The sagittal plane is the plane of body movements which are best seen from either side of the body.

5 Linear movement in this instance is a movement occurring at the hip joint that results in the lower limb moving forward in an approximately straight line during the swing phase of gait.

6 Circumduction in this instance is a movement occurring at the hip joint that results in the lower limb moving forward in an arc during the swing phase of gait.

7 An inverted thigh describes an orientation of the thigh in which the knee joint is closer to the midline of the body than the hip joint, when viewed from the front or back.

8 The base of gait is the side-to-side distance between the heels on consecutive steps.

Figure 11.31 Original questioned footage.

Figure 11.32 Additional questioned footage 1.

Figure 11.33 Additional questioned footage 2.

Figure 11.34 Additional questioned footage 3.

moderately strong evidence for the proposition that the figure seen in the first of additional sets of footage was the figure in the first of the original sets of footage and limited evidence for the proposition that the person seen in the other two sets of additional footage was the same person seen in the first of the original sets of footage.

The reduction in the strength of evidence derived from the additional sets of footage was the result of several factors. In the first set of the additional recordings, there were many clips captured at a reasonable frame rate that showed a considerable number of steps, but the lighting, resolution, and contrast were variable. As a result, the clarity with which features of gait could be repeatedly seen also varied. Furthermore, some of the clips showed limited numbers of consecutive steps, and in some of the clips showing large numbers of consecutive steps, the line of progression changed, thereby potentially altering the subject's gait. Although there was a good match between the features of gait seen to be exhibited by the two figures, and no features of gait were observed that would have precluded them from being the same person, the limitations described were attenuating factors that resulted in the strength of the evidential conclusion as to the footage being of the same person being at the moderately strong level. In the second set of additional footage, attenuating circumstances included a limited number of consecutive steps being taken in a straight line and the subject having to walk in a series of arcs to negotiate various obstacles. Those features of gait that could be determined showed a relatively good match with those exhibited by the figure in the first of the original pieces of footage, and no features of gait were observed that would have precluded them from being the same person. However, in view of the limited number of steps seen and the arcuate line of progression, the strength of evidence derived was restricted to limited. The third set of additional footage had only one clip of limited quality and it showed a limited number of sometimes erratic steps. Those features of gait that could be determined showed some matches with those exhibited by the figure in the first of the original pieces of footage, and again there were no features of gait that would have precluded them from being the same person. The strength of evidence derived was therefore restricted to limited as a result of the lower quality of that footage.

Independent verification was undertaken of this second stage of the work, and the observations and conclusions agreed. The addendum report was then submitted to the commissioning agency.

The forensic gait analyst was called to give evidence in week 2 of the subsequent trial. At the preliminary meeting with the prosecution team, two points for discussion were identified by the analyst.

1. It became clear at the meeting that the first set of footage originally analyzed was to be used at trial as the reference footage for all comparisons. This footage was analyzed before what was now known to be the first set of questioned footage. However, as neither of the recordings was captured in an environment that implied guilt, and as the footage was at the time believed to be the questioned footage, the possibility of cognitive bias having occurred was considered not to have been elevated. Nevertheless, the report was subsequently rewritten to highlight this change and then resubmitted for court use. The nature and extent of the instruction given by commissioning agencies can be variable, and it is often necessary to engage in discussion with the agency to establish exactly what is required. In this case, although the original task was thought to be relatively straightforward, further discussion, had it taken place, may have highlighted differences in the identification of the reference footage before the trial.
2. Second, it became clear during the preliminary meeting that it had yet to be established in court that the figure in the reference footage was the defendant. To establish this fact, police officers would need to be called to give evidence to this effect, and the analyst could not therefore present his or her evidence at that point in the trial. The amount of discussion occurring between the commissioning agency's trial team and the analyst can vary considerably, ranging from a long meeting several weeks before the trial to a quick exchange before entering the witness box. Had there been a substantive meeting before the start of the trial, the order of the witnesses could have been amended. It is strongly recommended that the analyst makes contact with the commissioning agency's trial team, before the trial, and discusses the nature of the gait analysis evidence, how it should be presented, and how it might fit with other evidence.

Outcome: The analyst presented the forensic gait analysis evidence to the court eight days later, after the amended report had been submitted and after the police officers had presented their evidence. The trial lasted more than four weeks, and forensic gait analysis was only one facet of a complex and diverse range of evidence. At the conclusion of the trial, the defendant was found guilty of all 10 offenses as charged.

Key Learning Points:

- Ensure that both the analyst and the commissioning agency are clear as to the task required
- Check the quality of the footage before accepting a commission
- Understand and be aware of the possible implications of cognitive bias
- Independently verify your work in line with the essential standards required in forensic science and practice
- Communicate with the trial team before the start of the trial

11.9 State of Wisconsin v. Travis Petersen

Refer Section 10.5 for the case detail.

References

Bhattacharya, J., Hyde T., and Tu P. 2014. *Health Economics*. Basingstoke: Palgrave Macmillan.

Keereweer, I. 1998. The Nike Project – Results barefoot identification. *Information Bulletin for Shoeprint/Toolmark Examiners* 4: 129–138.

Kennedy, R. 1995. Barefoot Impressions. Paper presented at the Canadian Identification Association Annual Conference, Halifax, July 2015.

Learning Radiology. 2015. *Thalidomide-induced Phocomelia*. Learning Radiology. http://learningradiology.com/archives2009/COW%20365-Thalidomide/thalidomidecorrect.htm (Sampled 15th March 2016).

Lucock, L.J. 1980. Identification from footwear. *The Chiropodist* 35: 343–350.

Vernon, W. 2000. "The functional analysis of shoe wear patterns." PhD Diss., Sheffield Hallam University.

Glossary of Podiatric Terms

abduction: movement of the foot away from the midline of the body.
adduction: movement of the foot toward the midline of the body.
ball (foot): the part of the foot beneath the five metatarsal heads.
biomechanics: the application of mechanical laws to living structures, specifically to the locomotor system of the human body.
bunion/hallux abducto valgus: an enlargement of the first metatarsal head with rotation and lateral deviation of the big toe.
calcaneum: the heel bone.
callus/callous: a hardening and thickening of the skin usually associated with a boney influence.
contracted/retracted toes: a condition in which the toes are pulled back and may not contact the ground properly during stance.
corn/clavus: a discrete hard and painful area often associated with a hammer toe.
it usually has a deep "core" that presses on a subdermal nerve.
distal: farthest away from the central location of the body or part in question, such as the toes are distal to the heel.
dorsal/dorsum: upper surface of the foot.
dorsiflexion: upward movement of the foot.
eversion: the plantar surface tilts away from the midline of the body, lowering the inner border of the foot.
fibrous corn: a corn usually of very long standing duration that shows the presence of fibrous tissue.
foot zones: the sectioning of the foot into three sections (rearfoot-30%, midfoot-30%, and forefoot-40%) that can be used in the comparison process.
gait: any form of locomotion, such as walking, running, etc.
Greek ideal: a foot with a long second toe length versus the big toe.
hallux limitus: a condition in which the movement of the joint of the big toe is limited restricting its ability to bend during walking.
hallux rigidus: a condition in which the joint of the big toe is immobile, leading to a stiff toe and inability to bend during walking.
hallux valgus: a condition in which the big toe is deviated away from the midline of the body toward the midline of the foot.

hammer toe: a common toe deformity with prominence of one of the toe bones where a painful corn often develops.

hyperextended toes: a condition in which the toes are excessively extended beyond the normal range of movement.

hyperpronation: an excessive pronatory movement of the foot.

id lines: morphological descriptors (e.g., arch line, heel line, web ridge line) that are used in the dimaggio overlay comparison process.

interdigital: the area between the toes.

inversion: the plantar surface tilts toward the midline of the body; elevation of the inner border of the foot.

involution: a condition in which the nail curves inwards at the edges.

intractable plantar keratosis: a deeply nucleated keratotic lesion on the bottom of the foot that may leave its mark as an area of increased pressure on a receiving surface.

lateral: farther from the midline.

malleoli: the bones that can be seen as medial and lateral protrusions of the ankle.

mallet toe: a form of a hammer toe with a deformity at the end of the toe, creating a downward pressure that may be useful in the examination process.

medial: nearer to the midline.

metatarsal formula (parabola): the order in which the metatarsophalangeal joints of the ball of the foot are encountered when approaching these from a distal position.

metatarsalgia: a term denoting pain in the metatarsal area secondary to different etiologies.

metatarsophalangeal joint: joints situated within the ball of the foot, where the metatarsals join with the proximal phalanges.

midfoot: section of the foot situated between the forefoot and heel.

multinucleate corn: a corn that shows the presence of more than one white nucleus as a result of pressure in the area.

nevi: small benign pigmented lesions of the skin; often described as "moles."

onychogryphosis: grossly thickened and deformed toenail that when neglected takes on the appearance of a ram's horn.

pedal evidence: physical evidence related in some form to the human foot, e.g., bloody footprints and foot impressions in dirt. it may also include associated deformation of the shoe upper or an image on the sock liner secondary to the foot that housed it that can be used in the comparison process.

pes cavus: a foot type in which the arch is markedly accentuated and the toes are retracted with the forefoot, usually being situated lower than the heel when viewed in a relaxed position from the side.

pes planus: a true flat foot.

phalanges: toe bones.
plantar: pertaining to the sole of the foot.
plantarflexion: downward movement of the foot.
plantar verruca(e) [plantar wart(s)]: one or more lesions on the bottom of the foot that may leave their mark by an area of increased pressure or break in continuity on a receiving surface.
podometrics: the science of foot measurements.
pressure point: area of the foot (usually a toe) that shows minor signs of having rubbed against an enclosing shoe.
pronation: a triplane motion of the foot consisting of abduction, dorsiflexion, and eversion of the calcaneus, which is often labeled as the valgus (flat) foot type.
proximal: nearest to the central location of the body or part in question, such as the heel is proximal to the toes.
running: double-float phasic gait.
supination: a triplane motion of the foot consisting of adduction, plantar flexion, and inversion of the calcaneus, which is often labeled as the cavus (high arch) foot type.
step length: the distance between one-foot plant and the next, e.g., right foot to left foot.
stride length: the distance between one-foot plant and the next of the same foot, e.g., right foot to the next right foot plant.
tailor's bunion: an enlargement of the joint situated on the outer aspect of the ball of the foot.
toe formula: the order in which the toes are encountered when approaching these from a distal position.
toe-off: that phase of gait just before the foot leaving the ground, whereby the foot is now acting as a rigid lever.
valgus: an abnormality or deformity in which the foot is turned or forced outward; used to describe a pronatory attitude (flat foot).
varus: an abnormality or deformity in which the foot is turned or forced inward; used to describe a supinatory attitude (high arch).
vascular corn: a corn that has been complicated by the presence of blood vessels within the affected area.
walking: double-stance phasic gait.

Index

D

E

H

I

J

K

L

V

W

For Product Safety Concerns and Information please contact our EU representative GPSR@taylorandfrancis.com Taylor & Francis Verlag GmbH, Kaufingerstraße 24, 80331 München, Germany

Batch number: 10726532

Printed by Printforce, the Netherlands